Financial Systems at the Crossroads

Lessons for China

Financial Systems at the Crossroads

Lessons for China

Editors

Wing Thye Woo
University of California at Davis, USA

Yingli Pan
Shanghai Jiaotong University, China

Jeffrey David Sachs
Columbia University, USA

Junhui Qian
Shanghai Jiaotong University, China

World Scientific

ICP Imperial College Press

Published by

World Scientific Publishing Co. Pte. Ltd.

5 Toh Tuck Link, Singapore 596224

USA office: 27 Warren Street, Suite 401-402, Hackensack, NJ 07601

UK office: 57 Shelton Street, Covent Garden, London WC2H 9HE

Library of Congress Cataloging-in-Publication Data

Financial systems at the crossroads : lessons for China's choice / edited by Wing Thye Woo (University of California at Davis, USA), Yingli Pan (Shanghai Jiao Tong University, China), Jeffrey David Sachs (Columbia University, USA), Junhui Qian (Shanghai Jiao Tong University, China).

pages cm

Includes bibliographical references and index.

ISBN 978-9814566810 -- ISBN 9814566810

ISBN 978-9814566827 (pbk.) -- ISBN 9814566829 (pbk.)

1. Finance--China. 2. Financial institutions--China. 3. Banks and banking--China. I. Woo, Wing Thye.

HG187.C6F566 2014

332.0951--dc23

2013030510

British Library Cataloguing-in-Publication Data

A catalogue record for this book is available from the British Library.

In-house Editor: Alisha Nguyen

Typeset by Stallion Press

Email: enquiries@stallionpress.com

Printed in Singapore by B & Jo Enterprise Pte Ltd

Foreword

Since the launch of the reform and opening-up policy, China's economic growth has been marked by eye-catching achievements for more than three decades. However, with the new economic landscape after the Global Financial Crisis and the cumulated changes in some important domestic factors that support long-term growth, China's economy is facing much tougher challenges. With the declining availability of internal resources, shrinking of external markets, and increasingly unstable monetary and financial policies all over the world, China's economic growth model, which relies on cheap labor, cheap capital, cheap resources and expanding external markets, is no longer sustainable.

China is standing at a critical turning point for reform and transformation of its economy. The transformation of China's economy requires the composition of demand to shift from exports to internal absorption, and the growth of the supply side to be based more on improved efficiency and less on massive factor input. Because the optimum accumulation and allocation of capital is fundamental to the success of the required transformation, the reform of the financial system and its orderly development is a key task for China.

For the first six decades of the People's Republic of China, the state kept interest rates artificially low, and allocated the cheap capital administratively to facilitate industrialization. With the reform and opening-up of the economic system at the end of the 1970s, the financial sector has also experienced market-oriented reforms and is now partially open to the world. But, in general, financial sector reforms have been inadequate compared with the current and future demands for economic transformation. This lag in the financial reform could worsen the imbalance in the industrial structure and increase systemic financial risks. It is therefore important to accelerate the orderly development of the financial sector to promote the transformation of the economy in a safe, effective and sustainable manner.

The book "**Financial Systems at the Crossroads: Lessons for China**" is produced by an international team of financial experts led by Wing Thye Woo (Fudan University and University of California at Davis), Pan Yingli (Shanghai Jiaotong University), Jeffrey Sachs (Columbia University) and Qian Junhui (Shanghai Jiaotong University). The first part of the book starts by discussing the key problems in the financial markets and regulatory supervision in the United States, Japan, Scandinavia and other wealthy countries, and then summarizes the important lessons from the international experience. The second part of the book presents a comprehensive discussion about how to create an orderly and effective financial system for China that will facilitate the transformation of China's economy and enable sustainable development.

China has now entered a critical phase in its efforts to address the great challenges created by the complexity of economic system reform, especially in the financial market component of reform. As a strong supporter of financial sector reform, I am heartened that this book can help guide the architects of the new financial system and the participants in the reform effort in their work. A modern financial sector will help China to converge to the living standard in the developed countries.

Tu Guangshao
Executive Vice Mayor
Shanghai Municipal Government
Shanghai, China

Preface

China achieved middle-income status in 2006,[1] a milestone still denied to its three large neighbors, India, Indonesia and the Philippines, which were all richer than China in 1978. However, continued fast progress by China to high-income status cannot be taken for granted. Four of the largest economies in Latin American — Argentina, Brazil, Chile, and Mexico — have been in residence in the middle-income category at least since 1960. And, after being hailed by the World Bank in 1993 as an East Asian Miracle economy, catch-up growth in Malaysia stopped in 1994, leaving Malaysia trapped at 30% of the living standard of the United States for the last 18 years.

Our research on economic growth in other countries has led us to the conclusion that China's successful economic transition from middle-income to high-income cannot be achieved by the present dualistic policy regime of state-led industrialization facilitated by state-directed allocation of capital, and enthusiastic private-sector participation, mostly, in light industries and in the low and medium value-added portions of the service sector. The Soviet Union achieved middle-income status without private-sector participation, but it ended in economic collapse in 1991. The achievement of middle-income status in Malaysia (with the China-style policy regime of state-private dualism) has been followed by economic stagnation

[1]This is according to the Catch-Up Index (CUI) in Chapter 1 ("The Major Types of Middle-Income Trap That Threaten China's Growth," by Wing Thye Woo) in *A New Economic Growth Engine for China: Escaping the Middle-Income Trap by Not Doing More of the Same*, World Scientific and Imperial College Press, 2012, edited by Wing Thye Woo, Ming Lu, Jeffrey D. Sachs and Zhao Chen. CUI is the ratio of the country's per capita GDP per capita to US per capita GDP, with both measured in purchasing power parity units. In Woo's classification, middle-income begins with CUI at 20% and high-income begins at 55%.

because of policy inaction from the government's short-sighted attitude of "if it ain't broke, don't fix it."

Among the fundamental policy changes that China must now make in order to avoid falling into the middle-income trap is its financial-sector policy. The next phase of China's growth will require drastic financial-sector reform to generate a more efficient pattern of investment (to assist small and medium private enterprises to grow into global companies); and introduce new financial instruments that will reduce investment risk and facilitate home ownership and human capital formation. International experiences have shown, however, that the use of financial markets to accelerate economic development could sometimes be as dangerous as riding a tiger. The Japanese economy has been stagnant up to today following the bursting of its real estate and stock market bubbles in 1990. The implosion of the US financial system in September 2008 and the subsequent European financial crisis have produced prolonged high unemployment.

This book shows that the fact that the developed economies have yet to produce a financial system that is absolutely safe to use should not be allowed to justify delaying the needed restructuring of China's financial industry. The Antai College of Economics and Management at Shanghai Jiaotong University, the School of Economics at Fudan University and the Earth Institute at Columbia University have collaborated to convene an international team of leading financial experts to study the causes of financial disasters internationally to identify the regulatory framework to guide the emergence of efficient financial institutions that are prudent; and to specify the required institutional mechanisms to prevent and resolve systemic collapse. The Jiaotong–Fudan–Columbia research team then examines the specific circumstances of China to come up with a comprehensive agenda to reform China's financial sector.

This book is written to suit a broad audience, for the analysts and students interested in the financial industry, and for China-watchers interested in the development trajectories of China that have high probabilities of appearing. This is a handbook for developing a financial system that is efficient, innovative and resilient. This is also a research monograph on China's financial industry that identifies the policy choices for accelerating the pace of financial sector development.

An earlier draft of this book was published in Chinese in September 2013, as *Shizi Lukou de Jinrong Tixi: Guoji Jingyan yu Zhongguo Xuanze* (*Financial System at the Crossroads: International Experiences and China's Choice*). Major changes have been made only in Chapter 1 ("Mobilizing China's Financial Sector Efficiently and Safely for Sustaining Economic Transformation and Strengthening Global Financial Stability"). Two new sections were added (a) The Potential Future International Status of the RMB and Shanghai's Financial Industry, and (b) Modernizing the Financial Sector Safely and Entrenching Financial Firefighting Capability.

We are grateful to Max Phua, Michael Heng, and Alisha Nguyen of World Scientific Publishing, Dean Zhou Lin of the Antai College of Economics and Management at the Shanghai Jiaotong University, and Dean Yuan Zhigang of the School of Economics at Fudan University for their kind support for this project. Their optimistic confidence that our book would help advance the discussion in China on financial sector reform gave the research team the required encouragement to persist in its effort to understand the global experience in financial sector development and to come up with creative reform options for the specific situation in China. We can report that our team has done a good job, and had enjoyed the analytical challenges of this project.

Editors:

Wing Thye Woo (*Fudan University & University of California at Davis*)
Yingli Pan (*Shanghai Jiaotong University*)
Jeffrey Sachs (*The Earth Institute at Columbia University*)
JunhuiQian (*Shanghai Jiaotong University*)

Contents

List of Contributors

Jean-Louis Arcand
jean-louis.arcand@graduateinstitute.ch

Jean-Louis Arcand is Director of the Centre for Finance and Development, Professor of International Economics, and Head of the Ph.D. program in Development Economics at the Graduate Institute of International and Development Studies in Geneva, which he joined in 2008. He is a Founding Fellow of the European Union Development Network and Senior Fellow at the Fondation pour les études et recherches en développement international. He was Assistant and then Associate Professor at the University of Montréal, and Professor at the Centre d'Etudes et de Recherches en Développement International (CERDI). He holds a Ph.D. in Economics from MIT. His research focuses on the microeconomics of development. He has been a consultant to international organizations as well as to several national governments. He is currently leading impact evaluations in half a dozen countries, with the topics being investigated ranging from HIV-AIDS, to food security.

Peter Boone
pb@effint.org

Peter Boone is Chairman of Effective Intervention, a UK based charity in the United Kingdom. He is also a research associate at the Centre for Economic Performance, London School of Economics, and a non-resident Senior Fellow at the Peterson Institute, Washington D.C. where his current research interests include issues surrounding financial market regulation and stability. Previously, Dr. Boone worked at Brunswick UBS, a Moscow-based investment bank, and later was a Principal at Salute Capital Management, a UK-based hedge fund. Dr. Boone has worked as a resident macroeconomic advisor in Russia, Mongolia, Poland and Ukraine. He has advised on sovereign and corporate debt restructurings in the former Soviet Union, Eastern Europe and Latin America.

Seppo Honkapohja
Seppo.Honkapohja@bof.fi

Seppo Honkapohja is a Member of the Governing Board of the Bank of Finland. He was Professor of International Macroeconomics, University of Cambridge in 2004–2007. He has held Professorships with Academy of Finland, University of Helsinki and Turku School of Economics and Business Administration. He is Member of Academia Europaea and of Finnish Academy of Science and Letters, Fellow of the Econometric Society and of the European Economic Association, and recipient of an Honorary Doctorate from University of Turku. His research focuses on macro and monetary economics. His publications in English include over 80 articles and over 20 authored or edited books.

Simon Johnson
sjohnson@mit.edu

Simon Johnson is the Kurtz Professor of Entrepreneurship at MIT's Sloan School of Management. He is also a senior fellow at the Peterson Institute for International Economics, a co-founder of BaselineScenario.com, a member of the Congressional Budget Office's Panel of Economic Advisers, and a member of the FDIC's Systemic Resolution Advisory Committee. He is also a member of the private sector Systemic Risk Council founded and chaired by Sheila Bair. He is a regular contributor to NYT.com's Economix, Project Syndicate, and Bloomberg. He is also a contributing business editor at the Huffington Post. Professor Johnson is the co-author of *13 Bankers: The Wall Street Takeover and the Next Financial Meltdown* (2011) and *White House Burning: The Founding Fathers, Our National Debt, and Why It Matters to You* (2012) From April 2007 through August 2008, Professor Johnson was chief economist at the International Monetary Fund.

Hongzhong Liu
hzliu@fudan.edu.cn

Hongzhong Liu is Professor of Finance at Fudan University; Vice Dean of the Institute of Financial Studies, Chairman of Department of International Finance. He is also a Director of China Financial Society, Director of China International Financial Society and Director of Shanghai Financial Society.

Huw McKay
hmckay@westpac.com.au

Huw McKay is executive director and senior international economist at the Westpac Bank in Sydney, Australia. He is the Bank's spokesperson on pan-Asian economic and market issues.

Jing Nie
jing.nie@durham.ac.uk

Jing Nie is a Ph.D. candidate in Accounting and Finance at Durham University Business School, United Kingdom. She had graduated with a M.Sc. in Finance from University of Leicester. She specializes in multinational finance, international financial markets, risk management under exchange rate uncertainty and Chinese currency issues.

Kiyohiko Nishimura
nisimura@e.u-tokyo.ac.jp

Kiyohiko G. Nishimura is Professor of Economics at the University of Tokyo. Before returning to academia, he was Deputy Governor of the Bank of Japan for five years until March 19, 2013, one of the most turbulent periods in the history of the world economy and central banking. He has been particularly influential in the debates over macro-prudential policies, especially in pointing out the critical importance of demographic factors on property bubbles and financial crisis. He received his B.A. and M.A. from the University of Tokyo, and Ph.D. from Yale University. He was Associate Professor (1983–1994) and Professor (1994–2005) at the University of Tokyo, before joining the Bank of Japan as its Member of the Policy Board (2005–2008), and then as Deputy Governor (2008–2013).

Yingli Pan

panyl@sjtu.edu.cn

Yingli Pan is Professor of International Economics and Finance and Director of Research Center for Global Finance at Antai College of Economics and Management, Shanghai Jiao Tong University. Professor Pan is a member of Advisory Committee of Shanghai Municipal People's Government and the deputy director of Shanghai Research Institute of International Financial Center. She received her Ph.D. degree from East China Normal University in 1992. She spent one year in New York University as a Fulbright Study Scholar. She had headed the Department of Finance at East China Normal University. Her research fields include macroeconomics, international economics and finance. Her published books include the *Transformation of Chinese Economy and Finance* (2012), *International Financial Centers: Historical Experience and China's Future* (2010).

Junhui Qian

jhqian@sjtu.edu.cn

Junhui Qian is Associate Professor at Antai College of Economics & Management, Shanghai Jiao Tong University. He obtained his Ph.D. in economics from Rice University in 2007. His research interests include econometric theory, monetary theory and policy, and economic reform of China. He has published academic papers in the Journal of Econometrics and policy-oriented articles in newspapers. He is currently teaching econometrics, intermediate macroeconomics, and Chinese economy.

Tai Qin

fduqintai@gmail.com

Qin Tai is a Ph.D. candidate at Fudan University. He specializes in financial markets and international finance.

Jeffrey D. Sachs
sachs@ei.columbia.edu

Jeffrey D. Sachs is Director of The Earth Institute, Quetelet Professor of Sustainable Development, and Professor of Health Policy and Management at Columbia University. He is Special Advisor to United Nations Secretary-General Ban Ki-moon on the Millennium Development Goals, and Director of the UN Sustainable Development Solutions Network. He is co-founder and Chief Strategist of Millennium Promise Alliance, and is director of the Millennium Villages Project. Sachs is a syndicated columnist whose monthly newspaper columns appear in more than 80 countries. He has authored three bestsellers in the past seven years: *The End of Poverty* (2005), *Common Wealth: Economics for a Crowded Planet* (2008), and *The Price of Civilization* (2011). His most recent book is *To Move the World: JFK's Quest for Peace* (2013).

Wing Thye Woo
wtwoo@ucdavis.edu

Wing Thye Woo is Executive Director of the Penang Institute in George Town (Malaysia), Professor at University of California at Davis, Chang Jiang Professor at the Central University of Finance and Economics in Beijing, Distinguished Professor at Fudan University in Shanghai, and Director of the East Asia Program within The Earth Institute at Columbia University. His current research focuses on macroeconomic management of open economies, and on the growth the East Asia economies, especially, China, Indonesia and Malaysia. He helped in 2001 to establish the Asian Economic Panel (AEP), a forum of about 80 specialists on Asian economies which meets triannually to discuss important Asian economic issues; and he is the Managing Editor of the Asian Economic Papers. In 2012, he published *A New Economic Growth Engine for China: Escaping the Middle-Income Trap by Not Doing More of the Same* and *Ranking the Liveability of the Major Cities in the World.*

Jun Wu
junwu@sjtu.edu.cn

Jun Wu graduated from East China Normal University in 1997 with M.Phil. in Finance. After teaching in the Department of Finance at Tongji University for six years, she went to Hong Kong University of Science & Technology and obtained an M.Phil. in Economics in 2007. Wu Jun is now a Ph.D. candidate in Finance at Shanghai Jiao Tong University. Wu Jun has published articles in well-known journals such as *China International Finance Review*, *International Economic Review*, and *Journal of World Economy.*

Xinru Wu
xrwu@finance.ecnu.edu.cn

Xinru Wu is Professor of Finance in East China Normal University. Dr. Wu specializes in macroeconomics, exchange rates and international finance. He is the author of three books: *Macroeconomics, Financial Engineering*, and *Growth Effects of Capital Account Liberalization*; and he has published more than 20 papers in journals including *World Economy, Journal of Finance and Economics*, and *China Finance.* Dr. Wu participated in the National Ministry of Education Planning Fund Project, "RMB Real Effective Exchange Rate Index Construction and Technical Support." Dr. Wu won the second prize in the Fifth Shanghai Social Science Research competition for his paper entitled "Determining the Basis for a Reasonable Level of the RMB Exchange Rate."

Yingfeng Xu
yingfeng.xu@ualberta.ca

Yingfeng Xu is Associate Professor in the Department of Economics at the University of Alberta. He graduated with a Ph.D. in economics in 1989 from the University of Buffalo. Dr. Xu's research interests are in international trade and finance, economic development, and the Chinese economy. He has published extensively both on economic theory and policy oriented empirical studies. He has consulted for the Asian Development Bank.

Zhichao Zhang
Zhichao.Zhang@durham.ac.uk

Zhichao Zhang (OXON) is Lecturer in International Finance at Durham University, United Kingdom. He is Deputy Chairman of Chinese National Society for the World Economy and Chairman of Shanghai Research Centre for International Finance. He specializes in Chinese currency issues and international monetary relations. His main research areas include capital controls, exchange rate determination, Chinese exchange rate policy, management of China's foreign reserves, foreign reserve accumulation and dynamics in emerging markets, sovereign wealth funds, and dynamic stochastic general equilibrium modeling of the Chinese economy.

Si Zhou
si.zhou@durham.ac.uk

Si Zhou is Research Assistant at Durham University Business School, United Kingdom. His research interests include mutual funds, portfolio management, corporate finance, merger and acquisition, Bayesian decision making and empirical asset pricing.

John Qi Zhu
john.qizhu@gmail.com

John Qi Zhu is currently Assistant Professor of Finance at School of Management, Fudan University. He is also a fellow at the Wharton Financial Institution Center and the Research Center for Global Finance at Shanghai Jiao Tong University. He received his Ph.D. and Master's Degree from Emory University and Southern Illinois University Edwardsville, respectively, after his undergraduate study in economics at East China Normal University. His research interests focus on empirical asset pricing issues in the global and Chinese financial markets, such as jump-diffusion modeling, household portfolio allocations, predictive regressions, and finance-growth nexus. He has published papers in journals such as the *Financial Analyst Journal* and *Pacific Basin Finance Journal*. He is currently teaching the valuation and financial econometrics courses in the Master of Finance program. He has been awarded the National Natural Science

Foundation of China Research Grant, Shanghai Pu Jiang Program for Talented Overseas Returnees and a University-wide teaching prize when he was at the Shanghai Jiao Tong University.

Xi Zhu
zhuxi97@sjtu.edu.cn

Xi Zhu is Associate Professor in the Department of Economics at Shanghai Jiao Tong University. His research focuses on micro-economic issues in development economics, including household behavior, access to finance and policy evaluation. Xi Zhu completed his Ph.D. in Economics at Tsinghua University in 2006. He has been a visitor at the Department of Economics at Texas A&M University.

SECTION I

ANALYTICAL OVERVIEW

Chapter 1

Mobilizing China's Financial Sector Efficiently and Safely for Sustaining Economic Transformation and Strengthening Global Financial Stability

Yingli Pan, Jeffrey David Sachs, Wing Thye Woo and John Qi Zhu

The Interactive Nature of Modern Economic Growth

Just as it is necessary for the diet of a person to change when she moves from baby-hood to girl-hood, a country should also change its economic policies after reaching a different stage of economic development in order to facilitate if not enable the progression to the next stage. Without the change in both cases, subsequent performance would, at best, be below potential. The worst outcome from policy paralysis would not just be stagnation, but stagnation, followed by decay, and, then, by collapse. In short, one should always be skeptical about the adage "if it ain't broke, don't fix it" because the absence of policy changes could be due as much to ignorance and complacency as to caution based on the realization that our understanding of the world is imperfect.

In order for a leader to excuse her policy inaction by claiming to be being prudently cautious, she also has to claim that the state

A part of this chapter draws on Yingli Pan's research project on "The evolution and reconfiguration of the international monetary system." We acknowledge gratefully the financial sponsorship from Mr. Shi Zhengfu, Chairman of Comway Capital Group and Director of the Research Center of New Political Economy in Fudan University. We have benefited from constructive comments from Professor Yang Chaojun, Antai College of Economics & Management, Shanghai Jiaotong University. Liu Jianfeng and Feng Xuhui of the Institute of Contemporary Finance, Shanghai Jiaotong University helped with data collection.

of our knowledge about the economic growth phenomenon is too inadequate to justify policy activism to quicken economic growth. Our considered judgment is that the degree of policy activism to pursue depends on, one, the analytical and implementation capacity of the state agencies, and, two, the stage of economic development. Clearly, if the leadership is ignorant and badly-advised on economic matters, or if the project implementation process is dysfunctional to the extent of being counter-productive, then economic stagnation from policy inaction could be preferable to a quicker economic collapse from wrong policies.

The stage of economic development matters because the lower the stage of economic development, the more we know about what to do to accelerate economic growth, and the more ways we also know how to do it. This is because the lower the stage of economic development, the larger is the number of countries that have already graduated from that stage, and hence the larger the pool of collective experiences for us to draw upon for guidance on how to facilitate economic development out of that particular low stage.

It is correct to say that the voluminous literature on the economic growth of Western Europe, the overseas offshoots of Western Europe, and Japan over the last two hundred years[2] had provided good guidance to policymakers in South Korea and Taiwan to launch successful catch-up growth in their economies in the mid-1960s. It is therefore also correct to say that, in 2013, we know more about what to do, and know more ways, to sustain economic growth in middle-income China than we know about what to do to sustain growth in the high-income United States.

China entered into the middle-income category in 2006,[3] a milestone still denied to its three large neighbors, India, Indonesia and Philippines which were richer than China in 1978. However, Woo *et al.* (2012) have warned that continued fast progress by China to high-income status cannot be taken for granted. Four of the five largest economies in Latin American — Argentina, Brazil, Chile,

[2]A particularly helpful example of the literature would be Simon Kuznets (1966).

[3]This is according to the Woo's (2012) Catch-Up Index (CUI) which is the ratio of the country's per capita GDP per capita to US per capita GDP, with both measured in purchasing power parity units. In Woo's classification, middle-income begins with CUI at 20% and high-income begins at 55%.

and Mexico — have been in residence in the middle-income category at least since 1960. Furthermore, the secular decline in the Catch-Up Index (CUI) value of Venezuela, the fifth member, from its petroleum-induced high-income status pushed Venezuela down into middle-income status in 1980. And Malaysia is a nearer and more recent warning about the middle-income trap; Woo (2011). After having been hailed in 1993 by the World Bank (1993) as an East Asian Miracle economy, catch-up growth in Malaysia stopped in 1995.

Another way to describe the absence of catch-up growth in these large Latin American economies and Malaysia is to say that they are no longer experiencing what Simon Kuznets (1966) had called Modern Economic Growth (MEG). MEG is the type of economic growth that began in Western Europe in the late 18th Century, and it is distinguished from earlier types of growth on several dimensions: a sustained high growth rate in per capita output, large shifts in the composition of output, an increasing diversity in goods and services produced, and rapid institutional and ideological adjustments. MEG is not just magnification of quantities, it is also comprehensive transformation of qualitative features. MEG is the synergy produced by the two mutually-supportive phenomena of growth and transformation and not an outcome produced by technological progress alone. In short, the quintessential feature of MEG is continual change across the board, and this is the basis of our opening statement that a country should "change its economic policies after reaching a different stage of economic development in order to facilitate if not enable the progression to the next stage."

Our research on economic growth in other countries has led us to the conclusion that China's successful economic transition from middle-income to high-income cannot be achieved by the present dualistic policy regime of state-led industrialization facilitated by state-directed allocation of capital, and enthusiastic private-sector participation, mostly, in light industries and in the low and medium value-added portions of the service sector. The Soviet Union achieved middle-income status without private-sector participation but it ended in economic collapse in 1991. The achievement of middle-income status in Malaysia (with the China-style policy regime of state-private dualism) has been followed by economic stagnation because of policy inaction from the government's short-sighted attitude of "if it ain't broke, don't fix it."

Among the fundamental policy changes that China must now make in order to avoid falling into the middle-income trap is its financial sector policy. The role of the financial system is not just to mobilize savings but also to allocate them to the most productive uses. On both of these fronts, China has much to do. To get a sense of what needs to be reformed, and the priority of the different reforms, we first review the historical process that has created the present financial system.

The Evolution of the Financial System

The two primary tasks that the state has set for the financial system since 1949 are, one, to support the rapid industrialization of the country, and, two, to help maintain social stability. The financial system is of course only one of several policy instruments used to promote industrialization and keep social peace.

During the 1952–1978 period of Stalinist socialism where there was central planning and state ownership of all production units, the only type of financial institution that was needed for these two tasks were cash-disbursement cum payments-clearing institutions. The specialized banks established in the central planning period were cashiers to dispense budgetary allocation to support projects in the particular economic sector or economic activity, e.g., Agricultural Bank of China, and People's Construction Bank. The evolution of the financial system since the initiation of market-oriented reform at the end of 1978 is the consequence of trying to carry out these two tasks in the face of policy reforms in other parts of the economy to permit the Chinese economy to converge to a predominantly private market economy in order to initiate and sustain MEG.

Up to the end of 1978, the primary source of revenue to finance industrialization was the agricultural sector. From 1952 to 1978, the state underpriced agricultural products greatly and overpriced the industrial products in order to generate large profits for the state-owned enterprises (SOEs) to hand over to the state treasury. Chinese economists have analogized the gap between the artificially low agricultural prices and the artificially high industrial prices to the gap between the blades of a pair of scissors that is opened to be in the cut position, and they have hence called this resource-transfer instrument the "price-scissors mechanism."

Bi Sisheng (2003) estimated that the state took approximately 800 billion yuan from the agricultural sector during the 1952–1985 period by means of the price-scissors mechanism. During this same period, investments in physical assets for the SOEs totaled 1,442 billion yuan, in which 845.1 billion yuan came from the government. This indicates that the capital diverted by the "price-scissors mechanism" accounted for 95% of the government investment in fixed assets in SOEs and 55% of the overall investment in fixed assets in SOEs.

At the end of 1978, the Chinese government began to relax the ban on the private sector by allowing a dual-track system in the agricultural sector. The part of output that was beyond the state-set quota (which had to be sold at the state-set price to the state purchasing agency) could be sold in the newly-legalized free markets. For the financial sector, the marketization process that began in 1979 was noteworthy because it initiated a new round of the monetization of the Chinese economy. Monetization was then boosted further by the steady reduction over time in the number of agricultural products that had state-set prices.

The financial phenomenon of monetization helped the state to finance industrialization by increasing its seignorage revenue with large-scale money creation that did not cause high inflation. From 1979–1992, the average annual growth rates for M2, GDP, and CPI were 26.2%, 6.5% and 9.5% respectively, and the ratio of M2 to GDP rose from 25% in 1979 to 94% in 1992.[4] Figure 1 shows that after the high inflation in the 1993–1996 period, which signaled the near completion of this round of monetization and hence a tighter connection between money growth and inflation, the state reduced its collection

[4]The exception to price stability was 1988 when CPI increased by 18.8%, a development that was socially destabilizing. This positive aspect of monetization for China's macroeconomy was noted in McKinnon (1991); and a number of scholars have computed the seignorage revenue from the monetization, e.g., Zhang Jie (1997, 2001), Xie Ping (1996), and World Bank (1996).

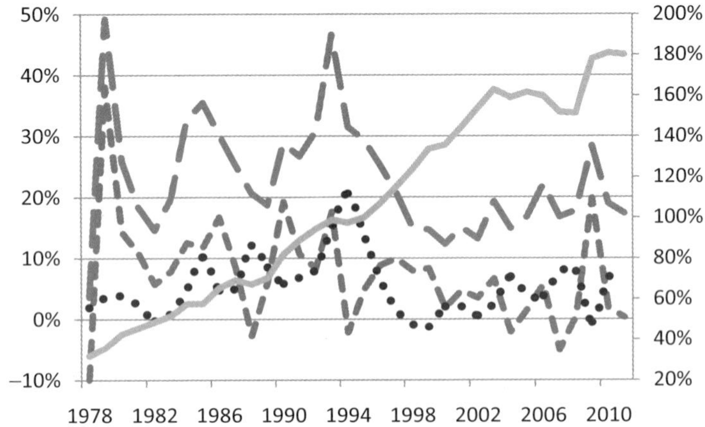

Figure 1. Monetary indicators in China.
Source: China Statistical Yearbook (2012) and Zhang (2011).

of seignorage revenue by reducing the subsequent annual M2 growth rate to less than 20.

Figure 1 also reports a commonly used indicator of seignorage revenue known as "excessive supply of M2" which is calculated as the M2 growth rate minus the (real) GDP growth rate minus the inflation rate.[5] The collection of seignorage revenue was lower in the 1996–2010 period than the 1978–1995 period.

The financial system assumed increasing importance starting in 1985 when the fiscal strength of the central government began to be reduced by the termination of the price-scissors mechanism in 1985, by the reform of the industrial and service sectors that began in 1984, and by the decentralization of fiscal and economic power to the provinces that began in 1983–1984. The price-scissors mechanism had been rendered inoperative by, one, the marketization of agricultural

[5]The exception to this was in 2009 when M2 grew 28% to counter the deflationary effects of the Global Financial Crisis.

production and distribution was almost complete by 1985 — which meant no more artificially low agricultural prices — and the marketization of the industrial sector that began in 1984 and led to fewer and fewer artificially high (relative) prices for industrial products.

The great increase in prosperity in the countryside brought by the agricultural reforms emboldened the government to also use the dual-track mechanism in 1984 to reform the industrial and service sectors. The government signed profit-sharing agreements with the SOEs, allowed them broad discretion in the use of their share of the profits (e.g., for bonus payment and capacity expansion), permitted them operational autonomy (e.g., in what and how to produce, and the replacement of permanent workers with contract workers), and allowed them to sell the above-quota output in free markets. The government also legalized the establishment of collectively-owned i.e., owned by the local instead of the central or provincial government non-agricultural enterprises in the rural area. These rural enterprises are famously known as township and village enterprises (TVEs). In many locations, and increasingly over time, many TVEs were private enterprises masquerading as collectively-owned enterprises.

One unintended outcome of this array of changes in agricultural and industrial pricing and in the regulation of private economic activities was a much larger-than-expected drop in the fiscal power of the federal government. After an initially impressive performance by the SOE sector upon enactment of the enterprise reform, the financial situation of the SOE sector deteriorated sharply. From 1985 to 1994, an average of 5.6% of annual GDP was redistributed to SOEs every year in various forms of subsidies through budgetary channels. Within this 5.6 figure was a declining trend in central government support. The steady weakening of central government's fiscal power caused the subsidies to SOEs to decline over time from 7.5% of GDP in 1985 to 2.2% in 1994 despite the mounting losses in the SOE sector.

The government kept the SOEs afloat (and hence suppressed unemployment from appearing) by channeling implicit subsidies in the form of loans from the state-owned banks (SOBs). Between 1987 and 1995, the average deficit of public sector amounted to 11.16% of GDP, of which 63.53% are financed by the banking sector. Such loans were classified as "government subsidiary loans"

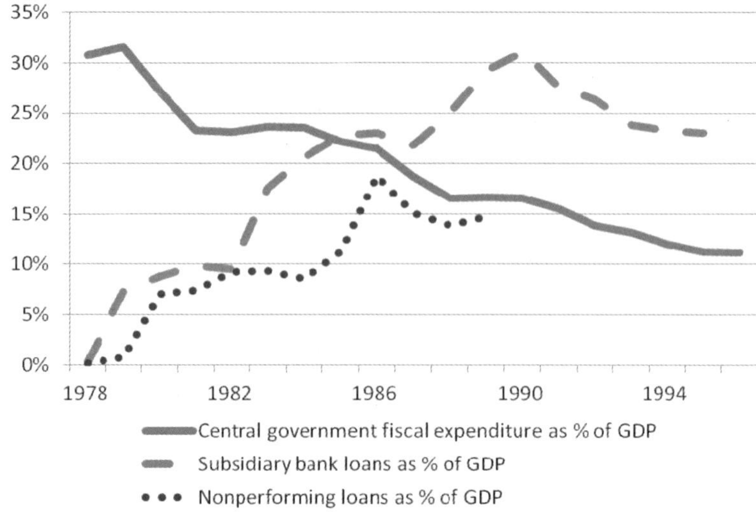

Figure 2. Fiscal expenditure versus bank loans.
Source: Statistical Yearbook of China and Zhang (2011).

whose sub-categories included "loans for national stability," "loans for Chinese New Year," and "payroll loans."

The government of course also used loans from SOBs to fuel the growth of the industrial sector, i.e., bank loans substituting for capital injection from the budget. The average debt-to-asset ratio of SOEs in 1994 rose up to 80%, and 80% of the SOE's had debt ratios higher than 90% (Zhang, 2001).

Figure 2 plots the shares of fiscal expenditure and subsidiary banking loans as a percentage of annual GDP between 1979 and 1996. Figure 2 also shows the profile of non-performing loans (NPLs) as a share of GDP. There was a significant substitution effect between the fiscal expenditure and subsidiary banking loans as well as a positive association between the ratio of NPLs and the share of subsidiary bank loans to the GDP. Against this background, the banks offered sufficiently high interest rates to absorb household savings, effectively taking on the function of government taxation. Banks effectively assumed the fiscal function of government by extending low-interest loans to SOEs.

The market estimate in 1998 of aggregate NPLs as share of total assets for China's four largest SOBs was about 48%. China's entry to the WTO in 2001 with a commitment to open the domestic financial industry in 5 years to foreign institutions created an urgent demand for the immediate recapitalization of the SOBs to clean up their balance sheets in order to have equal cost competitiveness against the foreign banks.

There were a number reasons in the 1985–1996 period for the large losses in the SOE sector which created this tremendous amount of NPLs in the SOBs. First, the operational autonomy granted to the SOE managers allowed them to engage in embezzlement and asset-stripping. Second, the managers expanded investment recklessly because they were operating under the soft-budget situation where profits were privatized via embezzlement and the losses were socialized via bank loans. Third, the soft-budget constraint allowed the SOEs to continue to be less efficient than the TVEs e.g. by having excess workers. Fourth, the competition from the TVEs reduced the profitability of the SOEs. Clearly, without fundamental reforms of the SOEs, the generation of more NPLs in the future was unavoidable.[6]

The next significant transformation of the financial system occurred in the 1997–2006 period to address the risk of a systemic collapse caused by a bankrupt banking system, a point that was made clearly in the regional economic conflagration in 1997–1998 known as the Asian Financial Crisis. The government had to end the chronic NPL problem in the SOBs, and to strengthen the cost competitiveness of the domestic banks before China's expected accession to WTO.

The termination of the chronic NPL problem at the SOBs had two components — one internal and one external to the financial sector. The first component to solving the NPL problem was to inform the national heads of the SOBs that they would be fired if the NPL ratio were to go up for two consecutive years. The incentive to be more cautious in extending bank loans was passed down the chain of command by a similar commitment to dismiss the heads of the provincial branches of the banks if these branches were to report consecutive increases in the NPL ratio.

[6]See Fan and Woo (1996) and Sachs and Woo (2000) for a review of the debate on the causes of the losses of the SOEs.

The second component to ending the chronic NPL problem was to end the endemic losses of the SOEs, the primary cause of the NPLs in the portfolios of the SOBs. The government launched a boldly comprehensive reorganization of the SOE sector to restore the financial health and boost the economic vitality of the SOE sector by privatizing most of the small and medium SOEs and some of the large SOEs, by improving the internal incentives of the remaining SOEs to maximize profit; and by reducing the reliance of firms on bank loans to finance investment. In 1997, the China Securities Regulatory Commission issued Document No. 15 that specified that "securities market and institutions should serve the reform and development of SOEs" and "(securities market and institutions) should endeavor to raise supplementary capital for the SOEs in order for them to acquire other financially struggling SOEs that might still have upside potential."

Most of the remaining SOEs were corporatized, and part of their shares were sold in the Shenzhen and Shanghai stock exchanges to bring in strategic investors and independent directors to help monitor and advise the operations of the SOEs. The corporate bond market was also enlarged along with the two stock exchanges in order to wean the enterprises from the habit of financing the bulk of their investment with bank loans. Figure 3 plots the market shares of IPO capitalization of firms by different ownership forms in the 1990–2012 period. The market shares for SOEs were always 60% to 80% of total annual IPO financing.

It must be pointed out however that the government also distorted the financial markets to help make the balance sheets of the SOEs look better. For one, the central bank kept the interest rate on bank deposits low in order to keep the lending rate paid by the SOEs low. For another, the government limited the public listing of firms (to the great disadvantage of the privately-owned firms) in the two domestic equity markets to raise the price–earnings (P/E) ratio, and thus lower the cost of equity financing. As part of China's industrial policy of promoting future important industries, the state especially favored SOEs in targeted industry sectors in the public listing selection process. Figure 4 plots the average P/E ratio for the IPO firms during the same period. Figure 5 compares the annual

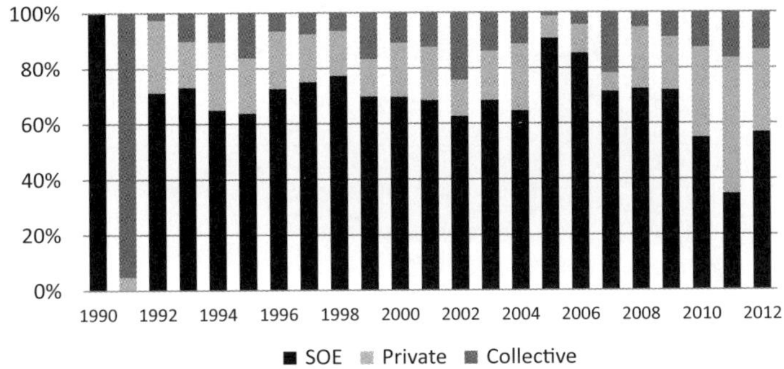

Figure 3. Proportion of A-share IPO capitalization by ownership.

Note: State-owned enterprises (SOEs) include the central and provincial SOEs; Collective enterprises include foreign-owned enterprises, collectively-owned enterprises, public enterprises, etc.

Source: The classification of firms by ownership is from Wind Info.
All data are from April 2013 Wind Info and author's own calculations.

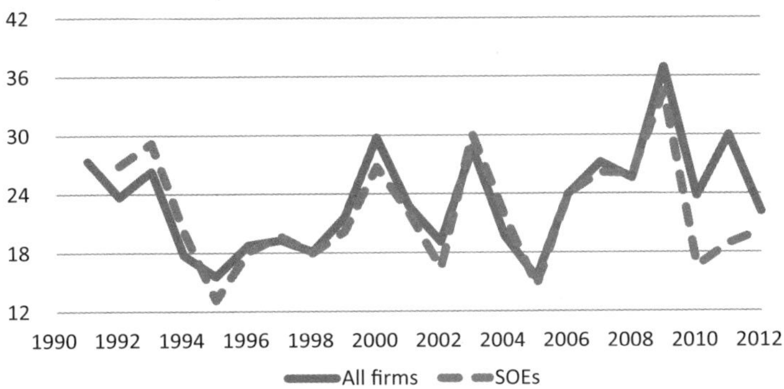

Figure 4. Average IPO P/E ratio.

Note: 1. State-owned enterprises (SOEs) include the central and provincial SOEs. 2. IPO price-earnings ratio = Total market cap at IPO/Total net earnings in the previous year.

Source: All data are from Wind Info and author's calculations.

dividend yields of A-share stocks to the one-year rate for deposits and the one-year rate for bank lending.

To summarize, the endemic losses of the SOE sector were addressed by a decisive program of restructuring the SOE sector

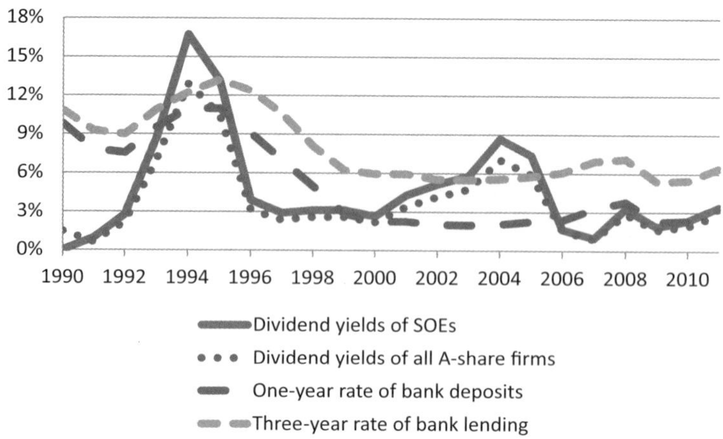

Figure 5. Dividend yields and lending rates.

Note: 1. State-owned enterprises (SOEs) include the central and provincial SOEs. 2. dividend yield = total annual cumulative dividend in the last 12 months/ year-end market capitalization.

(especially the mass privatization of the small and medium SOEs and the government-sponsored strategic restructuring of the remaining large SOEs), and by a financing program that supplies the SOE sector with cheap household savings mobilized through the tightly-regulated equity markets and the state banking system. These moves succeeded in turning around the financial position of the SOE sector by the early 2000s, and, hence, stopped the creation of new NPLs.

The government implemented an equally comprehensive restructuring of the SOB sector in order to remove the systemic risks of the bankrupt banking system and prepare it to compete against the foreign banks that would come in upon China's entry into WTO. The government set up asset management companies that bought a large portion of the NPLs at face value from the SOBs, introduced a central bank refinancing scheme for the SOBs, and injected capital directly from public saving and foreign reserves. The SOBs were also corporatized and listed in the stock market to bring in foreign strategic investors. The most important means of recapitalizing the banks was to boost their profitability by setting a sustained large margin between the lending rate and the deposit rate; and then to use the retained earning to increase core capital of the banks. By 2006, all major SOBs except for the Agricultural Bank of China had completed asset restructuring, met the international standards for prudential operation, and successfully made initial public offerings in the global equity markets.

With the completion of split-share structure reform in 2006, state-owned equities in public SOE's become "true" common shares with the equal provision of valuation and liquidity, see Inoue (2005). The aggregate profit of the banking sector in 2006 was 10 times the amount of just two year ago. Stock indices began to soar. The year 2006 would have been the ideal moment for the Chinese government to complete its withdrawal from its half-century-long financial repression policies and transform the financial system from a government-dominated one to a market-oriented one. If market interest rates had been introduced, the regulatory quota system for the stock issuance phased out, the restrictions on private small and medium banks relaxed, and financial supervisory capacity strengthened beginning in 2006, China's economic growth in 2013 would most likely be more robust and sustainable. Unfortunately, little or no progress has been made on these fronts, making the 2007–2013 the lost years in financial sector development. It is now imperative to immediately launch initiatives that would remove the remaining repressive financial policies to give China a modern financial system, which can support its economic growth to jump over the middle-income trap.

The Financial-Sector Reform Agenda

Most of the studies on the progress of financial development in China use an array of stock-flow ratios like the M2 to GDP ratio and the stock market capitalization to GDP ratio. As the M2 to GDP ratio has increased from 124 percent in 1998 to 188 percent in 2010, and the capitalization of the Shanghai and Shenzhen stock markets has climbed from an average of 30 percent of GDP in 1997–2005 and 53 percent in 2006-2012, it is common for many China analysts to report steady progress in the financial development of China.

However, two recent studies have suggested that this steady upward march of the stock-flow ratios like M2-GDP hides some unfavorable trends in China's financial sector, that could trigger a financial collapse: (1) Hongzhong Liu and Tai Qin (Chapter 8: "The Structural Friction in China's Banking System: Causes, Measurement and Solutions"), and (2) Jean-Louis Arcand (Chapter 9: Credit Rationing, Bank Bailouts, and the Deleterious Impact of Credit: Evidence from China). These two studies lend credence to our warning at the beginning of this chapter that the "worst outcome from policy paralysis [exemplified by little or no progress in financial sector reform in the 2007–2013 period] would not just be stagnation, but stagnation, followed by decay, and, then, by collapse."

Hongzhong Liu and Tai Qin (Chapter 8) challenge the conventional view that there has been progress (albeit, not enough) in China's financial development. They develop a price indicator instead of using the usual quantity indicator to measure the level of financial development. Their price indicator is the spread between the shadow ("social") rate of return on bank loans and the actual rate of return on bank loans. The size of the spread measures the degree of misallocation of the bank loans — the smaller the spread, the more efficient is the bank sector. Liu and Qin found the disturbing result that the spread between the shadow rate of return and the actual rate of return on bank loans has widened over time, from 1.02 percentage points in 2003 to 2.38 in 2005, to 3.25 in 2007 and then to 3.76 in 2010.

Hongzhong Liu and Tai Qin identifies the cause of the increasing inefficiency to come from two factors

- the disproportionate amount of bank loans that was allocated to state-controlled companies, and
- the average productivity of the state-controlled companies being lower than the average productivity of domestic private companies.

Jean-Louis Arcand (Chapter 9) also shares Hongzhong Liu and Tai Qin's assessment that China's financial sector has become more dysfunctional over time. In an earlier analysis of cross-country data (Arcand, Berkes and Panizza. (2012), he finds that an increase in a stock-flow ratio (e.g. M2-GDP ratio) when it is at a low value has positive impact on economic growth, but there is a threshold value for the ratio beyond which an increase in the ratio would be harmful to economic growth. Specifically, this earlier study found that the marginal effect of financial development on economic growth becomes negative when credit to the private sector reaches 100 percent of GDP.

In a new paper in this volume, Jean-Louis Arcand finds that this reversal from good effect to bad effect is generated in a simple model with endogenous default probability, credit rationing, and bailout of state enterprises. The important point is that the presence of a bailout leads to a level of loans which is "too large" with respect to the social optimum. When Jean-Louis Arcand tests this model on Chinese data, he finds an empirical regularity that has hitherto gone unnoticed in the Chinese context: there is a large, negative, and statistically significant impact of outstanding loans on the economic performance of counties.

Financial reform is now clearly overdue. The most important requirement in the formulation of the financial-sector policy is the recognition by the Chinese government that the role of a government in a middle-income country has to be substantially different from that of a government in a low-income country if dynamic catch-up growth is to continue. Specifically, the Chinese government should now no longer focus primarily on raising funds cheaply to promote industrialization because China is now a highly industrialized economy. The remaining part of industrialization is small, and the issue there is not the quantity but the quality of industrial expansion.

Furthermore, the fiscal position of the Chinese government is now strong enough that it does not need to distort the financial sector in order to finance its support for industrialization indirectly. Fiscal revenue grew at an average 20% per year since 2001, and fiscal revenue has climbed from 10.7% of GDP in 1997 to over 20% of GDP in the past few years. The rapid appreciation of land price has rendered the government even more secure fiscally, and so the government should fund its industrialization efforts directly and give up its direct intervention in the allocation of financial resources.

The time is ripe for financial transition.[7] The financial transition can only be achieved through a comprehensive reform agenda for

[7]The concept of financial transition was introduced for the first time by Yingli Pan in 2010 in the article "Why We Should Accelerate Financial Transition" that appeared in the "THINKER" column of *Jiefang Daily*; Yingli Pan (2012). Also see Yingli Pan (2001) for an innovative perspective on the need for financial transition that is based on combining Marxian political economic theory on income distribution with modern economic theory on resource allocation.

the financial system. As Hu Jingtao pointed out in his report at 18th Party Congress, all reforms should be market-oriented, giving the market a bigger and more effective role in resource allocation. Therefore, the over-arching objectives in the new growth-oriented financial sector policy that the Chinese government should adopt are "efficiency" and "stability" and not "industrialization." The government focuses primarily on ensuring that the financial market is channeling funds efficiently to the most productive uses, and that the financial market does not pose a systemic threat to the economy. This new operational stance will foster a well-functioning, market-oriented financial ecosystem whose prudential aspects are closely monitored.

In order to switch to the financial-sector policy that will facilitate China's graduation from middle-income status to high-income status, four key sets of financial reforms need to be undertaken:

1. Enlarge the financial sector by diversifying the range of financial institutions and the range of financial assets, paying particular attention to the increase in equity issuance by private domestic firms;
2. Deregulate and modernize the banking sector;
3. Update the international dimensions of the financial sector to be in line with globalization and China's emergence as a major economic power; and
4. Insert shock-absorbers and circuit-breakers into the financial system to increase the resilience of the system to financial malfeasance and financial melt-downs; and build up the financial fire-fighting capability of the regulatory agencies to minimise the costs of financial institution failure and to prevent financial contagion.

The stock and bond markets: Diversifying the financial sector while enlarging it

The range of financial instruments that finances investment is too narrow. In 2011, 80% of the external financing of Chinese enterprises came from bank lending, while corporate bond issuances and equity offerings accounted for 12% and 8%, respectively. This means not only that the banking sector bears 80% of the risk from investment, it also means the banking sector is a systemic risk to the economy.

The failure of the banking sector will certainly bring down the entire Chinese economy. It is therefore prudent to diversify the sources of working capital and investment capital. The corporate bond market must expand significantly to provide much more working capital, and the equity markets must grow several folds to make them more important than the banks in supplying investment capital.

The first fundamental step in enlarging the stock market quickly and improving its efficiency greatly is to reform the regulatory quota system for equity issuance by granting equal market access to firms of different ownership, and allowing more qualified firms to be listed. Private enterprises have been discriminated against in the approval process for listing, and the resulting smaller number of listed companies depressed the cost of equity financing to benefit the SOEs that are favored in the listing. The unusually high P/E ratios also discourage business executives from taking a long-term view in the management of the SOEs because they incentivize business executives to immediately cash in their shares for profits. The approval process for listing must become blind to the ownership form of the applicant, and become more permissive to increasing the number of listings in order to increase the supply of equity offerings for lowering the P/E ratios.

The second fundamental step in increasing the size and efficiency of the stock market is to strengthen the rule of law in the operations of the stock market. Guo Shuqing, Chairman of the China Securities Regulatory Commission, was correct in his remarks on December 8, 2012 at the opening ceremony of the Shanghai Stock Exchange Forum that integrity and the rule of law are the two cornerstones of a fair and efficient capital market as well as the prerequisites for effective resource allocation. The essential elements of the rule of law include, but not limited to, a robust legal system, thorough implementation of the law, harsh punishment of dishonest behavior, and institutionalized check and balance of power.

The government also should improve the working of the stock market by:

- establishing a specialized court for financial issues, and grant it judicial independence to enhance its effectiveness in law enforcement and to mete out punitive penalties;

- introducing a legal framework in which small and medium investors can initiate class litigation suits against listed companies or financial institutions for compensation for their fraud-induced losses;
- specifying the minimum payout ratio to regulate the distribution policy of public firms;
- observing strictly the policies regarding the penalty of delisting poor performance firms;
- scrutinizing closer the veracity of data supplied by listed firms to protect investors, especially the small ones, from financial statement fraud (for instance, steel firms sometimes misreport their steel production capacity so as to hide the extent of their excess capacity); and
- prosecuting foul plays, such as predatory pre-IPO investment, to the full extent.[8]

An effective financial supervisory and regulatory system would be essential to guarantee both the efficient allocation of financial resources and the shared benefit from economic growth.

There has been more talk than action on scaling up the size of the corporate bond market in the last decade. Part of this unhappy situation is due to over-cautiousness by the relevant state agencies, and the second part of the delay is caused by reluctance to allow the participation of private companies. While these two defects should be addressed decisively, we see that the difficulties of growing the corporate bond market had been compounded by the absence of a large, liquid secondary market in government long-term bonds. The existence of a well-developed government bond market would have greatly increased the credibility of the institutional credit rating system. Sovereign credit has traditionally been the greatest intangible asset for a modern economy by facilitating the government to raise a large sum of money to accomplish projects of great national importance. Moreover, as a traditional Chinese saying, "what the sovereign does, the people will follow," a gold standard system of infallible

[8]Criminality is a phenomenon that is common in both developing and well-developed financial markets. The case of the USA is laid out by Jeffrey Sachs (2013) in Chapter 2 of this book.

sovereign credit would exemplify the practice of integrity and fiduciary duties for all bond market participants.

We suggest that one way of accelerating the development of the government bond market is to set up a well-functioning municipal bond market. China's municipal governments have immense difficulties in raising funds at reasonable costs for profitable infrastructure projects because there is no reputable credit rating system. We propose that a few qualified municipal governments be allowed to issue RMB-denominated municipal bonds in the Hong Kong market as well as in the domestic market. These particular municipal government issuers would then be obliged to comply with the legal practices of Hong Kong in protecting creditors' interest and be subject to various market disciplines set by global investors. The acceptance of these municipal bonds by global investors would increase the creditworthiness of these bonds to Chinese investors and allow funds to be raised cheaper than at the present. The other municipal governments that have equally transparent public finances which are as sound as the public finances of the Hong Kong-listed municipal governments should then be able to raise funds at almost the same lower costs.

We recognize of course that a vibrant market for municipal bonds requires that the present system of local finance be revamped to give most local governments stable and adequate local revenue bases to support most of their local expenditure. For example, the size of central-to-local fiscal transfers should be reduced by allowing some of the central taxes to become local taxes (e.g. lower the central income tax and allow provincial income taxes). And the revenue from land sales by local governments should be replaced by a system of local property tax.

The banking system: Deregulation and modernization

The banking system has been very profitable in the last decade, particularly in the recent sub-period. According to the *2012 Development Report of China's Top 500 Enterprises* released by China Enterprise Confederation, China's Big-Four Banks (i.e., ICBC, ABC, BOC, and CCB[9]) and Bank of Communications jointly

[9]ICBC = Industrial and Commercial Bank of China, ABC = Agricultural Bank of China, BOC = Bank of China, and CCB = Construction Bank of China.

accounted for 5.7% of the 500 enterprises total revenue but 32.2% of the total profit. For the 272 largest manufacturing firms, they accounted for 42.7% of total revenue and 25% of total profit. In a survey of the branches of the Big-Four Banks and 131 enterprises in 15 cities of 5 northwestern provinces conducted by the Hanzhong Sub-branch of BOC, it was found that the operating margin of the banks had a year-on-year growth of 61.5% in 2012 Q1,[10] while the enterprises experienced a decline of 9.6%; Yang and Dai (2012).

The large profits of the banks are due to several reasons:

- there is a lack of competition in the banking sector, which is not surprising given that four banks dominate the sector, making implicit collusion easy to do, and that all four banks are controlled by the state; and
- the state-set margin between the deposit rate and the lending rate (which are both dictated by the state) has been wider since 1999, with the deposit rate set particularly low.

In short, the high profit margin of the banking sector is the result of the institutional distortions (i.e., economic inefficiencies) in the financial system.

There is another inefficiency in the banking system that is potentially threatening to the systemic stability of the economy. This inefficiency is created by the banks' standard practice of approving loans based on the availability of collateral. Because collateral-based lending is naturally biased towards real estate purchase, manufacturing equipment investment, and infrastructure project construction by local governments, it fosters excess capacity in these three activities at the expense of working capital and investment capital to new enterprises in general and to agricultural and service sector enterprises in particular.

The continuing supply of cheap bank loans to the manufacturing sector maintains the over-expansion of low-end production, and covers the losses of inefficient firms, hence delaying industrial upgrading and postponing structural adjustment. The outcome is that the manufacturing sector exhibits chronic over-capacity, particularly in

[10]The year-to-year growth in the banks' operating margin in 2011 Q1 was 27%.

machinery and chemical industries. With the eventual realization of the expected excess capacity in the near future, the credit risk accumulated in the banking system would bankrupt the banks, and there would be an economic downturn unless the central government can take the NPLs on as its fiscal obligation.

The banking sector needs fundamental reforms. The number and variety of banks must be increased. Entry into the banking sector should be eased for small and medium private banks because only they are motivated to lend to small and medium private enterprises. Some of the branches of the Big-Four Banks should be spun off and privatized. The original parent banks may retain a minority, 10–20%, of the equity in the newly established community or township banks to better facilitate or complement the interbank businesses with the local banks which lack branch banking capacities.

The spinning-off of branches from the large SOBs will generate other benefits as well such as:

- It eases the capital shortages of the commercial banks.
- It terminates the risk transmission mechanism that translates all risk into government liability because of the too-big-too-fail branch banking regime.
- A large number of small retail banks will better serve individual clients and small businesses, and
- Large SOBs may realign their business priority towards the global markets, contributing more to the internationalization of the Yuan.

The control of the deposit rate and the loan rate should be phased out quickly. There is no need to keep a wide margin between the two rates because the recapitalization of the biggest state banks had been completed by 2006. The central bank should commit to maintaining positive real interest rates and not to keeping interest rates low.

China should establish a deposit insurance system. The government should consider setting the insurance premium to be positively correlated with bank size in order to restrain the empire-building instinct motive of bank managers.

The emergence of a strong small-medium banking sector will reduce the dominance of the state-controlled banks and hence make the economy less vulnerable to their collapse. The entry of private banks (domestic and foreign) will reduce the probability of any one of the big four state banks would remain too big to fail, and hence reduce the soft-budget protection enjoyed by the now monopoly state banking system. The privatization of some units of the SOBs, and the emergence of large domestic private banks will also help in strengthening the budget constraints perceived by the managers of SOBs. The development of a modern banking system with a major role for the private sector will thence increase the quality of bank loans along with the increase in the quantity of bank loans

Updating the international dimensions of financial policy

China is now the second largest economy and is projected to become the largest economy in the world in the next decade. This process has already brought a significant change in the international division of labor as exemplified by the decimation of the US manufacturing sector. This process might also bring about equally large shifts in the economic architecture of the world, e.g., the emergence of an Asian economic bloc, amendments to the governance of international financial institutions like the International Monetary Fund and the World Bank, and new international initiatives on the regulation of capital flows, and financial sector supervision.

To be in line with the large structural changes in the Chinese economy, it is necessary that China's exchange rate regime be changed to accommodate and promote these changes. In Chapter 10 of this book, Wu *et al.* (2013) identified the medium-term and long-term choices of RMB exchange rate regime. For the medium-term, they recommend that China implement an exchange rate management with the characteristics of "Basket, Band, and Crawl" (BBC). Specifically, they suggest setting up a dynamic target zone for management of the effective exchange rate where the central parity rate (based on the Balassa–Samuelson hypothesis about relative labor productivity growth) maintains an annual 2% appreciation in terms of the real effective exchange rate, with the width of the target zone set to allow +/−5% fluctuation for the movements of the RMB exchange rate around the central exchange rate. For the long term, they recommend that China implements a monetary regime that combines a floating exchange rate system and generalized inflation targeting.

Also, in line with China's growing impact on the world economy, it is natural for her currency, the Renminbi (RMB), to become an international vehicle currency, a currency that is used to denominate the prices of goods and financial assets traded among foreign countries. In Chapter 11 of this book, Yingli Pan *et al.* (2013) believe that against the background of the gravity center of the global economy moving towards Asia and a multi-polar global economy being formed, the main reform direction should be to create a multiple reserve currencies system that has an internal stabilizing mechanism. RMB internationalization is an integral component of this reform package. They suggest that RMB internationalization proceeds in two phases. In the early phase, the key task is to transform the Chinese economy and the financial system and foster international demand for the RMB. In the later phase, the task is to open the capital account and increase substantially the supply of RMB for global use.

Reform measures to promote financial openness include issuing licenses to foreign financial institutions to conduct RMB-denominated business, and allowing merger with and acquisition of branches from SOBs. It is desirable to pursue policies that favors capital outflow to incentivize large enterprises and financial institutions to go overseas.

The Potential Future International Status of the RMB and Shanghai's Financial Industry

To Wing Thye Woo (2013a), the truly important international aspects of China's financial reform are not, one, whether or when the RMB will be internationalised; and, two, whether and when Shanghai should be allowed to become an international financial center (IFC). He points out that once China's capital account is open like that of Taiwan's, as it would inevitably be, the RMB would automatically be internationalised like the Swedish Krona and the Swiss Franc (because the foreigners could use it freely); and Shanghai would automatically be eligible to be an IFC like Stockholm and Geneva (because foreign residents would be able to participate in China's stock and bond markets, and the Shanghai branches of foreign banks would be able to operate in any currency).

Woo (2013a) identifies the fundamentally important international consequences of China's financial reform to be:

1. whether the RMB would become an international vehicle currency (IVC) like the US$ and the Euro, i.e. be in the small sub-set of internationalised currencies that other countries would commonly use to denominate the prices of their traded goods and to denominate the international loans amongst themselves; and
2. whether Shanghai would become a 1st-tier international financial center (1-IFC) like the two present members, London and New York City (NYC), in which the value of transactions in each is markedly higher (a quantum leap higher) than in the other IFCs like Frankfurt, Tokyo, Zurich, Hong Kong and Singapore.

Woo's (2013a) review of the financial history of the UK£ and the US$, and of London and NYC leads him to advance five propositions.

First, a city would be eligible to be a 1st-tier IFC (1-IFC) only after its national currency is already an IVC. Because foreigners would hold a significant amount of this country's currency as working capital, they would deposit these funds in this country's banks or branches of foreign banks in that country. This first proposition is based on the UK£ and the US$ becoming IVCs before London and NYC emerged as 1-IFCs.

Second, after a city has been a 1-IFC for a long period, the maintenance of this status does not depend on the national currency continuing to be an IVC. For example, London is still a 1-IFC today even though the UK£ is no longer an IVC.

Third, the transaction cost of using a foreign currency as the medium of exchange is inversely related to the size of the global use of that currency. And, similar economies of scale also exist in the use of a particular international financial center by foreign investors. There are three implications from the virtuous cycle nature in the use of internationalised currencies and international financial centers:

1. the number of internationalised currencies that would become IVCs is small,

2. the number of international financial centers that would become 1-IFCs is small, and
3. the membership of IVCs and 1-IFCs has a bias towards the status quo.

Fourth, the financial market in an IVC and 1-IFC country has three characteristics:

1. **openness**: there are no restrictions on the international movement of capital and on entry into the financial industry
2. **broadness (sophistication)**: there is a rich menu of financial instruments being traded and a wide range of financial institutions offering differing services, i.e. financial market sophistication is very high; and
3. **calmness (safety)**: the central bank maintains satisfactory overall stability (e.g. price stability and a satisfactory steady growth rate) and an efficient, robust and reliable payments and settlement mechanism; the prudential regulators keep fraud, manipulation, and excessive speculation at low levels; the legal system is predictable and transparent in the protection of private property and in adjudication of disputes; and the macro-prudential authorities display adequate financial firefighting capability (e.g. in-place procedures to take over and manage failed banks in the short-term, and then to re-capitalise and privatize them in the medium-term).

Fifth, the successful convergence to IVC and 1-IFC status requires the country to have been an overwhelming economic force vis-a-vis other countries (i.e. to have great relative economic strength) for a substantial period of time. The United Kingdom enjoyed global economic leadership for over one hundred years because the Industrial Revolution had began there. In 1914, the US-UK GDP ratio was 2.1, but the US$ was not an IVC. This suggests that a relative economic strength of 2.1 does not qualify as "overwhelming economic strength"[11] A decade later, in 1924, the

[11]Unless otherwise indicated, the GDPs used in the GDP ratios in this chapter are measured in PPP terms, data from Angus Maddison (2010).

US$ had eclipsed the UK£ as the most important IVC, and the US-UK GDP ratio was 3.2 and still increasing[12]

One could say that the challenger is not big enough to displace the existing currency hegemon when its GDP is 2.1 times that of the incumbent, and is big enough to do so when its GDP is 3.2 times that of the incumbent. The tipping point for when GDP-ratio (relative economic strength) is sufficiently high to transform a currency into an IVC through overwhelming economic force is somewhere in the 2.1 to 3.2 range.

Much of the literature on IFC has tended to emphasize Proposition 4 as the basis of a city becoming a 1st-tier IFC i.e. the openness, breadth, and calmness of a financial market determines whether it would emerge as a 1-IFC. A few observers like Charles Kindleberger (1967) have emphasized that Proposition 5 is the fundamental market force that propels a city into 1-IFC status i.e. *the city must not only have a large, sophisticated open, and safe financial industry but, more fundamentally, it has be located in a country that has a GDP that is or was disproportionately larger GDP for a substantial length of time*[13] (An open large economy would inevitably also be a large trader in absolute terms.)

The plausibility of the importance of Proposition 5 in deciding the 1-IFC outcome is confirmed by the failure of the Japanese Yen to develop into a significant international vehicle currency in the early 1990s, and hence the failure of Tokyo to join London and NYC in the ranks of 1st-tier IFCs. Specifically, the Japan-US GDP ratio in the 1970–2000 period never reached the level of relative economic strength of the US-UK GDP ratio of 2.1 in 1914 and 3.2 in 1924. The Japan-US GDP ratio doubled from 0.2 in 1963 to peak at 0.41 in 1991 and then declined to 0.31 in 2008. The entire increase in the Japan-US GDP ratio in the 1961-1991 period was due to the standard of living in Japan soaring to that in the United State (i.e. technological catch-up). Half of the decrease in the GDP ratio in 1991–2008 period was due to the decline in the growth rate of Japan's population, and

[12]The GDP ratio reached 6.5 in 2012, and the UK£ was no longer an IVC.

[13]"For better or worse — and opinions differ on this — the choice of which language and which currency is made not on merit, or moral worth, but on size." Charles Kindleberger (1967).

half to the faster increase in the US rate of technological progress and capital accumulation[14]

Huw McKay (Chapter 6: "Tokyo's Ultimately Failed Bid for First Tier International Financial Centre Status: Why Did It Fall Short and What Are the Lessons for Shanghai?") adds an intriguingly interesting dimension to the above conclusion that Japan never had the overwhelming economic force that would naturally make the Yen into an IVC, the stepping stone toward 1-IFC status. McKay raises the possibility that there was a period of time in which IVC status could have been achieved if the Japanese government had made this quest for IVC status an overwhelming policy priority and hence had intervened decisively to promote the pricing of manufactured exports and of raw materials imports in Yen. Such focused intervention would have broken the "legacy mindset that was holding back progress toward the IFC goal."

> The argument here is that Japan was too timid in working towards denominating its major commodity imports in yen, particularly where benchmark prices were negotiated rather than traded on an exchange. After all, just as it was the world's largest exporter of manufactures in 1985, it was the largest steel producer with almost one quarter of global output, and it was also the largest importer of fuel and mining products in the same year, narrowly surpassing the United States ... While with hindsight we see that this was a temporary situation, we can be certain that many contemporary observers would have expected that ranking to persist having been caught up in the "Japan as number 1" euphoria of the times. (Huw McKay, Chapter 6)

McKay attributes the absence of active promotion of Yen as an IVC as the result of two factors:

1. the Japanese government did not elevate "the goal of becoming a first tier IFC ... above other competing objectives ... [and so] the necessary intermediate steps ... [were not] achieved in timely fashion ... Japan's ambivalence to the IFC goal can be read through the succession of official studies on yen internationalisation, trade invoicing, the financial system's international competitiveness and

[14]The Japan-US ratio in GDP per capita was 39% in 1961, 85% in 1991 and 73% in 2008; and the Japan-US ratio in population was 52%, 49% and 41% respectively. The Jaspan-US ratio in population is expected to fall to 30% in 2030.

the like, that spanned more than two decades of 'further discussion' ..."; and

2. the Japanese government thought that it had time on its side because it did not expect that Japan's economic strength would start weakening steadily in 1992 vis-a-vis the United States

Woo (2013c) sets the background for thinking about the international financial policy choices for China with the following four observations. First, under some circumstances, a country could find itself in a dual equilibria situation: an ordinary IFC equilibrium like Paris and a 1-IFC equilibrium like New York City.

Second, the experience of the United States in the 20th Century suggests that if

- the relative economic strength of the country grows rapidly over time, and
- if the country's financial sector is marked by financial openness (e.g. few restrictions on capital account transactions), financial depth (e.g. the total value of transactions in the market is very high and the market operates in a highly competitive setting), financial breadth (e.g. existence of a wide variety of financial instruments and of financial institutions), and financial calmness (e.g. in place are financial regulations that are transparent, predictable, and prudentially-effective , and monetary-financial authorities that have effective financial firefighting ability to restructure failed large financial firms and to prevent financial contagion),

then market forces would naturally first push the country's currency into IVC status, and then push the country's largest financial market into 1-IFC status. In this case, the dual equilibria situation is temporary.

Third, in a dual equilibria situation, appropriate state actions might be able to accelerate the movement from the ordinary IFC equilibrium to the 1-IFC equilibrium. For example, a country could first identify the types of international transactions in goods and financial assets where it has significant market power, and then push for the transactions in some of these markets to be priced in the country's currency.

Fourth, while all the sets of circumstances that would enable a country to face a dual equilibria situation in its international status, one such set would be a large economic weight (e.g. a disproportionately large GDP and big trader across a large number of world markets), and a deep, broad and calm financial market.

The implications from the above four observations is that the Swedish Krona and Stockholm could not have become, respectively, an IVC and a 1-IFC regardless of how aggressively the Swedish state had intervened in the 1900–2008 period to promote these two objectives. As the Sweden-USA GDP ratio never reached anywhere near critical level (e.g. it did not even exceed 0.05 at any time[15]), Sweden never had to worry about the dual equilibria dilemma in the 20th Century.

In this context, Huw McKay's analysis could be interpreted as saying that Japan possibly faced the dual equilibria dilemma in the 1980–1997 period when the Japan-USA GDP ratio peaked in the 0.37 to 0.41 range; and the probability for policy intervention to jolt the Yen into IVC status was highest before 1991 when the relative GDP ratio was rising strongly. The crucial question for Huw MacKay's analysis is whether Japan's peak relative economic strength of 0.4 was enough to generate a dual equilibria outcome. We suspect not because, after all, the US$ was not an IVC when US relative economic strength was 2.1, which is five times that of Japan in 1991.

Woo (2013b) calculates what he expects China's relative economic strength to be in the future by using the decomposition of:

$$
\begin{aligned}
&\text{China's Relative Economic Strength}^{16}\\
&\quad = [\text{GDP}_{\text{China}}/\text{GDP}_{\text{USA}}]\\
&\quad = [(\text{GDP/L})_{\text{China}}/(\text{GDP/L})_{\text{USA}}] \times (\text{L}_{\text{China}}/\text{L}_{\text{USA}})\\
&\quad = (\text{standard of living ratio}) \times (\text{labor ratio})
\end{aligned}
$$

In 2008, the situation was

- $(\text{L}_{\text{China}}/\text{L}_{\text{USA}}) = 4.3$
- $[(\text{GDP/L})_{\text{China}}/(\text{GDP/L})_{\text{USA}}] = 0.2$
- China's Relative Strength $= [\ \text{GDP}_{\text{China}}/\text{GDP}_{\text{USA}}\ ] = 0.2 \times 4.3 = 0.86$

[15]Sweden-USA GDP ratio reached its peak at 0.04 in 1931–1940.

[16]As noted earlier, GDP is measured in PPP US$

For estimates of relative China-US economic strength in the future, Woo (2013b) assumes that

- (L_{China}/L_{USA}) will decline from **4.3** but will remain big. In the new steady-state equilibrium in, say, 2050, $(\mathbf{L_{China}/L_{USA}}) = \mathbf{3.2}$[17]; and
- 2 Catching-Up Scenario Assumptions
  - Scenario A: $[(\mathbf{GDP/L})_{China}/(\mathbf{GDP/L})_{USA}] = \mathbf{0.3}$, the Middle-Income Trap outcome
  - Scenario B: $[(\mathbf{GDP/L})_{China}/(\mathbf{GDP/L})_{USA}] = \mathbf{0.8}$, the Successful Catching-Up outcome

Woo (2013b) calls the "standard of living ratio" the Catch-Up Index (CUI). The CUI value for the Middle-Income Trap scenario is based on the average CUI value for the five largest Latin American countries (Argentina, Brazil, Chile, Mexico and Venezuela) being about 0.3 in 1960 and 2008. The CUI value for Malaysia has stayed at 0.3 in the 1994-2008 period.

The CUI value for the Successful Catching Up scenario is based on the average CUI value for the five largest Western European countries (France, Germany Italy, Sweden and United Kingdom) being about 0.7 in 1960 and 2008. So the assumed value of 0.8 is not a probable understatement of the Catching-Up outcome.

The Relative Economic Strength outcome under

- *Scenario A*: $[GDP_{China}/GDP_{USA}] = 0.3 \times 3.2 = 1.0$
- *Scenario B*: $[GDP_{China}/GDP_{USA}] = 0.8 \times 3.2 = 2.6$

As mentioned earlier, when the US-UK GDP ratio was 2.1 in 1914, the US$ was not an IVC, and when the US-UK GDP ratio was 3.2 in 1924 *and increasing*, the US$ had become an IVC. If China is stuck in the Middle-Income Trap and has a long-run relative economic strength of 1.0, we think that China would not find itself in a dual equilibria situation, i.e. there is low probability that the RMB would become an IVC and Shanghai a 1-IFC.

---

[17]The value of 3.2 is computed from the population projections of the World Bank (accessed 16 January 2014): http://web.worldbank.org/WBSITE/EXTERNAL/TOPICS/EXTHEALTHNUTRITIONANDPOPULATION/EXTDATASTATISTICSHNP/EXTHNPSTATS/0,,contentMDK:21737699~menuPK:3385623~pagePK:64168445~piPK:64168309~theSitePK:3237118,00.html.

However, if China is successful in catching up to the living standard of the United States to possess steady-state relative economic strength of 2.6 (which is between 2.1 and 3.2), we think that China would have a choice between Shanghai being an ordinary IFC and Shanghai being a 1-IFC. The RMB would be eligible to become Vehicle Currency but since China's relative economic strength would not grow over time, there is **no overwhelming natural market forces to ensure an IVC outcome**. The Chinese state would therefore have to implement decisive action to encourage international traders and international creditors to price their transactions in RMB if RMB is to be an IVC and Shanghai a 1-IFC

We think that the Chinese government should see the IVC and 1-IFC objectives as worth pursuing. This is not only because these two developments would benefit China (e.g. the creation of a new high value added financial service industry, and the lowering of costs in international transactions) but also because the world would also benefit tremendously from these two developments, which would amount to increasing the supply of a basic global public good. Specifically, the emergence of RMB as an IVC would help meet global demand for international reserves and for diversification of reserves, and this would strengthen global financial stability fundamentally by addressing an important systemic confidence problem[18]

To summarise, the policy agenda to ensure that the RMB would be an international vehicle currency and Shanghai be a 1st-tier international financial center would require three sets of actions:

1. root and branch reform of China to ensure that China would leap over the Middle-Income Trap (such a reform agenda is given in Woo, Lu, Sachs and Chen, 2012).

[18]In the present global monetary system where the US$ is the primary global reserve currency, there is a **non-sustainable tradeoff between** the need for additional global liquidity to accommodate the growth of the international economy **and** the requirement for confidence in the US$ as the global reserve currency. The larger is the amount of US$ held by non-US businesses and foreign governments, the greater is their concern about the ability of the US government to maintain the purchasing power of the US$. This present day tradeoff not identical to the Triffin dilemma. Robert Triffin (1960) had expressed the skepticism about the continued ability of the US over time to swap gold for US$ freely as required by the Bretton Woods Monetary System.

2. internal actions to strengthen the international competitiveness of Shanghai as an international financial center by establishing a financial sector that is open, deep and broad; and ensuring that there is adequate macro-prudential monitoring of the financial sector, and having macroeconomic and financial firefighting teams ready if things go awry; and
3. external actions to promote pricing in RMB by seeking to set prices in RMB for export goods (manufacturing) and import goods (raw resources) where China has market power; and seeking to set value in RMB in purchases of foreign financial assets (which should be possible because China is a creditor not debtor)

Modernizing the Financial Sector Safely and Bolstering Financial Firefighting Capability

The discussion of how to avoid systemic financial crisis can usefully begin by analysing the recent financial collapses in a number of advanced economies, and then identifying their lessons for developing countries like China which are seeking to reform their financial sectors to support Modern Economic Growth. Jeffrey Sachs examines the record financial malfeasance in the United States in the last thirty years in Chapter 2 ("Wall Street Lawlessness"). Peter Boone and Simon Johnson investigate the roots of the systemic imprudence in the financial institutions of the developed countries in Chapter 3 ("Systemic Lack of Prudence in Wealthy Nations: Avoiding the Dark Side of Financial Development"). Seppo Honkapohja identifies the reasons for the financial crises in Finland, Norway and Sweden in the 1980s in Chapter 4 ("Lessons from the Financial Liberalization in the Nordic Countries in the 1980s").

Jeffrey Sachs (Chapter 2) finds that one of the features of the 2008 financial crisis is the epidemic of lawlessness among America's major investment banks, commercial banks, hedge funds, financial conglomerates, and stock exchanges, collectively known as Wall Street. Major Wall Street firms have been repeated lawbreakers, and as a result have faced dozens of lawsuits and criminal actions regarding corporate practices at the core of the business. The startlingly common aspect of these legal actions is that, with few exceptions, senior Wall

Street managers do not face personal risks as a result of corporate malfeasance. When settlements in the SEC cases are reached, the defendant firm typically pays a fine but has been allowed to "neither admit nor deny wrongdoing" (a practice that has been, correctly, criticized by Federal court judge Jed Rakoff as not serving the public interest). The fine is often a small fraction of the gains that accrued to the company as a result of its malfeasant behavior. Without no judgment of guilt or acknowledgement or denial of wrongdoing, no further action is taken against senior management (e.g. a revocation of an manager's right to engage in banking).

It is useful to examine the Jeffrey Sachs paper in some detail because most of the causes for the widespread financial malfeasance that he identifies exist in all capitalist economies in similar degrees. Jeffrey Sachs argues that there are five main structural reasons for the intrinsic proclivity for US financial institutes to engage in overly risky transactions:

1. the CEO's are inadequately supervised;
2. the firms are highly leveraged operations;
3. the equity-based compensation scheme for CEOs;
4. the financial industry is under-regulated; and
5. the political power of Wall Street in Washington D.C.

Large US companies have limited liability, are generally publicly owned, and are characterized by highly dispersed shareholdings rather than ownership by a family or a small number of core investors. Because of the dispersed shareholding and limited liability, shareholders generally free ride on the public good of corporate governance. The upshot is that the CEOs have considerable authority with relatively low oversight from the board of directors, whose appointments are frequently made at the suggestions of management.

Banks tend to have an extremely high leverage ratio compared with non-financial corporations because the bank's job is to take on debt from depositors, other banks, and the financial markets, to invest in assets. Using a simple numerical example, Jeffrey Sachs shows that high leverage increases the shareholder's appetite for risk beyond the social optimum. The ability to leverage is facilitated, in general, by the presence of deposit insurance and by the implicit expectation of government bailouts of bank creditors in the event of a crisis. In the run-up to the 2008 financial crisis, US investment banks and European commercial banks had the highest leverage, a remarkable average of around 30 (total assets relative to equity), while US commercial banks were less highly leveraged at around 10, still a very high leverage ratio compared with non-financial companies.

In Jeffrey Sachs's view, a major factor in the soaring compensation of CEOs in the last three decades was the increasing use of equity-based compensation, especially in the form of stock options. He extends his simple numerical example on leverage to clarify how stock options increase the CEO's appetite for risk beyond those of the shareholders. The combination of highly leveraged firms and CEO pay packages laden with stock options is strong motivation for a CEO to treat his enterprises as an enormous gamble for riches.

The process of financial deregulation started in earnest in the early 1980s in the savings and loan (S&L) industry. Within a few years, the entire sector was bankrupt, in effect "looted" by its CEOs, in the words of economists George Akerlof and Paul Romer (1993). Insolvent S&Ls took advantage of federal deposit insurance to attract new deposits, and then used deposit inflows to make payments of phantom profits and other insider payments to the owner-managers of the S&Ls. In the end, the federal government had to pay off the depositors, while many corrupt owners of bankrupt S&Ls walked away with fortunes.

The most important act of deregulation was the Gramm-Leach-Bliley Act of 1999, which repealed of the 1933 Glass-Steagall Act, a major part of Great Depression financial reform that separated deposit-taking activities and investment banking activities. Glass-Steagall was repealed in 1999 with strong bipartisan artisan support. The leading architect of the repeal, Treasury Secretary Robert Rubin, immediately became Chairman of Citigroup, a new financial conglomerate (formed in a $140 billion mega-merger of Citicorp and Travelers Group, one of the largest mergers in history) made possible by the deregulation.

Jeffrey Sachs attributes the extremely low personal risk of any penalties from financial malfeasance that senior Wall Street managers face, and the steady deregulation of the financial industry to the enormous political power of Wall Street in Washington. The money flows mainly in two forms: as campaign contributions and as lobbying outlays, much of which end up in political pockets indirectly through hiring politicians into lobbying firms (and law firms).

More controversially, Jeffrey Sachs hypotheses that there has been a change in the moral zeitgeist in the United State that has increased the acceptability of self-serving or illegal behavior. He makes the case that super-high managerial compensation is not the social norm in the rich capitalist countries by citing the case of a leading and highly successful Swedish CEO, Percy Barnevik, who engineered a retirement package typical of a US CEO. When the news of the retirement package became commonly known several years later, the public outcry forced the retired CEO to recant the arrangement and to step down from other public positions. In the United States, however, the social restraints on high compensation packages have diminished, thereby making it easier for US CEOs to take the opportunity to increase their own paychecks.

Based on his overview of Wall Street lawlessnes, Jeffrey Sachs suggests the following seven areas for the greatest attention in trying to promote financial sector development safely:

1. Limit the leverage of financial institutions because it promotes excessive risk-taking or outright looting.
2. Implement tougher scrutiny and regulatory limits on compensation packages of CEOs as in the European Union. Shareholders should have an automatic vote on compensation packages, and the use of stock options should be limited to avoid excessive risk-taking.
3. Increase significantly the higher levels of marginal taxation, in part to tamp down the incentives for managerial abuse.
4. Legislate CEOs and senior managers to face *personal* liability for major acts of malfeasance committed by their companies during their watch. Personal liability could include the loss of license to practice, forced resignation from office, a ban on bonuses, and personal liability for a portion of corporate fines and civil settlements in cases where CEO responsibility or negligence can be determined.

5. Bring criminal prosecutions against firms and individuals for large-scale financial malfeasance.
6. Bar Wall Street firms from lobbying activities and senior bank managers from making campaign contributions.
7. Undertake research on how to restore ethical norms on Wall Street.

Peter Boone and Simon Johnson (Chapter 3) document that prudent financial regulation, broadly defined, has proven difficult to do in wealthy nations. The economic incentives and political forces that promote undercapitalized financial institutions, over-leveraged production firms, and unfinanced public entitlements have consistently and invariably won out over prudent management across Europe, the US, Canada and Japan. This outcome has placed much of the wealthy world on a path with intermittent, but growing financial crises. In particular, these countries are addicted to methods of economic management that are debt-financed (e.g. re-capitalizing banks by issuing new government debt) because they have ageing populations, and the future generations are not represented in the policy-making process.

Successive financial crises are bailed out with additional debts, adding to deficits caused by ageing populations and limited political incentives to balance budgets. Rapid growth tends to obscure insolvencies, and these difficulties usually surface only when growth prospects turn down. Once large undercapitalized systems and structural budget deficits have developed, it is very difficult to change course, leading to financial traps with rising dangers. Inflation, financial repression, and new crises will be outcomes of this systemic lack of prudency in wealthy nations.

While Peter Boone and Simon Johnson "are sceptical that adequate changes can be achieved [in the developed economies] without crisis," they see the possibility that the rapidly growing economies (like China) might be able to avoid the same outcome if they take the following three sets of actions now.

First, China must promote the safety of financial institutions by

1. enlisting the energy of creditors to monitor the financial institutions by passing strict no bailout laws which require creditor bail-in before public funds can be used;

2. requiring financial institutions to have large buffers of equity and contingent capital; and
3. strengthening regulation by imposing multi-year restrictions on the participation of former financial regulators in private financial firms, i.e. stopping revolving-door practices between the state and the private sector.

Second, China must promote stable public finance by:

- enforcing balanced budget rules through constitutional amendment (this requirement will keep current spending in check but it cannot prevent over-promises on pensions);
- implementing means-test requirement for pensions because this would reduce size of the group lobbying for high pension at expense of future generations
- increasing transparency in the financial implications of fiscal actions, e.g. there should be a nonpartisan agency (like the Congressional Budget Office) that makes projections on the budget; and
- institute regular auditor-general reports and prosecute malfeasance

Third, China must recognise that financial bubbles usually cannot continue for extended periods without the complicity of the central bank. The US Federal Reserve under Alan Greenspan encouraged bubbles by giving implicit bail-out guarantees to systemically-important financial institutions (e.g. Long Term Capital Management, Bear Stearns). It is therefore important to create an independent "Financial Stability Oversight Board" to look over the shoulders of the central bank and the other financial regulators. The existence of this independent financial sector overseer will increase the emergence of whistle-blowers whose timely warning would help prevent financial collapses.

Seppo Honkapohja (Chapter 4) reviews the process of liberalization in the Nordic countries in the 1980s and discusses the reasons why Finland, Norway, and Sweden drifted into financial and economic crises. He arrives at four key conclusions.

The first conclusion is that the Nordic countries paid too much attention on the "how to" and too little attention on "what is". There was a lot of attention on what would be the optimum sequencing of policy actions to dispense with the system of financial market and capital account controls. There was insufficient attention to (1) how the different markets and production sectors would adjust to the policy actions; and (2) what conditions the banks and other market institutions were in. It was thought that firms and households would know how to adjust to the new system and would do so in a flexible way. However, it turned out that both banks and their customers moved toward the new equilibrium too rapidly, causing a credit boom, an asset price bubble and, in the end, a banking crisis.

The Nordic countries did not realize sufficiently that liberalization leads to increased risks and, hence, that a new kind of behavior was needed. Prudential supervision did not have a significant role in the period of a controlled financial system, because the control mechanism by itself had secured the stability of banks to a very large extent. How could the existing institution of prudential supervision which was not needed under the controlled system could have been counted on to start working adequately right away upon financial deregulation?

It is important that all the parties involved understand the need for changing ways of thinking and business practices. Traditional ways of thinking can become a trap, which should be avoided. Market-based financial systems are inherently less controllable and thus market participants must prepare for new risks and uncertainties that were absent in a system of financial repression. Risk management and supervision become very important with financial deregulation.

Seppo Honkapohja's second conclusion was that strengthening the capital base of banks and reforming their supervisory systems are important steps to make in advance of the major liberalization steps.

The third conclusion was that the Nordic countries should have known that it would be very difficult to maintain fixed exchange rates after they have moved to market-based financial systems and have freed cross-border capital flows. The combination of free capital flows and a fixed exchange rate regime can generate immense speculative pressures, which make the defense of the exchange rate costly.

The fourth conclusion is that it is important to try to time the main parts of the liberalization so as to avoid a business-cycle upswing.

Seppo Honkapohja points that the sheer size of China's economy makes its liberalization process different from that of most countries. The reforms in China could have major spillover effects on other countries, and they might well take actions in response to the Chinese reforms. China should hence take into account in the planning of its financial deregulation the international repercussions of its financial sector reform and the possible foreign reactions to it.

To summarise, these three papers by Jeffrey Sachs, Peter Booue and Simon Johnson, and Seppo Honkapohja propose three sets of actions to modernise the financial sector safely and to bolster prudential oversight and financial firefighting capabilities. The first set seeks to reduce the incentives and means of financial institutions and their managers to engage in excessive risk-taking by

- requiring the government to prosecute financial institutions for financial malfeasance, and to make their managers bear personal liability for illegal acts by their firms;
- replacing bailouts of creditors and stockholders with bail-ins,
- increasing the buffer of capital requirements, and
- reducing the leverage ratios of financial institutions, and the use of equity-based compensation for the managers

The second set of reforms is to change the cosy, self-serving relationship between the financial industry and the political establishment by:

- limiting the amount that financial industry can spend on political donations; and
- stopping the practice of revolving door employment pattern between Wall Street and Pennsylvania Avenue by putting multi-year delay in switching jobs between employment in these two places.

The third set of reforms is to strengthen the regulatory capability of the state financial agencies, and to limit the ability of the central bank and fiscal authorities to destabilise the macroeconomy by:

- establishing an independent Systemic Financial Stability Oversight Board to audit the conduct of monetary policy of the central bank to (1) end the practice of the "Greenspan put" to bail out the culprits of irrational exuberance, (2) prevent the bias toward the defence of an overvalued currency, (3) audit the work of the financial agencies in approving new financial instruments and in prosecution of financial fraud, and (4) monitor the readiness of the slew of federal financial agencies to handle the orderly restructuring of failed financial institutions and to prevent financial contagion in the country and across countries; and

- passing a law to stop the bias toward debt-financed state spending by (1) requiring the federal budget be balanced over the business cycle, and (2) establishing an independent Fiscal Mediation Board to craft the overall expenditure-revenue reconciliation.

Final Remarks

We end this chapter with three final remarks.

First, the emergence of a more robust and efficient financial sector would protect China's growth from protectionism as well. The Global Financial Crisis has greatly increased attention on the chronic imbalances in global trade and incited strident justifications for US protectionism against China's "beggar-thy-neighbor" policies.[19] The prevention of foreign protectionism is in essence, a new growth driver for China, and the key is the modernization of China's financial system.

Because China's trade account surplus is largely caused by the difference between its savings and investments, it has become fashionable to call for China to adopt consumption-led growth by reducing savings and investments.[20] This is from the GNP identity:

$$\mathrm{CA} = (S - I) + (T - G),$$

[19]See, for example, Krugman (2010a, 2010b); Wolf (2010); Landler (2010); and the hard-hitting editorial "Will China Listen?" published in *The New York Times* (2010). See Woo (2008) for a detailed discussion on the causes of US–China trade tensions.

[20]For example, Lardy (2007) wrote that the more desired growth path is one marked by "a reduction in China's national savings rate" (p. 10), and by a reduction in "China's excessive rate of investment" (p. 10). The latter "is a prerequisite to a successful transition to a more consumption-driven growth path" (p. 10).

where

$CA =$ current account balance,
$S =$ non-governmental savings,
$I =$ non-governmental investments,
$T =$ government revenue, and
$G =$ government expenditure.

We note, however, that

- this adjustment recipe of a lower investment rate is at its essence a call for China to grow slower and delay its economic catch-up with the advanced economies;
- what is truly economically unnatural, is for China to have been putting its savings abroad when the rate of return on domestic investment is so much higher than the rate of return on US Treasury securities; and
- China's "over-savings" could just as accurately be described as China's "under-investment."

The true cause of China's chronic trade surpluses is the inability of China's financial system to intermediate all of domestic savings into domestic investment, and the best cure is to eliminate this dysfunctional aspect by modernizing the financial system through freeing up entry to private financial institutions, both foreign and domestic.[21] Financial sector modernization will not only lower the savings rate and raise the investment rate but also establish new investment financing mechanisms that will channel investments toward the non-tradeable sector (e.g., a proper actuarially-based, forward-looking credit system that will re-direct non-collateralized mortgage loans to housing for new rural migrants away from collateralized investment loans to the existing export and import-competing industries). This cure will reduce trade inbalance and forestall the protectionism that would lower China's growth imbalance and rate and harm the international economy.

[21] Liu and Woo (1994) shows formally and empirically that an underdeveloped financial system, *ceteris paribus*, raises the savings rate and hence increases the current account balance.

Our second concluding remark is on the great concern in China about the safety of the transition to IVC Status and 1-IFC Status. It is prudent to note from international experiences that the use of financial markets to accelerate economic development could sometimes be as dangerous as riding a tiger. The Japanese economy has been stagnant up to today following the bursting of its real estate and stock market bubbles in 1990. More recently, the implosion of the US financial system in September 2008 and the subsequent European financial crises have produced prolonged high unemployment.[22]

In our opinion, the fact that the developed economies have yet to produce a financial system that is absolutely safe to use should not be allowed to justify delaying the restructuring of China's financial industry. The key is to study the foreign experiences carefully and to think critically about how the foreign lessons on building an efficient financial sector safely should be modified to take China's circumstances into account – a task that has been done in this book. It is also important not only to prevent financial failures with effective monitoring and appropriate regulation but also to possess financial firefighting ability to put out financial conflagration.

This concern for safety during financial transition is most strongly seen in the Chinese debate on whether, when and how the capital account should be opened. The concern is that capital account liberalization could bring,

- first, the danger of excessive foreign capital inflows that would cause asset bubbles and inflation; and,
- then, the danger of an abrupt sudden reversal of the foreign capital flow that would panic domestic capital into joining the flight, and thus precipitate the collapse of the RMB and financial system, and trigger a cessation of normal trade credit, resulting in an import compression that would deepen the output decline.

This is a valid concern but this potential cost of financial openness has to be compared with the benefits from financial openness. The

[22]Carlos Diaz-Alejandro (1985) has wryly summarised the Latin American experience with financial reforms in the 1970s as "Good-Bye Financial Repression, Hello Financial Crash."

fact is that there is no way to eliminate the possibility of this disaster but we can undertake actions to minimise the probability of it occurring (e.g. require a large capital buffer and low leverage ratios), and actions to maximise our ability to control the disaster quickly and rebuild expeditiously afterward (e.g. set up a Resolution Trust Corporation).

Furthermore, the view that the capital account should not be opened until effective financial monitoring and prudential regulation systems are in place is untenable. The realities are that:

1. financial regulation is learned best in the classroom *and* in the marketplace. The recent establishment of the Shanghai Free Trade Zone (SFTZ) will allow the emergence of an off-shore international financial center to give real-life training for China's financial regulators to recognise the signs of a developing financial storm and defuse the situation; and to handle efficiently the recapitalization and reorganization of failed financial institutions.
2. a financial market is not either open permanently or shut permanently, the degree of openness at any point in time is a policy choice at that point in time. As we will argue, a capital account once opened could always be partially closed temporarily without long-run adverse consequences if the closure is done for the right reasons like stopping a financial panic.

When a financial disaster occurs, the most important action is to prevent it from spreading. In a large financial crisis that is causing massive capital flight to occur, the normal tools of management like raising the interest rate to high levels and imposing macro-austerity are usually ineffective. The Hong Kong dollar (HK$) was attacked four times in the 1997–1998 period where speculators sold the HK$ and took a short position on the Hang Seng Index. The first three speculative attacks (October 20–23, 1997, June 10–12, 1998, August 4–6 1998) were successfully defeated by high interest rates, but each successive attack was significantly larger in scale. The scale grew each time because, in each subsequent attack, more of the general public were panicked into joining the strategic financiers (who had started the panic) in the sell-off of HK$ and Hong Kong stocks. The Hang

Seng Index suffered a major loss each time along with the fall in the Hang Seng Index Futures.

The fourth speculative attack on the HK$ started occurred on August 13, 1998, and the Hong Kong Monetary Authorities (HKMA) took the extraordinary actions of, one, buying the HK$ but now putting it back into the banking system to prevent the interest rate from rising; and, two, buying the blue-chip stocks on such a large-scale that the Hang Seng Index and the Hang Seng Index Futures actually went up. This HKMA counter-attack worked very well because there has not been another speculative attack on the HK$ since September 1998, and the HKMA made HK$30 billion (US$4 billion) in profits when it sold off the blue-chip stocks. It should be noted that what HKMA did go against a fundamental principle of central banking which is that a central bank should not print money to buy private company shares because this action amounts to the nationalization of private property.

The lesson here is that extraordinarily adverse financial market developments can be contained only with extraordinary state actions that break the general public sense of panic about asset values and the economic future. The free fall of the Malaysian ringgit, and with it, the free fall of the Malaysian stock market, was stopped in September 1998 only after Malaysia imposed temporary capital controls.

For both Hong Kong and Malaysia, their "extraordinarily unfair confrontations with private capital by changing the rules of normal finance" have not resulted in any long-term reduction in their access to international financial markets or in the growth of their financial industries. This is because private capital recognises that the only iron rule that matters for profit-maximization is that long-run economic stability and normal economic growth are preserved, and these non-textbook methods of economic management were effective in maintaining this iron rule.

Just as the belief that "a capital account, once opened, must always be kept open" is overly dogmatic, the belief that "the financial market is always efficient in its working" is equally overly dogmatic. The deep collapse in the Asian Financial Crisis of 1997–1998 and the Global Financial Crisis of 2008–2009 and the galloping bull markets in the two-year periods before both collapses are undeniable examples of financial panic and irrational exuberance, respectively. Hence, another step that China should take to strengthen global financial stability and to increase the safety of opening its capital account and financial industry is to take leadership at the global level (e.g. at the G20 summit, and at the United Nations) to push for a global transactions tax on capital movements — push for a Tobin (1978) tax (a currency transaction tax) — to induce investors to take a more long-term view of their overseas investment.

Our final concluding remark is on whether there is the issue of speed in the internationalization of the RMB. As pointed out at the beginning, the phenomenon of economies of scale in the use of a particular currency in international transactions means that the number of IVCs is a small one. The "natural IVC oligopoly" could consist of, say, two or three members. If any one of the Indian Rupee, the Russian Ruble and the Brazilian Real were to join the US$ and the Euro as IVCs before the RMB, the RMB would be denied IVC status forever, and Shanghai be denied 1-IFC status forever.

Clearly, if Russia, Brazil and India would not come close to China's economic strength in the coming half century, there is no reason for China to complete capital account liberalization and financial sector opening in the next twenty years until China is completely satisfied that it has made every preparation possible to ensure that the deregulation would not generate the slightest perturbation to its economy. China could repeat what Japan did, which is to take two decades to decide whether, when and how to promote its own currency to be an IVF and a reserve currency (McKay, Chapter 6).

So could India pose a challenge to China's ascent to IVC and 1-IFC status given that India's GDP per capita in PPP$ today is only half of that of China's? The answer is yes because the competition between them stretches over a long time span.[23]

The Chinese-US living standard ratio (LSR) is 20 percent today, and we had termed China's catching-up to be completed when the ratio reaches 80 percent. Going by the observation that the Taiwan-US LSR had risen from 20.7 percent in 1973 to 67.1 percent in 2008, which is an increase of 1.3 percentage points per year, we will assume that China

[23]Georges de Menil alerted us to this point in private communication.

continues its higher-than-normal economic growth and hence raises the China-US LSR by 1.5 percentage points annually. The US-China LSR will reach 80 percent in 2050, and, with the China-US population ratio (LR) at 3.2 in that year, China-US relative economic power in 2050 would be 2.56 percent, as calculated earlier.

If we assume that India continues to grow slower than China, at 1.3 percentage points annually, then the India-US LSR would be 62 percent in 2050, i.e. the India-China LSR would be 77.5 percent. However, because the India-US population ratio (PR) will be 4.2[24] then, India-US relative economic power in 2050 will be 2.60, just pipping China in the economic power race.

If the India-US LSR were to grow at 1.5 percentage points a year just like the China-US LSR, then India-US relative economic power in 2050 would be 2.9. And if the India-US LSR were to grower faster, say 1.7 percent points annually, then India-US relative economic power would be 3.3 in 2050.

In short, among the conditions required for China's ascent to IVF and 1-IFC status is that India's economic growth rate for the next forty years would not come close to that of China. This is a prerequisite that has no basis. In any case, it would not be rational for China to base its dream of the RMB being an IVC and Shanghai being a 1-IFC on the hope that its competitor would not be able to achieve exactly what it has done.[25]

As China is unlikely to be able to out-compete India for IVC and 1-IFC status on the basis of relative economic strength, China will have to out-compete India in the attractiveness of its financial market. To do so, China has better get on with the deregulation and opening of its capital account and its financial industry, and with building up its financial firefighting capacity in order to build a competitive lead for China's financial industry over India's in openness, sophistication, and safety.

---

[24]Computed from the population projections of the World Bank (accessed 15 January 2014): http://web.worldbank.org/WBSITE/EXTERNAL/TOPICS/EXTHEALTHNUTRITIONANDPOPULATION/EXTDATASTATISTICSHNP/EXTHNPSTATS/0,contentMDK:21737699~menuPK:3385623~pagePK:64168445~piPK:64168309~theSitePK:3237118,00.html

[25]This hope is unrealistic because the average annual growth rate of India in the 2003–2010 period (which includes the 2008 severe downturn) was 8.4 percent.

References

Akerlof, GA and PM Romer (1993). Looting: The economic underworld of bankruptcy for profit. *Brookings Papers on Economic Activity*, 2, 1–74.

Arcand, J-L (2014). Credit rationing, bank bailouts, and the deleterious impact of credit: Evidence from China. In WT Woo, Y Pan, JD Sachs and J Qian (eds.), *Financial Systems at the Crossroads: Lessons for China*. London, UK and Hackensack, NJ: Imperial College Press & World Scientific Press.

Arcand, J-L, E Berkes and U Panizza (2012). Too much finance. IMF Working Paper WP/12/161.

Bi, S (2003). *Cutting-edge Research on China's Agriculture, Rural Areas, and Farmers*. Beijing: People's Daily Press.

Boone, P and S Johnson (2014). Systemic lack of prudence in wealthy nations: Avoiding the dark side of financial development. In WT Woo, Y Pan, JD Sachs and J Qian (eds.), *Financial Systems at the Cross Roads: Lessons for China*. London, UK and Hackensack, NJ: Imperial College Press & World Scientific Press.

China Securities Regulatory Commission (1997). Notification on print and distribute Comrades Zhou Zhengqing and Chen Yaoxian's speeches on the forum of take advantage of the stock market and accelerate state-owned enterprise reform. China Securities Regulatory Commission, No. 15 Document, October 6.

Diaz-Alejandro, C (1985). Good-bye financial repression, hello financial crash. *Journal of Development Economics*, 19(1–2), 1–24.

Editorial (2010). Will China listen? *The New York Times*, March 17.

Fan, G and WT Woo (1996). State enterprise reform as a source of macroeconomic instability: The case of China. *Asian Economic Journal*, November.

Honkapohja, S (2014). Lessons from the financial liberalization in the Nordic countries in the 1980s. In WT Woo, Y Pan, JD Sachs and J Qian (eds.), *Financial Systems at the Crossroads: Lessons for China*. London, UK and Hackensack, NJ: Imperial College Press & World Scientific Press.

Inoue, T (2005). Reform of China's split-share structure takes shape. *Nomura Capital Market Review*, 8(3), 42–59.

Kindleberger, CP (1967) *The Politics of International Money and World Language* (Essays in International Finance, No. 61). Princeton, NJ: Princeton University Press.

Krugman, P (2010a). Chinese New Year. *The New York Times*, January 1.

Krugman, P (2010b). Taking on China. *The New York Times*, March 15.

Kuznet, S (1971). Modern economic growth: Findings and reflections. Lecture to the memory of Alfred Nobel, December 11. Available at http://www.nobelprize.org/nobel_prizes/economic-sciences/laureates/1971/kuznetslecture.Html.

Lardy, N (2007). China: Rebalancing economic growth. In Bergsten, F, B Gill, N Lardy and D Mitchell (Eds.), *The China Balance Sheet in 2007 and Beyond*. Washington, DC: Center for Strategic and International Studies and the Peterson Institute for International Economics.

Liu, L-Y and WT Woo (1994). Saving behavior under imperfect financial markets and the current account consequences. *Economic Journal*, 104(424), 512–527.

Liu, H and T Qin (2014). The structural friction in China's banking system: Causes, measurement and solutions. In WT Woo, Y Pan, JD Sachs and J Qian (eds.), *Financial Systems at the Crossroads: Lessons for China*. London, UK and Hackensack, NJ: Imperial College Press & World Scientific Press.

Maddison, A (2010). *Statistics on World Population, GDP and Per Capita GDP, 1–2008 AD*. Available at http://www.ggdc.net/MADDISON/oriindex.htmthat.

McKay, H (2014). Tokyo's ultimately failed bid for first tier international financial centre status: Why did it fall short and what are the lessons for Shanghai? In WT Woo, Yingli Pan, JD Sachs and J Qian (eds.), *Financial Systems at the Crossroads: Lessons for China*. London, UK and Hackensack, NJ: Imperial College Press & World Scientific Press.

McKinnon, R (1993). *The Order of Economic Liberalization*. Shanghai: Shanghai Joint Publishing Company and Shanghai People's Publishing House.

Pan, Y (2001). A research on the evolution and duality of fictitious economy. *Journal of East China Normal University (Philosophy and Social Sciences Version)*, (5).

Pan, Y (2012). *Research on China's Economic and Financial Transition*. Shanghai: Gezhi Press and Shanghai People's Publishing House.

Pan, Y, Y Xu and J Wu (2013). Chapter 11: The internationalization of the renminbi in accordance with China's national interests and global responsibilities. In Woo, WT, Y Pan, JD Sachs and J Qian (Eds.), *Financial Systems at the Cross road: Lessons for China's*. Singapore: Imperial College Press & World Scientific.

Sachs, JD (2013). Chapter 2: Wall street lawlessness. In Woo, WT, Y Pan, JD Sachs and J Qian (Eds.), *Financial Systems at the Cross roads: Lessons for China's*. Singapore: Imperial College Press & World Scientific.

Sachs, JD and WT Woo (2000). Understanding China's economic performance. *Journal of Policy Reform*, 4(1).

Statistics Division of the Investment in Fixed Assets, National Bureau of Statistics of China (1997). *Statistical Yearbook of the Chinese Investment in Fixed Assets: From 1950 to 1995*. Beijing: China Statistics Press.

Tobin, J (1978). A proposal for international monetary reform. *Eastern Economic Journal*, July/October, 153–159.

Triffin, R (1960). *Gold and the Dollar Crisis: The Future of Convertibility* New Haven, MA: Yale University Press.

World Bank (1993). *The East Asian Miracle: Economic Growth and Public Policy*. Washington D.C.: World Bank.

World Bank (1996). *World Development Report 1996: From Plan to Market*. Beijing: China Financial & Economic Publishing House.

Wu, X, Y Pan, Z Zhang, J Nie and S Zhou (2013). Chapter 10: The otions for reforming the renminbi exchange rate regime. In Woo, WT, Y Pan, JD Sachs and J Qian (Eds.), *Financial Systems at the Cross roads: Lessons for China's*. Singapore: Imperial College Press & World Scientific.

Wolf, M (2010). China and Germany unite to impose global deflation. *The Financial Times*, March 16.

Woo, WT (2008). Understanding the sources of friction in U.S.–China trade relations: The exchange rate debate diverts attention away from optimum adjustment. *Asian Economic Papers*, 7(3), 65–99.

Woo, WT (2011). Understanding the middle-income trap in economic development: The case of Malaysia. Invited World Economy Lecture delivered at the University of Nottingham, Globalization and Economic Policy (GEP) conference, Globalization Trends and Cycles: The Asian Experiences, Semenyih, Selangor, Malaysia, January 13. Available at http://www.nottingham.ac.uk/gep/documents/lectures/world-economy-asia-lectures/world-econ-asia-wing-thye-woo-2011.pdf.

Woo, WT (2012). China meets the middle-income trap: The large potholes in the road to catching-up. *Journal of Chinese Economic and Business Studies*, 10(4), 313–336.

Woo, WT (2013a). *Renminbi Shanghai yu Zhongguo Jinrong Gaige Zhilu* (The Fate of the Renminbi and Shanghai in China's Financial Reform Strategy. *Shanghai Zhengquan Bao* (Shanghai Securities News), November 19, 2013 (published in Chinese).

Woo, WT (2013b). *"Xiangdui Jingji Shili" Jueding Reneminbi de Guoji Diwei* ("Relative Economic Strength" is the Determinant of the International Status of the Renminbi). *Xin Jing Bao* (The Beijing News), December 3, 2013 (published in Chinese).

Woo, WT (2013c). The Future Status of RMB as an International Currency and Shanghai as an International Financial Centre: Is China Dreaming? Public lecture, Bank of Finland, Helsinki, December 10, 2013.

Woo, WT (2013d). Renminbi jueqi? (Renminbi rising?). *Caijing*, December 17, 2013 (published in Chinese). Available at http://comments.caijing.com.cn/2013-12-17/113699789.html. English language version distributed by Project Syndicate (www.project-syndicate.org).

Woo, WT, M Lu, JD Sachs and Z Chen (Eds.) (2012). *A New Economic Growth Engine for China: Escaping the Middle-Income Trap by Not Doing More of the Same*. London: World Scientific and Imperial College.

Xie, P (1996). *The Choice of China's Financial Institutions*. Shanghai: Shanghai Yuandong Press.

Yang, Q and S Dai (2012). Survey on the reversed rate of return on capital between the banking sector and real economy. *China Finance*, (20).

Zhan, X (2012). Beware the potential threat of industrial transfer, lest it should be transformed into real risk. *China Finance*, (20).

Zhang, J (1997). China's monetization process, financial control and reform dilemma. *Economic Research Journal*, (8).

Zhang, J (2001). *Institution, Gradual Transition and China's Financial Reform*. Beijing: China Financial Publishing House.

SECTION II

UNDERSTANDING THE IMPORTANT LESSONS FROM THE INTERNATIONAL EXPERIENCE

Chapter 2

Wall Street Lawlessness

Jeffrey D. Sachs

One of the features of the 2008 financial crisis is the epidemic of lawlessness among America's major investment banks, commercial banks, hedge funds, financial conglomerates, and stock exchanges, collectively known as Wall Street. Major Wall Street firms have been repeated lawbreakers, and as a result have faced dozens of lawsuits and criminal actions regarding corporate practices at the core of the business. The conclusion of this chapter is that the massive financial law breaking reflects the basic elements of criminal behavior: means, motive, and opportunity. In short, through changes in law, regulation, and ethical environment, Wall Street has become a haven of criminality and corruption.

Let me be clear up front: there are many honest people working on Wall Street, yet the industry behavior taken as a whole, and including the major companies and leading figures, has displayed a flagrant lawlessness and brazenness.

The goal of this chapter is to analyze the behavior of senior Wall Street executives who have directed the operations of their firms, and directed or at least overseen much of the lawlessness. They live in an environment of mass and unchecked greed, unhampered by law or social norm. They have the means, motive, and opportunity to commit large-scale financial crimes. The result is pervasive lawlessness that has done grave damage to the US and world economy. Solutions will require action on several fronts: criminal prosecution, personal liability, changes in compensation systems, regulatory reforms, and a restoration of professional norms and ethics.

I will proceed in four sections. The first section sets the scene, describing the general atmosphere of lawlessness on Wall Street. The second section covers the means of crime. The focus is on managerial discretion, managerial compensation, lack of personal liability of key actors, and public bailouts. The third section covers the motive of crime. The focus is on the culture of greed and uncontrolled corporate compensation. The fourth section covers the opportunity, focusing on the era of deregulation and the revolving door of politics and finance. The total effect is an environment conducive to pervasive malfeasance.

Wall Street Lawlessness

The 2008 financial crisis has uncovered a remarkable wave of financial malfeasance during the past 10–15 years. Table 1 offers several examples. In many cases, the settlement with the US Government, including the payment of hefty fines, is made without an admission of guilt. Yet the record often speaks for itself pointing to the certainty of unethical behavior (e.g., deceit) whether or not it is actually illegal behavior.

The full extent of financial malfeasance is of course unknown, and bad behavior can be called "criminal" only when the U.S. Department of Justice or a state attorney general successfully prosecute a company for financial crimes, something that federal and state justice officials have been reluctant to do for both political and practical reasons. Yet dozens of civil lawsuits by the U.S. Securities and Exchange Commission (SEC), and dozens more private suits between financial firms, have exposed pervasive financial wrongdoing. Table 1 offers a representative selection of such cases. There have been repeated settlements — both fines to the SEC and payments by defendants to plaintiffs — to end these cases, but few admissions of wrongdoing, and only a small number of criminal convictions. To close its cases, the SEC has routinely allowed defendant firms to pay a fine "without admitting or denying the allegations." Some federal judges, notably Judge Jed Rakoff of the US Southern District of

Table 1. Selection of charges of financial malfeasance.

Type of fraud	Firms involved	Brief description of allegations	Dates of fraud	Scale of fraud	Penalties
Deceiving investors	Bank of America; Merrill Lynch	Bank of America failed to disclose material information to shareholders prior to their vote to approve the merger with Merrill Lynch.[a]	2008–2010	$5.8 billion — discretionary bonuses that false statements and misrepresentations allowed BofA to pay Merrill Lynch executives in 2008; $4.5 billion — the net loss that Merrill Lynch incurred in October 2008, which BofA failed to disclose to shareholders; $70 billion — the value Bank of America's shareholders lost in 3.5 months between deal's announcement and closing.	$183 million in penalties to the SEC; $2.7 billion plus paid out so far in settlement in class-action lawsuit related to its acquisition of Merrill Lynch.
Deceiving investors	Citigroup	Citi lied to its shareholders regarding tens of billions of dollars in toxic mortgage-backed securities (MBS) on its books.[b]	2/2007–4/2008	Citigroup lost $27.68 billion in 2008, and by March 2009 its market value had sunk roughly $250 billion from the start of the class period. The bank underwrote $70 billion in collateralized debt obligations (CDOs) from 2004 to 2008.	$590 million settlement to shareholders; $730 million accord with bondholder.

(Continued)

Table 1. (*Continued*)

Type of fraud	Firms involved	Brief description of allegations	Dates of fraud	Scale of fraud	Penalties
Deceiving investors	J.P. Morgan; Credit Suisse	J.P. Morgan Securities LLC and Credit Suisse Securities (USA) misled investors in offerings of residential MBS.[c]	2005–2007	J.P. Morgan made \$2.7 million, while investors lost at least \$37 million. Credit Suisse pocketed \$55.7 million in compensation, while investors lost more than \$10 million.	\$417 million settlement with SEC. J.P. Morgan — \$296.9 million; Credit Suisse — \$120 million.
Market rigging	UBS; Royal Bank of Scotland; Barclays	LIBOR/collusion — Lawsuit filed by Freddie Mac, which lost money due to the artificially lowered interest rates.[d]	Approximately 1991–2012	\$3–5 billion total.	Still in court in the US; UBS, Barclays and Royal Bank of Scotland Group have been fined \$2.6 billion for their role in the scandal in Europe. Barclays: \$450 million (2012); Royal Bank of Scotland: \$612 million (2013); UBS: \$1.5 billion (2012).

(*Continued*)

Table 1. (*Continued*)

Type of fraud	Firms involved	Brief description of allegations	Dates of fraud	Scale of fraud	Penalties
Deceiving investors	Ally Financial, Bank of America, Barclays, Citigroup, Countrywide Financial, Credit Suisse, Deutsche Bank, First Horizon, Goldman Sachs, HSBC, J.P. Morgan, Merrill Lynch, Morgan Stanley, Nomura, RBS, Société Générale, GE	Violations of federal securities laws and common law in the sale of residential private-labeled MBS to Fannie Mae and Freddie Mac.[e]	9/2005–11/2007	Losses on more than $200 billion in MBS.	Cases pending. Bank of America paid $2.8 billion to Fannie Mae and Freddie Mac; UBS will pay $885 million; Citigroup and GE settled for undisclosed amount.
Financial fraud (fraudulent misrepresentation)	Merrill Lynch; Goldman Sachs; Deutsche Bank	Misrepresentations in the firms' marketing and sales of auction rate securities.[f]	8/2008	$330 billion market	Merrill Lynch: $125 million; Goldman Sachs: $22.5 million; Deutsche Bank: $15 million. Also required to buy back billions in frozen, illiquid securities.

(*Continued*)

Table 1. (*Continued*)

Type of fraud	Firms involved	Brief description of allegations	Dates of fraud	Scale of fraud	Penalties
Mortgage/ foreclosure abuses	Goldman Sachs; Morgan Stanley	Morgan Stanley's Saxon Mortgage Services subsidiary and Goldman Sachs' Litton Loan Servicing were rubber-stamping home foreclosure documents without any proper review or understanding of what they were signing.[g]	2007–2008	Affected over 220,000 borrowers.	\$557 million in cash payments and other assistance to help mortgage borrowers: Goldman Sachs: \$330 million and Morgan Stanley: \$227 million.
Mortgage fraud	Deutsche Bank; MortgageIT	Deutsche Bank and MortgageIT falsely certified that they properly assessed the default risk of borrowers, qualifying loans for insurance by the Federal Housing Administration (FHA).[h]	1999–2009	FHA paid insurance claims on more than 3,200 mortgages totaling over \$368 million.	\$202.3 million in damages and penalties.

(*Continued*)

Table 1. (*Continued*)

Type of fraud	Firms involved	Brief description of allegations	Dates of fraud	Scale of fraud	Penalties
Deceiving investors	Goldman Sachs	Goldman Sachs structured and marketed a synthetic CDO that hinged on the performance of subprime residential MBS, without disclosing to investors that the investment vehicle (Abacus) had been designed in consultation with hedge fund manager John Paulson, who chose securities he expected to decline in value and had shorted the portfolio.[i]	4/2007–1/2008	More than $1 billion in losses for investors.	$550 million in SEC fines — $250 million to harmed investors; $300 million to the US Treasury. £17.5 million fine by Britain's Financial Services Authority.
Insider trading	Goldman Sachs; Procter & Gamble; Galleon Group	Rajat K. Gupta, Goldman and P&G board member, provided Galleon Management founder and hedge fund manager Raj Rajaratnam with confidential information Rajaratnam used for insider trading.[j]	10/2008–5/2010	$23 million in illicit profits and loss avoidance.	$150 million and criminal and civil penalty for Rajaratnam, who received an 11 year prison sentence; $17.9 million fine and 2 years in prison for Gupta.

(*Continued*)

Table 1. (*Continued*)

Type of fraud	Firms involved	Brief description of allegations	Dates of fraud	Scale of fraud	Penalties
Tax evasion (facilitation)	Deutsche Bank	Deutsche Bank helped 2,100 customers evade taxes through 2,300 financial transactions using tax shelter deals.[k]	1996–2002	Enabled reporting of over $29 billion in fraudulent tax losses.	$553 million settlement with the I.R.S. and Southern District of New York.
Tax evasion (facilitation)	UBS	UBS was accused of conspiring to assist 52,000 American clients evade US taxes.[l]	2000–2007	Prosecutors allege UBS helped clients hide $20 billion, thereby evading $300 million a year in taxes.	$780 million in fines, penalties, restitution, and interest.
Ponzi scheme	Bernard L. Madoff Investment Securities; Ascot Partners	Madoff ran a "Ponzi scheme," paying returns to his investors from their or other investors' money, rather than from profit earned.[m]	Disputed beginning (somewhere between the 1970s and 1990s) — 10/2008	Estimates of Madoff's Ponzi scheme range from $55–65 billion; of that, $17.3 billion represents money invested; the rest are fake profits.	The total amount available for compensating Madoff victims is now just under $10 billion, including a $7.2 billion settlement. 150 year sentence for Madoff.

(*Continued*)

Table 1. (*Continued*)

Type of fraud	Firms involved	Brief description of allegations	Dates of fraud	Scale of fraud	Penalties
Mortgage/ foreclosure abuses	Bank of America; Wells Fargo; J.P. Morgan; Ally Financial; Citigroup	Abusive practices included improper foreclosure on homeowners where so-called robo-signers hired by banks signed foreclosure affidavits without reviewing the documents, resulting in unlawful foreclosures.[n]	2008–2011	750,000 people affected.	$25 billion total. Ally Financial: $310 million; BofA: $11.82 billion; Citigroup: $2.2 billion; J.P. Morgan: $5.29 billion; Wells Fargo: $5.35 billion.

[a]Fitzpatrick *et al.* (2012).
[b]Raymond and Vaughan (2013).
[c]Silver-Greenberg (2012).
[d]Touryalai (2013).
[e]Son and Kopecki (2011) and Benson and Logutenkova (2013).
[f]Dover (2008).
[g]Morran (2013).
[h]United States Attorney's Office, Southern District of New York (2012).
[i]Dealbook (2010) and Nicholson (2010).
[j]U.S. Securities and Exchange Commission (2011a) and Agence France Presse (2013).
[k]Protess and Browning (2010).
[l]Dealbook (2009).
[m]Sandler (2012) and Henriques (2010).
[n]Rizzo (2012).

New York Court, have heatedly criticized this SEC practice, arguing that it is not in the public interest to have cases end without a finding of wrongdoing, but the practice has continued nonetheless.

The lawsuits have involved the following types of behavior:

Investor fraud. Many Wall Street companies have been sued both by the SEC and private plaintiffs over charges of misrepresenting the true value of marketed securities, especially securities such as CDOs tied to MBS.

Reporting fraud. Many Wall Street companies have been charged with issuing false reports to shareholders, creditors, and regulators about the balance sheets and investment activities of the companies.

Insider trading. Several hedge funds and other investment funds have been charged with criminal and civil offenses related to insider trading.

Mortgage origination fraud. A host of companies have been charged with a range of fraudulent activities regarding mortgage origination, for example, false claims that mortgages were eligible for federal mortgage insurance.

Foreclosure fraud. Many companies have been charged with illegal actions regarding mortgage foreclosures.

Facilitation of tax evasion. Major banks have been charged with facilitation of massive tax evasion, through concealment of various types of offshore activities.

Money laundering. Major banks have been charged with help to terrorist and other illegal organizations in international money laundering.

Market rigging. Major banks have been charged with market rigging in interbank loans (LIBOR), electricity markets, and other markets.

Several major Wall Street investment banks and financial conglomerates, including Goldman Sachs, J.P. Morgan, and Citigroup, have paid fines and settlements related to charges of investor fraud in the marketing of toxic assets, especially MBS and other CDOs. The

Federal Home Finance Administration (FHFA) has sued 17 major financial firms for defrauding the mortgage institutions Freddie Mae and Fannie Mac;[1] two of the defendants, Citigroup and GE, have settled by paying fines to FHFA, while the others face trial in 2014. Several large hedge funds, most recently SAC Capital Advisors, have been charged with insider trading and fraudulent reporting. Here is a *partial* alphabetical list of companies that have paid fines or settlements in lawsuits regarding financial malfeasance since 2005:

AIG, Bank of America, Barclays, Bayou Group, Bear Stearns, Brookstreet Securities, Countrywide Financial, Citigroup, Credit Suisse, Deutsche Bank, Diamondback Capital Management, First Horizon, Galleon Group, GE Capital, Goldman Sachs, HSBC, Hudson Capital Partners, J.P. Morgan, Lehman Brothers, Madoff Investment Securities, Merrill Lynch, Morgan Stanley, Nomura, Peregrine Financial, Quantek Asset Management, Royal Bank of Scotland, S2 Capital, SAC Capital, Société Générale, Tiger Asia Management, UBS, Wachovia, Wells Fargo, Whitier Capital.

To highlight the extent of malfeasance by just one firm, Table 2 lists the settlements paid by J.P. Morgan since 2005. Once again I underscore that many of these cases were settled without an admission of wrongdoing, but the extent of the charges and their specificity make clear that J.P. Morgan often acted in profoundly unprincipled and unethical ways.

One consequence of the financial crisis and exposure of pervasive malfeasance has been the collapse of public confidence in the banking system and financial services industry, especially since many of the same firms involved in illegal activities were also rescued by public-sector bailouts and low-interest Federal Reserve credits in the wake of the 2008 crisis. From Figure 1, we see that public confidence in the banks fell from 60% (great deal/quite a lot of confidence) in 1979 to just 22% in the wake of the financial crisis. By 2013, confidence had crept up only slightly, to 26%, still far below the confidence levels before 2008.

[1]Van Voris and Hurtado (2011).

Table 2. J.P. Morgan selected fines.[2]

Date	Behavior/Allegations	Penalties
April 2011	J.P. Morgan was one of several banks called out in a class-action lawsuit for overcharging or wrongfully foreclosing on active-duty military personnel. The company apologized, paid out $27 million in cash, cut interest rates on home loans and returned houses that were wrongfully foreclosed upon.[a]	$56 Million.
June 2011	The SEC sued J.P. Morgan for misleading buyers by allegedly failing to inform investors that a hedge fund assisted in picking and betting against securities in a CDO J.P. Morgan had sold in 2007.[b]	J.P. Morgan paid $153.6 million to settle the charges without admitting or denying the allegations.
July 2011	In response to a suit by federal and state authorities, J.P. Morgan settled allegations that it rigged the bidding process for reinvesting bond transactions that affected 31 state governments.[c]	The bank paid $229 million to settle the charges without admitting or denying the allegations.
August 2011	The Treasury Department alleged the banking giant violated sanction orders by conducting transactions with people or entities tied to Iran, Sudan, Cuba, and Liberia.[d]	$88.3 million civil penalty.
February 2012	Along with Bank of America and a few smaller lenders, J.P. Morgan settled consumer litigation that claimed the banks processed checks by size — rather than by chronological order — so they could charge unwarranted overdraft fees.[e]	$110 million.

(Continued)

[2]Strochlic (2013).

Table 2. (*Continued*)

Date	Behavior/Allegations	Penalties
March 2012	J.P. Morgan was sued by pension funds and investors for investing their funds in a risky structured investment vehicle that failed at the height of the global financial crisis in 2008.[f]	$150 million settlement without admitting wrongdoing.
November 2012	The SEC charged J.P. Morgan with misleading investors about the quality of mortgages that underlay MBS it sold.[g]	The bank settled the charges for $296.9 million without admitting or denying guilt.
January 2013	Ten banks, including J.P. Morgan Chase, agreed to an $8.5 billion settlement with the Office of the Comptroller of the Currency and the Federal Reserve over "robo-signing" and other alleged abuses of the foreclosure process. The banks were to pay $3.3 billion to harmed borrowers and provide a combined of $5.2 billion in assistance in the form of principal reductions or mortgage modifications.[h]	J.P. Morgan Chase did not disclose its share of the settlement.
March 2013	J.P. Morgan Chase agreed to return $546 million to former customers of MF Global Holdings, the investment firm run by former New Jersey governor Jon Corzine that collapsed in 2011. While it did not admit wrongdoing, J.P. Morgan had been threatened with a lawsuit if it did not return the cash that had been transferred from MF Global during the firm's chaotic final days.[i]	$100 million.

[a]Feeley (2011).
[b]Son *et al.* (2011).
[c]U.S. Securities and Exchange Commission (2011b).
[d]U.S. Department of the Treasury (2011).
[e]Stempel (2012a).
[f]Stempel (2012b).
[g]Silver-Greenberg (2012).
[h]Olick (2013).
[i]Associated Press (2013).

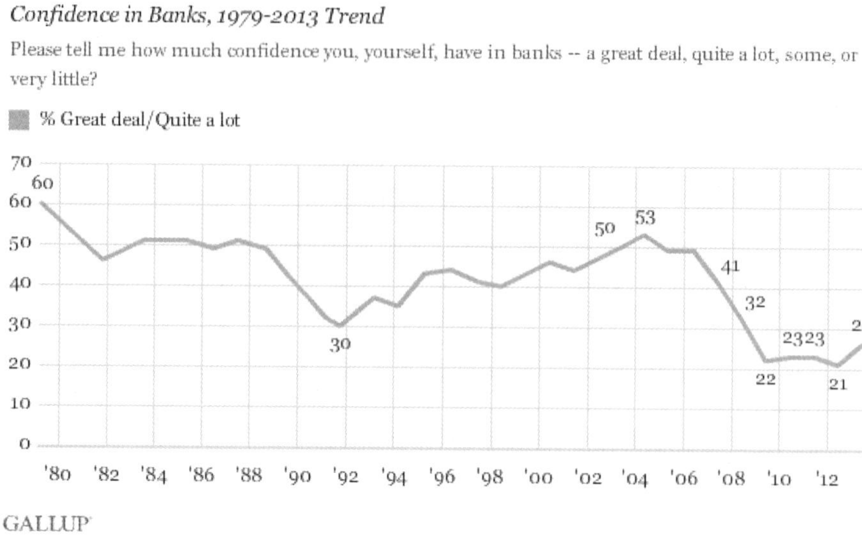

Figure 1.[3]

The flip side of this crashing confidence has been soaring incomes of the bank managers. Wall Street has been enjoying a quarter-century boom in bankers' earnings, a boom that was only partly dented by the 2008 crash and bailout. One shorthand measure of the compensation boom is the bonus pool enjoyed by the New York City securities industry, a figure that is reported annually by the New York State Comptroller.[4]

Figure 2 shows the inflation-adjusted bonus per securities industry employee, compared with median annual earnings of full-time male workers. Clearly the past quarter century has marked an extraordinary era of soaring bank incomes. In 1985, bank bonuses are 40% below median male earnings. At their peak in 2006, they are 4.5 times the median earnings, and as of 2012, roughly 2.5 times the median earnings.

The surge in banker compensation is strongly related to the deregulation of the financial sector, a point made powerfully by

[3]Jacobe (2013).
[4]Office of the State Comptroller 2013.

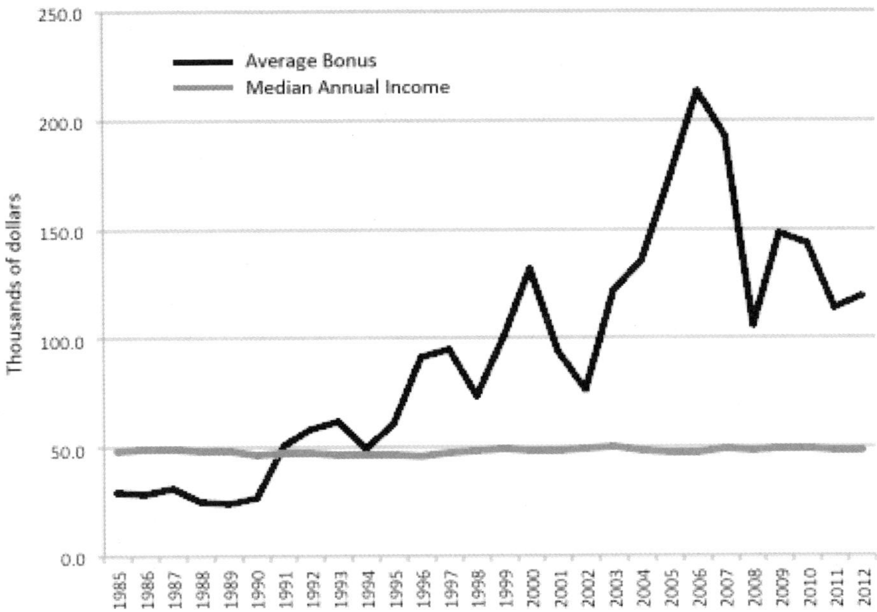

Figure 2. Comparing Wall Street bonuses with median male income.

Philippon and Reshef (2009). They calculate a relative wage of the financial sector and compare it with an index of financial deregulation. Their results are shown in Figure 3. During the 1910–1920s, the relative wage of the financial sector is high, and financial deregulation is low. With the 1929 Great Crash and the onset of the Great Depression, the financial sector is brought under strict regulation and the relative wage of the financial sector declines sharply and stays low for half a century. Beginning in the early 1980s, financial deregulation begins, and the relative earnings in the financial sector begin to climb. By the early 2000s, the financial sector is substantially deregulated and relative earnings are back to the levels of the 1920s.

The Means of Financial Crime

In American capitalism, major corporate malfeasance generally begins at the top, with the responsibility of the CEO and the management team. This is because of the power vested in the American CEO, and the relative lack of oversight of the CEO by the corporate board

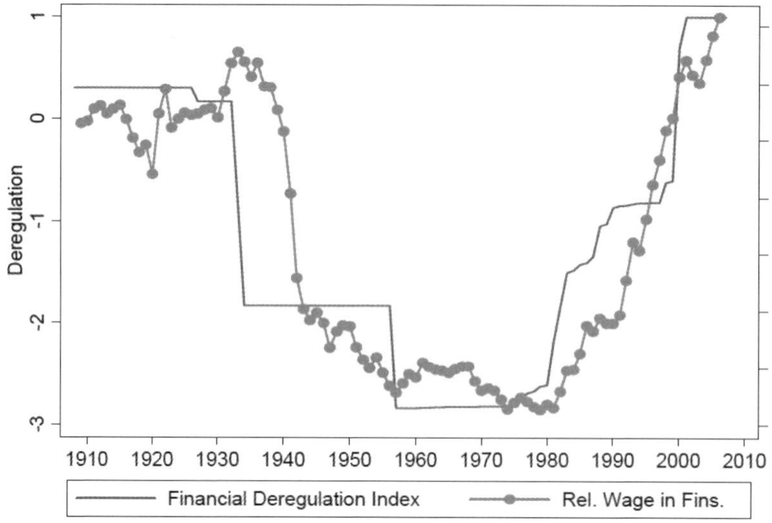

Figure 3. Relative financial wage in banking and financial deregulation. *Source*: Philipon and Reshef (2009, Figure 6).[5]

or other entities. The lack of oversight gives both the means and the motive for financial crime.

The CEO in US managerial capitalism

Our starting point is the distinctive form of US capitalism that places corporate decision-making in the hands of senior management, notably the Chief Executive Officer (CEO) and his senior management team. Large US companies are generally publicly owned, and with highly dispersed shareholdings rather than ownership by a family or a small number of core investors. The companies are incorporated, so that the dispersed investors have limited liability. Because of the dispersed shareholding and limited liability, dispersed shareholders are likely to free ride on the public good of corporate governance. CEOs have considerable authority with relatively low oversight. One result is a natural tension between shareholders and managers that has been recognized since the classic study on

[5]Philippon and Reshef (2009).

The Modern Corporation and Private Property by Adolf Berle and Gardiner Means (1932).

Two major mechanisms are supposed to align management and shareholder interest. The first is a strong and independent board of directors. Yet a massive scholarly literature documents the chronic weakness of the US board of directors in governing the enterprise and overseeing top managers. Board members typically follow the recommendations of management, and many members of the board sit at the behest of management. Many CEOs are simultaneously the chairmen of the board of directors as well. The weakness of boards in the US context is especially damaging because of the highly dispersed ownership structure of most large US publicly traded corporations.

The second is corporate compensation based on shareholder value, through stocks and stock options as part of the pay package of senior managers. The use of equity-based compensation took off in the 1980s, leading also to an overall massive increase in the compensation packages of top managers. Equity-based compensation may to some extent reduce potential conflicts between managers and shareholders but it opens an entirely new set of problems involving the incentive by CEOs to manipulate corporate practices in order to boost share prices, either at the expense of the true long-term value of the company or at the expense of non-equity stakeholders such as the company's creditors.

Shareholders also have remarkably little say in CEO compensation. This remains the purview of the board, and normally of a compensation committee of the board. The compensation committee typically operates at the behest of the CEO, so when times are good for the company the CEO effectively sets his own compensation package. In the Dodd–Frank legislation that followed the 2008 financial crash, shareholders were given slightly more influence on compensation, through a "say on pay" clause, by which shareholders can render an advisory position to the board on a proposed compensation package through a shareholder vote.[6] This is evidently an extremely limited power, as it is only advisory and depends on disgruntled and

[6]Dodd–Frank Wall Street Reform and Consumer Protection Act 2010.

decentralized shareholders successfully mounting a campaign against a proposed compensation package.

Corporate leverage

A second distinguishing feature of American companies, and especially Wall Street firms, is the high level of leverage. The American tax system encourages leverage since interest payments are tax deductible from corporate earnings, while dividend payments are not. American companies face a large range of lenders, both in the form of bonds and bank loans. Banks have a special incentive for leverage, since the Federal Deposit Insurance Corporate (FDIC) guarantees bank deposits up to a limit, and the federal government more generally guarantees banks' liabilities through emergency bailouts under the "Too Big To Fail" doctrine.

Leverage gives both managers and shareholders an incentive to engage in overly risky practices, since shareholders and managers (through equity-based compensation) capture the corporate gains while creditors share in the corporate losses. Consider a simple illustration. A debt-free corporation with a value of 100 faces a risky business opportunity paying +40 with probability one half and −60 with probability one half. Risk-neutral shareholders would clearly decline the opportunity, which has an expected return of −10. Now suppose that the same company is once again worth 100, but with equity value of 30 and debt of 70, and so leverage of 3.33 (=100/30). Now, the business opportunity would lead to a corporate value of +70 (=30 + 40) with probability one half, and a value of 0 (i.e., bankruptcy) with a probability of one half. Expected shareholder value rises from 30 to 35 (=½ × 70). The shareholders of leveraged firm would take the gamble even though it has a negative social return.

CEO compensation in equity options can make the situation even worse, leading managers to accept risky bets that the shareholders would not. Suppose for example that the same company is not quite so leveraged, with equity value of 60 and debt of 40. Clearly the shareholders would not accept the risky investment, since the company would end up with a value of 100 with probability one half and zero with probability one half, or a value of 50.

Now suppose that the CEO has stock options on the company that are in the money when the corporate value reaches 70. Suppose, for example, that the CEO compensation is given by: Base Salary + Bonus, where the Bonus is equal to \$1 million × (Equity Value − 70) if the Equity Value is greater than 70, and is equal to 0 if the equity value is below 70. Without the investment, the CEO's bonus is worth zero. The options are out of the money. With the investment, the CEO's bonus would be \$30 million with probability one half, and zero with probability one half. Clearly, the CEO will want to undertake the risky investment, even though the shareholders are left worse off. The fact that compensation is in the form of a stock option, rather than outright equities, exacerbates the CEO's taste for socially harmful risk taking.

We see that high leverage increases the shareholder's appetite for risk beyond the social optimum, and that stock options increase the CEO's appetite for risk even beyond those of the shareholders. The combination of highly leveraged firms and CEO pay packages laden with stock options can turn into a lethal brew in which the CEO treats the enterprises as an enormous gamble for riches.[7]

Banks tend to have an extremely high leverage ratio compared with non-financial corporations. This is the bank's job, to take on debt from depositors, other banks, and the financial markets, to invest in assets. It is also facilitated, in general, by the presence of deposit insurance and by the implicit expectation of government bailouts of bank creditors in the event of a crisis. In the run-up to the 2008 financial crisis, US investment banks and European commercial banks had the highest leverage, a remarkable average of around 30 (total assets relative to equity), while US commercial banks were less highly leveraged at around 10, still a very high leverage ratio compared with non-financial companies. The data are shown in Figure 4.

The combination of high leverage and deposit insurance can prove even more toxic than reckless risk taking. It can lead to outright illegality and "looting" of the financial firms by their own managers. A CEO backed by government deposit insurance (or by the prospect

[7]Bolton *et al.* (2011).

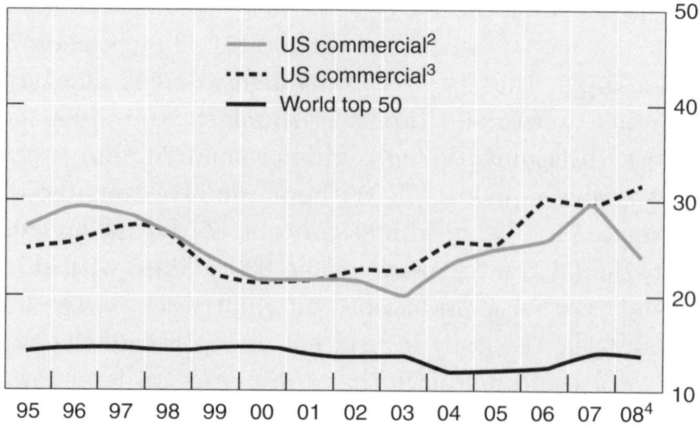

Figure 4. Leverage ratios of banks (BIS).
Source: The role of valuation and leverage in procyclicality.[8]

of a government bailout of the bank's creditors more generally) can attract depositors (or creditors more generally) even for an insolvent bank. The inflow of deposit funds can be used, if regulators are not diligent or are complicit in the crime, to make direct or hidden payments to insider interests, including the CEO, leaving the ultimate bill to the government.

The era of banking deregulation

In addition to CEO governance and high leverage, the third major characteristic of Wall Street in the decades before 2008 was deregulation, something we already noticed in Figure 2. The deregulation movement in the US began in the 1970s and has covered many aspects of the economy, including health and safety, environment, labor, and finance. Regarding Wall Street, financial deregulation dramatically expanded the range of products that banks could market (e.g., market-backed securities and other derivatives), the prices on those products, the accounting rules and prudential rules governing

[8]Working Group of the Financial Stability Forum and the Committee on the Global Financial System 2009.

the banks, and the kinds of banking activities that could be combined within a single financial company.

The first wave of deregulation came in the early 1980s in the savings and loan (S&L) industry, which at the time was a specialized set of banks and institutions to finance housing and real estate. The new Reagan Administration, inheriting a financially weak savings and loan industry, opted for deregulation, on the ostensible grounds that deregulation would speed the recovery of the floundering industry. Various kinds of regulatory restrictions on the industry were lifted, including the interest rates that S&Ls could pay on deposits; accounting treatment of intangible assets such as goodwill; and the range of investments that S&Ls could undertake.

The deregulation did not solve the industry's problems. Quite the contrary. Within a few years, the entire sector was bankrupt, in effect "looted" by its CEOs, in the words of economists George Akerlof and Paul Romer (1993). Insolvent S&Ls took advantage of federal deposit insurance to attract new deposits, and then used deposit inflows to make payments of phantom profits and other insider payments to the owner-managers of the S&Ls. In the end, the federal government had to pay off the depositors, while many corrupt owners of bankrupt S&Ls walked away with fortunes. Only a few were charged with crimes. Within a few years, the result was the financial gutting of the S&Ls, and total resolutions costs to the government of around \$150–175 billion as cited by Akerlof and Romer (1993, p. 36).

The most important act of deregulation was the Gramm–Leach–Bliley Act of 1999,[9] which repealed of the 1933 Glass–Steagall Act,[10] a major part of Great Depression financial reform that separated deposit-taking activities and investment banking activities. Glass–Steagall was repealed in 1999 with strong bipartisan support. The leading architect of the repeal, Treasury Secretary Robert Rubin, immediately became Chairman of Citigroup, a new financial conglomerate (formed in a \$140 billion mega-merger of Citicorp and Travelers Group, one of the largest mergers in history)[11] made

[9]Gramm–Leach–Bliley Act 1999.
[10]Banking Act of 1933.
[11]Martin (1998).

possible by the deregulation. Citigroup brought together a deposit-taking bank (Citibank), with insurance, investment banking, proprietary trading, and hedge-fund activities. The Federal Government bailed out Citigroup in 2008.[12] During the period 1999–2009, Rubin received $126 million in compensation before the federal rescue of the firm, including compensation made possible by the federal bailout.[13]

The Motive for Financial Crime

If the means of financial crime includes poorly supervised CEOs, highly leveraged companies, and deregulation, the overwhelming motive for financial crime is greed. Financial crimes aim at enrichment, especially of the senior managers of the banks. Yet greed is always present. The motive for crime was strengthened, however, by several specific factors that made crime more profitable to the bank CEOs. These include changes in the compensation package, in the tax code, and in the cultural environment.

The changing compensation package

Beginning in the early 1980s, CEO compensation began to soar. The increases in the financial sector were even more extraordinary than elsewhere. A major factor in the soaring compensation was the widespread adoption of equity-based compensation, especially in the form of stock options. These were given favorable tax treatment on the one hand, and strong normative backing from leading business professors like Harvard Business School's Michael Jensen, who argued that stock options would align the incentives of CEOs and shareholders to overcome agency problems within the firm.[14] CEO compensation took off like a rocket, from around 40 times average earnings of workers in the early 1980s to hundreds of times average earnings by the 1990s.[15]

The financial sector is marked by extraordinary, indeed unprecedented compensation packages for industry leaders. This reflects the

[12]Wilchins and Stempel (2008).
[13]Cohan (2012).
[14]Jensen and Murphy (1990).
[15]Sachs (2011, Figure 2.5, p. 21).

widespread use of stock options, large end-of-year bonuses on Wall Street, and remarkable compensation systems in particular parts of the industry such as hedge funds. The hedge-fund "standard package" is the so-called two-and-twenty package. The hedge-fund manager receives a fee of 2% of all assets under management, plus 20% of the profits earned, subject to a partial carry-forward and offset of past losses. Hedge-fund managers do not sacrifice compensation (e.g., from the 2% of assets) as a result of outright losses. The minimum compensation two-and-twenty package is therefore 2% of assets under management.

The results of this hedge-fund compensation rule can be stunning. In 2012, several hedge-fund managers took home more than $1 billion in annual compensation.[16] Even more remarkably, some of the $1-billion-plus recipients did not even beat the market, receiving their extraordinary pay as a result of the level of assets under management, not as a result of superior investment performance. This is the case, for example, of Ray Dalio, manager of Bridgewater Associates, who took home a *reported* $1.7 billion in compensation in 2012 despite falling short of average market returns. Similarly, SAC manager Steven A. Cohen received a reported $1.4 billion in compensation, also having fallen short of the market.[17] Indeed Cohen not only fell short of the market, but also of the law. SAC was indicted on insider trading charges in July 2013.[18]

Tax breaks for the rich

High-income earners have enjoyed increasingly favorable tax treatment since 1980, enabling the rich to keep a growing share of their steeply rising take-home pay. The tax benefits have come in a variety of ways: (1) a sharp cut after 1980 in the top marginal tax rate on personal income tax; (2) a sharp cut after 1980 in the tax rates on capital gains and dividend income; (3) special tax benefits for hedge-fund managers in the form of low tax rates on "carried interest," the tax category for hedge-fund compensation. Figure 5 shows the

[16] Cresswell (2013).
[17] La Roche (2013).
[18] Lattman and Protess (2013).

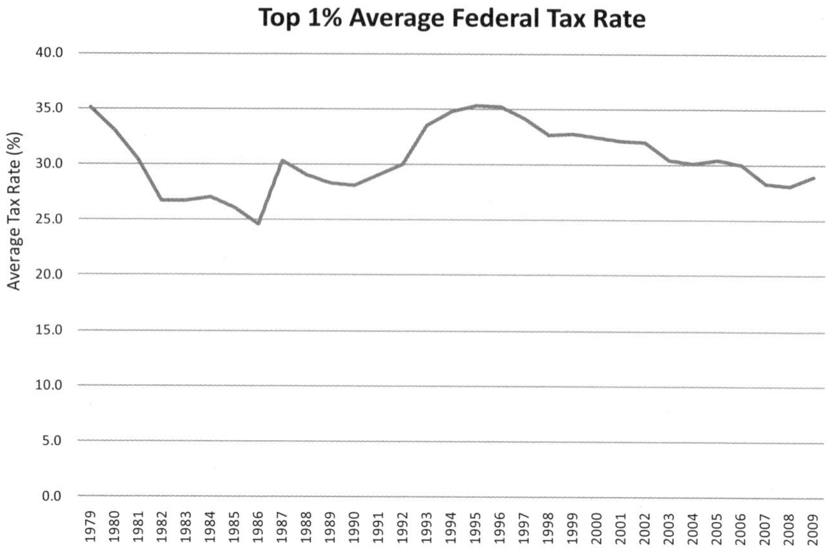

Figure 5.

Source: Data from Tax Policy Center (Urban Institute and Brookings Institution).

declining average personal income tax payments for households in the top 1% of income.

Changing social norms

The social milieu influences the scale of CEO compensation and the acceptability of self-serving or illegal behavior. A notable case in point involved a leading and highly successful Swedish CEO, Percy Barnevik, who engineered a retirement package typical of a US CEO. When the news of the retirement package became public several years later, the public outcry forced the retired CEO to recant the arrangement and to step down from other public positions.[19] Such public pressure almost disappeared in the US context from the 1980s onward. CEOs have long reveled in their mega-packages and face no practical public pressures for moderation.

The epitome of CEO excess is a fictional movie character, financier Gordon Gekko, with his famous slogan that "greed is good."

[19]Goodley (2002).

Yet serious studies of financial-market ethics suggest that Gekkoism is an accurate depiction of Wall Street mores. A recent survey of Wall Street financiers revealed a Wall Street ethos of success at any price.[20] Some of the major conclusions include:

- More than half of respondents — 52% — felt it was likely that their competitors have engaged in unethical or illegal activity to gain an edge in the market; 24% felt employees at their own company likely have engaged in misconduct to get ahead;
- Misconduct is still widespread in the financial services industry; 23% of respondents indicated that they had observed or had first-hand knowledge of wrongdoing in the workplace;
- 29% of respondents believed that financial services professionals may need to engage in unethical or illegal activity in order to be successful;
- More than one-quarter of all financial services professionals — 26% — believed the compensation plans or bonus structures in place at their companies incentivize employees to compromise ethical standards or violate the law;
- An alarming number of financial services professionals, 24% of respondents, likely would engage in insider trading to make $10 million if they could get away with it;
- Shockingly, and consistent with recent and high-profile criticism of the culture within the financial services industry, a full 28% of respondents felt that the financial services industry does not put the interests of clients first.

There may be a deeper cultural phenomenon at play, of serious concern for moral behavior. Many studies in recent years have revealed that students and professionals in economics and business tend to be less cooperative, more self-serving, and more subject to corruption that individuals coming from fields.[21] A recent study has similarly showed that in a battery of experimental situations, individuals of higher socioeconomic status tend to cheat more, not less, than individuals of lower socioeconomic status. Countless recent

[20]Labaton Sucharow LLP (2013).
[21]See, for example, Frank *et al.* (1993).

sociological studies have also found that the degree of social trust in the US has declined markedly in recent decades.[22] The upshot of all of this may be that social restraints on high compensation packages have diminished in the US during the past three decades, thereby making it easier for CEOs to take the opportunity to increase their own paychecks. This has been the strong conclusion of one influential analyst of CEO pay.[23]

The Opportunity for Financial Crime

The means of financial crime is the very high discretion of senior bank managers, unchecked by regulation or board oversight. The overwhelming motive of financial crime is greed, in a context where mega-compensation has become normal and socially sanctioned (or at least expected). The opportunity for financial crime comes from the legal and political milieu facing Wall Street senior managers. Senior Wall Street managers face extremely low personal risk of any penalties or adverse consequences in response to their financial malfeasance. This is most importantly a result of the enormous political power of Wall Street in Washington.

Wall Street political power

Wall Street is one of America's four mega-lobbies, alongside the military–industrial complex, health care, and big oil. A lobby achieves its political might through several channels: a large share in corporate profits, large financial payments in Washington, and an active revolving door between the sector and senior political positions. The financial sector ranks very high in every one of these dimensions.

The share of financial-sector profits in overall corporate profits rose from low levels before financial deregulation to around one-quarter of all corporate profits on the eve of the financial crisis. We can see this increase in Figure 6, where the share of the financial sector in total profits rises from under 10% in 1985 to above 20% after

---

[22]Putnam (2000).
[23]Bebchuk and Spamann (2010).

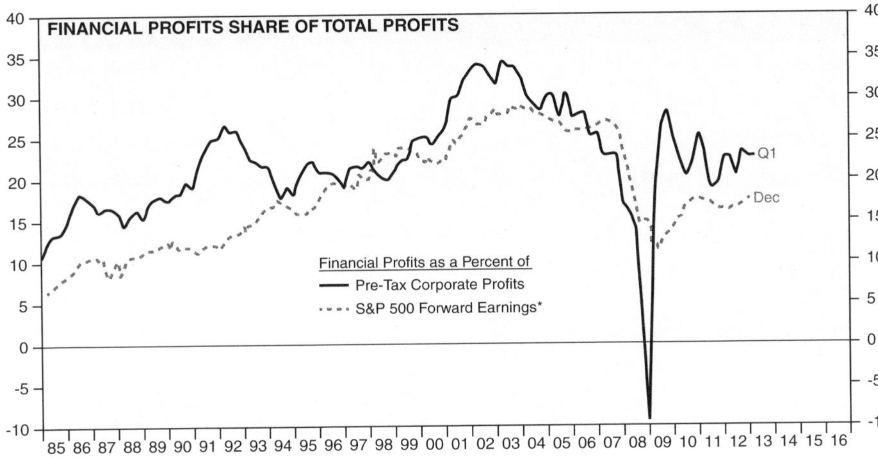

* Using consensus 12-month forward earnings forecasts.
Source: US Department of Commerce, Bureau of Economic Analysis and Thomson Reuters I/B/E/S.

Figure 6. Financial profits share of total profits.

2000, with the exceptional collapse in 2008. This massive profitability gave enormous political leverage to the sector.

The industry has not been shy in throwing some of its soaring profits towards politicians, and the politicians were not shy in receiving it. One can credit Bill Clinton with bringing Wall Street investment banks back towards the Democrats in 1992. They were repaid handsomely with an administration that aggressively championed financial deregulation. Barack Obama has maintained the aggressive courtship of Wall Street during his Presidency and especially his two campaigns for the Presidency, both of which were heavily financed by Wall Street. Yet both political parties, and hundreds of top politicians in Washington, enjoy Wall Street largesse. The money flows mainly in two forms: as campaign contributions and as lobbying outlays, much of which end up in political pockets indirectly through hiring politicians into lobbying firms (and law firms), lavish fundraisers, and other means.

Figures 7 and 8 show the rundown on lobbying outlays and campaign contributions by corporate sector. In Figure 7, we see that the financial sector has been the second largest sector in lobbying (following health care and a miscellaneous category). Total registered

Sector	Total
Misc Business	$5,549,911,554
Health	$5,493,818,976
Finance/Insur/RealEst	$5,491,167,679
Communic/Electronics	$4,494,912,573
Energy/Nat Resource	$4,087,109,545
Other	$2,953,969,509
Transportation	$2,838,099,261
Ideology/Single-Issue	$1,820,437,730
Agribusiness	$1,655,007,427
Defense	$1,575,774,971
Construction	$602,483,234
Labor	$548,471,641
Lawyers & Lobbyists	$396,457,969

Figure 7. Corporate lobbying by sector, totals for 1998–2013. *Source*: Opensecrets.org.[24]

Rank	Sector	Amount	Dems	Repubs
1	Finance/Insur/RealEst	$2,928,928,155	43%	54%
2	Other	$1,760,700,838	50%	48%
3	Misc Business	$1,739,227,874	40%	55%
4	Ideology/Single-Issue	$1,522,573,763	57%	41%
5	Lawyers & Lobbyists	$1,521,381,893	70%	29%
6	Health	$1,109,575,365	43%	54%
7	Communic/Electronics	$956,518,808	58%	39%
8	Labor	$811,617,232	87%	7%
9	Energy/Nat Resource	$623,557,316	29%	68%
10	Construction	$594,353,047	32%	64%
11	Agribusiness	$567,080,253	32%	67%
12	Transportation	$486,039,345	32%	67%
13	Defense	$179,929,505	43%	57%

Figure 8. Campaign contributions by sector of donor, all federal elections 1990–2012.[25]

[24] OpenSecrets.Org Center for Responsive Politics (a).

[25] OpenSecrets.Org Center for Responsive Politics (b).

lobbying outlays since 1998 have totaled an extraordinary $5.5 billion. In Figure 8, we see that the financial sector has been far and away the largest campaign contributor as well. (Note that for purposes of allocating campaign contributions, each individual campaign donor is assigned to a corporate sector based on employment.) Adding overall federal election cycles since 1990, financial sector donors have contributed $2.9 billion, divided 43% to Democrats and 54% to Republicans. No other sector comes even close. In the 2008 election cycle, financial-sector contributions reached $513 million, and in 2012, $662 million, in both cases by far the largest single sector.

The flow of money is at the core of the Wall Street — Washington relationship, but personal arrangements augment the financial ones. The Wall Street — Washington revolving door is notorious. Wall Street leaders staff the top jobs in the White House and Treasury, and politicians and staff are routinely tapped for regulatory positions. Politicians, their family members, and staff are also regularly assured of highly lucrative employment in lobbying organizations.

History will record that Robert Rubin forged the most important network of personal linkages between Wall Street and Washington over the past two decades, an act of private service that was phenomenally lucrative for many people, not least for Mr. Rubin himself. Rubin arrived at the White House in 1993 direct from being Co-Chair of Goldman Sachs. After serving Clinton as top economic advisor (1993–1995), he became Treasury Secretary (1995–1999), during which time he presided over the repeal of Glass–Steagall, and led the opposition to the regulation of derivatives markets.[26] Four months after leaving the Treasury he became the Chairman of Citigroup, the financial conglomerate that was made possible by the end of Glass–Steagall.[27] In that capacity, Mr. Rubin earned a total compensation of $126 million during 1999–2009. In 2008–2009, Citigroup required hundred of billions of dollars of government guarantees and loans to stay afloat after its massive involvement in the subprime bubble.

---

[26] *The Wall Street Journal.*
[27] Stempel and Wilchins (2009).

Mr. Rubin oversaw the crucial economics appointments in both the Clinton and Obama Administrations. His acolytes in the Obama Administration have included Lawrence Summers, Director of the National Economic Council; Gene Sperling, Summers' successor; Peter Orszag, director of the Office of Management and Budget; Timothy Geithner, Secretary of Treasury; Jack Lew, director of the Office of Management and Budget and Secretary of the Treasury; Michael Froman, Deputy National Security Advisor for International Economic Affairs; and Jason Furman, Chairman of the Council of Economic Advisors; among others. This includes nearly every senior economics official. Even the Obama White House team outside of Mr. Rubin's immediate orbit also shared extensive Wall Street experience, including: Rahm Emmanuel, Chief of Staff (Wasserstein Parella, Freddie Mac); William Daley, Chief of Staff (J.P. Morgan); Tom Donilon, National Security Advisor (Fannie Mae); and many others.

Regulatory, legal, and political environment

With few exceptions, senior Wall Street managers do not face personal risks as a result of corporate malfeasance. There are a few notorious exceptions: Bernie Madoff went to jail for the Ponzi scheme he lead. A few individuals engaged in insider trading have gone to jail. Yet most of the financial malfeasance has resulted, at most, in fines or cash settlements paid for by the company rather than any individuals. The shareholders end up footing the bill for malfeasance committed by the managers.

Most of the Federal prosecutions have been civil lawsuits brought by the SEC. The Department of Justice has filed almost no criminal charges against top officials of Wall Street CEOs for financial companies, and very few criminal cases with the company as defendant. (A recent exception is the federal criminal prosecution against SAC Capital Advisors hedge fund, but with no charges against the CEO Steven A. Cohen, and without any evident risk to the billions of dollars in compensation earned by Cohen.) Before becoming Obama's Attorney General, Eric Holder worked for Covington and Burling, a corporate law firm that represents Wall Street firms including Goldman Sachs.

When settlements in the SEC cases are reached, the defendant firms typically pay a fine but has been allowed to "neither admit nor deny wrongdoing," a practice I noted earlier that has been heatedly criticized by Federal court judge Jed Rakoff as not serving the public interest.[28] The fine is often a small fraction of the gains that accrued to the company as a result of its malfeasant behavior. Without no judgment of guilt or acknowledgment or denial of wrongdoing, no further action is taken against senior management (e.g., a revocation of a manager's right to engage in banking).

A notable feature of the US political scene is the any lack of political consequence whatsoever to CEOs whose firms pay fines to settle cases of financial malfeasance. Rubin continues to be a senior advisor to Obama. Goldman Sachs CEO Lloyd Blankfein has continued to be a valued White House guest, as has J.P. Morgan's Jamie Dimon. Not only did the financial malfeasance of their companies not bring any professional loss or cost whatsoever, the firms in question faced little regulatory, political, or moral pressure to replace the CEO who had presided over the incidents in question.

[28]In S.D.N.Y. (2011), Rakoff argued: "Here, the S.E.C.'s long-standing policy — hallowed by history, but not by reason of allowing defendants to enter into Consent Judgments without admitting or denying the underlying allegations, deprives the Court of even the most minimal assurance that the substantial injunctive relief it is being asked to impose has any basis in fact . . . A consent judgment that does not involve any admissions and that results in only very modest penalties is just as frequently viewed, particularly in the business community, as a cost of doing business imposed by having to maintain a working relationship with a regulatory agency, rather than as any indication of where the real truth lies."

And in his decision S.D.N.Y. (2009), he noted: "Overall, indeed, the parties' submissions, when carefully read, leave the distinct impression that the proposed Consent Judgment was a contrivance designed to provide the S.E.C. with the facade of enforcement and the management of the Bank with a quick resolution of an embarrassing inquiry — all at the expense of the sole alleged victims, the shareholders. Even under the most deferential review, this proposed Consent Judgment cannot remotely be called fair . . . Oscar Wilde once famously said that a cynic is someone "who knows the price of everything and the value of nothing." Oscar Wilde, Lady Windermere's Fan (1892). The proposed Consent Judgment in this case suggests a rather cynical relationship between the parties: the S.E.C. gets to claim that it is exposing wrongdoing on the part of the Bank of America in a high-profile merger; the Bank's management gets to claim that they have been coerced into an onerous settlement by overzealous regulators. And all this is done at the expense, not only of the shareholders, but also of the truth."

A Case Study: Goldman Sachs, John Paulson, and Abacus

The Abacus case is exemplary of the nature of financial fraud and the failures of legal enforcement or practical accountability. Abacus refers to a synthetic CDO that offered a payout structure based on an underlying set of MBS. Goldman Sachs created the synthetic CDO and from 2004–2008 marketed it to two buyers, ABN Amro and IKB Deutche Industriebank. When the underlying MBS went into default, the CDO also defaulted, causing ABN and IKB to lose around $1 billion. The SEC charged that Goldman Sachs violated the Securities Act of 1934 and the Securities Exchange Act of 1933 by committing various acts of financial fraud or deceit in the sale of the CDO to the two investors.

The full story, explained in the SEC complaint,[29] is that the hedge-fund manager John Paulson approached Goldman Sachs with the plan to create a synthetic CDO *designed to go into default* within a short period after their sale. (The underlying MBS were selected for inclusion in the CDO with the knowledge that they were on the verge of default.) Paulson would purchase a credit default swap (CDS) from Goldman Sachs that would pay Paulson in the event of default of the CDO.

Goldman Sachs would sell the CDO to unsuspecting investors. Those investors would pay Goldman Sachs for the CDO, and in turn, upon the default of the CDO, Goldman Sachs would in turn pay Paulson. Goldman Sachs would make a profit by taking fees on its management of the overall process. Just as planned by Goldman and Paulson, the two unwitting investors paid around $1 billion for the CDO, which quickly defaulted. Goldman Sachs then paid nearly $1 billion to Paulson using the funds it had received from ABN and IKB.

The SEC's fraud charge was based on the fact that Goldman Sachs failed to disclose the role of John Paulson in creating a CDO designed to fail, and Paulson's plan to buy a credit-default swap on the toxic CDO. In short, Goldman Sachs sold the Abacus security to

[29]Securities and Exchange Commission v. Goldman, Sachs & Co. and Fabrice Tourre (2010).

investors with a plan based on the fact that the security would soon go into default.

Goldman Sachs did not dispute the main facts of the case. The firm's main defense was simply that the investors should have done their own due diligence and that Goldman had no responsibility to alert the investors to Paulson's plan. The SEC invoked, among parts of the law, Section 10b-5 of the Securities Act of 1934, which states that it is unlawful for any person to "engage in any act, practice, or course of business which operates or would operate as a fraud or deceit upon any person, in connection with the purchase or sale of any security."

In the event, Goldman Sachs paid the SEC a fine of $550 million.[30] It neither admitted nor denied wrongdoing. Incredibly, Paulson was never charged with any wrongdoing whatsoever, even though he was party to the alleged fraud. On the contrary, Paulson walked away with a clean $1 billion in earnings from the deal, and was hailed as a conquering hero on Wall Street. Predictably, many Wall Street traders rallied to Goldman's defense, saying that an investment bank selling toxic securities has no reason or responsibility to notify potential buyers that the securities have been designed to fail.

The Abacus case was repeated in broad strokes by several other investment and commercial banks, often working hand in hand with other hedge funds such as Magnetar. Typically, European banks and investors were the ones that purchased the toxic CDOs, while the investment banks and hedge funds walked away with the earnings. The SEC imposed fines from other banks for similar activities (including J.P. Morgan, $153.6 million,[31] and Citigroup, $285 million, in an agreement that is still pending in an appeals court). Yet none of the banks admitted nor denied wrongdoing. Hedge funds involved in engineering these deals generally walked away with large profits.

Lessons for Financial Market Reform

Wall Street malfeasance of the kind involved in Abacus played an enormous role in the 2008 financial crisis, in fomenting the subprime

[30] Dealbook (2010).
[31] Stempel and Lynch (2011).

housing bubble and then in expanding it even after the housing market peaked in 2005–2006. Without fraudulent behavior of many sorts, the crisis would have been much smaller. With better incentives and oversight, the boom and bust cycle might have been avoided entirely.

The US has done little to rectify the organizational, regulatory, legal, political and moral weaknesses that created the financial catastrophe. Wall Street remains largely out of control, or one might better say in control of the levers of power. There seems to be little will to hold Wall Street leaders accountable for their actions, or even for that matter to have them pay honest taxes on the gargantuan compensation packages they successfully engineer for themselves.

Still, even if the US remains largely impervious to reforms, other countries can learn from the US experience. What it teaches is that the financial system is an interconnected process that requires policy interventions at many levels. Our brief overview of Wall Street lawlessness suggests the following areas for the greatest attention:

Leverage. The high leverage of financial institutions creates clear and present dangers of misbehavior, whether in terms of excessive risk or outright looting. Leverage is greatly exacerbated by deposit insurance and by deceptive accounting, e.g., the use of derivatives to misstate valuations on the balance sheet.

Compensation. CEOs should face much tougher scrutiny and regulatory limits on compensation packages. The European Union is right to adopt new limitations on bankers' pay, something that Washington has steadfastly refused to countenance for Wall Street. Shareholders should have an automatic vote on compensation packages, not merely an advisory say. The use of stock options should be limited to avoid excessive risk. One-way bets that raise incentives for excess risk taking, such as the two-and-twenty principle for hedge funds, should be barred by market regulation.

Personal taxation. The low effective tax rates faced by financial managers, e.g., in hedge-fund managers paying a top 15% tax rate on "carried interest," should be replaced by fairer, significantly higher levels of marginal taxation, in part to tamp down the incentives for managerial abuse.

Personal liability. CEOs and senior managers should face *personal* liability for major acts of malfeasance committed by their companies during their watch. Personal liability could include the loss of license to practice, forced resignation from office, a ban on bonuses and other compensation limits, and personal liability for a portion of corporate fines and civil settlements in cases where CEO responsibility or negligence can be determined.

Criminal prosecution. The justice system cannot function if the Department of Justice is unwilling or unequipped in expertise to bring criminal prosecutions against firms and individuals for large-scale financial malfeasance.

Campaign and lobbying funds. As highly regulated entities enjoying federal protection in the form of deposit insurance, preferential access to bank credit, and other support, Wall Street firms should be barred from lobbying activities and senior bank managers should be barred from making campaign contributions.

Ethical norms. As surveys, media interviews, and recent books have fully attested, the moral environment on Wall Street is profoundly degraded. Wall Street participants do not easily distinguish right from wrong, and believe that illegality and immorality are pervasive. Moral authority needs to be restored, though the ways to do that remain elusive and in need of a separate analysis.

References

Presse, AF (2013). Ex-Goldman Director Rajat Gupta fined $13.9 million for insider trading. *Business Insider*, July 17. Available at http://www.businessinsider.com/rajat-gupta-fined-insider-trading-2013-7.

Akerlof, GA and PM Romer (1993). Looting: The economic underworld of bankruptcy for profit. *Brookings Papers on Economic Activity*, 24(2), 1–74.

Associated Press (2013). JP Morgan, MF Global Trustee Reach Agreement. *Associated Press*, March 20. Available at http://bigstory.ap.org/article/report-jp-morgan-mf-global-reach-agreement.

Banking Act of 1933, Pub. L. No. 73-66, 48 Stat. 162 (1933).

Bebchuk, LA and H Spamann (2010). Regulating bankers' pay. *Georgetown Law Journal*, 98, 247–287.

Berle, Jr., AA and GC Means (1932). *The Modern Corporation and Private Property*. New York: Macmillan.

Benson, C and E Logutenkova (2013). UBS to pay $885 million to settle U.S. mortgage suit. *Bloomberg*, July 26. Available at http://www.bloomberg.com/news/2013-07-25/ubs-agrees-to-pay-885-million-to-settle-u-s-securities-suit.html.

Bolton, P, H Mehran and J Shapiro (2011). Executive compensation and risk taking. *Federal Reserve Bank of New York*.

Cohan, WD (2012). Rethinking Robert Rubin. *Bloomberg Businessweek*, September 30. Available at http://www.businessweek.com/articles/2012-09-19/rethinking-robert-rubin.

Cresswell, J (2013). Hedge fund titans' pay stretching to 10 figures. *The New York Times*, April 15. Available at http://dealbook.nytimes.com/2013/04/15/pay-stretching-to-10-figures/.

Dealbook (2009). UBS to pay $780 million to settle tax case. *The New York Times*, February 18. Available at http://dealbook.nytimes.com/2009/02/18/ubs-reaches-deal-over-offshore-banking-services/.

Dealbook (2010). Goldman settles with S.E.C. for $550 million. *The New York Times*, July 15. Available at http://dealbook.nytimes.com/2010/07/15/goldman-to-settle-with-s-e-c-for-550-million/.

Dodd–Frank Wall Street Reform and Consumer Protection Act, Pub. L. No. 111-203, 124 Stat. 1376 (2010).

Dover (2008). Three top Wall St. banks to buy back billions in auction rate securities. *The New York Times*, August 22. Available at http://www.nytimes.com/2008/08/22/business/worldbusiness/22iht-22auction.15532286.html?_r=0.

Feeley, J (2011). JP Morgan settles military mortgage suits for $56 million. *Bloomberg*, April 21. Available at http://www.bloomberg.com/news/2011-04-21/jpmorgan-chase-settles-military-mortgage-overcharging-suit-for-56-million.html.

Fitzpatrick, D, C Berthelsen and R Sidel (2012). BofA takes new crisis-era hit; Shareholder lawsuit tied to Merrill deal is settled for $2.43 billion; bill is surely set to increase. *The Wall Street Journal*, September 29. Available at http://online.wsj.com/article/SB10000872396390443843904578024110468736042.html.

Frank, RH, T Gilovich and DT Regan (1993). Does studying economics inhibit cooperation? *Journal of Economic Perspectives*, 7(2), 159–171.

Goodley, S (2002). Astrazeneca boss says sorry for pension. *The Telegraph*, April 26. Available at http://www.telegraph.co.uk/finance/2760859/Astrazeneca-boss-says-sorry-for-pension.html.

Gramm–Leach–Bliley Act, Pub. L. No. 106-102, 113 Stat. 1338 (1999).

Henriques, DB (2010). Deal recovers $7.2 billion for Madoff fraud victims. *The New York Times*, December 17. Available at http://dealbook.nytimes.com/2010/12/17/big-settlement-with-madoff-investor-near/.

Jacobe, D (2013). Americans' confidence in banks up for first time in years. *Gallup*, June 14. Available at http://www.gallup.com/poll/163073/americans-confidence-banks-first-time-years.aspx.

Jensen, MC and KJ Murphy (1990). CEO incentives — It's not how much you pay, but how. *Harvard Business Review*, 3, 138–153.

Labaton Sucharow LLP (2013). *Wall Street in Crisis: A Perfect Storm Looming.* New York: Labaton Sucharow's U.S. Financial Services Industry Survey.

Lattman, P and B Protess (2013). SAC Capital is indicted, and called a magnet for cheating. *The New York Times*, July 25. Available at http://dealbook.nytimes. com/2013/ 07/25/sac-capital-is-indicted/?_r=0.

La Roche, J (2013). The 10 highest paid hedge fund managers. *Business Insider*, April 15. Available at http://www.businessinsider.com/best-paid-hedge-fund-managers-in-2012-2013-4?op=1.

Martin, M (1998). Citicorp and Travelers plan to merge in record $70 billion deal: A new no. 1: Financial giants unite. *The New York Times*, April 7. Available at http://www.nytimes.com/1998/04/07/news/07iht-citi.t.html.

Morran, C (2013). Goldman Sachs, Morgan Stanley hit with $557 million settlement over foreclosure practices. *Consumerist*, January 16. Available at http://consumerist.com/2013/01/16/goldman-sachs-morgan-stanley-hit-with-557-million-settlement-over-foreclosure-practices/.

Nicholson, CV (2010). F.S.A. fines Goldman over Abacus investigation. *The New York Times*, September 9. http://dealbook.nytimes.com/2010/09/09/goldman-sachs-said-to-be-fined-30-9-million-in-britain/.

Office of the State Comptroller (2013). New York City securities industry bonus pool. *Office of the State Comptroller*, February 26. Available at http://www.osc.state.ny.us/press/releases/feb13/avgbonus.pdf.

Olick, D (2013). Banks pay big for robo-signing . . . again. *CNBC*, January 7. Available at http://www.cnbc.com/id/100359672.

OpenSecrets.Org Center for Responsive Politics (a). Lobbying, ranked sectors, 1998–2013. Available at http://www.opensecrets.org/lobby/top.php?showYear=a&indexType=c.

OpenSecrets.Org Center for Responsive Politics (b). Historical elections: Campaign contributions, totals by sector over time. Available at http://www.opensecrets.org/bigpicture/sectors.php?cycle=All&bkdn=DemRep&sortBy=Rank.

Philippon, T and A Reshef (2009). Wages and human capital in the U.S. financial industry: 1909–2006. National Bureau of Economic Research Working Paper No. 14644. Available at http://www.nber.org/papers/w14644.

Protess, B and L Browning (2010). Deutsche makes deal in tax case. *The New York Times*, December 21. Available at http://dealbook.nytimes.com/2010/12/21/deutsche-bank-settles-tax-shelter-case-for-553-million/.

Putnam, R (2000). *Bowling Alone: The Collapse and Revival of American Community.* New York: Simon & Schuster.

Raymond, N and B Vaughan (2013). Judge approves Citigroup $590 million settlement. *Reuters*, August 1. Available at http://www.reuters.com/article/2013/08/01/us-citigroup-settlement-idUSBRE9700T420130801.

Rizzo, P (2012). US files $25 billion settlement with banks on mortgage abuses. *NBC News Business*, March 12. Available at http://www.nbcnews.com/business/us-files-25-billion-settlement-banks-mortgage-abuses-409683.

Sachs, JD (2011). *The Price of Civilization.* New York: Random House.

Sandler, L (2012). Recovery comes slowly for Madoff victims. *Bloomberg Businessweek*, May 3. Available at http://www.businessweek.com/articles/2012-05-03/recovery-comes-slowly-for-madoff-victims.

Securities and Exchange Commission v. Goldman, Sachs & Co. and Fabrice Tourre, 10 Civ. 3229 (BJ) (S.D.N.Y. filed April 16, 2010).

S.D.N.Y. (2009). United States Securities and Exchange Commission v. Bank of America Corporation. Memorandum Order, No. 09 Civ. 6829, September 14.

S.D.N.Y. (2011). United States Securities and Exchange Commission v. Citigroup Global Markets Inc. Opinion and Order, No. 11 Civ. 7387, November 28.

Silver-Greenberg, J (2012). 2 banks to settle case for $417 million. *The New York Times*, November 16. Available at http://www.nytimes.com/2012/11/17/business/jpmorgan-and-credit-suisse-to-pay-417-million-in-mortgage-settlement.html.

Son, H, D Griffin and J Hamilton (2011). JP Morgan's $153.6 million settlement with SEC recalls case against Goldman. *Bloomberg*, June 21. Available at http://www.bloomberg.com/news/2011-06-21/jpmorgan-to-pay-153-6-million-to-settle-sec-allegations-over-housing-cdos.html.

Son, H and D Kopecki (2011). BofA resolves Fannie Mae, Freddie Mac loan-putback dispute. *Bloomberg*, January 3. Available at http://www.bloomberg.com/news/2011-01-03/bank-of-america-sees-2-billion-charge-on-home-loans-insurance.html.

Stempel, J (2012). JP Morgan settles overdraft fee case for $110 million. *Reuters*, February 6. Available at http://www.reuters.com/article/2012/02/06/us-jpmorgan-overdraft-settlement-idUSTRE8151F520120206.

Stempel, J and D Wilchins (2009). Robert Rubin quits Citigroup amid criticism. *Reuters*, January 29. Available at http://www.reuters.com/article/2009/01/09/us-citigroup-rubin-idUSN0930738020090109.

Strochlic, N (2013). JP Morgan chase's crazy fine tally. *The Daily Beast*, May 8. Available at http://www.thedailybeast.com/articles/2013/05/08/jpmorgan-chase-s-crazy-fine-tally.html.

The Wall Street Journal. Robert Rubin. Available at http://topics.wsj.com/person/R/robert-e-rubin/550.

Touryalai, H (2013). Libor still big threat for banks as Freddie Mac sues dozens over losses. *Forbes*, March 20. Available at http://www.forbes.com/sites/halahtouryalai/2013/03/20/libor-still-big-threat-for-banks-as-freddie-mac-sues-dozens-over-losses/.

U.S. Department of the Treasury (2011). JP Morgan chase bank settles apparent violations of multiple sanctions programs. *U.S. Department of the Treasury*, August 25. Available at http://www.treasury.gov/resource-center/sanctions/OFAC-Enforcement/Pages/20110825.aspx.

U.S. Securities and Exchange Commission (2011a). SEC obtains record $92.8 million penalty against Raj Rajaratnam. U.S. SEC, November 8. Available at http://www.sec.gov/news/press/2011/2011-233.htm.

U.S. Securities and Exchange Commission (2011b). SEC charges JPMS with fraudulent bidding practices involving investment of municipal bond proceeds. U.S. SEC, July 7. Available at http://www.sec.gov/litigation/litreleases/2011/lr22031.htm.

United States Attorney's Office, Southern District of New York (2012). Manhattan U.S. attorney recovers $202.3 million from Deutsche Bank and

MortgageIT in civil fraud case alleging reckless mortgage lending practices and false certifications to HUD. United States Department of Justice, May 10. Available at http://www.justice.gov/usao/nys/pressreleases/May12/deutschebankmortgageitsettlement.html.

Van Voris, B and P Hurtado (2011). BofA, JPMorgan among 17 banks sued by U.S. for $196 billion. *Bloomberg News*, September 3. Available at http://www.bloomberg.com/news/2011-09-03/jpmorgan-bofa-among-17-banks-sued-by-fhfa-over-196-billion-in-securities.html.

Wilchins, D and J Stempel (2008). Citigroup gets massive government bailout. *Reuters*, November 24. Available at http://www.reuters.com/article/2008/11/24/us-citigroup-idUSTRE4AJ45G20081124.

Working Group of the Financial Stability Forum and the Committee on the Global Financial System (2009). The role of valuation and leverage in procyclicality. Committee on the Global Financial System, CGFS Papers No. 34. Basel: Bank for International Settlements.

Chapter 3

Systemic Lack of Prudence in Wealthy Nations: Avoiding the Dark Side of Financial Development

Peter Boone and Simon Johnson

"*First of all, let's recognize that this is a once-in-a-half-century, probably once-in-a-century type of event.*" Alan Greenspan quoted by AFP, September 14, 2008.[1]

"*It is the worst crisis since World War II and it could have been the worst crisis since World War I if leaders hadn't taken the important decisions.*" Jean-Claude Trichet, quoted by AP, August 9, 2011.[2]

"No matter how much the government redistributes income, unless it succeeds in creating wealth through continuous economic growth . . . it could . . . cause the foundations of social security, which serves as an anchor for our peace of mind, to become shaky." Shinzo Abe, Prime Minister of Japan, Policy Speech to the Diet on January 28, 2013.[3]

Introduction

Over the last seven decades, citizens in wealthy nations have enjoyed an unprecedented combination of growth and economic security. A young child born at the end of the Second World War arrived into a world with a simple, and comparatively tiny, financial system.

[1]Available at http://afp.google.com/article/ALeqM5i6u55aefaUf_RXJC4-5kcva-gyWQ
[2]Available at http://news.yahoo.com/trichet-sees-markets-worst-crisis-since-wwii-08412-5504.html
[3]Available at http://www.japantimes.co.jp/news/2013/01/29/national/policy-speech-by-prime-minister-shinzo-abe-to-the-183rd-session-of-the-diet/#.UYgFP8FwaUk

For war-torn Europeans and Japanese, physical gold was the safest means of savings. For Americans, the banking system was simple and small; few people could afford more sophisticated financial products. Today that grown child benefits from a large, complex and integrated financial system. She probably receives a state pension and health-care (at least when retired in the United States), she has her own private pension, she keeps money in banks, she has insurance policies to protect her assets and loved ones, and she may own bonds and equities (or mutual funds with claims on the same).

In order to provide these functions the financial system has grown very large relative to the economy — for example, in the United States, rising from around 1% of GDP before World War II to around 8% at the time of the crash in 2008. And, due to its "life or death" role in every person's life, the stability of this system has become sacrosanct.

In this chapter, we argue that the perceived stability of the system may be illusory — and also very costly, in the sense that the measures used to support financial stability have unintended adverse consequences on the rest of the economy. To develop and sustain this large system, several ingredients were essential that literally took centuries to develop. Nations needed reasonably stable and predictable macroeconomic outcomes. They required institutions and legal infrastructure which were credible, so that rule of law, contracts and property rights were trusted. They needed a central bank to act as lender of last resort to the financial system, while limiting dangers from moral hazard and regulatory capture that could plague such institutions. Given the inevitable pressure to bail out financial systems, a reasonably functioning regulatory system which investors could trust was also essential.

Wealthy nations are now at risk of failing, in varying degrees, on all these points. Most importantly, long-term macroeconomic stability cannot be taken for granted. The financial sector crisis of 2008–2009, reflects our inherent inability to regulate and maintain a well-capitalized financial system. Based on our assessment of reforms to the system taking place now, we anticipate there will be more and larger financial sector crises in the future. The ingredients which led to the downfall of regulatory systems have not changed, and the incentives to misuse the system for policy makers and those working in the financial sector still exist. There are now many voices calling for more capital and tougher regulation, but this always occurs in the aftermath of a crisis. With the large bailouts in 2008–2009, moral hazard is secure and well entrenched.

A second factor contributing to further instability is the ageing of the population. Most state-managed pension systems in wealthy nations face insolvency (in the sense that their current funding structure is not enough to maintain current benefit levels, see for example, OECD). This is widely recognized, and there are attempts to address solvency issues. As we discuss in this chapter, solutions generally involve promises to cut future benefits while continuing to pay generous benefits to the current elderly. For some nations, such as Italy and France, the required future cuts in replacement ratios to keep pension systems solvent are very large. There are bound to be serious battles against cuts as they start to kick-in in coming years.

However, our main concern is that the politicians we elect show a bias toward debt financing when faced with tough choices regarding spending, taxes and bailouts. Some empirical estimates suggest many nations have little or no "fiscal space" left to absorb debts (Ghosh *et al.*, 2011). Fiscal data generally underestimates state indebtedness because it excludes off balance sheet items such as unfinanced entitlement programs. Even so, since 1970, general government debt levels have trended upwards in all G-7 nations. We argue, the pressure to use debt finance in most nations will rise even further in the future as the enfranchised population ages (especially if interest rates remain low).

In this respect, we do not believe the recent financial crisis is a "once in a century" or even a "once in 50 years" event. Rather, it is an event which should be expected to occur again, and potentially with greater hardships, given the path most advanced nations are on. The growing and large size of our financial system, alongside our inherent inability to properly regulate the system, means that it will regularly fail and bailouts will be needed to support it.

Japan is the furthest along this dangerous path. In 1995, Japan's working age population peaked and it is projected to decline by 43% from 1995 to 2050 (Statistics Bureau Japan, 2012). The country suffered a major credit crisis in 1990. The national pension and social security system remains heavily underfinanced. Despite the crisis in the early 1990s, Japan's growth rate, after adjusting for the change in working age persons, has been similar to other wealthy nations over the last two decades. There are no "lost decades" apparent from comparing Japan's growth or unemployment with other G-7 nations. Even so, Japanese policy makers have seemingly lost control of fiscal deficits. The gross government debt stock has risen from 67% to 238% of GDP from 1990 to 2012 (IMF).

The recent decisions of the Abe government to promote a new fiscal expansion, as well as appointing a Bank of Japan governor prepared to embark on massive monetary stimulus, would not resolve Japan's problems. A nation with near full employment, and near the wealthiest in the world, is unlikely to see durable growth from massive monetary and fiscal stimulus. Japan needs something far different: They need policies which deal with the unfinanced pension programs, and plans to cut budget deficits and move to surpluses so that the debt burden passed on to the younger generation is sustainable. Mass immigration is one solution, or, tough changes to spending and taxation. This is not what the Abe government is proposing.

There is a long tradition of heavily indebted governments attempting to inflate away debts, and in this context Japan's monetary stimulus makes sense. The Japanese hope that local savers and investors will accept negative real returns on their savings. It is hard to believe that rational investors and savers can be tricked for long, so more forceful tactics of "financial repression" will be needed (Reinhart, 2012). In this regard, Japan's monetary stimulus, suggests a path for other indebted nations. Large implicit taxes can be raised through seigniorage. If inflation is not too high, such opaque gains are politically more palatable than direct taxes. However, this is a fragile path which politicians should understand is fraught with risk.

Europe faces many similar problems which were exacerbated by the introduction of the euro, and the rapid private and public debt accumulation in the periphery. The solutions to problems in Cyprus, Ireland and Greece present alternative paths that nations may follow. During this process, the officials at the Troika (European

Commission, European Central Bank, and International Monetary Fund) and national governments have all proven willing to take measures which surely break the spirit of national laws and international treaties, as well as essentially confiscate property in an ad hoc manner in order to address an issue which had been simmering (and often hitherto bailed out by the same actors) for several years.

Hence, the solutions being practiced in Japan and Europe, each point to clear dangers which might eventually unwind the seven decade long process of building our stable financial system. In Japan, they are gambling with inflation and capital flight, hoping that investors and savers will afford negative real returns on Japanese debt. In Europe's periphery, they have bailed out immediate problems leaving large debts, and, at times they have essentially confiscated property. There are some positive changes: public pensions are being adjusted, and in Europe, a German-led plan to improve fiscal discipline may impose needed long term restraints. However, neither the US, nor Europe, nor Japan have achieved regulatory systems which avoid the need for periodic large bailouts, or liquidations. It seems that many of the ingredients necessary to make financial systems function well are now being challenged.

There are no simple solutions to these complex problems. In an old joke, when a lost Englishman in Dublin asks directions, the Dubliner responds: "I know where you want to go, but I would not start from here." This is the important conclusion for rapidly growing nations. Once financial systems become heavily leveraged, growth slows, and entrenched interest groups fight for the status-quo, it becomes very difficult to change direction without first facing crises. While there is no magic solution that prevents these errors, there are examples of institutional changes that shift the balance of power toward stability, or at least avoiding mistakes.

We are skeptical the wealthy nations can resolve problems without a series of further crises. However, we point out measures that will help delay, or mitigate the risk of crisis. And, we point out policies (such as balanced budget rules, and required bail-ins of creditors), which, had they been implemented regularly long ago, might have helped prevent nations from getting to the difficult situations they are stuck in today. We focus on three areas of reform: First, measures to strengthen political power in favor of better capitalized institutions. Second, measures to strengthen political power in favor of fiscal stability. And finally, measures to improve transparency.

The Rise of Giant Finance

Figure 1 illustrates the rapid growth of financial assets in G-20 nations. Prior to the great depression, financial assets were largely government debts, bank loans and credits, and corporate bonds. The investors were corporates and wealthy families and individuals. The great depression scaled back or destroyed large parts of the financial system. War and greater regulation prevented the system from growing.

The great burst of finance which we are focused on really began in the 1970s, coinciding with the end of the Bretton Woods system which included fixed exchange rates and some capital controls.[4] This growth reflects multiple factors. By the 1970s, the first of the post-war baby boom generation were entering the workforce, and starting to buy insurance, save at banks, and maintain pension

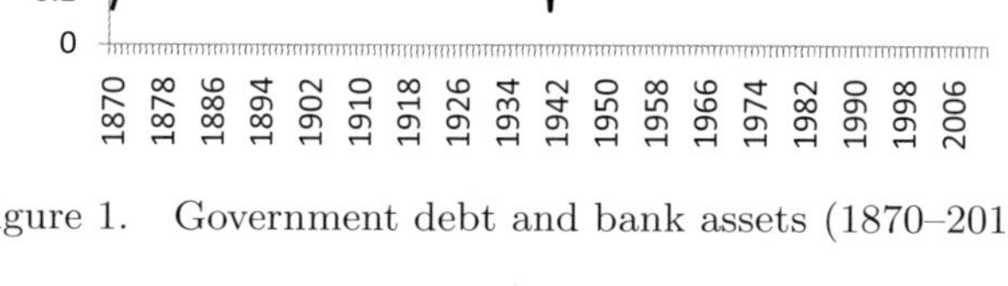

Figure 1. Government debt and bank assets (1870–2011).

Notes:

1. Government Debt/GDP from IMF Historical debt statistics, 1880–2011.
2. Bank Assets/GDP from, 1870–2008. The data is based on historical statistics from Australia, Canada, Denmark, France, Germany, Italy, Japan, the Netherlands, Norway, Spain, Sweden, Switzerland, the United Kingdom and the United States.

Source: Schularick and Taylor (2012).

[4]The discipline of maintaining reserves in a fixed exchange rate system, like under a gold standard, can check deficit financing.

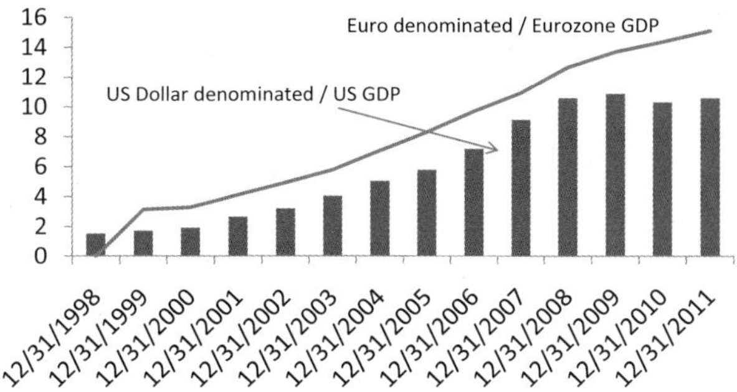

Figure 2. Outstanding nominal value of interest rate derivatives (1998–2011).
Source: Bank for International Settlements and Bloomberg.

funds. Additionally, governments and regulators relaxed restrictions on activities. This permitted increased leverage. Derivatives markets took off. By June 2012, as shown in Figure 2, the outstanding nominal value of derivatives contracts reached $179 trillion in Europe and $164 trillion in the United States, or 14.9 and 10.5 times GDP respectively.[5]

This large financial system is intrinsic to most people's personal security. It manages the payment system, our insurance, our savings, and our pension payments when we are too old to work. These factors mean that governments will invariably intervene to stabilize the system if there are problems, and such intervention will often involve spending taxpayer funds. For these reasons, state regulation of the

[5]Banks often have multiple contracts which, when netted off, lead to far lower exposures. The net market value of exposures at June 30, 2012 was 7.9 trillion of euro contracts, and 7.4 trillion of US dollar contracts. The netting off of contracts is considered acceptable by regulators because if a client of a bank enters into liquidation, banks are permitted to immediately net the value of funds owed in different derivative contracts. However, there are two important instances where gross exposures matter. First, since the "netting procedure" during liquidation requires creditors to determine pricing of the contracts, there is significant risk that creditors will manipulate pricing to their benefit. This would mean that liquidating banks with larger gross exposures would fare worse than those with small gross exposures. Second, in the event of a breakup of the euro currency union, the denomination of the 178 trillion dollars in gross contracts would need to be assessed. It would not be reasonable to net two similar contracts if, post exit from the euro, one of the contracts would be denominated in a different currency. Data is calculated by authors from Bank for International Settlements, B. f. I. (2012). Semi-Annual OTC Derivative Statistics at end-June 2012. Geneva.

financial system is essential. It also explains why moral hazard, and implicit subsidies to finance due to their "too big to fail" and "too important to fail" position, always exists.

Financial systems face regular crises. The IMF database on systemic financial crises shows that between 1970 and 2011, 80% of G-20 nations experienced at least one systemic banking crisis. On average, when comparing data from three years into the crisis to one year before, cumulative output fell 28.6% and public debt increased by 14.6% of GDP. Central banks injected an average 21.2% of liquidity, measured as a fraction of deposits and non-resident liabilities, into the banking system (Laeven *et al.*, 2012). Often central bank bailouts are kept secret, so official figures probably understate the sums used and the frequency of problems. In the IMF data, Canada is not listed as suffering a systemic banking crisis in 2008–2009, yet Canada's banks received 7% of GDP in emergency assistance in March 2009 (MacDonald, 2012).[6] These IMF figures also do not capture other finance-related crises. For example, the bail-out of long-term capital management in the United States, and the unwinding of the tech bubble and related recession and losses in the insurance sector, are not reported as systemic banking crises in the United States, although they are clearly major finance related failures.

Figure 3 repeats a figure from (Boone and Johnson, 2010) which we referred to as the "Doomsday Cycle." We argued that repeated financial crises reflect a common cycle across nations. After each crisis, policy makers tighten up on regulation in response to popular demands for corrections. This is when we get new revisions to the Basel accords in order to de-risk and improve capital, new regulation for the financial sector, etc. After several more years, the pressures to relax regulations start. Policy makers have great incentive to relax regulations in order to create credit booms and improve prospects

[6]Beyond this large liquidity provided to Canadian banks, the cosy relation between government and banks in Canada also permits substantial implicit transfers at times of crisis. In January 2009, the CEO of Toronto Dominion Bank, Edmund Clark, rallied investors to buy preference shares that the bank was trying to issue by stating: "Maybe not explicitly, but what are the chances that TD Bank is not going to be bailed out if it did something stupid?" (*Bloomberg News*, January 23, 2009).

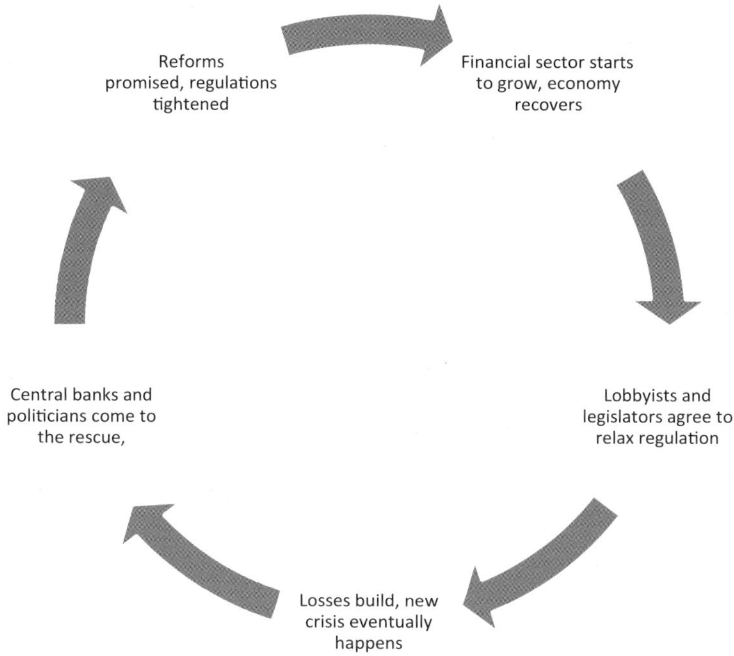

Figure 3. The Doomsday cycle.

Source: Boone and Johnson (2009).

ahead of elections. The financial sector gains profits if they can operate with more leverage.

Once this relaxing phase starts, credit grows, and the economy tends to do well. During these periods regulation is especially difficult. It is hard to discern whether the growth is sustainable, or instead driven by policy changes which have led to dangerous accumulation of poor credits or financial excess.

Lehman Brothers' liquidation presents a sobering example of how far reported data can be from the true underlying solvency of banks. In Figure 4, we compare key indicators from the last balance sheet Lehman Brother's reported before they went into liquidation in 2008, to a conservative estimate of the post liquidation balance sheet. In its pre-liquidation balance sheet, Lehman Brothers reports $639 billion of assets and $23 billion of tier one capital (which roughly matched their reported equity of $26 billion). They reported risk adjusted

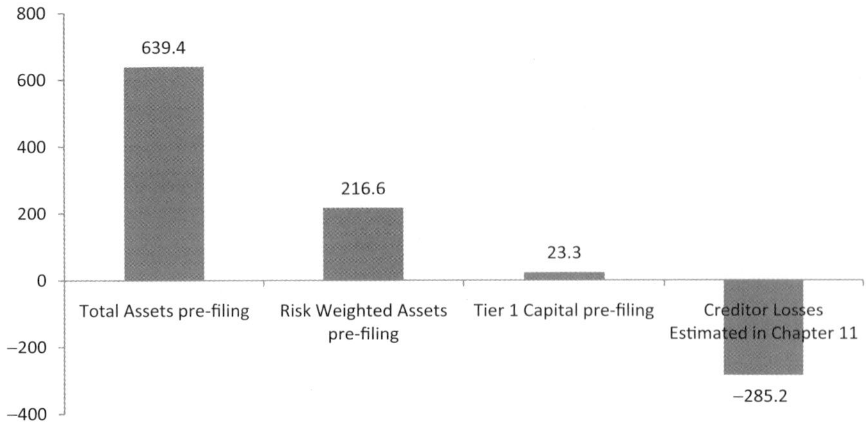

Figure 4. Lehman Brothers key risk indicators before and after filing for bankruptcy.

Source: Bloomberg.

assets of \$216 billion. This implied a tier one capital ratio of 10.7%, which is comparable to the latest requirements in Basel III.[7] On those simple measures, one would assume that Lehman senior creditors should be fairly safe in liquidation.

However, Lehman's US trustee filings show unsecured creditors with claims of \$361 billion are expected to recover only \$76 billion. Even if we assume that all other creditors are repaid, the total loss for these creditors is an astonishing \$285 billion. Equity is of course wiped out. These creditor losses are more than Lehman's total risk-weighted assets. Risk-weighted assets are supposed to measure the true value at risk from Lehman's investments.

There are numerous potential reasons for these losses, but no accurate figures. Some part is surely due to derivatives. Lehman was reported to have 930,000 derivative contracts outstanding, with a nominal value of \$35 trillion, over two times US GDP (Kimberly, 2012) at the time of liquidation. Safe Harbour rules

[7]The new Basel III regulations demand minimum tier one capital of 8.5%. The definition of tier one capital and risk adjusted assets has been narrowed to effectively further raise capital requirements when compared to Basel II.

permit contract partners to immediately terminate such contracts and net out the claims. In over the counter, illiquid markets, it is likely that counterparts generated favourable pricing for themselves.[8]

Lehman's losses probably also reflect the weak position regulators have when checking accounts. Large regulated institutions are responsible for valuing assets, determining risk-weighs, and calculating liabilities. A regulator can audit the process, including a small sample of specific valuations or decisions. In cases where regulators question specific decisions, bank officials will have substantial informational advantages, as well as legal and accounting support, when compared to a regulator.

The Lehman liquidation also suggests there are large costs to the liquidation process. Once a bank is liquidated, its ability to manage assets is curtailed, and fire sales may lead to lower valuations than could be earned when it was operating. Since market participants will often be aware of assets held by a liquidating bank, they may be able to take advantage of weak governance during liquidation, and the need for rapid sales, to make profits at the cost of the estate.

The Lehman liquidation sends two clear messages. First, it suggests, we should be extremely sceptical regarding a regulators' ability to measure the true state of a bank's capital position. This is not a unique case. In July 2012, the European Banking Authority (EBA), the supervisory body for banks in the European Union, reported its pan-European stress test results for large banks. They concluded Dexia bank required no extra capital, yet three months later, Dexia was on the verge of bankruptcy and required a large bailout from the French and Belgium governments.[9] In July 2011, Irish banks

[8]For example, the Lehman estate is currently suing the Federal Home Loan Bank of Cincinnati (FHLBC) for losses incurred when FHLBC closed a swap transaction with Lehman, paying a valuation $43 million less than the price FHLBC agreed for an identical contract with a different counterparty the following business day. United States Bankruptcy Court Southern District of New York (2013). Lehman Brothers Special Financing Inc. vs. Federal Home Loan Bank of Cincinnati: Adversary Complaint.

[9]Available at http://www.guardian.co.uk/business/blog/2011/oct/05/europe-bank-stress-tests-dexia

also passed similar EBA tests, although months later they required major bailouts.[10]

Second, the Lehman crisis illustrated to markets and policy makers that bank liquidations are no longer feasible. The collapse of Lehman created great uncertainties for other institutions, and contributed to market collapse and a race to safe havens which ensued in the coming months. This lesson has dangerous implications: creditors of major banks learned that policy makers were sure, in the future, to bail them out at virtually any cost.

In our Doomsday Cycle, we argued that, once the aftermath of crisis is well behind, the regulatory system gradually loses discipline, and new risks build up. Regulators are unable to measure the risks, and with a credit boom underway, poor lending and accounting practices can be hidden for years. The accumulation of losses and poor practices eventually leads to another crisis. The crisis may not be in banks — it could be in hedge funds, or insurance companies, or some other systemically important leveraged business. When crises occur, our central banks and governments step in to ensure the system is stable. They lower interest rates, bail out institutions, and they increase fiscal spending.

The total cost of financial crises is rarely considered in its entirety. The US Treasury has very aggressively argued that its bailouts were profitable for US taxpayers, because they managed to get back more than what they directly gave out.[11] However, their argument is misleading when considered more broadly. The IMF projects general government debt of the United States will rise from 54% of GDP at end of 2008 to 89% of GDP at end of 2013. The Federal Reserve lowered the Fed Funds rate from 5.25% in August 2007 to 0.25%

---

[10]The results for Irish banks were reported on July 15, 2011. Available at http://www.centralbank.ie/press-area/press-releases/Pages/2011EU-WideBankStressTestResultsfor-IrishBanksPublished.aspx

[11]For example, on January 23, 2013 the US Treasury website reports, "During 2013, we expect to make significant additional progress winding down TARP's investment programs and recovering taxpayer dollars. We also continue to expect that the financial stability programs that Treasury, the Federal Reserve, and the FDIC put in place during the crisis are likely to result in an overall positive financial return for taxpayers" (highlights in original text). Available at http://www.treasury.gov/connect/blog/Pages/Winding-Down-TARP-A-Progress-Report.aspx

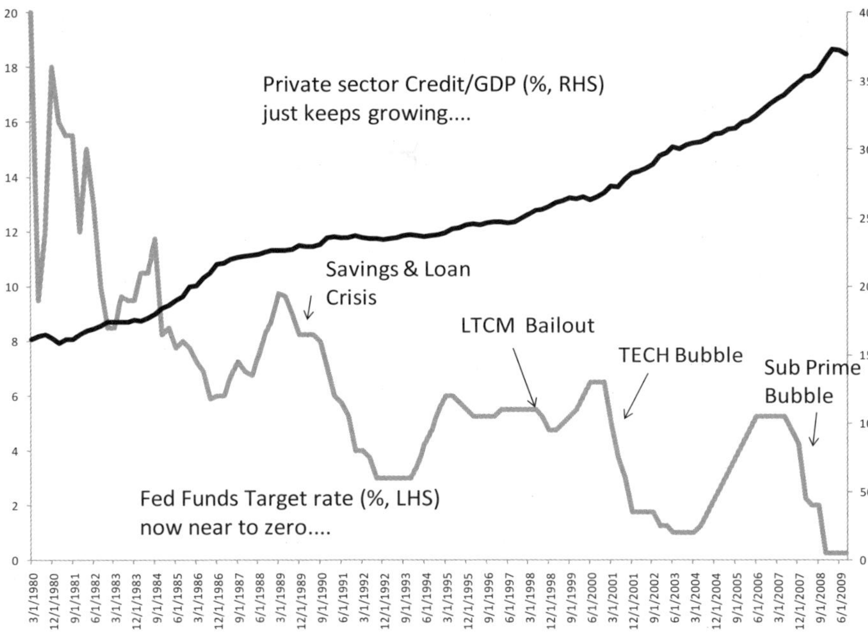

Figure 5. Fed funds rate, credit growth, budget deficits.
Source: Bloomberg.

today. Savers are subsidizing the financial sector in order that it can rebuild capital. The costs to societies of these crises are invariably obfuscated by large indirect transfers and subsidies.

The fact that financial systems are hard to regulate, and they face regular crises, is not necessarily a concern. If they can survive each crisis intact without too large costs, and the system rebuilds itself, then it may simply be a painful necessity. However, this enormous financial system which we have created is only 40 years old, and it is still growing. Figure 5 illustrates a worrying trend. Here we show the pattern of interest rates and one measure of total credit. The point here is that the policy response has been growing over time to the crises. We are now at a point where the Federal Reserve has lowered interest rates essentially to zero, and the budget deficit is the largest it has been in the post-war era. The same factors hold true for Europe.

The regular bailouts of our financial system have importantly contributed to rising indebtedness over the (short) history of large finance. However, while we see this as the main risk to financial security, the potential burden of old age pension systems is also large, and will play a growing role in the future to add to risks of instability.

The Rise of Pensions

Pensions are relatively new in our financial system. The earliest pensions were often discretionary awards from monarchs or religious leaders. The first systemic pensions were given to retired and injured soldiers. The world's first old age pension law was introduced in Germany in 1889, while the United Kingdom's first means-tested system was started in 1908.[12] Private pensions were rare. By 1900, there were just 12 private pension plans in the United States.[13] It was only after the World War II that a large fraction of the elderly people could count on state and/or private pensions in old age.

Figure 6 plots the replacement ratios of state pension programs (i.e., the fraction of final salary which your pension replaces at retirement) against the total assets held by both public and private pension funds for OECD nations. There is very large variation in pension fund assets across nations. In many nations, there are very little pension fund investments, while others, such as Israel and Netherlands, have well over 100% of GDP invested in pension funds.

One reason some nations do not have large pension funds is that the state provides for generous pensions. Most state systems are primarily "pay-as-you-go." The logic for pay-as-you-go systems is enticing: if every worker in the nation paid a fixed proportion of their income into a pool, and that pool was divided amongst retired persons, then so long as incomes and the number of workers grows, the sums paid to retired people can be large and growing. Indeed, if growth is rapid enough, then pay-as-you-go systems can essentially generate fantastic returns to savers.

---

[12] See Thane (2000).
[13] See Clark (2003).

However, the solvency and rationale behind pay-as-you-go pensions systems relies on multiple assumptions. You need a state that is capable and prepared to tax people and maintain the system far into the future. You also need growth. If growth is slow, then young people may be better off saving their funds in bonds, or investment projects, rather than contributing to the state pension system.

The main issue with most pay-as-you-go systems is that the initial promises were excessively generous — or even unrealistic. The Greek program, until recent revisions, was an extreme example. Workers were able to retire at age 65 or after 37 years of service on full pensions, meaning someone who began work at 20 would retire at 57. In general, workers received 70% of their final salaries as payments, plus a supplement that took receipts to 90% of final salaries. Since the state system was generous and pay-as-you-go, the public saw no need for pension savings (see Figure 6). With the

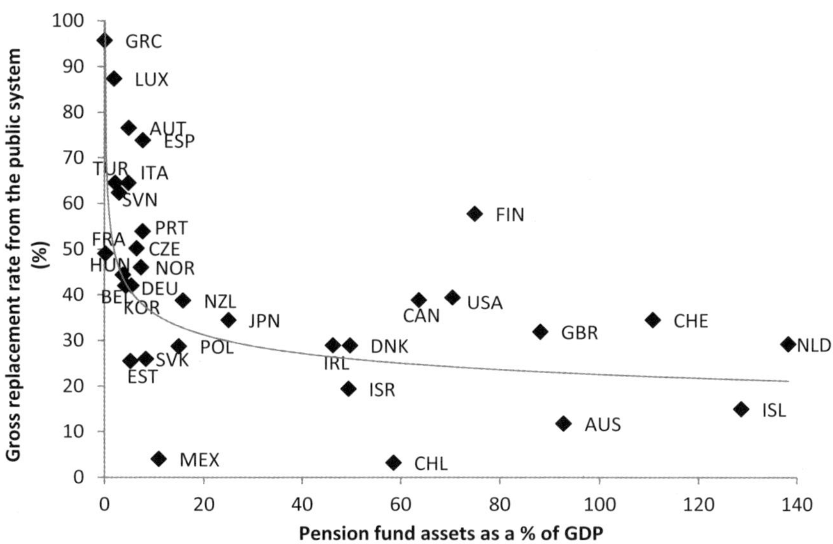

Figure 6. Pension fund assets (private and public) and public pension replacement ratios (2011).

Notes:

1. Pension fund assets do not include insurance based pension contracts.
2. The public pensions refer to pay-as-you-go system replacement rations.

Source: OECD (2012).

population aging, and making only small contributions in taxes, this was clearly an unsustainable program. Yet the government created it and workers managed large strikes to prevent changes until the crisis of 2010.

The French also have few assets in pension funds. This is because, like the Greek system, the main pension programs in France are pay-as-you-go. There is a standard state system with an unsustainably generous pay-out. There is also a mandatory supplementary system which essentially operates as pay-as-you-go. When workers retire, their pensions are determined through a point program based on their past contributions. The annual pay-out to pensioners roughly matches annual contributions.

The French public pension system, with a 50% replacement ratio (Figure 6), is not as generous as the Greek system. Further, the pension a retiring person will receive is calculated based on the available funding for the future. Hence, as the French population ages and retires, there will be less and less funds available to pay out to each new retiree. According to the IMF, the French replacement ratio will fall from 50% to approximately 38% by 2050. So, by design, the system appears solvent. However, it is only solvent if workers are prepared to accept the rapidly declining replacement ratios which are needed.

Japan and the United States both have partially financed public pension systems. The US Social Security Trust by law is not permitted to receive funding from the budget. It collects payroll taxes and pays out benefits. Any surpluses are invested in US government bonds. Japan manages a similar system, although the Japanese payroll taxes are not adequate to cover long term benefits of recipients, so an annual government contribution is needed.

However, the difference between the Japanese and US systems, vs. pay-as-you-go systems, may be less than it appears. A financially backed system is not much different from a pay-as-you-go system if the government issues bonds to pension funds, and then uses the pension contributions for current spending. For example, the US government can issue debt to the social security trust funds, and then run larger budget deficits. As the population ages, the government would need to run surpluses in order to repay the pension funds.

That is not much different from the French system where the government needs to raise taxes in the future if it is to maintain current replacement ratios.

During times of crisis there will be large pressures on pension funds to purchase government debts. Politicians can use regulatory powers to force or incentivize pension funds to buy national debts.[14] Japan's largest pension fund, the Government Pension Investment Fund, holds 67% of its assets in domestic bonds, with over 50% of those in government debt. The pension fund will probably make significant losses on these bonds (at least compared to alternative investments) under the new inflation targets of the Bank of Japan described below. The Spanish government ordered the state pension funds to buy government bonds as private markets became reticent to finance its deficit, leaving the pension funds holding over 90% of assets in government debt.[15] The demands from the state that pension funds take inordinate risks, or make losses, in order to finance government deficits is the logical result of weak fiscal discipline.

Dynamics of Lack Fiscal Control

> *"Any idiot can face a crisis; it's this day-to-day living that wears you out."*
>
> *Anton Chekhov*

The security of our large financial systems today is intrinsically linked to government debts. Regulators have universally declared national debts are "risk-free," making them critical components of our banks, insurance companies and pension funds' capitalization.

Figure 1 illustrates rapid growth of general government debts alongside other debts since the 1970s. We do not believe this is a coincidental correlation. Once governments gain access to reliable long term debt finance, it is very difficult to avoid using it. Debt is used to bail out financial systems, to finance recessions, and to cover current regular spending. Debt is understated, because some of the promises governments make do not show up in official statistics. For

[14] Ireland recently changed regulatory rules to encourage Irish pension funds to increase their purchases of Irish debt.

[15] Spain drains fund backing pensions. *The Wall Street Journal*, January 3, 2013.

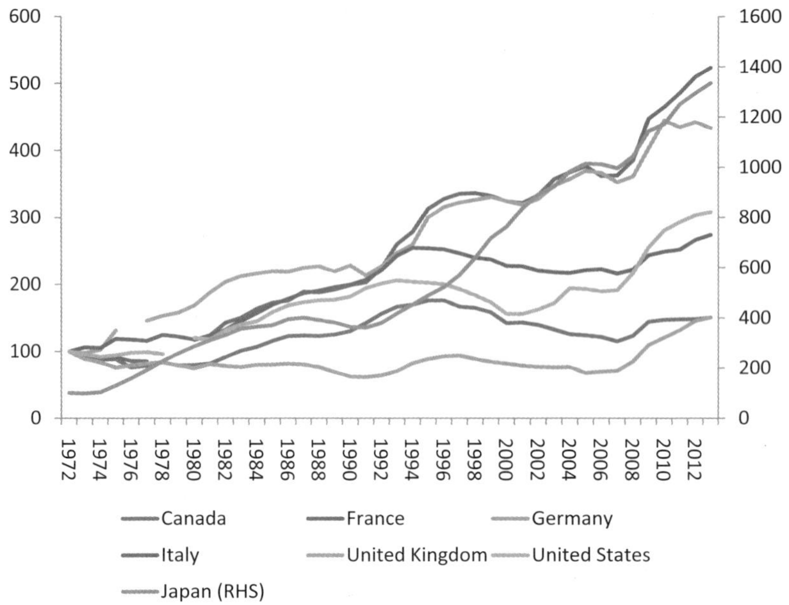

Figure 7. Gross debt/GDP for G-7 nations (1972 = 100, LHS y-axis for all except Japan).

example, the projected large funding deficits of most pay-as-you-go pension systems, unfinanced health entitlements, and off balance sheet items, are not recorded as debts.

Figure 7 shows the time series pattern of gross debt to GDP in G-7 nations since 1972 (the year Bretton Woods ended). In every G-7 nation, we see a clear upward trend in debt levels. The pace of growth varies from an increase of the debt/GDP of 1.25 times (Canada and the United Kingdom) to almost 14 times for Japan. It is clear that, with the recent crisis, government debt accumulation is not slowing.

In Figures 1 and 7, we reported gross government debt. Sometimes commentators report net debts, where they subtract out financial assets of nations. This matters most for Japan and the United States, where state pension funds hold large amounts of bonds.[16] We include these bonds as debts because they will be needed to finance

[16]Some nations have reserve assets, or debts which will be repaid from dedicated revenue streams. Adjusting gross debt for these financial assets, or excluding such debts, would not change the qualitative arguments in this chapter.

the future pension payments, and even so, both nations' pension systems are underfunded. For all nations in Figure 7, there is no attempt to include remaining unfunded pension obligations, and we have not included any financial assets.

In recent years, Central Banks in Japan, the United Kingdom and the United States have purchased large amounts of government bonds. It is also tempting to subtract these debts from gross government indebtedness. These bonds are purchased by central banks in exchange for "cash" (reserve money — i.e., zero interest perpetual liabilities of the central bank). The banks and investors who hold this cash generally anticipate inflation will be low, and they choose to maintain a large liquidity balance. If circumstances change, such that investors no longer want large liquidity balances, central banks state they are prepared to sell bonds back to the market to withdraw cash from the economy. To the extent they hold onto the bonds, central banks require the debt to be repaid, in order to be able to maintain their own capitalization. Hence, it is not appropriate to argue that central bank purchases reduce liabilities of the general government.[17]

The rising trend in national debts, which has accelerated very recently, raises concerns that wealthy nations may be en route to new financial crises where the solvency of the state itself is questioned. State insolvencies can lead to outright default, but they are more likely to lead to inflation and financial repression (discussed later). In either case, risk premiums on debt (risk of inflation or of default) may eventually rise, and since government bonds underlie the "risk-free" capital of large parts of our financial system, such changes could lead to the largest systemic failures yet.

We can never be sure how much debt any nation can safely issue before risk premiums will start rising in a dangerous manner. In a recent IMF working paper (Ghosh *et al.*, 2011), the authors attempted to measure "fiscal space," i.e., how much extra debt markets would tolerate, by examining the historic response of fiscal policy (measured by the primary budget balance) to changes in the debt stock. If, when debt stocks rise, policy makers raise the primary

[17]It is appropriate to transfer the annual profit and losses from these transactions to the government.

surplus enough to finance it, then investors may be confident that higher debts will be repaid. This is a very weak test — it merely calls on governments to show willingness to reduce budget deficits enough to finance the interest costs of additional debt. Even so, after examining 23 advanced nations past fiscal responses to deficits, and their projected debt levels in 2015, they concluded nine nations were at or near their limits to build additional debts. They warned that Iceland, Ireland, Spain, the United Kingdom and the United States were probably nearing their limits but still had some room beyond 2015 debt levels. They concluded Greece, Italy, Japan and Portugal were probably very near or beyond limits for sustainability.

Similar results were found for Japan, the United Kingdom and the United States in a separate study (Ito *et al.*, 2011). These authors found that since 1970, Japan's fiscal regime has been on an explosive path (in the sense that, there was no tendency to adjust budgets as debt levels rise). However, they found that during the pre-war era under the gold standard, as well as during the 1950s–1970s, which they attribute to balanced budget rules introduced by the US commanding forces after World War II (but could also be linked to discipline from Bretton Woods), Japan's debt policies were not on this explosive path.

This literature paints a bleak picture for several nations, and it correctly captured difficulties in Europe's periphery. However, it fails to explain why there is a consistent upward trend in indebtedness in all G-7 nations since 1972. Indeed, in the fiscal space models, if debt levels continue to drift upwards, then eventually all nations will reach their debt capacity, and at that point every nation would be on a path to crisis.[18]

When authors conclude that nations have bearable debt burdens, they make a key assumption that the behavioral response of nations to debt problems remains the same in the future as it was in the past. We anticipate that the responsiveness of fiscal policy to debt levels may weaken in many wealthy nations. Ageing populations will increase the median and average age of voters, and this will

[18]It also does not take into account off balance liabilities such as unfunded pension schemes.

place more pressure on spending for health and pensions. The elderly are more likely to support debt finance as they are not required to repay it. Even if debts are on an unsustainable path, any crises may occur well after their lifetimes.

Low interest rates also reduce incentives to cut budget deficits. Business lobbies and households with mortgages are key actors who pressure governments to cut deficits, hoping to reduce interest rates. This was a major factor behind Bill Clinton's steps to reduce the deficit during his first term in office (Johnson and Kwak, 2012). However, real interest rates are at historic lows now, and they may remain very low for an extended period due to ageing and the need to recapitalize parts of the economy.[19]

Low interest rates also buttress the lobbies calling for more spending. Given high levels of leverage, it is no surprise that in the aftermath of crises companies and households try to rebuild capital. This drives up savings rates and lowers interest rates. It is reasonable to argue there is no better time for governments to invest in the future, as well as support demand, since the costs of such support are low compared to the benefits (Summers and DeLong, 2012).

In the depths of crisis, there is near unanimous agreement that policy makers must appropriately provide emergency liquidity to prevent bank runs, and support the unemployed. Often the same people the administered the nation into the run up to the crisis, turn now to design rescue programs for banks, and new spending program for governments. The interest groups in favor of spending align with financial sector lobbyists calling for delays to reforms (in order to support lending). There is little appetite for tough reforms.

Once the economy does start recovering, reform seems less pressing. President Obama's 2014 budget recommendations imply budget deficits would continue for a decade, and the US Debt/GDP levels

---

[19]In a series of articles with forecast simulations, Auerbach *et al.* (1992) attempts to empirically examine the ramifications of aging societies for growth and budget finance. They conclude growth rates will slow, investment declines, and at least for a period, interest rates will be low due to the large pool of savings held by the elderly. National savings rates fall as the elderly spend their past investments. These conclusions are modified, somewhat, by the types of pension and other entitlement programs, but the general pattern remains in most circumstances. See Auerbach *et al.* (1992).

would stabilize around current levels. Instead of truly focusing on reigning in debt accumulation while dealing with an ageing society, the implicit compromise in Washington has been to postpone measures on entitlements and revenues, while continuing stimulus spending *via* deficit finance.[20] In the United Kingdom, while the current recession is far less severe than in 1991–1993, or the early 1980s (as measured by unemployment), the government is running significantly larger budget deficits than in those recessions. Britain's conservative government is coming under enormous pressure from opposition, as well as the IMF and US government officials, for excessive "austerity." From 2009–2012, the government has run cumulative deficits of 36% of GDP, and under the current program, deficits will continue such that the Debt/GDP ratio only stabilizes in 2016.

Across advanced economies, Germany currently stands out as a nation where sound financial policies are publicly supported. However, even Germany has built up large public debts, and let its banking system sink into crisis, during the last three decades (see Figure 7). The former President of the European Central Bank, Jean Claude Trichet, regularly reminds audiences that it was the Germans and French who backed efforts to weaken Europe's stability and growth pact last decade. Today, Germany's new demands for fiscal rectitude probably reflect its (possibly temporary) role as a large creditor to other EU nations. Those credits arose as it provided well over 25% of GDP in opaque Bundesbank financing, as well as direct support, to peripheral EU nations.[21]

These dynamics implies that government debt accumulation tends to follow a step function. At each crisis governments let budget deficits increase, and they use debt to bail out systemic and favored institutions. When the crisis ends, there is little appetite to reign in budgets or stick to tough regulations, so debt stays at the higher level

[20] Jeffrey Sachs puts in perspective how far the current political debate over good policy is from the problems facing the United States over coming decades. See Sachs (2011).

[21] Bundesbank financing is provided through the euro system payments mechanism. These claims of the Bundesbank on troubled EU nations amounted to over 25% of German GDP at end of 2012. Any losses on these loans should legally be shared amongst euro system nations.

until the inevitable next crisis occurs. Thus, the Debt/GDP ratios continue to rise.

Unless we properly deal with our proclivity for regular financial crises, as well as our tendency to resolve both current problems and crises with debt finance in the public sector, then we will continue on the path to crisis. Japan presents a good example of this dangerous path.

Japan's dangerous path

When Japan's growth started slowing in the 1980s, the Bank of Japan mistakenly spurred credit expansion believing there was room for stimulus. This generated one of the greatest real estate and equity bubbles of all time, followed by a similar collapse. At market values, the value of the emperor's palace in Tokyo was briefly greater than the value of all land in California. From the peak to trough, Tokyo commercial land prices fell 83%. Equities fell 82%.[22]

The crisis generated bank failures and recession; however, as measured by GDP per working age person, as seen in Figure 8, the

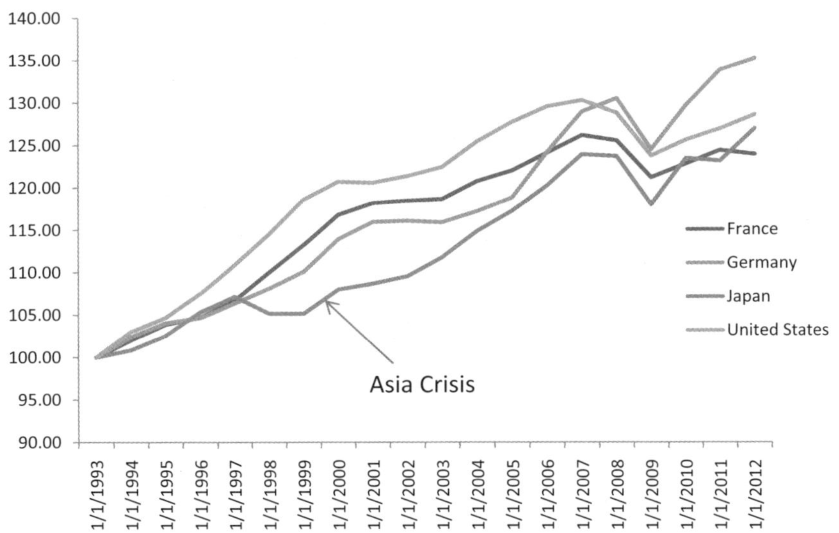

Figure 8. GDP per working age population in selected G-7 nations (1993 = 100).

[22]Land and equity prices from Bloomberg.

economy fared surprisingly well. Figure 8 crudely adjusts Japan's post-crisis economic performance for the change in working age population and compares it to selected large advanced nations. When comparing GDP per working age person, one can hardly conclude Japan has suffered the "two lost decades" often referred to in the press and academic literature. Japan's slower growth can largely be attributed to demographic decline. Wages and prices have been flexible enough to keep unemployment rates low. Despite the crisis, the Japanese post-crisis unemployment rate peaked at 5.5%, and is currently 4.1%. The nation remains one of the wealthiest in the world.

Japan's slow growth due to ageing is understandable and would not normally be a concern, but the real crisis is fiscal. The problems have stemmed from the inability of Japan's political system to wrest control of budget deficits. In the aftermath of the crisis, the budget moved from a 1.3% GDP surplus in 1989 to a deficit of 11.0% of GDP in 1998. There was a good case for temporary stimulus when asset prices collapsed; however, the deficit has remained large ever since. Japan's gross debt to GDP ratio rose from 70% in 1989 to 238% at end of 2012. The government does have $1.2 trillion of foreign exchange reserves (22% of GDP) but this hardly dents the debt.

Japan's debt situation is worse than these numbers imply. Like other wealthy nations, Japan created a generous pension program for the elderly, which is now underfunded. The program did accumulate some government bonds in a social security fund and those can be used to partly pay pensions in the future, but they are not adequate to maintain benefits promised by the system. Doi Doi *et al.* (2011) calculate that in order to create a sustainable debt path, such that the Debt/GDP ratio returns to the current levels by 2100, the Japanese government would need to raise revenue/GDP from 33% currently to 40%–47% immediately. They conclude Japan is on an explosive fiscal path.

There appears little chance that the Japanese are going to raise revenues quickly or adequately. Any plans to reduce pension benefits are highly opposed. An Asahi Shimbun poll in January 2013 showed 68% of Japanese opposed suggestions to reduce pension benefits instead of raising consumption taxes. The government plans to raise the consumption tax between 2012–2015 by enough to increase tax revenues 2.5% of GDP, but this also is not popular. When asked in a January 2012 opinion poll, 46% of Japanese opposed the move, while 40% supported it. The polls suggested that the main opposition to tax increases emanates from a belief that the government would be better to reduce spending.[23]

Strong opposition to measures that would correct Japan's fiscal problems contributes to procrastination. That opposition is only likely to grow. We calculate that as of 2009, 36% of voters received state pensions in Japan.[24] They are sure to be strong, well-organized proponents against change.

How long can procrastination last without causing a debt crisis? At some point, if this trajectory is not changed, there will not be enough willing buyers of Japanese bonds. Due to the large savings pool in Japan and low investment, factors which reflect the early stages of an ageing population, interest rates have remained low. The world's largest pension fund is Japan's Government Pension Investment Fund, and it plays a key role buying these bonds. Increasingly, whether it be banks, insurance companies, or pensions, Japanese savers effectively are buying government bonds with their savings (Iwaisako, 2012). The government has not been disciplined — yet — by rising interest costs, and savers have not yet experienced any losses.

In theory, very large levels of debt can be supported so long as investors believe ultimately it can be repaid with a reasonable return. However, Japan's ageing population would be far better off today if their savings had been backed by investments which generate real returns, such as greater corporate and sovereign assets

[23]Poll conducted February 11–12, 2013 with 1,741 responses. See http://mansfieldfdn.org/program/research-education-and-communication/asian-opinion-poll-database/listofpolls/ 2012-polls/asahi-shimbun-regular-public-opinion-poll-2142012/

[24]There are 103 million eligible-aged voters, and at end 2009 there were 37 million pension recipients. See http://www.google.com/hostednews/afp/article/ALeqM5ivVoNXz5-jCRPbnoEQ8rprN7BHtlQ?docId=CNG.8c338e3b1bec49650ef90f296bedf8dc.531 and see http://www.nationmaster.com/graph/dem_par_ele_vot_age_pop-parliamentary-elections-voting-age-population.

outside Japan, similar to the activities of Singapore and Norwegian investment programs. Instead, Japanese savers today are (often unwittingly) seeing their savings channeled into government bonds, where the government then spends those savings on current spending. The only source of funds to repay these bonds is the income from future generations of Japanese taxpayers. The number of these taxpayers is getting smaller each year.

What next?

Japan's plight illustrates the problems that wealthy, ageing societies face.

The ingredients that contribute to rising debts and procrastination over solutions are prevalent in many other nations. The United States suffers from political deadlock within Congress and the administration,[25] France suffers from a population that is prone to strike against tough policies,[26] and Germany has proven unwilling to resolve its own banking system issues. In the United Kingdom, the government's gradual program of debt reduction has met with large political opposition. So long as interest rates remain low, it is often easier to issue debt rather than cut spending or raise taxes.

The results of procrastination are best seen in Figure 1. Over the last 30 years, nations have built larger and larger debts. As populations age, bank crises continue, and more people are dependent on state pension funds and other entitlements, the ability of the government to resolves these issues will get even more difficult. How might it end? We focus on two worrisome possibilities.

[25]In the United States, like Japan, there is strong opposition to a reduction in Social Security or Medicare provisions (Johnson and Kwak, White House Burning, 2012). The Republicans adamantly oppose tax increases and have veto power within the Congress. Cuts to discretionary spending and raised taxes for the wealthy, have limited scope but are so far the only means to bring in deficits. The main advantage that the US maintains is high immigration and moderate fertility rates, so the population continues to grow and it remains relatively young (at least compared to Japan and many European countries).

[26]In 2010, Sarkozy's government announced changes to the pension program, with the main plan being to increase the age of retirement from 65 to 67 (60 to 62 for early retirement) through gradual rule change over eight years. Opponents to the reforms quickly organized 14 national strikes, which lead to substantial shut downs of airports, rail and business. When Francois Hollande won election in 2012, he reversed part of these reforms.

Abenomics and financial repression

On December 26, 2012, Shinzo Abe was elected Prime Minister for the second time. His policy platform includes monetary and fiscal stimulus with structural reforms to improve long run growth. The fiscal spending will increase Japan's budget by 2% of GDP, bringing the 2013 estimated general government deficit to 9.7% of GDP.[27] Structural reforms announced in June are unlikely to have much effect on economic growth.[28] The hope is that a burst of stimulus can create growth which will reduce the budget deficit later.

The novelty in Abe's program (commonly called "Abenomics") is the monetary policy. Governor Kuroda, newly appointed at the Bank of Japan (BOJ), is promising measures that will double the base money supply over two years. The BOJ will also increase purchases of risky assets. The aim of these measures is to pressure investors to take more risk. The results in the first few months were a sharp depreciation of the real value of the yen, and a rally in stocks, taking both to levels last seen in 2008. Bonds rallied modestly, reflecting the opposing forces of higher inflation, and large scale bond purchases by the Bank of Japan, on their prices. The Bank of Japan is committed to raising inflation to 2% per year within two years.

For a country with rapidly growing debts, an ageing population, and large fiscal deficit, these moves show signs of desperation. The fiscal stimulus is motivated by political need rather than economic logic. In his electoral campaign, Abe promised a new wave of spending to interest groups that were feeling pain from Japan's far too insufficient attempts to cut back on spending.

The inflation target has more logic. If the government is successful at keeping nominal interest rates low, while raising inflation, then it could be possible to improve debt sustainability over the medium term. For example, Doi *et al.* (2011) estimate that if the

[27]Bloomberg Consensus forecasts on May 7, 2013.

[28]Given Japan is already one of the wealthiest countries in the world, and unemployment rates are low, the scope for productivity increases and greater output must naturally be limited. Abe's structural reforms included promises to create tax free zones, liberalization of the electricity sector, and some hints of liberalization in retail and wholesale trade. Some of these changes could generate greater productivity; however, none will contribute significantly to resolving the serious fiscal problems we have outlined.

government policy could, ceteris paribus, generate a 1% reduction in the real interest rates, then they could save 2% of GDP on needed tax increases.[29] But, as these numbers suggest, the gains from the inflation are small compared to the size and immediacy of Japan's problem. Further, in the current policy package, these gains are offset by the extra fiscal spending.

There is a long history of nations attempting to print money in order to resolve fiscal problems. The money printing usually ends in high inflation and sometimes defaults. For Japan, the hope is that, despite negative real interest rates, savers will continue to buy government bonds at low interest rates. This can be done for some period of time, but faced with relentless losses on such securities; smart investors can find means to generate better returns by avoiding such bonds.

In our new world with large and liquid financial markets, it is hard to believe that Japanese interest rates will stay low for long if inflation really does return. Inflation offers opportunities for banks to structure derivatives based on commodities, or foreign assets, which provide savers with returns which protect them. The government can respond to reduced demand for bonds with "financial repression" tactics (Reinhart, 2012). For example, they can use regulations to force banks and insurance companies to hold government bonds as capital. However, with the debts growing, and better returns elsewhere, it may be difficult for the Japanese to keep interest rates low.

The dangers of this new policy are clear. With gross government debt at 238% of GDP in 2012, a large part of the banking system, pension funds and insurance rely on these government bonds for their solvency. If interest rates rise, so that bonds values fall, the capital of the financial system will fall. Further, since pension and insurance benefits are often partly linked to inflation, the liabilities of these groups may rise when bonds fall due to inflation. To achieve its rather modest goals (which as we stated above do not resolve Japan's fiscal

[29]These authors' calculations are based on a program to stabilize Japan's public Debt/GDP ratio such that in 95 years it returns to its current level. In a representative scenario, tax revenues need to immediately rise to 44.1% of GDP from 32.9% of GDP in 2010 in order to ensure Japan's Debt/GDP ratio returns to the 2010 ratio by 2205.

issues), Abenomics relies on the vast mass of Japanese savers being willing to maintain buying large sums of debts, and growing annually, despite the real returns on those instruments being negative for many years to come. This seems a dangerous bet.

Liquidations, defaults, confiscation

Recent actions in the European Union show alternative "end games" to the dangerous insolvencies wealthy nations suffer. The novel aspect of the European Union is that each nation is not able to issue its own currency. Since there is no lender of last resort (such as the BOJ), it is possible for a nation to default, and nations do not have unlimited resources to bail out their financial systems. Further, there is a disciplinary force at the European Commission which monitors nations' fiscal programs.

The disciplinary force has both positive and negative aspects. When Greece ran into problems, the Troika demanded large, long-term fiscal changes. Most importantly, the insolvent pension system has been dramatically revised, with benefits cut sharply and contributions increased. In one step, the Greeks turned a highly insolvent system into a solvent system.

However, the Cypriot bailout is the most interesting because it points out the potential institutional dangers that arise when dealing with wealthy nation insolvencies. The problems in Cyprus stemmed from an insolvent banking system. The Cypriot banks were large investors in Greek government bonds, so when the Troika forced a Greek default, the Cypriot banks became instantly insolvent. Despite this, the ECB continued providing emergency lending to Cypriot banks, while the Troika and Cypriots negotiated over a rescue plan.

Over one year later, on March 15, 2013, the Troika arranged a meeting after markets closed on a Friday evening to discuss a bailout plan. To the surprise of the Cypriots, for the first time in any bailout program in Europe, the Troika called for a "tax" to be imposed on all bank deposits. After some negotiation, with threats that the ECB would pull all funding to Cypriot banks if no agreement was reached, all sides agreed to a tax on both insured and uninsured deposits. This agreement soon failed when the Cypriot parliament voted it down.

The decision to make insured depositors pay for the needs to recap banks was one step too far.

After one more week, a new final agreement between Cyprus and the Troika was complete. This agreement has many components which should make investors worry. In place of a tax on deposits, the most insolvent bank was liquidated. In the process of this liquidation, all emergency lending from the ECB to that bank was transferred to a second bank (Bank of Cyprus, or BOC). The decision to make this transfer was important from the point of view of the ECB, but arguably it did not follow the spirit of the law or treaty arrangements. Under treaty arrangements, emergency lending to commercial bank is a risk of the Central Bank of Cyprus, and if they fail, then of the Euro system. The lending is not a liability of the government, and it is certainly not a liability of the Bank of Cyprus. Of course, the leadership of the ECB was determined to not be responsible for losses on this lending, and they were able to strong arm the Cypriot government to force it upon the Bank of Cyprus. The losers in this arrangement were the depositors at the Bank of Cyprus. They were forced to take haircuts (up to 60% of deposits) to ensure the bank had adequate capital. Those haircuts would have been less if the bank could have avoided the ELA financing.

This willingness to make deals outside the spirit of the law reflects momentary political expediency. There have been many other examples in the European Union. For example, after promising to "never let Greece default," the Troika agreed a plan to change Greece's law and write down private sector debt as far as needed to make Greece appear solvent. The large write downs ignored fair treatment of similar seniority credit, such as bilateral credits and bank creditors who were fully bailed out. In Ireland, when the large local banks became clearly insolvent, the ECB refused to consider any bail-in of bank creditors to reduce the burden on tax payers.

The ad hoc and varying nature of Troika actions towards creditors in insolvent nations is worrisome. The over-riding reason for decisions appears to be political expediency. French and German banks were large creditors to Greek and Irish banks, but not to Cypriot banks. The nations being bailed out were small, and faced with the alternative of a messy exit and default from the euro zone, they have few real alternatives but to accept what is ordered.

By breaking the laws and institutions which have made our financial systems be able to develop and grow over the last six decades, these ad hoc variations in the "bankruptcy regime" for nations in the EU, albeit in a small manner so far, threatens the very foundations of our financial systems.

Lessons for Rapidly Growing Nations

For advanced economies, it may already be too late to extricate themselves from high leverage, excessive government promises and growing debts, and ageing populations. Rapidly growing nations have better opportunities.

The most important factor to delay problems is continued growth. Macroeconomic policies including immigration and fertility promotion could offset the impact of ageing. Canada, the United Kingdom and the United States are particularly benefitting from immigration. However, not all nations are prepared to take such measures, and some may not be attractive in the future in any case.

Social and institutional change is ultimately necessary. We are skeptical that adequate changes can be achieved without crisis. It is easy to design and discuss rules that make the system appear safer (as we do in the subsections which follow), but the real problem is that few people wish to impose these rules consistently over many years. Japan's example shows how easy it is for our socio-political systems to become content with highly unsustainable policies so long as there is no obvious immediate cost to them. At present, governments can issue debt cheaply, and with each new "bail out" programs from central banks, equity and bond markets rally. With such outcomes, politicians calling for concrete, immediate measures that create new discipline and an end to bailouts and deficits, have little hope of success.

Strengthening the political balance in favor of capitalized financial institutions

One key problem is the balance of political forces weigh against stability. In the financial sector, powerful firms can lobby and work with current politicians to relax or avoid regulation, and ultimately generate excessive credit expansions and other risks. Tax payers are the main losers from such deals, but we have managed to postpone payments by issuing debts, so ultimately it is future generations who pay for current excess. If we cannot strengthen the institutions that support better capitalized finance, and social support for such institutions, then we are unlikely to succeed at breaking the Doomsday Cycle.

A first step to improving the political balance is to enlist the energy of creditors in favor of better capitalized entities. Creditors set the price for leverage at institutions, and they can monitor them. If creditors expect they will lose money in crises, then they will be more likely to monitor and price risk appropriately.

The problem for policy makers is that promises to bail-in creditors are time inconsistent. The Lehman example shows how destructive liquidations are. Both creditors and financial institutions have an incentive to make the system complex and interconnected, thus, forcing policy makers to bail them out or bear enormous systemic costs.

There are measures that nations and regulators can take. We can implement strict "no bailout" laws which require creditor bail-in before public funds can be used. We can also require simple capital structures which permit regulators to go after certain categories of creditors early in the process. Large buffers of equity and contingent capital, as called for in Basel III, will help. Clear laws and professional teams to implement resolution authorities are required. This can be helped by living wills.

Second, we can strengthen our regulators too. Presently, in many nations, policy makers and regulators can freely move between private and public service. In private service, they lobby against the same regulations they were supposed to support in public service. The fact that lucrative employment is available to regulators, and those setting policy, when they move later to the private sector is an important conflict of interest that probably prevents sound regulation. Multi-year restrictions which prevent such revolving door practices are common in some areas and should be applied to policy also (Bair, 2012).

Strengthening the political balance in favor of stable public finance

We believe there is a natural bias in advanced nations' political systems towards debt finance. This reflects ageing populations and lack of representatives from future generations who are expected to bear this debt. It also reflects opaque and very complicated accounting, which invariably permits politicians to obfuscate the true costs of such measures.

There are institutional examples of success. In the United States, balanced budget rules have largely worked to limit debt finance at the state level (Johnson and Kwak, 2010). The states subject to these rules have over-promised on pensions, but at least many parts of current spending were kept in check (Andonov *et al.*, 2012). The social security trust fund by law is not permitted to pay out more than it receives in specific payroll taxes. This rule has contributed to pressure to keep the fund reasonably solvent. Strict balanced budget rules take away the ability of governments to manage counter-cyclical fiscal policies, however, limited leeway can be introduced (through deficit ceilings, or, cyclical adjustments) which might permit rules to be binding but not so costly when deficits are justified.

It is also possible to import discipline. Ito *et al.* (2011) argue that Japan's commitment to the gold standard prevented the government from running up large debts in the pre-war era, and balanced budget rules installed during the post-war US administration maintained budget responsibility from 1950–1970. The European Union's first attempts to instill fiscal discipline on members with the "Stability and Growth Pact" completely failed, however, recently the euro zone member nations agreed to new budget rules which, if applied, would lead to large reductions in public debt levels over coming decades in the euro zone. But for nations such as Greece, the euro zone has already created enormous fiscal discipline and change in a very short period.

While rules might work for regional discipline, at the national level it would be difficult to get a majority in favor of truly binding implementation of rules limiting excessive debts. In the

United Kingdom, there is no capacity to make binding rules. Any new law could be easily rescinded by later governments, so it would not be credible. The United States, through constitutional amendment, is more able to generate lasting fiscal discipline through new rules; however, it is hard to get enough support to make such changes. The inflexibility of such rules brings its own dangers.

If the main underlying problem is that intergenerational transfer of debts is attractive to older generations, then winning support for institutional change that ends such transfers will be difficult. One common reason that proponents of national pension programs, and other benefit programs, often demand these be offered to every citizen, regardless of means, is in order to gain lasting political support for the project. If instead, means testing was introduced in order that the programs only go to those who need them most, then support would be reduced.[30]

Greater transparency

Transparency can be an important force to elicit change. The greatest progress has been made in budget accounting. In the United States, the Congressional Budget Office has developed into a respected arbiter when comparing long-term budget costs of alternative programs. The United Kingdom has recently created the "Office for Budget Responsibility" lead by respected leading economists to provide short and medium term outlooks on the budget, and checks with the Treasury's own forecasts. The United Kingdom project "The Whole of Government Accounts" produces an annual report on the state of the consolidated public sector balance sheet and cash flows, but implicit pension liabilities for government workers and national programs are not included in these accounts. The European Union has mandated "Eurostat" with the role of monitoring national statistics. Eurostat played a critical role correcting misleading Greek statistics, although for many years it appears to have ignored suspect reporting from member nations.

[30]As a redistributive program, national pension funds are inefficient relative to more targeted, smaller transfer programs.

However, there is very little progress with transparency at Central Banks. The lack of transparency starts with the discussion over policy measures. Some costs of repeated financial crises can be measured. For example, the misallocation of capital across sectors during financial booms and busts leads to lower average returns to savers. The ensuing losses lead to financial crises and bailouts, which have systemic costs. The low interest rates during the period where the financial sector recapitalizes itself are a cost to savers. The value of these losses (and gains during boom times) could be discussed openly, and some crude measures of their importance could be determined. Instead, the central banks and government officials do not discuss these issues. Few central bankers are willing to admit their institutions play integral roles in financial collapse.[31] They prefer to point out that most bailout money is returned often with interest, so central banks and tax payers make a profit.[32]

Central banks also provide an implicit subsidy to systemic institutions through the understanding that they will be bailed out during crises. The benefits can be crudely measured. By measuring the benefits, we also raise for debate a discussion on how to "level the playing field" to encourage a great number of non-systemic institutions could compete in the sector.

In Europe, there was large debate over funds provided through government budgets to the periphery, and these funds required parliamentary approval in most nations. However, there were far greater sums transferred through the euro system, with little oversight or monitoring. According to European treaties, the risk from the various

[31]Charlie Bean, the Deputy Governor of the Bank of England, is a rare exception. He received enormous criticism after sympathizing that savers seemed to be paying the biggest price for the financial crisis. In a Channel 4 TV news interview on September 27, 2010, Mr. Bean spelled out that "very often older households have actually benefitted from the fact that they've seen capital gains on their houses." Available at http://www.channel4.com/news/bank-of-england-savers-should-eat-into-cash.

[32]For example, in a speech on December 6, 2009 to the Economic Club of Washington, the chairman of the Federal Reserve, Ben Bernanke, remarked, "I do believe we're going to get back all the money, and indeed we'll be showing for the tax payers fairly significant extra income." Available at http://money.cnn.com/2009/12/07/news/economy/bernanke_speech/

lending programs (Emergency lending assistance, Long-Term Repurchase Operations, other repurchase operations, government bond purchases etc.) is borne by the euro system as a whole. If one member of the euro system could not retrieve their funds, the national central banks of other members would pay for the losses. This places the burden on the shoulders of taxpayers in other nations. The ECB has diverted trillions of euros in credits and yet discussions over the risks implied by these sums have been limited. One reason for limited discussion is the large sums in question point to the mistakes made by politicians when they created the euro area. They essentially created a system which can now only survive through bailouts that taxpayers may not be willing to approve if asked transparently to take such risks. The costs of this system are seen in bailouts, unemployment, and financial crises through the euro zone.

We believe there are two important ways that central banks could be better monitored. First, strong oversight from legislative branches makes sense. Central Banks are naturally worried that such oversight could compromise independent decision making. However, given the enormous sums of funding involved, we clearly need far greater capacity to audit and question the costs of the programs. If central banks grow wary of taxpayer revolts against bailout programs, then the credibility of efforts to ensure that creditors bear the costs will be enhanced. This could ultimately ensure the system is better capitalized.

Secondly, there is a role for an independent "Macro Stability Board" to monitor and report regularly on the general issues related to systemic risk in a nation, as well as providing indicative accounts for the costs of bailouts, and other activities of central banks. Such boards, if managed as strong independent institutions, could serve as public whistle blowers to help ferret out areas where public policy is leading to excessive risks, or unreported costs.

Some countries have tried to create these. In the United States, Dodd–Frank legislation called for the creation of the "Financial Stability Oversight Board." At least as proposed by Sheila Bair, this would have had independent standing and potential political clout.[33]

[33]See Bair (2012).

After hard negotiating, however, the US Treasury Secretary managed to gain the chair of the board, and the Chairman of the Federal Reserve Board of Governors is also on the board, alongside the heads of the major regulatory agencies. The make-up of this institution is inappropriate for the role of a whistle blower. These are the same groups who managed the economy in the run-up to previous crises, and did little to speak out against problems both ahead of and after the crises. The IMF can also contribute to this role in the international sphere. However, they too have proven incapable of providing strong independent advice as their major board members (the United States and Europe) dislike public criticisms.

We believe such boards need to be led by strong individuals who are independent of the existing financial, policy making, and regulatory institutions. In the United States today, Paul Volcker would be an ideal candidate. Unfortunately, there are seemingly few candidates like him who could pull this off — and he is currently 85 years old.

Such boards would need to be structured like national auditors, with annual budgets guaranteed through legislation, and the ability to gather information as required for their work in a confidential manner. Such institutions will naturally threaten most existing powers, and this makes them difficult to commence.

Access to data is essential — and the Macro Stability Board would need to be able to see all "supervisory" information on financial institutions. Again, the opposition from existing supervisors — for whom knowledge is power — would be intense.

Conclusions

We have argued that the rise of large financial systems over the last 50 years present unprecedented risks for stability in the future. The financial system has presented wealthy nations with the opportunity to levy costs on future generations through debt finance, and they appear to be using this ability to excess. Each time there is a financial crisis, nations use debt finance to bail out systemic institutions. There is a common tendency to run budget deficits. The growth of this system and debts, alongside weak capitalization, has contributed to regular and growing financial crises around the world. If our thesis is correct, this last financial crisis is not a "once in a century" event, but rather one of many even larger crises to come. Japan appears to be leading the way, but many more nations could follow.

Today's rapidly growing nations can reduce the dangers of falling into this same trap or at least reduce the costs when a crisis arise. While there is no "magic solution," the creation of strong institutions which provide increased transparency, and legislation which help check the growth of debts, while changing the political balance in favor of a better capitalized public and private sector, may be enough to keep dangers at bay.

References

Andonov, A, R Bauer and C Martijn (2012). Pension fund asset allocation and liability discount rates: Camouflage and reckless risk taking by US public plans? Available at http://ssrn.com/abstract=2070054.

Auerbach, AJ, J Gokhale and LJ Kotlikoff (1992). Assessing the impact of income tax, social security tax, and health care spending cuts on US saving rates. *Economic Review/Federal Reserve Bank of Cleveland (US)*, 28(4), 13–21.

Bair, S (2012). *Bull by the Horns: Fighting to Save Main Street from Wall Street and Wall Street from Itself.* New York: Free Press.

Boone, P and S Johnson (2010). Will the politics of global moral hazard sink us again? In Layard, R and P Woolley (Eds.), *The Future of Finance*, p. 288. London: London School of Economics.

Clark, RL, LA Craig and JW Wilson (2003). *A History of Public Sector Pensions in the United States.* Philadelphia: University of Pennsylvania Press.

Doi, T, T Hoshi and T Okimoto (2011). *Japanese Government Debt and Sustainability of Fiscal Policy.* NBER Working Paper Series No. 17305, August.

Ghosh, AR, JI Kim, EG Mendoza, JD Ostry and MS Qureshi (2011). *Fiscal Fatigue, Fiscal Space and Debt Sustainability in Advanced Economies.* NBER Working Paper Series No. 16782, February.

Ito, A, T Watanabe and T Yabu (2011). Fiscal policy switching in Japan, the US, and the UK. *Journal of the Japanese and International Economies*, 25(4), 380–413.

Iwaisako, T (2012) Saving-investment balance and fiscal sustainability of Japan: A view from the JGB market. Institute of Economic Research Discussion Papers No. 568, April. Hitotsubashi University.

Johnson, S and J Kwak (2010). *13 Bankers: The Wall Street Takeover and The Next Financial Meltdown.* New York: Pantheon Books.

Johnson, S and J Kwak (2012). *White House Burning: The Founding Fathers, Our National Debt, and Why It Matters to You.* New York: Pantheon Books.

Kimberly, AS (2012). An examination of Lehman Brothers' derivatives portfolio postbankruptcy — Would Dodd–Frank have made a difference? Available at http://media.hoover.org/sites/default/files/documents/Kimberly-Summe-Dodd-Frank-20110421.pdf.

Laeven, L, F Valencia and International Monetary Fund (2012). Systemic banking crises database: An update. IMF Working Paper WP/12/163, p. 33, June. Washington, DC: International Monetary Fund.

MacDonald, D (2012). The Big Banks' big secret: Estimating government support for Canadian banks during the financial crisis. Canadian Centre for Policy Alternatives No. 46, April.

OECD (2012). OECD Pensions Outlook 2012. OECD Publishing. Available at http://dx.doi.org/10.1787/9789264169401-en.

Reinhart, C (2012). Return of financial repression. *Financial Stability Review*, 16, 37–48.

Sachs, J (2011). *The Price of Civilization: Reawakening American Virtue and Prosperity*. New York, Random House.

Schularick, M and AM Taylor (2012). Credit booms gone bust: Monetary policy, leverage cycles, and financial crises, 1870–2008. *American Economic Review*, 102(2), 1029–1061.

Settlements, BfI (2012). Semi-Annual OTC Derivative Statistics at end-June 2012. Geneva.

Statistics Bureau Japan (2012). *Statistical Handbook of Japan 203*. Available at http://www.stat.go.jp/english/data/handbook/index.htm.

Summers, L and B DeLong (2012). Fiscal policy in a depressed economy. *Brookings Papers on Economic Activity*, 233–274. Available at http://www.brookings.edu/~/media/Projects/BPEA/Spring%202012/2012a_DeLong.pdf.

Thane, P (2000). *Old Age in English History: Past Experiences, Present Issues*. New York: Oxford University Press.

United States Bankruptcy Court Southern District of New York (2013). Lehman Brothers Special Financing Inc. vs. Federal Home Loan Bank of Cincinnati: Adversary Complaint.

Chapter 4

Lessons from the Financial Liberalization in the Nordic Countries in the 1980s*

Seppo Honkapohja

Introduction

The banking and economic crisis that took place in the Nordic countries in the 1990s has received a lot of international attention ever since its occurrence. The episode was the most serious economic and financial crisis experienced by advanced market economies in the period after WWII.[1] In particular, the drop in aggregate output of nearly 15% in Finland in a period of two-to-three years was a surprising and unusual event.[2] The very low frequency of financial crises in advanced economies until the beginning of 1990s should be contrasted to the relatively frequent such crises in advanced market economies before WWII. Financial crises were also frequent in developing countries in the post WWI period.

*I am grateful to Tapio Korhonen for extensive assistance. Adam Gulam, Hanna Putkuri, and Juhana Hukkinen helped in specific aspects of work. Jarmo Kontulainen, Iikka Korhonen and Juha Tarkka provided useful comments. The views expressed are my own and do not necessarily represent those of the Bank of Finland.

[1]In the beginning of the 1980s, Spain suffered a serious banking crisis when measured in terms of fiscal costs from bank support. See for example Vives (2000). However, the Spanish GDP did not decline in that period.

[2]Reinhard and Rogoff (2008) compute the average of "big five crises" in advanced market economies before 2007 as a point of comparison for the discussion of the current crisis. The big five crises are those of Finland, Norway and Sweden in the 1990s, together with Spain in 1970s and Japan in the 1990s. Reinhart and Rogoff (2009) is an extensive treatise on different types of financial crises.

Subsequently, there have been a number of other financial crises in advanced market economies throughout the world. Some of these crises have been even deeper than the ones experienced by the Nordic countries, so that the latter are no longer unique. Nevertheless, it is instructive to study why the Nordic countries ran into the deep economic and financial problems. Though some concurrent external factors had an influence on the Nordic crises (especially on Finland), it is evident that the root causes were closely connected with the liberalizations of financial and foreign exchange markets in the 1980s and the widespread capital and credit controls in these markets in the period just before the liberalizations.

In this chapter, I discuss in some detail the processes of financial liberalizations in the Nordic countries in the 1980s and the reasons why three of the four Nordic countries — Finland, Norway and Sweden — gradually drifted into systemic financial crisis. The emphasis on the liberalizations makes this chapter complementary to the substantial literature that focuses on the Nordic financial crises.

There are a number of discussions of the Nordic financial crises in the existing literature. These articles largely focus on the crisis period and the management and resolution of the crises. Several of these studies also contain overviews of the period leading to the crisis, but the treatments are relatively short.[3] I will not consider the crisis management procedures in this chapter. For this topic, see Honkapohja (2009) and references therein. Denmark managed to avoid the fate of Finland, Norway and Sweden as it experienced some banking problems but they never became systemic. I hope perspectives presented in this chapter are of some use for emerging economies that are thinking about initiating a process of financial liberalization.

It should be noted at the outset and is further explained that it is difficult to give precise descriptions and make detailed comparisons of the liberalizations in different countries. Instead, I discuss at a general level different issues and problems that emerged during

[3]See, for example, Drees and Pazarbaşioğlu (1998), Englund (1999), Honkapohja and Koskela (1999), Steigum (2004), Honkapohja *et al.* (2009), Honkapohja (2009), Jonung *et al.* (2009), Englund and Vihriälä (2009), Steigum (2009), and Vastrup (2009). Rautava (1994) gives some more details about the liberalization period in Finland.

the liberalization. The four countries had their own assessments and decisions about the steps in the liberalization. Understandably, the discussion emphasizes the Finnish experiences to a significant extent as Finland is my home country.

General Background

The four Nordic countries (Denmark, Finland, Norway and Sweden) are similar, roughly of the same size and small economies. In total, their population was about 22 million people at the end of the 1970s. Sweden is the largest and in the decades after WW II the wealthiest of the four countries, because it managed to stay outside the war. Finland was the weakest of these countries, partly because it suffered big losses during the war.

Nordic countries are known as being egalitarian, socially cohesive countries with strong western democratic traditions. The mutual ties between these countries are wide-spread. The common Nordic labor market was created already in 1954.

A good example of the close ties between the economies is the fact that the countries experienced the economic crisis nearly concurrently. The Danish crisis took place earlier and was much milder and different from the other crises. As an oil-producing country, the Norwegian crisis had some special features. The crises in Finland and Sweden were similar and occurred at almost the same time, though some special features made the Finnish crisis deeper than the Swedish one.

Figures 1–4 provide the basic data on the Nordic countries (levels of real GDP, levels of consumer prices, current accounts as percent of GDP, and exchange rates against the German mark). It is seen from Figure 1 that with the exception of Sweden, GDP growth was relatively rapid, as the countries were catching up with the most advanced economies. The 1990s crises are clearly visible in the data, especially for Sweden and Finland. Figure 2 illustrates that rates of inflation were higher than those in Germany and the United States. Nordic countries experienced current account problems to varying degrees (see Figure 3) and the exchanges rates of the Nordic currencies depreciated against the German mark after

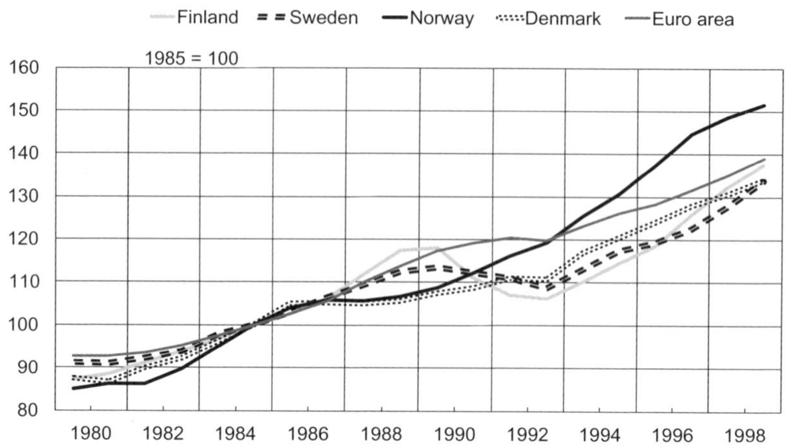

Figure 1. Levels of gross domestic product 1980–1999.

Source: Eurostat.

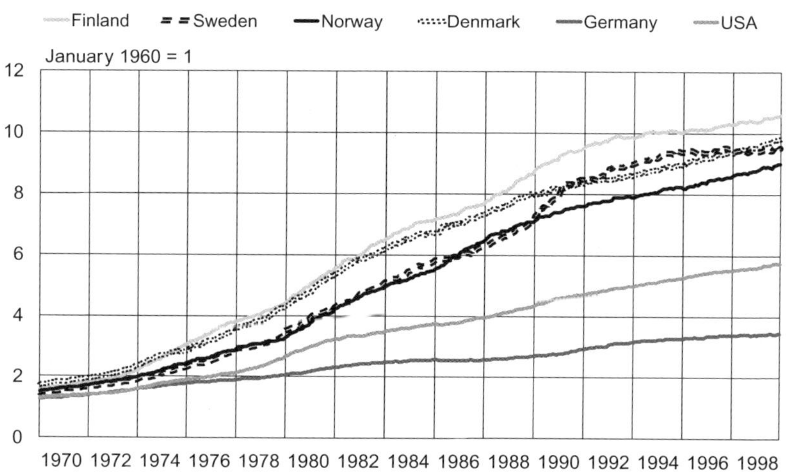

Figure 2. Consumer price levels in 1970–1998.

Source: OECD.

the breakdown of the Bretton Woods system. The depreciations are shown in Figure 4.

The economic significance of the public sector is big in all four countries, and in some areas it was even bigger in the decades after the war. The state had strong influence in social policies and the

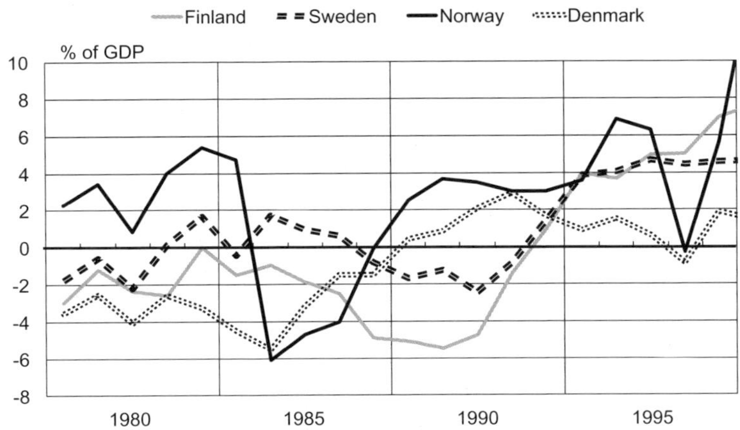

Figure 3. Current accounts in percent of GDP in 1980–1999.
Source: European Commission.

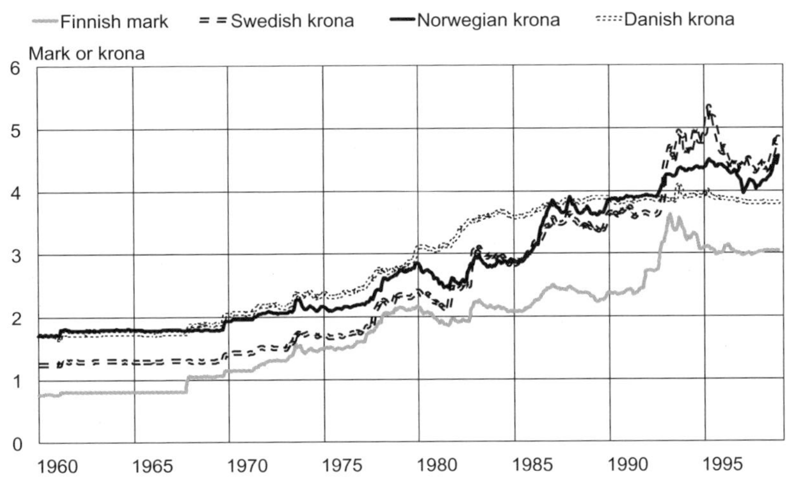

Figure 4. Exchange rates against the German Mark in 1960–1999.
Source: Bank of Finland.

economy. Nordic governments used to own major corporations and financial institutions. Public ownership of businesses has gradually declined since 1990s. The state regulated many societal functions until the 1980s by use of licenses and permits. For example, price controls were used to varying degree.

The role of incomes policies was central. Together with labor market organizations, the state often made agreements about wage contracts and, as part of the agreements, sometimes the state even made commitments about some fiscal and monetary policy actions. Incomes policy was actually the primary means to control inflation. This approach was unsuccessful in the Nordic countries and especially in the 1970s and 1980s, inflation was mostly quite rapid in these countries (see Figure 2).

Comprehensive control of financial and foreign exchange markets was particularly pronounced in the decades after WWII, though some aspects of this control were inherited from the economic depression in the 1930s. However, it must be emphasized that the system of financial repression was mostly an instrument of the growth and industrialization policies of the post-WWII decades.[4] Rationing of the real economy was largely given up soon after the war. As in the rest of Europe, foreign trade and other current account transactions and payments were liberalized already at the end of 1950s. Import duties were important until the start of the European integration process, but only agriculture remained under wide protection in the Nordic countries.

Basic Features of the Control Systems for Capital Movements and Financial Markets

In the first decades after WWII, major Western European economies also began to liberalize capital movements, but in Nordic countries all central elements of capital movements were controlled until the 1980s.[5]

Long-term capital movements in and out of the country required a permit from the authorities. The permits were given only for investments. Short-term financial investments, like foreign deposits, were

[4]Tarkka (2009) discusses the Finnish regulation system from the 1950s to the 1980s. Abilgren (2007) discusses the liberalization period and credit dynamics in Denmark.

[5]See e.g., Prasad and Rajan (2008), Korinek (2011), and Jeanne *et al.* (2012) for recent discussions of the issues and problems in opening the capital movements. The older literature on capital controls is surveyed in Dooley (1995). See Edey and Hviding (1995) for a broad discussion of the older empirical experiences in financial liberalization.

not as a rule allowed in either direction. Of the major items in capital movements, trade finance which was immediately tied to foreign trade was relatively free. In contrast, foreign exchange for travel was rationed. Also some specific transactions, such as certain direct investments were traditionally free in some countries.

Control of capital movements helped to maintain fixed exchange rates among other things. Nordic countries were part of the Bretton Woods system of the fixed dollar-based exchange rate system until 1971. The system was based on the so-called adjustable peg. In the year 1973, Denmark (which then joined the European Union), Norway, and Sweden attached themselves to the European exchange rate cooperation mechanism (the so-called "snake") — in practice to the German Mark.[6] The latter two countries were not able to remain in the system and resigned from it after a few years. They began to use a trade-weighted currency basket, which Finland had already adopted.

Though the possibility of using floating exchange rates was occasionally discussed, the system of fixed exchange rates was not questioned until it broke down after strong market pressures in 1992. This happened first in Finland and soon after in Sweden and Norway. The choice of the exchange rate system was primarily political. The exchange rate provided an anchor especially to incomes policies. At the same time the exchange rate acted as a backstop policy instrument in case of negative economic shocks and competitiveness problems. A major consequence of exchange rate and income policy was that inflation expectations were elevated.

Similarity and integration of Nordic economies was very visible also in the currency markets. International investors tended to view the countries similarly. Typically, pressures on the exchange rate moved from one country to the others — especially between Norway, Sweden and Finland. These countries often devalued, and had to devalue, in response to each other. Denmark was geographically and also in terms of its economy and financing, somewhat closer to Central Europe.

---

[6]The "snake" was created in Europe as system to manage exchange rates after the breakdown of the Bretton Woods system.

In practice, central banks managed the currency controls. Independence and duties of central banks in exchange rate and monetary policies differed somewhat. Fixing the exchange rate was *de facto* duty of governments[7] and setting the most important interest rates were in practice under the direct control of the government (e.g., in Norway) or indirectly *via* representatives of the parliament (in Finland).

In all Nordic countries, control of domestic financial markets was concentrated primarily in banks, but also other financing activities were in general regulated.

In the 1960s and 1970s, quantitative control of credit in the Norwegian economy was the most wide spread among European countries. A financing budget ("*nasjonalbudsjettet*") was prepared annually and approved by the public authorities. The budget contained the main features of how financing for the whole economy was allocated to the different sectors. This financing budget was in reality a guideline and significant deviations from it happened in practice, especially in later years. In Sweden and Denmark, quantitative rationing of finance focused on bank lending. In Sweden a large part of bank funds were directed to the government that financed, e.g., housing. In Finland, different constraints on lending were used only from time to time and banks usually did not significantly fund the government. In all countries more or less binding directives about allocation of finance were given in addition to the general quantitative control.

In Denmark, securities markets were wide spread and relatively free, but especially in Norway and Finland bond markets were small and did not function well. In all four countries, governments fully or partly owned special financing institutions, which were used to direct financing in the economy.

Banks were mostly privately (or mutually/cooperatively) owned, but they were heavily under state control. Private commercial banks largely dominated the banking sectors. The role of local saving and cooperative banks varied somewhat between the four countries.

[7] In Sweden, this duty was formally the prerogative of the council of the Riksbank.

Banks operated under tight constraints. Quantities and allocation of credit were controlled directly or indirectly and interest rates of bank deposits and lending, and thus the interest margin, were regulated. In addition, deposit and lending rates were controlled through taxation. Foreign items and currency positions of banks were controlled. Also fees charged by banks were controlled. Liquidity of banks was secured by central bank funding, which was also used to regulate banking by means of various marginal rate schedules.

This system guaranteed a banking system that was stable in terms of balance sheets and profits. A particularly notable feature of the system was that loan losses were kept very low. At the same time, the banking system grew a lot in terms of personnel and its operational efficiency was low. In some countries there were attempts to limit this growth, e.g., by controlling establishment of branch offices of banks. Competition among banks in this environment could not be based on genuine market competition but rather on supply of secondary customer services and advertising. Banks were almost viewed as a branch of the government.

Objectives of Financial Repression

Control of capital movements was necessary to protect independence of domestic monetary policy. Controlling of domestic financial markets was easily achieved until the 1970s. The economies of all Nordic countries were somewhat isolated internationally and ties to other countries largely consisted of trade relations. In Sweden, some important international companies had been created. Another important feature was that all Nordic countries were open economies in terms of foreign trade already in the 1970s. Their international trade was large and it was conducted under market conditions. The countries were significant exporters, for example, in forest and engineering industries.

Financial isolation of the economy was considered important, because it was desired to have the interest rates as a policy instrument and keep the level of these rates low. Investments by companies and households were also supported by generous tax benefits. For example, interest payments on loans were largely or fully tax-deductible. Investment was supported in order to achieve rapid growth. Economic thinking giving a minimal role for the interest rate as a policy tool was also in behind the low interest rate system.

Support policies for investment led to undesirable developments in many respects. Low levels of nominal interest rates, tax benefits and fast inflation made real interest rates mostly negative in 1970s. This led to very strong excess demand for loans at times, which in turn developed excessively strong customer ties between banks and borrowers. A bank almost guaranteed a loan, provided there was sufficient advance saving. These kinds of practices were harmful when the markets were liberalized.

On the other hand, firms were usually able to secure funding easily and cheaply, often at negative real rates, for investment into real capital formation. This favored debt financing in firms and led to high degrees of indebtedness. Especially large exporting companies tried to benefit from foreign funding because of the tightness of domestic financial markets. Interest rates on foreign currency loans were relatively low, but there was an associated currency risk. This weak financing structure of firms was detrimental when the markets were liberalized and the real interest rates rose sharply.

Control of credit continued for several decades and economic agents adjusted to the system. There were fears of instability that might follow from giving up rationing. It is also truc that the period of financial repression was also a period of relatively rapid growth. Though fluctuations in growth were large at times, financial crises were avoided. Control of capital movements kept, for example, current account deficits manageable. On the other hand, it is evident that the system of controls and restrictions led to significant inefficiency in the use of economic resources. The policy of allocating finance and low interest rates resulted in very high investment rates in the Nordic economies. Especially in Norway and Finland, investment was commonly 25%–30% of GDP and sometimes even above this level. In view of these high investment rates, the growth rate of the economies remained modest.

Starting points of the liberalization

During the period of financial repression, the system was often criticized, but expressions of satisfaction with it were also wide-spread in the society. Pressure to liberalize came mostly from abroad. International organizations, IMF, OECD and EU, attempted to liberalize markets and also international capital movements. It was nevertheless the growth of international trade, internationalization of firms, and development of international financial markets that gradually broke the foundations of controls and restrictions especially from the 1970s onward.

Liberalization of foreign finance was started in Denmark in the 1960s, but clear steps of liberalization begun only toward the end of 1970s. Genuine freedom of money and currency markets took place only during the 1980s in the four countries.

The liberalizations led to some volatility in macroeconomic developments, aspects of which can be seen from Figures 1–4. In particular, current account deficits had been persistent (with Norway being an exception) and the deficits worsened during the process of liberalization. Moreover, the countries experienced lending booms to varying degrees and there were also major increases in real estate and share prices. Figures 5–7 show growth rates of bank lending, real house prices and real share prices in the four countries.[8]

It is in general, difficult to measure the degree of freedom and regulation in different countries. As a result, it is also difficult to compare the Nordic countries in their processes of liberalization.[9] IMF has tried to create indices of degree of regulation of international capital movements. Even nowadays, foreign finance is not fully free in any country; some limitations, for example on export of cash notes, exist in order to restrict criminal activities.

Interpretations of individual regulations and liberalization activities are correspondingly uncertain. Often the image that emerges from listing liberalization activities of different countries is

[8]Danish data is not included in Figure 5 for reasons of comparability.

[9]See Englund and Vihriälä (2009) for illustrative figures of the liberalization steps in Finland and Sweden.

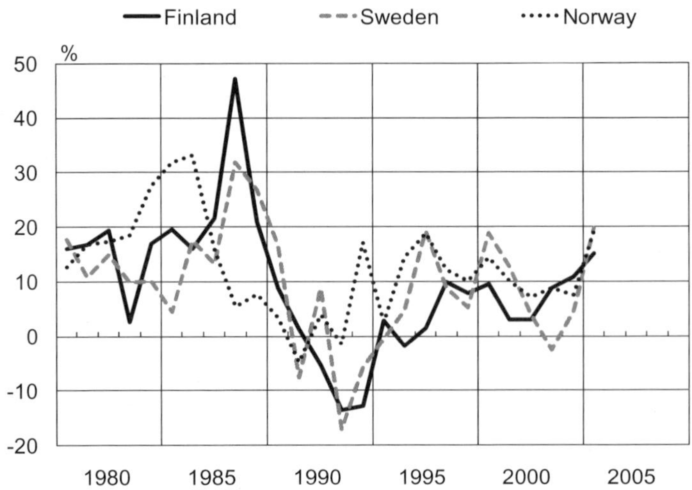

Figure 5. Growth of bank lending 1980–2005.

Note: Denmark is not included.

Source: OECD and Bank of Finland.

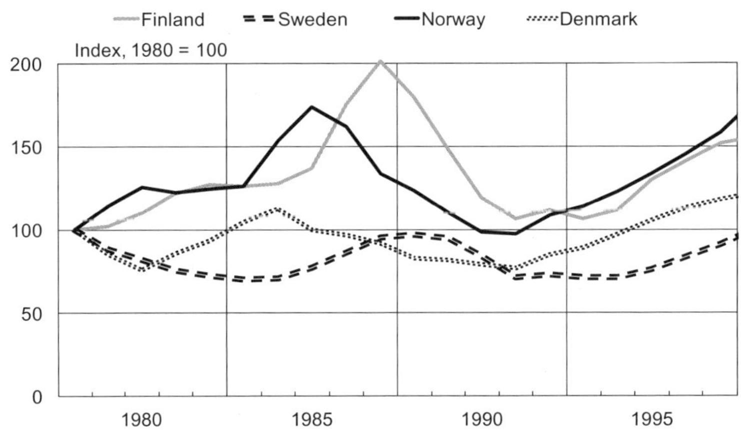

Figure 6. Real house prices in 1980–1999.

Note: Nominal houses prices deflated using the consumer price index.

Source: Statistics Finland, Statistics Sweden, Norges Bank, Statistics Norway and Bank of Finland.

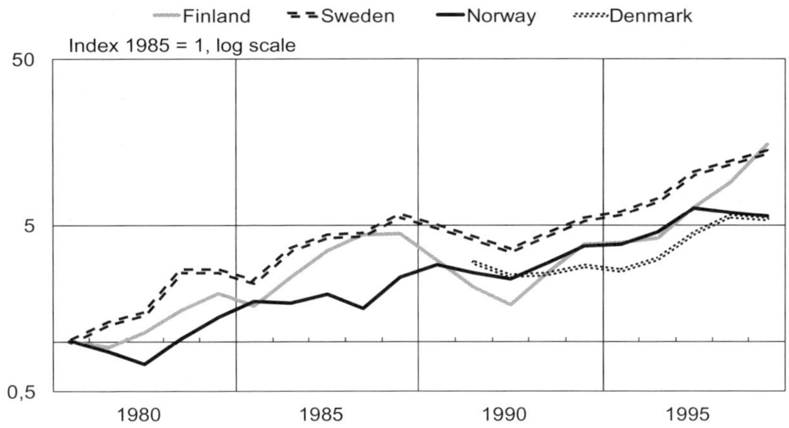

Figure 7. Real share prices 1980–1999.

Note: Normal share prices deflated using the consumer price index.
Source: IMF, ECB and Bank of Finland.

incomplete and even misleading. A seemingly modest action may have surprisingly large effects especially when the state of the market or economy changes in an essential way. On the other hand, a seemingly large action may mean that some existing realities are just confirmed. For example, if control of certain currency transactions has already been quite liberally applied, then the formal freeing of these transactions is not a significant decision.

The tight controlling of financial transactions in Nordic countries relied on a "negative principle" in which the main rule was a ban: regulations indicated allowed activities and everything else was forbidden. As markets became more developed and relatively free, the rule book became very thick. For this reason, it was and still is difficult to compare the rules of regulating countries and their significance.

Another difficulty was that the rules, for example, in permits were applied in a variable fashion. Permits were granted at times stringently or loosely depending on the business cycle or currency market pressures. Countries can also differ with respect to the degree of avoidance of regulation, both legally and illegally. Nordic countries are constitutional states, so that evasion of controls was undoubtedly limited, excluding the last period of regulation. In the final stages, frustrations with the leakages and loopholes in the controls speeded up the abolishing of the restrictions. Evasion of regulations was mostly fully legal after the increase in the possibilities for avoidance in well-developed markets.

In the final stages of controls and restrictions, there was also a move to the "positive principle," so everything that was not forbidden was permitted. In these stages, specific activities were kept forbidden. For example, in Finland, foreign currency loans for households were permitted only in the last stages of liberalization — luckily, as this did not have time to worsen the economic crisis in the 1990s.

Importance of the order of liberalization

Objectives in the reform of the framework of economic policies in part, determine how the liberalization of different markets is carried out. Freeing of financial and foreign currency markets limits the domestic leeway of economic policy in essential ways. In an economy with repressed financial markets, it is possible to fix all three of the following instruments: exchange rate, domestic interest rate, and the quantity of finance. As is well known, in free markets, it is impossible to fix all three of these and the remaining magnitudes are determined by the markets. This is called the impossible trinity.

This simple fact was in principle understood in the Nordic countries but at the same time it was difficult to accept the lack of the policy autonomy in practice. There should have been a willingness to give up a fixed exchange rate or interest rate policy when capital movements were freed. However, political realities precluded this, except in Denmark. The consequence was a difficult balancing act between the adjustable peg and interest rate policy. The outcome was evidently suboptimal in all countries.

Everything looks much clearer with the benefit of hindsight. There have been a lot of criticisms stating that liberalization was not executed in accordance with a coherent and consistent plan. Already during the liberalization process, studies were made in the different countries about the appropriate ways to move ahead with the liberalization. It is difficult to say to what extent the formulated guidelines could have been applied in practice. In the initial stages of the process it was not widely accepted or perhaps even considered desirable that the objective was to move to fully deregulated markets and capital movements. Almost until the end of the process the intention was to maintain some controls on at least a part of the capital movements. The deeper European integration process starting at the end of the 1980s was the main reason for a complete liberalization of financial activities.

As was already said, pressures to liberalize financial and foreign exchange markets came partly from international policy cooperation and partly from market pressures as the economies gradually become more internationalized. Capital movements became more elastic as a result of increasing foreign trade, the emergence of multinationals and the development and widening of their financing. Especially, companies doing foreign trade became associated with informal "grey" domestic financial intermediation outside the banking system and direct control of regulators. The grey financial market became widespread in the end of 1970s. It meant that it was impossible to try to control quantitatively the total financing of the economy, which had been a central objective earlier. The existence of grey markets influenced the decisions and their sequencing in the liberalization of markets.

There are two main dimensions in the liberalization of markets:

(1) Does one first liberalize domestic financial markets (quantities, interest rates on loans, deposit rates, distorting taxes) or international capital movements and currency markets?
(2) In what order are the different markets freed in terms of maturity and other characteristics (short-term finance, long-term finance, finance of different sectors, derivative markets etc.)

Further issues in the freeing of international capital movements include the following:

(1) Does one liberalize foreign currency denominated or domestic currency denominated quantities simultaneously or in some order?
(2) Does one liberalize import and export of capital in same ways and simultaneously?

(3) Does one liberalize in response to market pressure, i.e., free capital imports when there is pressure for capital exports and *vice versa*?
(4) In what situations and what degree is it justified to reverse steps in the liberalization?

The common view is that domestic financial markets should be liberalized first. The domestic markets would then be more ready to receive the pressures from opening the economy internationally. On the other hand, it has been argued that only the freeing of capital movement forces domestic financial markets to adjust to the new environment.

The Nordic countries moved in reality so that both domestic markets and foreign transactions, i.e., currency markets and capital movements were liberalized more or less in tandem. Some small foreign operations were in fact freed first. However, most important domestic deregulation activities were carried out faster and somewhat ahead of important liberalizations of capital movements.

By the early 1980s, it had become evident in all Nordic countries that there was no alternative to moving toward free domestic financial markets and also toward mostly free foreign capital movements. A market-based domestic financial system was operational in all these countries by the end of the second half of the decade. For example, market-based reference interest rates were created following the example of London LIBOR rates. The steering mechanisms of central banks were turned market-based and clear control rationing elements were discarded.

Nordic countries adopted somewhat different ways to carry out the process of liberalization of different markets. In general, it would have probably been justified to free long-term, foreign currency denominated operations as the first step. Denmark started with freeing sales abroad of long-term bonds and even of domestic currency denominated bonds. Financing of firms was released in any case in the first wave. Certain operations of banks and other financial institutions were freed gradually. The possibility of banks to give loans abroad was restricted even in the beginning of 1980s, when Nordic countries mostly avoided the international (Latin American) banking crisis of that time.

Liberalization of liquid items of banks and firms was an important issue from the view point of implementing monetary policy. If the sensitivity to negative economic shocks and potential fluctuations are big, foreign reserves of a country could be exhausted if devaluation speculations arose. On the other hand, revaluation speculations created difficulties for control of domestic liquidity which in turn led to risks of overheating and inflation.

Forward contracts in currencies to hedge commercial risk were allowed early subject to requirement of commercial base within limits, but derivatives markets in general were made free only in the last stages of liberalization.

Liberalization of markets was not quite a unidirectional process. On a few occasions controls rationing was tightened in some countries, when the deregulation steps were thought to endanger the orderly development of liquidity and possibilities of control by monetary policy.

Nordic countries followed the common international practice, according to which there was greater readiness to free capital imports than capital exports. This was understandable in a less than perfectly credible system of fixed exchange rates. In practice, there was an attempt to liberalize capital movements in a counter-cyclical way. If pressures to import capital were strongly easing domestic money markets, controls on capital exports were reduced, while control on capital imports was kept unchanged or was even tightened. On the other hand, when there were pressures to export capital, there was a tendency to reduce controls on capital imports. For a long time, structural reasons made it desirable to limit exports of capital. It was feared — and to some extent justifiably so on the basis of later evidence — that investors, including banks, would be wide-eyed and rush to make international investments. The control of capital exports exercised by central banks did not, however, usually deliver very good results.

During the period of controls, Nordic currencies did not have international markets. Nordic monies, especially the Swedish krona, were to some extent used as invoicing and settlement currencies in this period. As a matter fact, internationalization of a country's money was viewed with some caution. Of course, Nordic monies as small inflationary currencies were initially not much sought after by international investors. An example is that the foreign sales of Finnish markka-denominated debt securities were free, but there was very little investment in them until the early years of 1980s. Denmark was an exception as it allowed foreign sales of krone-denominated bonds and the amounts of these sales were non-trivial. This meant that, the Danish long rate of interest began to be determined from abroad to a large extent.

In particular, there were fears that large foreign investors might bring instability to the domestic money markets. Thus, there were attempts to restrict foreign investors' use of domestic currency right to the end of the liberalization period. On the other hand, it was increasingly contemplated that widening the base and diversity of investors might instead stabilize market developments. The possibilities of investing domestic currency abroad were naturally restricted as long as there was control of domestic money and financial market interest rates.

When international activities of corporations became wide spread and, for example, inflation slowed down, foreign demand for Nordic currencies significantly increased in the early years of 1980s. One reason was the occasionally high interest rate. As in Denmark, increased investments in the Finnish domestic markets created liquidity problems, which in fact led to the breakdown of the system based on tight controls. The outcome was a two-tier interest rate system, in which the importance of grey market rates increased gradually. Eventually, official interest rates did not reflect the cost of credit anymore. Consequently, monetary policy started to lose its grip of monetary developments in the economy.

Decisions about taxation are central policy questions in the liberalization of financial markets. Tax systems that favored debt finance were typical in the period of financial repression. This form of taxation had created distortions to different forms of finance. It would have been important to give up these tax benefits early on, but this turned out to be impossible for political reasons. Decisions concerning tax benefits for loans and deposits were made quite late in the liberalization process, and they were often done only at the time of the banking and economic crisis.

Timing of the liberalization

Liberalizations in the Nordic countries led to a variety of problems, which turned into full scale crises in the end. This outcome can be contrasted with the experiences of Western European countries which carried out the liberalization of markets earlier or concurrently. The latter mostly did not experience nearly as big problems as the Nordics. This was the case even though most other European countries had a steady policy with fixed exchange rates though with the support of the European Monetary System.[10]

The Nordic countries tried to free financial and foreign exchange markets gradually and carefully to avoid risks, but still they were unsuccessful. In contrast, and against the advice from numerous experts, Margaret Thatcher freed foreign capital movements and currency markets "overnight" in 1979 in the UK. Financial stability in Britain was not much disturbed by the speedy actions.

A regime of floating exchange rates was perhaps the main advantage for Britain in this reform, but also well-developed domestic markets and the city, as well as stability of the external environment, helped. It is evident that success depends a lot on the degree of stability in the foreign business cycle and financial developments at the critical stage of liberalization. Apparently, Denmark was successful in this respect, whereas, for Sweden and in particular Finland, the most critical stage of liberalization occurred in a very adverse external environment.

In practice, economic and political realities dictated timing of the liberalization in Nordic countries. Sometimes, measures were adopted under a lot of market pressure.

This meant that it was not always possible to carefully plan ahead the stages of the liberalization. Thus, some decisions were made

[10]Empirical evidence about the connection between banking crises and exchange rate regimes is mixed. See Domaç and Peria (2003).

in less benign economic circumstances and then, consequences of a reform measure could become unpredictable. This was the case, when under international pressures the price of oil fell sharply in 1985–1986. At that time, Finland and Sweden were using expansionary policies and, for example, capital imports were being liberalized. As a result of the fall in oil prices the international and domestic business cycle turned round very quickly and in fact, the policies were very badly timed. This contributed to the detrimental overheating of the economy, especially in Finland.

Controls and liberalization as backgrounds for the crises

Undoubtedly one of the basic mistakes in the liberalization was that the planning narrowly focused on the sensible execution of the liberalization process. One should have analyzed simultaneously how the prevailing financially repressed economy differs from a market based economy. It should have been important to aid the flexible adjustment of controlled markets and sectors to an unregulated system.

Attention on the adjustment of markets and sectors was insufficient in the Nordic countries. The starting point was too much in how and what order one can dispense with the system of controls. There was too little attention to the condition of banks, other market institutions and sectors. It was thought that firms and households know how to adjust and are able to do so in a flexible way to a new system requiring a very different kind of behavior. However, it turned out that both banks and their customers moved toward the new equilibrium too rapidly causing a credit boom, an asset price bubble and, in the end, a banking crisis.

It was not sufficiently realized that liberalization leads to increased risks. Prudential supervision did not have a significant role in the period of a controlled financial system, because the control mechanism by itself had secured the stability of banks to a very large extent. Some banking problems occurred in the decades after WWII, but there had not been any system-wide crisis in the Nordic countries. Such a possibility was not even contemplated, so that there was no readiness to manage a systemic banking crisis. Capital ratios of banks were quite low in the Nordic countries in the era of controls, with the exception of Denmark where, bank solvency was better.

Nordic countries naturally followed international trends in prudential supervision, but the practices of supervision were judicial and technical. The focus was solely on individual banks and their risk positions. It would have been important to focus on stable adjustment of the banking sector as a whole and macro risks of banks when the markets were liberalized.

Liberalizations led to major changes in the economic behavior of different sectors, which contributed to the emergence of economic and banking crises in all Nordic countries. Most important phenomena in the main sectors were the following:

(1) the unsatisfied demands for loans by households and small and medium-size businesses erupted,
(2) unhealthy financial structures (too much debt, too little equity) of firms were revealed,
(3) there was consequent weakness of firms in weathering fluctuations in financing costs and exchange rates,
(4) after the initial boom period, there was strong tightening of competition between banks and the excess capacity and incompetence of management became destabilizing factors, and
(5) significant instability in the fixed exchange rate regime arose from liberalized capital movements.

Especially households, including entrepreneurial ones, were faced with severe constraints during the period of credit control. Advance saving was required for housing loans and consumer loans were rare. Average household loan maturity was also very short. As the markets were liberalized, the built-in pressures erupted and the number of potential loan customers increased substantially. Banks responded to this increase in demands by preparing a quick expansion and household loans started to grow very rapidly.[11]

The same situation applied to small and medium-size firms to an extent. On the other hand, investments by firms had received a

[11]Gourinchas *et al.* (2001) discuss empirical evidence about lending booms and their aftermath.

favored financing and tax treatment, so that in part the situation of the firms was the opposite from that of households. Firms had too much, both domestic and foreign currency denominated debt to begin with. Especially in Finland, firms had taken excessive amounts of foreign currency loans. When the real rate of interest rose sharply in the course of the liberalization and when to exchange rate pressures emerged, the situation of many firms became difficult.

The banking system was inefficient and too big in terms of real resources (personnel, branch network) as a result of the financial repression period. Banks understood the need for change but they reacted in different ways. It would have been natural to trim personnel and activities, but some banks instead chose a strategy of expansion aiming to make use of their excess capacity at the expense of their competitors. This strategy was successful during the initial period of strong growth of the economy, but the economic depression which followed came as a surprise to these aggressive banks. In Finland, especially the savings banks and in Norway, some commercial banks got into overwhelming difficulties and were taken over by authorities and wound up. Banks were not used to face credit losses and — with the exception of Danish banks — with the deepening of the crises, they lost large percentages of their loan stocks.

The system of controlled finance had guaranteed a relatively stable development of the financial markets. Financial institutions, especially banks, were thought to be almost eternal. Crisis awareness and preparedness was insufficient among banks and also among government officials. The crises after liberalization transformed the Nordic financial market institutions in numerous and surprising ways. Some banks were wound up and merged to other banks.

Figure 8 shows that the realized loan losses soared with onset of the economic crisis. As already discussed, Denmark experienced the lowest losses as it avoided a systemic crisis. The Norwegian crisis was also gradual but became quite deep. In Sweden and Finland, the losses started to occur quickly. Correspondingly, Figure 9 shows that profitability of Nordic banks plummeted in the crisis years. In Denmark, banks' profitability fluctuated already in early 1980s as a result of the earlier liberalization and reforms, and the fall in

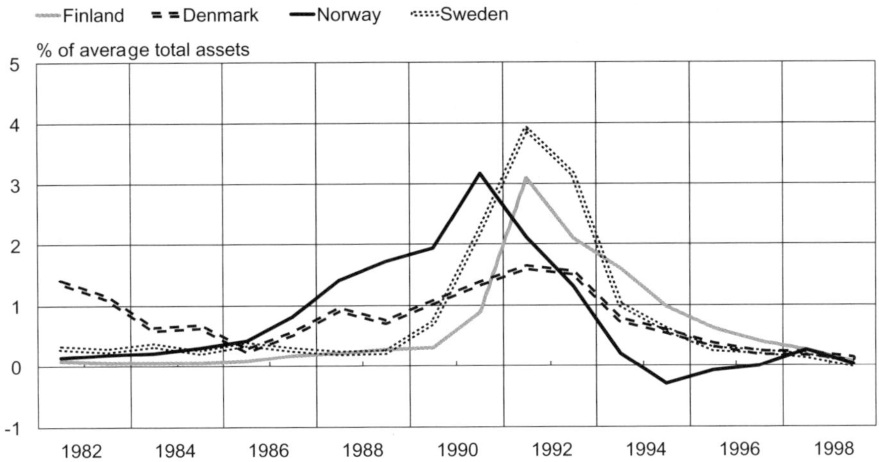

Figure 8. Loan losses of Nordic banks 1982–1999.
Source: National central banks.

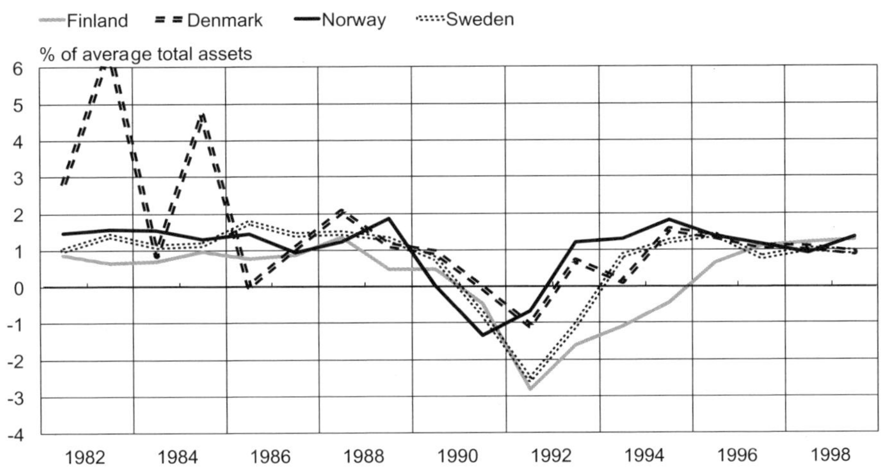

Figure 9. Operating profits of Nordic banks 1982–1999.
Source: National central banks.

profitability in the 1990s was then relatively small. It can also be seen that Norwegian banks did somewhat better in terms of profitability than Swedish and Finnish banks. Especially in Finland, the period of negative profits lasted quite a long time, about five years.

The crisis in Denmark was the earliest and mildest. Apparently, Denmark succeeded to liberalize early and in a relatively favorable external environment. Capitals ratios of Danish banks were much better than in the other countries and also growth of household indebtedness had been discouraged by tax measures since 1986. The Norwegian crisis differed from the Swedish and Finnish crises because of the oil producing sector. This sector strengthened the economy after the 1970s and the sharp fall of oil prices in 1986 mitigated the overheating of the economy. Therefore, the crisis in Norway primarily involved the banking sector and was not a serious economic recession.

Swedish and Finnish economies were overheated at the end of the 1980s right after the liberalizations. These countries would have required a calm period in order to repair the structural problems that had been created during the period of controlled finance and its liberalization. Unfortunately, the bubble burst almost concurrently with the onset of the international recession in the early 1990s. Exceptionally high interest rates and overvalued currencies made the problems worse. The 1991, the breakdown of the Soviet Union led to collapse of about 20% of Finnish foreign trade and major devaluation of the markka in conjunction with a large stock of foreign currency denominated loans contributed to the depth of the economic depression.

Instability of Nordic economies, especially of Finland, Sweden and Norway, in the last stages of liberalization and in the crises was clearly influenced by the aim of these countries to maintain a regime of fixed exchange rates on their own. In contrast, the Danish currency was supported by the European Monetary System and its credit facilities with financed foreign exchange interventions.

Strong devaluation and revaluation pressures on the currencies occurred during the period of liberalization. After the 1982 devaluations, the countries experienced pressures to import capital, while at times capital tended to move out. At the end of the decade, especially Finland and Sweden faced pressures from capital imports. The developments in Norway were somewhat different because of the oil.

As the international and domestic business cycle turned toward a recession at the turn of the decade, the countries had to face strong speculative pressures which led to high interest rate policies and deepened the recessions. Also the levels of international interest rates were high as a result of German interest rate policies. With liberalized foreign exchange markets, this had a full impact on the Nordic countries.

Under the pressures from recession Finland, Sweden and Norway had — after long and partly expensive defenses — to give up the fixed exchange rate system. Initially, there were suspicions about the floating exchange rate. However, a floating rate, combined with the adoption of inflation targeting regime, worked surprisingly well during the 1990s. Financial development was clearly much smoother than in the preceding decade. In a sense, the shift to a floating exchange rate in 1992 marked the end of long period of financial repression and its aftermath in the Nordic countries.

Are There Lessons for China?

At the outset, it must be noted that present-day China and the Nordic countries of 1970s and 1980s are in many ways quite different from each other. Size differences are the most obvious point. There are, however, also common characteristics. At a general level, problematic aspects of the earlier Nordic financial deregulation processes can in fact hold some potential lessons to the ongoing Chinese financial market liberalization process. One can add that the Nordic liberalization process has been well documented, so that the reasons for the subsequent financial crisis in early 1990s have been widely studied.

The main common features of the Nordics in 1970–1980s are, first, that the financial systems were very much centered in bank intermediated finance. In the 1970s and the beginning of the 1980s, numerous price or quantity controls were in place in the Nordic countries. Similar controls are in place in China today. In particular, credit controls limiting the quantity of domestic finance were extensively used in the Nordic countries and are also in use in China.[12]

[12]See e.g., Johansson (2012) and the references therein for overviews of Chinese financial system policies, their effects on internal and external imbalances. The study by Sedik and Sun (2012), considers the effects of capital flow liberalization and presents estimates of the effects of such policies on Chinese macroeconomic performance.

Second, controls of cross-border finance were widely applied in the Nordics. Aspects of trade finance were liberalized first, while the lifting of capital controls was largely carried out only in the second half of the 1980s. The situation is somewhat similar in China today: Juan in increasingly used in trade finance and direct investment in and out is partly liberalized, but many other dimensions of cross-border capital flows are controlled.

One general development in the Nordics in the 1970s and 1980s was that, the system of tight controls and financial repression gradually started to leak as the economies became more internationalized and the international operations of the biggest companies grew in scale. This kind of development creates strong pressures on the regulated financial system, so that the need for liberalization becomes more and more apparent. There are indications of this kind of development in China as only less than 40% of new loans to businesses came *via* banks and about 25% in the form of new instruments mediated by banks (BOFIT Weekly, January 18, 2013).

An important lesson from the Nordic cases has been that the liberalization of the financial system is a much more encompassing development than just technical lifting of the different controls on the system. It is important that all the parties involved understand the need for changing ways of thinking and business practices. Traditional ways of thinking can become a trap, which should be avoided. Market-based financial systems are inherently less controllable and thus, market participants must prepare for new risks and uncertainties that were absent in a system of financial repression. Risk management and supervision become very important.

Changes in the strategies of banks and other institutions in response to the free market environment can be hugely influential for the development of the financial system. This is one aspect where, for example, Finnish banks misjudged the new competitive environment. The aggressive strategies of some banks had very adverse longer term consequences, which were not foreseen in advance. A competitive financial system will affect the effectiveness of banks and other institutions. This can be one of the benefits of the liberalization, but the institutions must be ready to carry out the efficiency enhancing changes. It is important that the different players in the financial system understand the extent and consequences of the reforms, so that they can cope well in the new business setting. Strengthening of the capital base of banks and reforms of their supervisory systems are important steps to make in advance of the major liberalization steps.

The Nordic countries tried to maintain fixed exchange rates while they moved to market-based financial systems. This is very difficult once cross-border capital flows are largely free.

First, free flows and market-based finance imply the impossible trinity. One cannot simultaneously control domestic finance, interest rates and the exchange rate of the country's currency. In Nordic countries, there were attempts to influence domestic interest rates even after freeing of capital movements, which led to adverse outcomes as the interest rate differential between domestic and foreign rates widened accelerating the inflow of foreign finance. The Nordic countries were mostly facing current account deficits at the time of liberalizations, so there were pressures for weakening of their currencies. In the case of China, it is difficult to predict the direction of movement of the exchange rate if it were made free now. There might well be appreciation pressures for a floating renminbi.

A second lesson about free capital flows and a fixed exchanges rate is that the rate can become subject to speculative pressures, so that defense of the rate can be costly. This latter is, however, not likely to be an issue for China, given that its foreign exchange reserves are very large. Nevertheless, one may contemplate freeing of the exchange rate ahead of the main liberalization moves.

Good timing of the liberalization is crucial and mistakes in this respect can be one reason for an excessive boom and possible financial crisis. As discussed, this problem emerged for Finland, Norway and Sweden, whereas, Denmark avoided a large-scale crisis as it took steps of liberalization earlier. It is important to try to time the main parts of the liberalization so as to avoid a business-cycle upswing.

A related issue is the order of the liberalization, in particular between domestic and international aspects. It is a common view that domestic financial markets should be liberalized first, as then the domestic system can better withstand pressures from abroad. One could in principle envisage a reverse order, but one must then be prepared to have rapid reforms in the domestic system, should pressures emerge. It appears at present that China is moving faster with liberalization of capital flows than, for example, in freeing the interest rates charged by banks and in allowing foreign competition in banking. The Nordic countries tried to follow a gradual and cautious approach in their financial deregulation processes. This is a common way to proceed, though there have also been instances where the liberalization has proceeded fast with a "big bang." A case in point is United Kingdom in the late 1970s.

One final consideration for the Chinese liberalization process stems for the sheer size of its economy. The reforms in China will have international repercussions on other countries and other countries may well take policy decisions in response to the Chinese reforms. Here Nordic liberalizations cannot offer any guidance as the countries were and are small even as a group.

References

Abilgren, K (2007). Financial liberalization and credit dynamics in Denmark in the post World War II period. Danmark's National bank, Working Papers No. 47, October. Available at http://www.nationalbanken.dk/C1256BE9004-F6416/side/461C0281C902AFA9C125736E003820C9/$file/2007_Branche_DNWP_47.PDF.

Domaç, I and MSM Peria (2003). Banking crises and exchange rate regimes: Is there a link? *Journal of International Economics*, 61(1), 41–72.

Drees, B and C Pazarbaşioğlu (1998). The Nordic banking crisis: Pitfalls in financial liberalization. IMF Occasional Paper No. 161.

Dooley, MP (1995). A survey of academic literature on controls over international capital transactions. NBER Working Paper No. 5352, November.

Edey, M and K Hviding (1995). An assessment of financial reform in OECD countries. Economics Department Working Paper No. 154, January. OECD Paris.

Englund, P (1999). The Swedish banking crisis: Roots and consequences. *Oxford Review of Economic Policy*, 15(3), 80–97.

Englund, P and V Vihriälä (2009). Financial crises in Finland and Sweden: Similar but not quite the same. In Jonung, L, J Kiander and P Vartia (eds.), *The Great Financial Crisis in Finland and Sweden*, pp. 71–130. Cheltenham: Edward Elgar.

Gourinchas, P-O, R Valdés, O Landerretche, E Talvi and AV Banerjee (2001). Lending booms: Latin America and the world. *Economia*, 1, 47–99.

Honkapohja, S (2009). The 1990s financial crises in Nordic countries. Bank of Finland, Discussion Papers No. 5/2009, January. Available at http://ssrn.com/abstract=1427260 or http://dx.doi.org/10.2139/ssrn.1427260.

Honkapohja, S and E Koskela (1999). The economic crisis of the 1990s in Finland. *Economic Policy*, 14(29), 399–436.

Honkapohja, S, E Koskela, W Leibfritz and R Uusitalo (2008). *Economic Prosperity Recaptured: The Finnish Path from Crisis to Fast Growth*. Cambridge, MA: MIT Press.

Jeanne, O, A Subramanian and J Williamson (2012). *Who Needs to Open the Capital Account?* Washington, DC: Peterson Institute for International Affairs.

Johansson, AC (2012). Financial repression and China's economic imbalances. CERC Working Paper No. 22, April. Stockholm School of Economics.

Jonung, L, J Kiander and P Vartia (2009). The great financial crisis in Finland and Sweden: The dynamics of boom, bust and recovery. In Jonung, L, J Kiander and P Vartia (eds.), *The Great Financial Crisis in Finland and Sweden*, pp. 19–70. Cheltenham: Edward Elgar.

Korinek, A (2011). The new economics of capital controls imposed for prudential reasons. IMF Working Paper No. 11/298, December. Available at http://www.imf.org/external/pubs/ft/wp/2011/wp11298.pdf.

Prasad, ES and R Rajan (2008). A pragmatic approach to capital account liberalization. NBER Working Paper No. 14051, June.

Rautava, J (1994). The Finnish experience with financial market liberalization: Some lessons for economies in transition. In Bonin, JP and IP Székely (eds.), *The Development and Reform of Financial systems in Central and Eastern Europe*, pp. 196–213. Cheltenham: Edward Elgar.

Reinhard, CM and KS Rogoff (2008). Is the 2007 US sub-prime financial crisis so different? An international historical comparison. *American Economic Review*, 98(2), 339–344.

Reinhard, CM and KS Rogoff (2009). *This Time Is Different, Eight Centuries of Financial Folly*. Princeton, NJ: Princeton University Press.

Sedik, TS and T Sun (2012). Effects of capital flow liberalization — What is the evidence from recent experiences of emerging market economies? IMF Working Paper No. WP/12/275, November.

Steigum, E (2004). Financial deregulation with a fixed exchange rate: Lessons from Norway's boom-bust cycle and banking crisis. In More, TG, JA Solheim and B Vale (eds.), *The Norwegian Banking Crisis*, pp. 23–75. Norges Banks Skriftserie/Occasional Papers No. 33, May.

Steigum, E (2009). The boom and bust cycle in Norway. In Jonung, L, J Kiander and P Vartia (eds.), *The Great Financial Crisis in Finland and Sweden*, pp. 202–244. Cheltenham: Edward Elgar.

Tarkka, J (2009). Financial regulation in Finland from the 1950s until the 1980s. Stability at what price? In Gigliobianco, A and G Toniolo (eds.), *Financial Market Regulation in the Wake of Financial Crises: The Historical Experience*. Bancad'Italia Workshops and Conferences, Vol. 1, November.

Vastrup, C (2009). How did Denmark avoid a banking crisis? In Jonung, L, J Kiander and P Vartia (eds.), *The Great Financial Crisis in Finland and Sweden*, pp. 245–264. Cheltenham: Edward Elgar.

Vives, X (2000). Lessons from European banking liberalization and integration. In Claessens, S and M Jansen (eds.), *The Internationalization of Financial Services*, pp. 177–198. Alphen, the Netherlands: Kluwer Law International.

Chapter 5

Asian Financial Markets and Financial Internationalization in China

Kiyohiko G. Nishimura

Introduction

The objective of this chapter is to make some useful suggestions to help guide the deepening of the internationalization of China's financial markets. I begin by examining the current state of Asian financial markets: pointing out the improvements in their market structure since the Asian financial crisis, and the remaining vulnerability and shortcomings in the system. I identify five challenges:

(1) still lingering double mismatch of currency and maturity (especially maturity),
(2) bank-centered financial system with underdeveloped derivatives and securitization and high reliance of foreign financial institutions,
(3) necessity of developing reliable inter-bank collateralized transactions markets,
(4) necessity of developing new financial innovations suitable for changing economic conditions in Asia, especially with respect to rapidly ageing population, and
(5) financial inclusion.

Then, taking account of these characteristics of Asian financial markets, which also hold for the Chinese markets, I examine the current discussion on financial internationalization in China, often summarized in the phrase of "renminbi internationalization." Despite a remarkable increase in trade settlements in renminbi and the policies of the Chinese authorities encouraging them, I find severe limitation to the internationalization of renminbi through this way. The fundamental obstacle of the renminbi internationalization is the lack of free capital flow and guaranteed full convertibility. In fact, transaction costs, payments and settlement costs, and all other costs associated with fund flows generated by trades are related to the degree of openness of capital markets and their independence from non-market interference. Current attempts to have offshore markets to promote direct exchange between renminbi and other currencies are not likely to get extra miles for renminbi to lead to a quantum jump into internationalization.

Financial Markets in Asia: Their Characteristics and Vulnerabilities

Two financial crises and improved market structure

In the past two decades, Asian economies have experienced two financial crises: the Asian currency crisis of the late 1990s, and the recent global financial crisis. However, the impact of these crises was very different: severe in the former, and relatively mild in the latter. The difference is partly due to the improved resiliency of Asian financial markets, enhanced by cooperation among the governments and central banks of the region and its vicinity.

The Asian currency crisis highlighted the structural vulnerabilities in the region's economies: first, corporate finance remained highly dependent on banks, and second, there was the double-mismatch of currency and maturity in the region's financial sector, especially banks. As a result, Asian countries were vulnerable to sudden changes in global financial markets and their abundant savings were not being mobilized effectively within the region.

To rectify the problem of overdependence on banks, The Executives' Meeting of East Asia and Pacific Central Banks (EMEAP), consisting of eleven central banks and monetary authorities in the region, started the Asian Bond Fund (ABF) initiative to promote local-currency bond markets, a project giving members the opportunity to invest in bonds in Asia. In parallel, the governments of ASEAN + 3 member countries are now implementing the Asian Bond

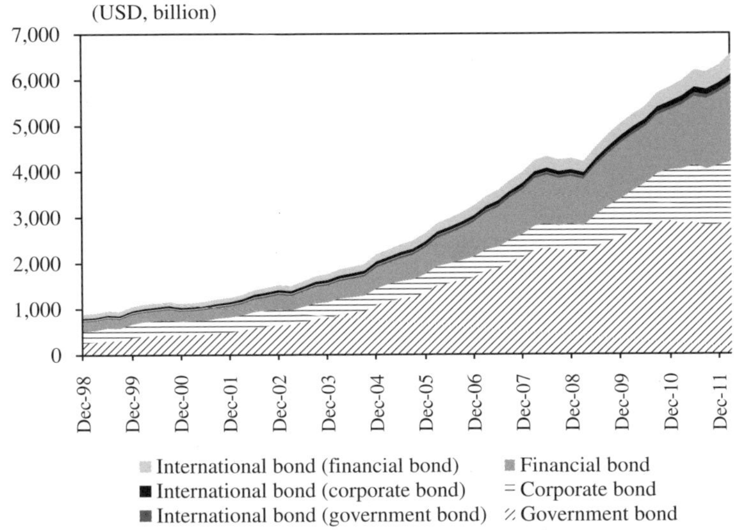

Figure 1. Size of bond markets: Asia (ex. Japan).

Notes:

- Asia is the aggregate of China (CN), Taiwan (TP), Hong Kong, (HK), Indonesia (ID), Malaysia (MY), Philippines (PH), Singapore (SG), Korea (KR), and Thailand (TH).
- Government bond, corporate bond and financial bond are local currency bonds issued by local residents. International bonds (offshore) are the aggregate of the foreign currency bonds issued by local residents and the bonds (both local/foreign currency) issued by non-residents.

Sources: IMF, BIS.

Market Initiative (ABMI) to foster deregulation and to create an environment conducive to investment. The results have been impressive: the local-currency bond markets in Asia have developed significantly, as shown in Figure 1, in terms of amount outstanding for both government and corporate bonds. The share of Asian-currency bonds in global bond markets increased from 2.1% at the end of 1996 to 8.4% at the end of 2011, although the improvement is rather uneven (Figure 2). What is remarkable here is that the presence of foreign investors in a number of local-currency bond markets in Asia is rapidly increasing, as shown in Figure 3. This can be attributed to the enhancement of the market infrastructure of these economies, not just because of improvements in the risk/return profile of these

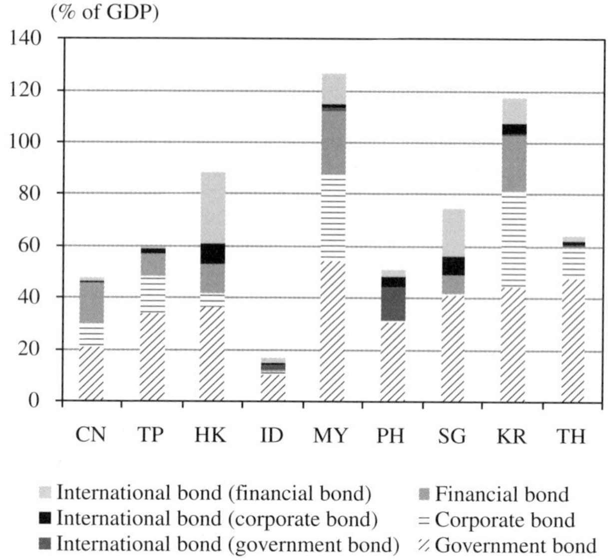

Figure 2. Comparison between jurisdictions.

Note 1. Asia is the aggregate of China (CN), Taiwan (TP), Hong Kong, (HK), Indonesia (ID), Malaysia (MY), Philippines (PH), Singapore (SG), Korea (KR), and Thailand (TH).

Note 2. Government bond, corporate bond and financial bond are local currency bonds issued by local residents. International bonds (offshore) are the aggregate of the foreign currency bonds issued by local residents and the bonds (both local/foreign currency) issued by non-residents.

Sources: IMF, BIS.

bonds in terms of the creditworthiness of the issuers and the relatively higher yields of the papers.

Moreover, there has also been a significant improvement in the problem of currency mismatch. The share of foreign lenders' loans denominated in local currencies has increased remarkably, as shown in Figure 3, although the maturities of such loans are still one year or shorter (which will be discussed later). It is worth mentioning here that some countries have implemented measures explicitly to reduce the mismatch. A case in point is the Republic of Korea which obliges local banks to hold a certain proportion of short-term foreign currency assets against short-term foreign currency debt.

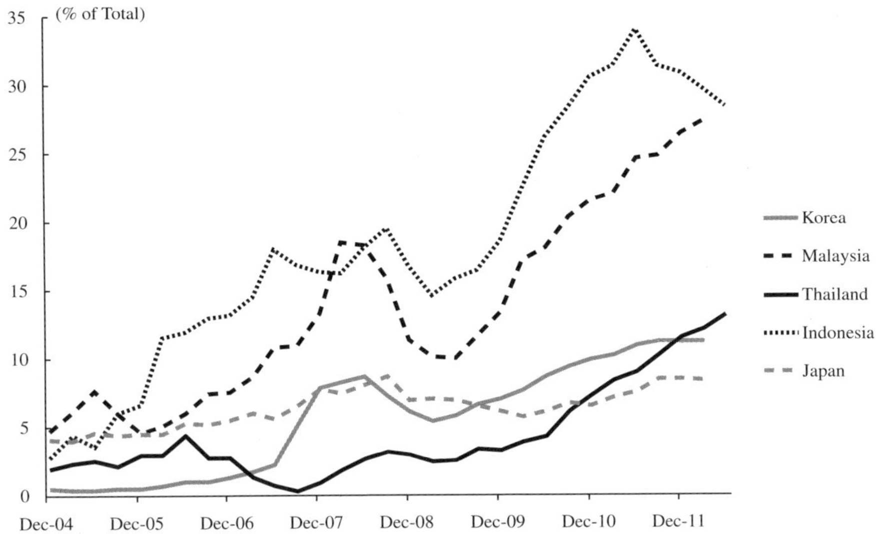

Figure 3. Foreign holding in local-currency government bonds.

Note: The percentage in local currency government bonds held by foreign investors relative to the amount of local-currency government bonds outstanding in a specific market.

Source: ADB.

The Asian economies have weathered a series of shocks starting from the bankruptcy of Lehman Brothers to the European debt crisis of today. The improved market structure described has contributed to this performance, together with good economic fundamentals and the relatively plain business models of banks in Asia.

Challenges to develop well-functioned financial markets with variety and depth

Many challenges, however, remain to make Asia (except Japan) as a region or a country in particular become a truly internationalized financial center. Although there have been improvements in some areas, as I have mentioned, I would like to raise the following four challenges to develop well-functioned financial markets with variety and depth found in developed regions. The first two are old problems that still remain, and the remaining three are relatively new challenges.

(1) *To solve double-mismatch of currency and maturity*

The first is about the double-mismatch of currency and maturity in the banking sector, especially maturity mismatch. As I have already mentioned, this problem was identified in the wake of the Asian financial crisis of 1997. When banks finance short-term money in foreign currencies, swap it to local currency, and invest in long-term domestic assets, they incur risks both in terms of currency and maturity. For some external reasons, if short-term foreign currency funding becomes difficult in the market, banks tend to face funding problems. Moreover, if their local currency depreciates significantly at the same time, they also encounter an increase in unhedged foreign currency liabilities in terms of local currency, and eventually have to deal with the deterioration of their balance sheets. In fact, when Lehman Brothers collapsed, such vulnerability emerged in some Asian economies.

This structural issue has not changed fundamentally in the past 10 years. As shown in Figure 4, cross-border credit denominated in local currencies from foreign banks to local residents has grown rapidly in the 2000s. However, their reliance on foreign currencies is still large compared with developed regions. Moreover, fundamental vulnerability continues to be found with respect to maturity mismatch as shown in Figure 5, although the mismatch has reportedly been improving to some extent.[1]

(2) *To change bank-centered financial structure and high reliance on foreign institutions*

Second, the bank-centered structure of the financial intermediary function also remains basically unchanged. Although it has gradually declined in some jurisdictions in recent years, the reliance of firms on indirect financing is still structurally high. Given this financing structure, when a large negative shock hits financial institutions, non-financial corporations are likely to find it hard to get a smooth debt

[1] In the BIS statistics on cross-border credit outstanding by maturity, it is not evident that borrowing of less than one-year maturity has been decreasing. However, the authorities report the considerable reduction in those of very short-term maturities.

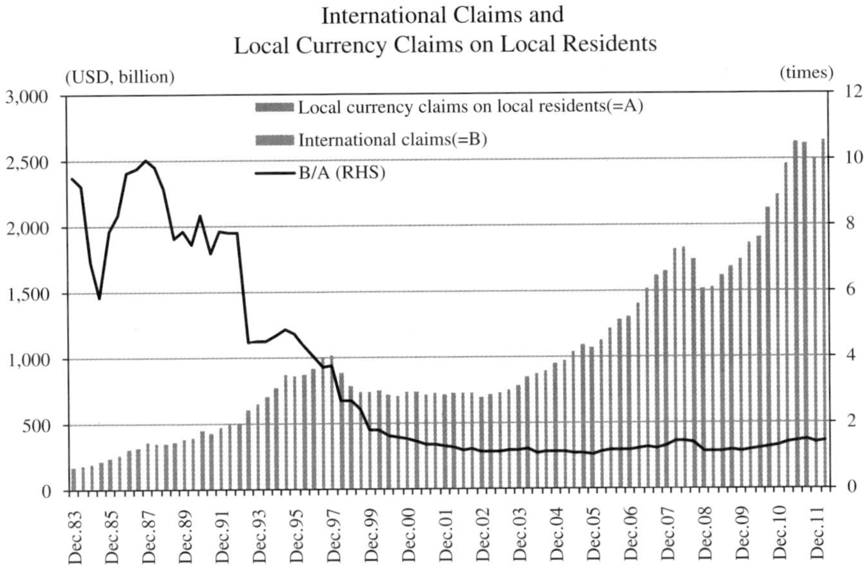

Figure 4. Double mismatch (1) currency.

Notes:

- Local Currency Claims are the local currency denominated claims held by local branches/subsidiaries of foreign banks on residents.
- International Claims are the claims (denominated mainly in foreign currencies) held by foreign banks on residents and the foreign currency denominated claims held by local branches/subsidiaries of foreign banks on residents.
- All figures are the aggregate of China, Hong Kong, Taiwan, Korea, Singapore, Malaysia, Indonesia, Thailand, and Philippines. Data from 1983 to 1999 is semi-annual, quarterly thereafter.

Source: BIS Consolidated Banking Statistics.

finance from these financial institutions, almost regardless of these non-financial corporation's financial soundness.

To put it in a different perspective, the Asian financial sector remains insufficient both in terms of its variety and its depth, in contrast with the strength of its non-financial sectors, especially manufacturing. High reliance on bank finance implies the underdevelopment of regional corporate bond markets. It is also often mentioned that the immature local derivatives market makes appropriate risk-taking transactions difficult, as risk-hedging instruments are limited

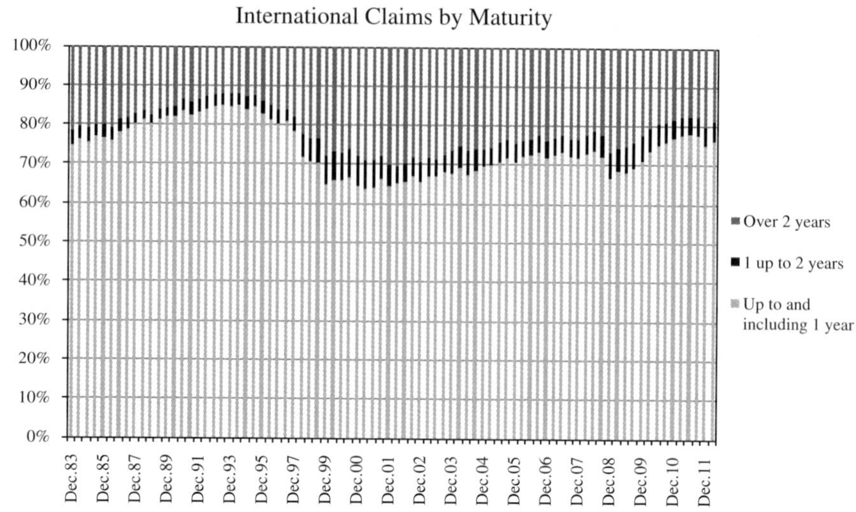

Figure 5. Double mismatch (2) maturity.

Notes:

- Local Currency Claims are the local currency denominated claims held by local branches/subsidiaries of foreign banks on residents.
- International Claims are the claims (denominated mainly in foreign currencies) held by foreign banks on residents and the foreign currency denominated claims held by local branches/subsidiaries of foreign banks on residents.
- All figures are the aggregate of China, Hong Kong, Taiwan, Korea, Singapore, Malaysia, Indonesia, Thailand, and Philippines. Data from 1983 to 1999 is semi-annual, quarterly thereafter.

Source: BIS Consolidated Banking Statistics.

(Figure 6). Moreover, owing to less-developed securitization markets in the region, Asian economies do not sufficiently enjoy the merits of the securitization schemes that attract a variety of investors depending on their risk-taking capacities (Figure 7).

From a wider perspective, there is still the issue of scant investment opportunities in Asian local currencies. Abundant savings in Asia have not been invested sufficiently within the region, and have thus, eventually been invested outside the region, such as in bonds in the United States and developed Europe.

Moreover, Asian region's funding relies heavily on foreign financial institutions. For example, in the areas of project finance and

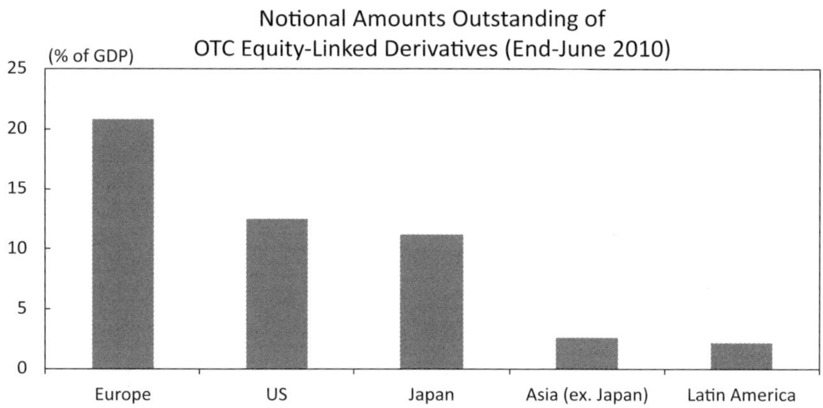

Figure 6. Underdeveloped derivatives market.

Note: 2009 GDP data is used for Cuba and North Korea. GDP data of Estonia, Bolivia, Colombia, Guatemala, Suriname, Cambodia, Fiji, Laos, Maldives, Myanmar, Nepal, and Papua New Guinea are estimates. GDP data of Latin America do not include the Falkland Islands (Islas Malvinas).

Source: BIS Triennial Central Bank Survey 2010; Bloomberg; IMF World Economic Outlook Database, September 2011; United Nations.

		Asia (ex. Japan)	Japan
% Change in Newly Issued Amount from 2006 to 2011			
	Corporate Bonds	376.4%	25.0%
	Securitized Products	-10.7%	9.5%
Securitized Products / Corporate Bonds (Newly Issued Amount in 2011)		3.5%	28.7%

Figure 7. Underdeveloped securitization market.

Source: Dealogic DCM Analytics.

trade finance, the Asian region has continued to depend considerably on foreign financial institutions, particularly European banks. In fact, in the wake of the European sovereign debt problem, net capital outflows were observed from August to December in 2011, except in October. Recent data suggests that capital flows returned to the region in January. As such, Asian financial markets have suffered from high volatility caused by the development of global capital flows, which is more or less the same problem they experienced in the Asian financial crisis. The background to this is that the market infrastructures, such as those of bond markets, remain less developed. Although the Asian bond market has certainly been developing as mentioned earlier, the corporate bond market, in particular, remains limited in its depth and liquidity.[2]

(3) *To develop reliable inter-bank collateralized transactions markets*

Third, a growing importance should be properly emphasized of reliable inter-bank collateralized transactions markets, including the repurchase agreement of securities, in order to develop deep and resilient financial markets. Short of a full blown crisis, but still relatively strained conditions such as found in the current European debt problem, market participants tend to prefer collateralized to uncollateralized transactions, when counterparty risks are strongly recognized among them. This indicates the utmost importance of having a solid market foundation of eligible bond transactions in order to secure stable financial transactions, regardless of rain or shine in financial conditions. In this regard, the cross-border collateral arrangement (CBCA) made between the Bank of Japan and the Bank of Thailand in November 2012, has the potential to be expanded throughout Asia. In fact, at almost the same time, a CBCA was announced between the Bank Negara Malaysia and the Monetary Authority of Singapore. Meanwhile, the EMEAP formed an action group, and has been discussing the promotion of CBCAs within the region.

[2]In Japan, although the amount outstanding of corporate bonds has been increasing, the market size continues to be limited compared to that of government bonds, and we have to admit that the market liquidity is low. There are also a limited number of issuances of corporate bonds with non-investment grades, which has long been an issue in Japan. Against this background, market participants established the "Forum on the Activation of Corporate Bond Market," and have been discussing a number of ways in which the market may be improved. Moreover, as the issuance of securitized products has stagnated since its peak in fiscal year 2006, we need to revitalize the securitization market as well.

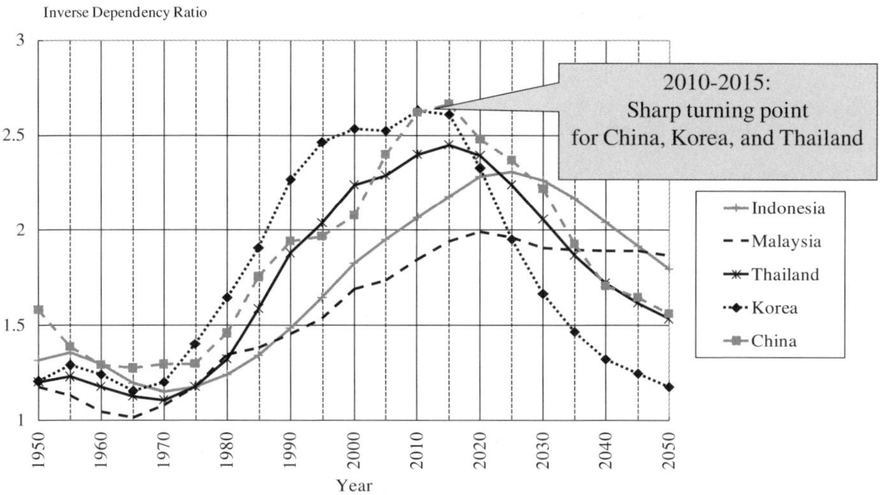

Figure 8. From population "bonus" to "onus".

Note: Inverse dependency ratio is the ratio of working-age population to the rest. This ratio shows how many people of working age have to provide for one dependent person.

Source: United Nations World Population Prospects: The 2010 Revision Population Database.

(4) *To foster financial innovation*

The fourth challenge is to develop innovative financial products, appropriate for an aging population in the region. In Asia, the population is aging at a steady but faster pace, not only in Japan but also in other economies such as China, Korea, and Thailand (Figure 8). Financial innovation is therefore essential to offer a flexible variety of enhanced financial products appropriate to the particular stage in the life cycle of the population. In this regard, the development of securitization seems a key factor. Although securitization, especially in its complex forms, has suffered from a negative image since the Lehman shock, simple, plain-vanilla type securitization products may contribute to the realization of appropriate risk-adjusted returns on financial transactions including lending, leading to more active operations of financial institutions. Moreover, as the credit intermediary channel becomes multi-layered to complement conventional lending, the risk tolerance of the financial system would be enhanced through risk diversification. Thus, it is important to "reinstall" useful securitization technologies into the system.

(5) *To enhance financial inclusion*

The fifth challenge is financial inclusion. From the perspective of developing deep financial markets, it is also important to improve infrastructures so that more of the world's population has access to financial services. There are reportedly more than 2.5 billion adults who are excluded from accessing financial services, and also tens of millions of small enterprises that are facing serious financing problems. Asia is no exception. In fact, meanwhile, there are some jurisdictions in Asia that rely significantly on so-called micro-finance. Micro-finance is indispensable particularly for the sustainable growth of emerging markets and developing economies, and as such has been a main agenda item of the G-20.

There is, however, one caveat. The main agents of micro-finance are non-bank financial institutions that, unlike banks, are not tightly supervised by the authorities, but which, like banks, take deposits and provide credit to customers. This means that it could become a risk factor in the financial system, if the market share of loans and deposits by micro-finance agents becomes non-negligible.

Financial Internationalization in China

There has been much discussion about financial internationalization in China, especially, with respect to the recent development of "renminbi internationalization," both in trade and financial data and policy discussion.

Generally speaking, the internationalization of a currency indicates that its settlement, calculation, and value-storage functions have expanded beyond a certain jurisdiction. To maintain these functions fully, the full convertibility of currency is always guaranteed, capital movements are liberalized, the payments and settlement system is established well to avoid various risks and international customs such as commercial contracts are adhered to. In other words, if these fundamental conditions are breached, or altered artificially or politically, true financial internationalization cannot be realized.

New kid on the block — Renminbi on the rise, but severe limitation persists

From this point of view, it is worthwhile looking at the recent development of so-called renminbi internationalization. In recent years, we have observed

(1) an increase in renminbi-denominated trade settlements,
(2) the establishment of an offshore renminbi market, and
(3) the expansion of renminbi-denominated financial products in Hong Kong.
(4) In addition, some central banks and monetary authorities in emerging markets and developing economies have recently announced the inclusion of the renminbi in their foreign currency reserves.

As such, the renminbi has been used increasingly in cross-border financial transactions, attracting greater attention from all over the world.

In particular, the Chinese authorities began taking steps towards currency internationalization by several attempts to improve the renminbi's settlement function. The Chinese authorities intended to reduce Chinese firms' excessive reliance on the US dollar in their trade settlements, and to mitigate the foreign exchange risks of huge US dollar holdings in the corporate and government sectors, as the impact of the Lehman shock spread throughout the global financial system.

Cross-border trade settlements in renminbi first started in July 2009 as a trial across a limited region, namely between 365 designated firms in the city of Shanghai and four cities of Canton Prefecture and ASEAN, Hong Kong, and Macau. The amount has since expanded to record just under RMB 600 billion (about JPY 7 trillion) in the third quarter of 2011 (Figure 9).

However, this remarkable increase in trade settlements does not guarantee internationalization of renminbi automatically. On the contrary, severe limitation persists that prevent further qualitative reap of renminbi toward internationalization. It should be noted that in order to make renminbi internationalized, firstly it should flow

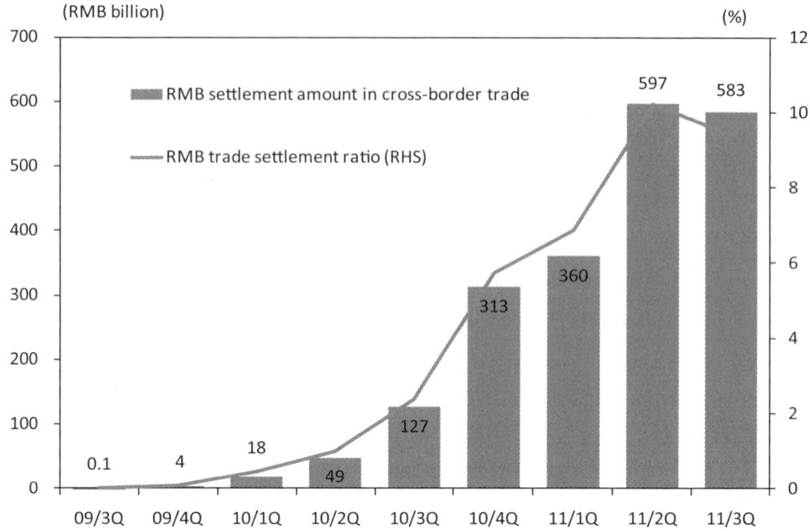

Figure 9. RMB trade settlement.

Source: People's Bank of China.

out of China, secondly it should find some investment opportunities offshore, and finally it should go back to China. This means that internationalization is not simply to use renminbi as international medium of exchange. It entails capital movement as its essential part.

In contrast, the development intended by China means simply that we can use renminbi for cross-border financial transactions that used to be settled only in foreign currencies, reducing exchange rate risks in foreign currency-mediated transactions. In particular, the development has not contributed significantly to the mitigation of capital regulations. While the volume of renminbi has increased in offshore markets as it is employed in cross-border trade settlements, there remains very limited room for offshore renminbi to flow back to the mainland under the current strict capital regulations imposed by the Chinese authorities.

There has been a growing need for developing offshore renminbi markets to meet the demand of agents who hold renminbi outside the mainland and wish to invest them in the market. In fact, the Hong Kong offshore market has been playing a major role in absorbing such

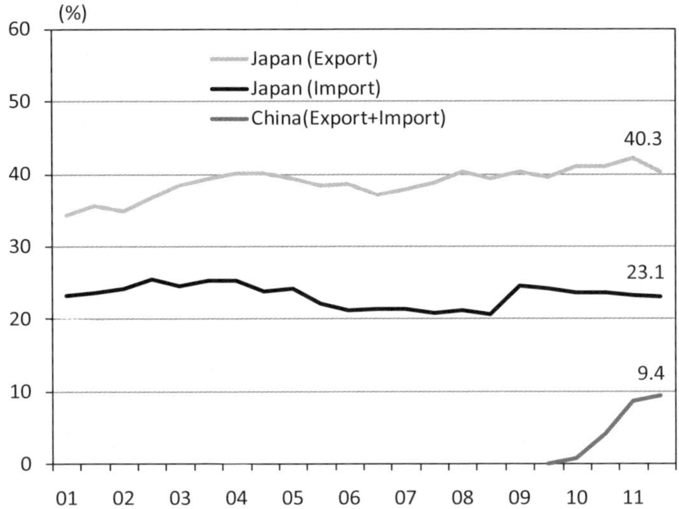

Figure 10. Local currency trade settlement ratio: Japanese yen and Chinese renminbi.

Note: Latest figure of China is 2011/3Q.

Source: Ministry of Finance Japan, People's Bank of China, National Bureau of Statistics of China.

offshore renminbi liquidity. Unlike the mainland markets, which are heavily regulated and whose prices do not reflect market participants' financial conditions as vividly as developed economies' markets, these unregulated or loosely regulated offshore markets reflect market participants' conditions rather well. However, it should be kept in mind that if one of closely connected markets are heavily regulated and inflexible, the other, which is not regulated and flexible, bears burden of adjustment of both markets and thus becomes overly volatile. This is a classic example of Le Chatelier's Principle expounded by Paul Samuelson. Thus, although unregulated Hong Kong offshore market provides useful market information, it still reflects some distortion in the heavily regulated mainland markets.

Thus, it would be implausible to assume that renminbi "internationalization" will be further developed without significant capital-flow deregulation. In fact, the current strict regulations on capital inflows to the mainland are gradually become an obstacle to the further development of offshore renminbi markets themselves.

The need for issuance of renminbi-denominated bonds, so-called dim-sum bonds, is after all limited. In the Hong Kong renminbi offshore market, the amount outstanding of issuance of dim-sum bonds is currently around RMB 70 billion, which is much smaller than renminbi-denominated deposits of about RMB 600 billion. If China wishes to promote further the internationalization of the renminbi, it may be necessary to address the issue of capital account liberalization.

The new initiative: Offshore markets in addition to Hong Kong

Let me now confine my focus solely on exchange risk reduction that Chinese authorities have in mind, and examine whether the attempt works well. In fact, the amount of trade between Japan and China, the two economic giants in Asia, has expanded by 2.5 times since 2001, reaching about JPY 26.5 trillion in 2010. During the same period, the number of firms that have extended their operations from Japan to China has increased by 1.5 times to about 22,000. However, the amount of trade settlements denominated in either yen or renminbi is very limited (Figure 11). Taking into consideration the long and profound ties between the two countries, as well as their importance to Asian regional trade, mitigating foreign exchange risks incurred by exporters and importers, and reducing their transaction costs, by promoting trade settlements denominated in both currencies would have considerable significance.

Currently, the US dollar is generally used as the intermediary currency when conducting currency transactions between yen and renminbi on foreign exchange markets. As a result, the price of the yen and renminbi is determined by the cross-currency rate of yen–US dollar and renminbi–US dollar, thereby requiring US dollar settlements. If a direct exchange market between the yen and renminbi is developed and has a certain degree of liquidity, one benefit will be a reduction in transaction costs, as the price will be set directly without the US dollar as intermediary. Moreover, without settlements in US dollars, there is also the merit of a reduction in currency settlement risks for financial institutions. As such, the development of financial

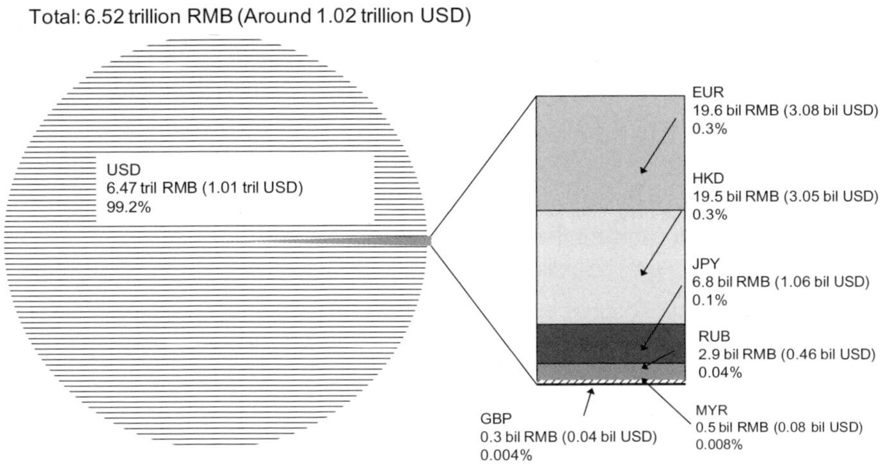

Figure 11. Direct exchange market between JPY and RMB: Trade amount at Shanghai inter-bank spot FX market (RMB/FX).

Note: Australian Dollar and Canadian Dollar started to be traded against RMB in November 2011.

Source: Peoples Bank of China, "China monetary policy report," 2011/3Q.

and foreign exchange markets denominated in yen and renminbi is an important issue for financial stability, not only for Japan and China but also for the rest of Asia.[3]

Although at surface direct exchange between the yen and renminbi seems very attractive in many ways, thorough examination suggests it is not so obvious. What are at stake are various costs and risks associated with trading, payments and settlement. The well-functioned payments and settlement system of dollar (and yen) transactions enables payment versus payment settlements reducing

[3]The leaders of Japan and China agreed on December 25, 2011 to enhance financial transactions between the two countries, specifically through promoting the use of the yen and renminbi in cross-border transactions between the two countries, and in support for the development of direct exchange markets between the two currencies. These agreed areas will be mutually promoted by establishing the "Joint Working Group for Development of Japan–China Financial Markets." Similarly, on January 16, 2012, the Hong Kong Monetary Authority and HM Treasury of the United Kingdom announced the establishment of a forum with the aim of mutually promoting offshore renminbi operations between Hong Kong and London.

risk considerably, which is lacking in renminbi transactions. The cost of using dollar payments and settlement system is not large because they are mostly on the per-trade basis, and large-sum transactions are rule of the game. In contrast, renminbi transaction costs (i.e., spreads) are high in reality for large-sum transactions even if posted transaction costs are not so high. This is because the renminbi market is a thin market lacking liquidity.

Here again, the issue is not simply exchange rate risk reduction, but the broad structural problems of reducing payments and settlement risks, increasing liquidity (of which convertibility is the essential part), and reducing costs of moving capital in and out of mainland China. That is, the issue is ultimately full convertibility of currency and liberalization of capital flows.

It should be noted that the Chinese financial markets share most of the vulnerabilities and challenges with other Asian financial markets that has been explained in the previous section. So, it is understandable that the Chinese authorizes, having in mind, vulnerabilities of their own financial markets, are very cautious in liberalizing capital movement and in allowing the foreign exchange market to determine the renminbi–dollar and other exchange rates. They rather move through patchworks of the existing systems. However, if they really want renminbi internationalization, these patchworks cannot be added up to a consistent framework. Sooner or later, if they still seek for renminbi internationalization, the time will come to decide on whether to have a comprehensive reform to allow free capital movement and full convertibility.

Future synergy between renminbi and yen

On one hand, as China climbs up the ladder of development, the renminbi has steadily and increasingly been used in settlements outside the mainland. Depending on developments in the liberalization of capital transactions, the presence of the renminbi is expected to increase. On the other hand, the yen has already been used internationally as a currency that is always tradable and has a well-established settlement infrastructure, in line with the US dollar, euro, and British pound. Then, a natural question arises: in the wake of renminbi internationalization, what is the role of yen?

The yen and Japanese government bonds will have an important role to play in the process of developing financial and foreign exchange markets in Japan and China, and thus in the whole Asian region. In this sense, there should be synergy between renminbi and yen.

First, to develop highly-liquid and deep bond markets, price transparency in the market is indispensable, as is a stable risk-free yield curve as the basis for pricing (a yardstick). The improved market-based function of interest rates formation is also an essential factor for the development of risky product markets, including corporate bond markets, as well as for determining appropriate foreign exchange rates that reflect economic fundamentals. In Europe, German government bonds function as a benchmark not only for financial products in Germany but also for fixed income products traded in the rest of Europe. Currently in Asia, Japanese government bonds are a leading candidate to act as such a benchmark, as they are always stably priced, and promptly traded and settled. Moreover, their issuance volume is large enough, and their credit rating is reasonably high.

In addition, there has been remarkable progress in improving the financial infrastructure, including the payments and settlement system. The issuance of Japanese government bonds is the largest in the world, and there exists a well-developed local currency-denominated bond market. Moreover, the payments and settlement system for Japanese government bonds, operated by the Bank of Japan, is expected to be improved noticeably in a couple of years with respect to its capacity, availability, and connectedness to other systems. As a result, the Japanese government bond market has maintained its high liquidity. Liquidity is essential for collaterals. In the previous section, it was explained that to have developed collateralized transactions markets is one of the major challenges in Asian financial markets. In this regard, to promote cross-border collateral arrangements between other Asian neighbors is of utmost importance, with the use of such highly-liquid Japanese government bonds as an effective means.

Concluding Remarks

As China climbs up the ladder of economic development rapidly, the internationalization of Chinese financial markets will sooner or later become absolutely necessary if the Chinese authorities want to transform the Chinese economy from mostly cheap-labor manufacturing economy to a truly advanced industrial economy. Also, as explained in section "Financial Internationalization in China," it has been increasingly evident that current, gradual and piecemeal approaches of "internationalization," still keeping very heavy hands on capital flows, are not likely to have sizable impacts on the scope, pace, and range of much-needed financial internationalization. This is because internationalization needs a systematic approach, involving intertwined development in payments and settlement system, the variety and depth of financial markets, and the mutual trust of market participants including the authorities. The most fundamental of all is that there should be no arbitrary and abrupt intervention by the authorities, which may jeopardize the stable functioning of the market. In this regard, we need more systematic approach explicitly taking into consideration complicated and sometimes hidden interaction among financial market participants and infrastructures in order to enable effective liberalization of capital flows.

At the same time, however, the authorities should be aware existing vulnerabilities in the present financial market structure, as expounded in section " Financial markets in Asia: Their characteristics and vulnerabilities." For example, although I have emphasized the importance of financial innovations to meet changing economic conditions such as population ageing, many so-called "new innovations" are often not of this kind of truly new innovation but simply new disguise of old speculative instruments of dubious origins. In the environment that people expect a "new age of internationalization," such "new instruments" are likely to emerge which are destabilizing in the end. We find many examples of this kind in the past financial internationalization and liberalization around the world, including the Japanese experience of the pre-bubble period.[4]

[4]See Nishimura (2011).

Reference

Nishimura, KG (2011). Macro-prudential lessons from the financial crisis: A practioner's view. In Kawai, M and E Prasad (eds.), *Asian Perspectives on Financial Sector Reforms and Regulation*, pp. 180–195. Washington, DC: Brookings Institution Press.

Chapter 6

Tokyo's Ultimately Failed Bid for First Tier International Financial Center Status: Why Did It Fall Short and What Are the Lessons for Shanghai?

Huw McKay

Introduction

Tokyo may once have had the potential to become a dominant international financial center (hereafter, IFC) to rival New York and London. History tells us that this apparent potential was left unfulfilled, with Tokyo having settled down as a very important but not dominant centre for international financial activity. This chapter will consider why Tokyo's apparent bid to ascend to the very top tier of IFCs was ultimately unsuccessful. The experience of Tokyo, Japan contains many lessons for Shanghai, China.

In the period from the early 1970s to the mid-1980s, Tokyo acquired many of the necessary characteristics for achieving top tier IFC status, but not all of them — and it did not do so quickly enough for them to bear fruit and mature before the underlying support from the spectacular rise of the economy went into reverse. Tokyo had not yet achieved equivalent status to New York or London during Japan's late 1980s zenith. Then, as the Japanese economy, its financial system and real and financial asset markets began to struggle in the early 1990s, the gap widened considerably. By the time of

The views expressed in this paper are the author's personal opinions and should not be ascribed to the companies of the Westpac Group.

the banking crisis of the late 1990s, which occurred simultaneously with the Asian financial crisis and the rise of the euro as a reserve currency competitor for the US dollar, the first tier IFC opportunity was lost.

The fact that establishing Tokyo as a first tier IFC was never a super-ordinate goal of national economic policy until the middle 1990s — in other words, it was never seen as a goal that other national policy objectives should be subordinated to until it was too late, and even then, somewhat ambivalently[1] — prevented a strategic approach to maximizing the obvious potential inherent in its earlier bid. A holistic effort is required to overcome the inherent disadvantages of a "latecomer" with aspirations to join the first tier. With hindsight, we can see that Tokyo was neither a genuine scale competitor for New York (Japan was never going to be able to double US output per head levels to overcome the population differential and become the world's largest economy) or a genuine competitor for London in terms of the concentration of expertise and support services, with the associated economies of scale and scope available to financial services firms operating out of that location. Even so, there is more that could have been done, and earlier, to maximize Tokyo's chances before the economy slowed, if the "bid" was "active" rather than "passive." Shanghai's chances are better, when one takes the long view, as it will be the financial hub of the world's largest economy for most of the time between 2016 and the final third of the century.[2]

Besides these top level judgments, more specifically this chapter concludes that the most important fundamental elements that

[1] I am indebted to Chalongphob Sussangkarn, a seminar participant at the Asian Economic Panel meeting in Penang, Malaysia, commenting on a previous version of this research, who poignantly noted that bureaucracies express their ambivalence for an initiative by deferring decisions through the establishment of committees, working groups, expert panels and so forth. On this measure, Japan's ambivalence to the IFC goal can be read through the succession of official studies on yen internationalization, trade invoicing, the financial system's international competitiveness and the like, that spanned more than two decades of "further discussion."

[2] For a discussion of a number of scenarios on global growth and world output shares between the present and 2100, see McKay (2012).

prevented Tokyo from ascending to the top tier of IFCs were as follows:

(a) The failure of the Japanese yen to become a genuine competitor for the US dollar as an international vehicle currency prior to the introduction of the euro.
(b) The relative and absolute decline of the performance of the Japanese economy and its financial markets from the early 1990s, which prevented the gains of the 1970s and 1980s from continuing to compound positively.
(c) Various accidents of timing in the global economic landscape that worked to amplify the power of incumbency for London and New York and to limit the degree of relevance attached to Japan. Most fundamentally, the time between Japan operating as a closed, financially repressed system with weak internal competitive dynamics (up to the Bretton Woods breakdown) and its late 1980s window of opportunity was just too short for it to realistically compete in terms of maturity, depth and sophistication with the incumbents.

These conclusions are reached following a systematic examination of Tokyo's absolute and relative IFC *bona fides* against rigorous criteria. The continual emphasis on absolute and relative positions is due to the acknowledged persistence (path dependency) associated with first tier IFC (and vehicle currency) status. It is not enough to merely meet the criteria oneself. One must be strong enough to also displace incumbents and take market share away from them. History shows that Tokyo was unable to meet the relative challenge in the long run.

The initial task is to define the vital traits of top tier IFCs that are critical to that status. The second is to assess Tokyo's first tier IFC candidacy through time against this framework. The third task is to integrate this assessment with a discussion of the global macroeconomic and macro-financial developments that defined the last three decades of the 20th century.

Finally, we apply the lessons of the Tokyo, Japan experience to the future challenges of Shanghai, China in the IFC arena, with a modest aside on the South Korean model. In considering the import of these conclusions for Shanghai, I am at pains to place the IFC goal in the broader context of China's ultimate macroeconomic objectives, its current growth model and the structural legacies that derive from it, alongside an assessment of desirable alterations to that model as its industrialization drive matures.

The intermediate policy actions required of China to accommodate an ultimate objective of achieving first tier IFC status will be a challenge to many internal interests that benefit from the parameters of the current system. However, such moves are inherently complementary with China's acknowledged need for transition towards a new growth model that sustains growth in aggregate living standards in an environmentally conscious way while simultaneously promoting equality of income and opportunity (McKay and Song, 2013). The new model that arises must emphasize domestic absorption and efficient capital and resource allocation, at the expense of over-expansion of productive capacity and the pursuit of foreign market share. Establishing a super-ordinate national objective to raise Shanghai to first tier IFC status would highlight that the Chinese authorities believe that an open, internationally competitive and sophisticated financial system can play a prime role in channeling resources to their most efficient uses, alongside requisite efforts to reduce the factor market distortions that have created the internal and external imbalances that the new leadership is seeking to redress.

The conclusion is that Shanghai will be advantaged *vis-a-vis* Tokyo due to the likely future scale of China's economic and financial footprint which indicates that the renminbi has an excellent chance to become a genuine international vehicle currency at some point. On the other hand, Shanghai at present is extremely disadvantaged by a lack of indigenous expertise and experience in international finance, and some pronounced shortcomings across the vast majority of the soft infrastructure demanded of first tier IFCs. China, of course, has time on its side to build such expertise, as it will be the world's largest economy for at least the next two generations. Even so, the imperative for a new growth model is more urgent than that, and the IFC goal may usefully serve as a galvanizing force in the overall reform process, assisting policymakers to move forward with focus and resolve.

Characteristics of first tier IFCs

The features of first tier IFCs that are considered critical are the following:

1. Unrestricted capital and financial accounts, including flows of portfolio equity, portfolio debt and derivatives, loans and other finance. While this criterion can be softened if the global financial architecture is not consistent with it (such as at the height of the Bretton Woods era), it is not negotiable at times of free flowing capital, such as today or in the final third of the "long" 19th century.
2. A convertible, internationalized currency that is acceptable as a store of value, unit of account, a denominator for unrelated third party real economy and financial transactions (especially debt, Thimann, 2010) and is readily able to be hedged in liquid markets. In other words, the local money must serve as an international vehicle currency. London's current status may only weakly meet this definition, but as the world's major centre for foreign exchange trading with a 40% market share, the supply of vehicle currencies other than the pound available in London is more than ample. Even in the Bretton Woods era, when the pound was deposed by the dollar, the euro–dollar market centered on London, because the global banks were already there and so was the international expertise (Baker and Collins, 2005; Schenk, 2005). Further, with many more euro changing hands in foreign exchange deals in London than on the continent, it has once again shown an ability to leverage its IFC advantages into concrete market share gains.
3. A liquid market for anchor risk free assets in the home currency: for example, British Consuls, French Rentes, UK Gilts, US Treasury securities. This blends with the characteristics of the home currency in criterion 2 to achieve reserve currency status. A highly regarded[3] sovereign issuer is therefore essential. Note

[3]The term "regarded" is used here in preference to "rated," as mature markets for sovereign debt existed well before ratings agencies became embedded in the global financial system, and formal ratings actions tend to lag well behind investor sentiment toward a troubled issuer — or one who has improved its balance sheet sufficiently to warrant a

that Japan's foreign long-term credit rating first reached AAA in February 1975 (Standard and Poor's Financial Services, LLC 2012). It lost that status in February 2002 and is presently rated AA minus, three notches below the risk free rating.

The combination of characteristics 2 and 3 is powerful. This combination ensures that the minimum level of foreign interest required to become a dominant center for the conduct of international financial business is present.

Additional characteristics that aid the competitive advantage of first tier IFCs are:

4. A market making central bank-primary dealer complex in the key financing vehicles of the day — whether the discounting of bills of exchange, government securities on repo/reverse repo or commercial paper. This was one factor in London's continued dominance over New York as an IFC in the late 1900s, despite the US economy becoming the world's largest in 1870. Prior to the creation of the US Federal Reserve System in 1913, following the 1907 financial crisis, there was no equivalent to the Bank of England's willingness to discount sterling bills in London or the liquidity of the markets it bestrode (Eichengreen, 2011).
5. A broad variety of financial assets to cater for the appetites of a diverse domestic and international investor base. This tends to prioritize the development of non-bank, arm's length financing channels (direct equity and debt raisings principally). London long held an advantage over its competitors in this space, with public and private issuers alike favoring its highly developed capital markets.[4] Even today, British Law is used for a large proportion of international bond issuance.[5] However, fiscal dominance

re-valuing of its debt. For a similar reason, the presence of rating agencies is excluded from the criteria for IFCs above. They are an implicit element of the support services outlined in criterion 7.

[4]Recent evidence shows that Paris was an impressive international financial center that was not as far behind London as one might have supposed during the *belle epoque* (Esteves, 2011; Flandreau and Gallice, 2005). At the very least, it was a very creditable number two to London at a time when New York was yet to find its feet.

[5]This was recently highlighted in the negotiations over the Greek sovereign debt restructuring, where some of its bonds were issued under local law and some under British law, with the latter disallowing re-denomination of the security from the original issue currency if Greece had left the euro.

can undermine an IFC's status in this field. For instance, major wars have generally left combatant sovereigns seriously indebted. Financially repressive and/or inflationary policies are then pursued to deal with the sovereign debt problem. This has obvious negative implications for IFC status.

6. A broad variety of financial institutions to cater for diverse intermediation functions. These institutions will also have a global footprint. At the very least, an internationally competitive cluster of banking, insurance and funds management firms must be present. Depending upon the regulatory situation, banks may be universal in scope (the early 20th century New York model), or deposit gathering and securities business may be separated (the US from the 1930s until the late 1990s, the UK's savings versus merchant banking model). What is important is that global demands are met and pre-empted, not that one particular institutional model is in place.
7. A legal framework that is transparent and predictable. This goes hand-in-hand with an independent judiciary and political stability. Other support services such as accounting, IT, and specialist higher education offer economies of scale and scope to financial institutions that choose to base their activities in IFCs. In the 19th century, London offered further benefits of agglomeration through its position as the center for maritime logistics and commodity trading (insuring cargoes, the Baltic exchange for the brokering of freight, the London Bullion Market and the London Metals Exchange).
8. A regulatory framework that is seen as a credible check on excesses without stifling innovation. While this may seem to be an ambiguous factor — given the tendency of private institutions to gravitate to the lightest touch jurisdictions — it is lower tier IFCs that must compete for business through a regulatory race to the bottom, not first tier IFCs.
9. A demonstrated ability to consistently and transparently allocate large amounts of capital to productive uses. It is in this "perception" that the advantages of a large scale and globally recognized funds management industry become very clear. Not even immense scale (think of Japan Post's massive deposit

pool for instance) can overcome a perception of backwardness or opacity.

10. A dynamic and cosmopolitan living environment that will be attractive to the world's leading financial professionals.[6]

Vehicle currencies, IFCs & the yen

The most important shortfalls in Tokyo's first tier IFC bid were arguably those pertaining to criteria 2 and 3. Japan failed to reach critical mass in terms of non-resident demand for the yen as it was unable to denominate the majority of its own trade in its own currency, which meant it was not able to assume a full role as an international "vehicle currency" and instead remained dependent on the US dollar for a large proportion of its international transactions. Non-residents were therefore not lured to Japanese financial markets in significant numbers. Japan was somewhat late to the game in providing foreign investors with a "risk free" yen denominated fixed income asset — it first allowed non-resident access to AAA rated sovereign bonds under "modern" conditions in the mid 1970s, and these bonds ceased to be perceived "risk free" sometime in the mid to late 1990s.[7] That is a narrow window. The combination of these failures left the yen short of achieving true inner circle reserve currency status. That is despite its well acknowledged "safe haven" status due to Japan's position as a large international creditor and its role as an IMF special drawing rights currency since the basket's inception in July 1974 (International Monetary Fund, 2001, Table 18.4, p. 951).[8]

---

[6] I am indebted to Dr. Lin See-Yan, a discussant of a previous version of this research, for highlighting the importance of this qualitative factor in IFC competition.

[7] There are many aspects here. The liberalization of inflow, the move away from balanced budgets to build a sizeable bond stock, liberalizing the sales of bonds outside the original "syndicate" of domestic financial institutions, the allowance of secondary market sales and the upgrade to AAA by the global rating agencies.

[8] Not all nations with the ability to achieve inner circle reserve status desire to do so. The Germans in particular have displayed an historical ambivalence towards reserve currency status, acknowledging that embracing the implications of the "Triffin Dilemma" (Triffin, 1978) — that a global reserve currency must be prepared to run current account deficits to furnish international monetary liquidity — was inconsistent with the anti-inflationary ethos that was deeply ingrained in the national psyche by the damage done in the 1920s hyperinflations.

Beginning with the 1984 report of the bilateral US–Japan "Yen–Dollar Committee," there have been a number of official and academic studies on the matter of internationalizing the yen, internationalizing Japanese financial markets and the use of the yen as an invoicing currency in trade (see for example, Japanese Ministry of Finance, 1998, 1999, 2003; Oi *et al.*, 2003; Sato, 1999; Aramaki, 2006; Ito *et al.*, 2011). The literature on international currencies, choice of invoice currency, and the currency denomination of bond issuance has also flourished with the introduction of the euro, the weakness of the US dollar since 2002 and China's evolving exchange arrangements and financial liberalization program (Siegfried *et al.*, 2007; Goldberg and Tille, 2008; Auboin, 2012; Aramaki, 2006; Cui *et al.*, 2009; Yun, 2005; Camps, 2006; Cohen, 2005; McKay, 2007; Dobson and Masson, 2009; Flandreau and Jobst, 2009; Thimann, 2010; Peng and Shu, 2010; Eichengreen, 2011, 2012; Maziad and Kang, 2012).

Nobel Laureate Paul Krugman's classic article on vehicle currency choice in international exchange (1980), is central to any discussion in this field. Krugman illustrated that in the presence of transactions costs that are negatively related to scale, there will be room for only a very small number of vehicle currencies in the global economy. The zero sum nature of the vehicle currency domain means that the advantages of size will compound and leave just a few currencies able to offer the low transaction costs required: scale will beget scale. That predicts that incumbency is very powerful in the vehicle currency arena and that consequently a high level of persistence in the choice of vehicle currencies will be evident in international exchange. That echoes the thesis put forward in 1967 by financial historian Charles Kindleberger that "For better or worse — and opinions differ on this — the choice of which language and which currency is made not on merit, or moral worth, but on size" (Flandreau and Jobst, 2009, p. 1).

Importantly for the prospective challenger in the vehicle currency domain, Krugman's dynamics are symmetric. The theory predicts that once a process of market share loss for an incumbent is in train, for whatever reason, its market share can unravel quickly and potentially irreversibly. Any momentum in favor of a greater proportion of transactions being undertaken in the currency of a rising power can be an accelerant to yet more transactions, as costs decline. A policy focus on encouraging own currency denomination in trade can assist to set these wheels in motion.

It appears that Japan certainly once had some momentum in its favor on this front. The proportion of Japanese exports invoiced in the yen rose rapidly between 1970 and 1985, moving from trivial levels at the outset of the period to two-fifths of all sales in 1985 (Sato, 1999; Oi *et al.*, 2003, Figure 1). Noting that Japan's share of global exports of goods and services had been rising strongly since 1960 (from 3% in 1960 to 5.7% in 1970 to 8.4% in 1985, Figure 2), with an even more pronounced increase in the area of trade most likely to be denominated in the currency of the exporter — manufactures (Grassman, 1973; McKinnon, 1979, Figure 3). Between 1980 and 1985, Japan surpassed Germany and the United States to become the world's largest exporter of manufactured goods.

The impact of the Plaza Accord and the associated reorientation of traded and non-traded activity among the G3 economies saw Japan fall back behind Germany and the United States by 1990. It should not be a surprise therefore that 1985 was the high point for yen denomination of Japanese exports. A 35% to 40% home currency share in export invoicing, as experienced by Japan between 1985 and 2002, is relatively low for advanced countries. Other major

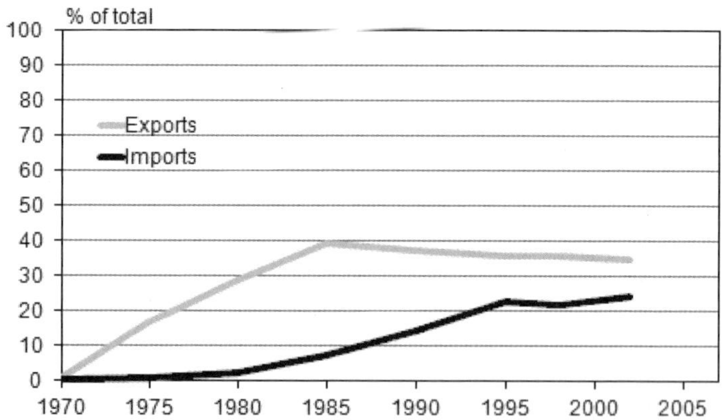

Figure 1. Share of Japanese trade invoiced in the yen.
Source: Sato (1999) and OI *et al.* (2003).

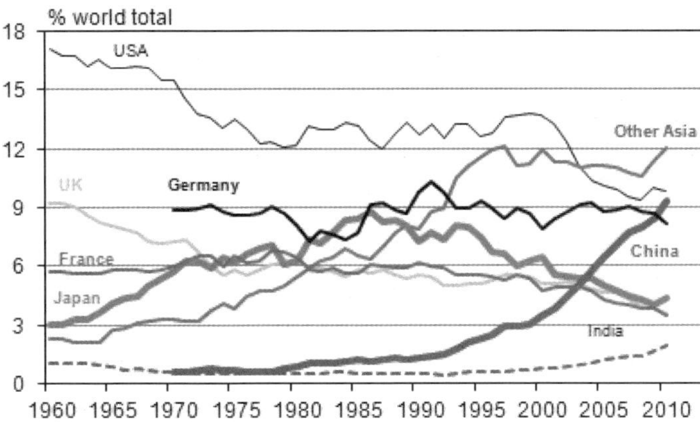

Figure 2. World export shares: Goods and services.

Source: WDI, Westpac.

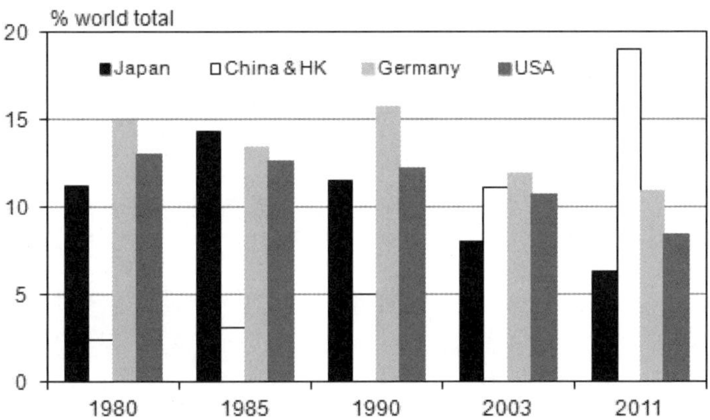

Figure 3. Manufacturing export shares.

Source: WDI, WTO.

economies range from one half (the United Kingdom), two-thirds to four-fifths (Germany, France and Italy) to almost 100% in the United States. An advanced, medium sized commodity exporter, Australia, denominates roughly one third of its exports in its own currency.

On the import side of the equation, yen denomination was much slower to move, and while it peaked later, it was at a lower level than for exports. The proportion of imports that were yen denominated remained trivial through the entirety of the 1970s before rising

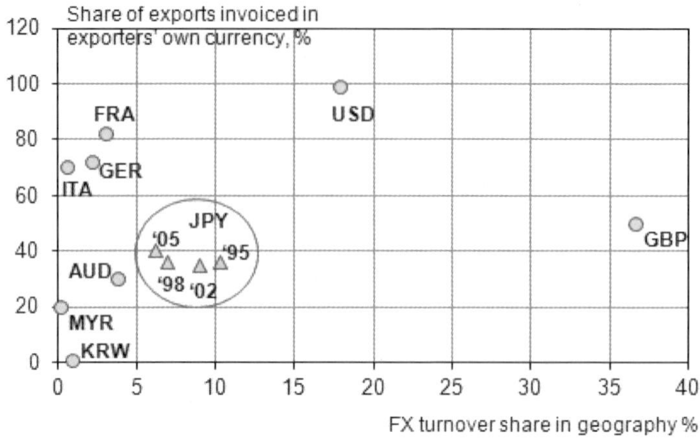

Figure 4. Trade invoicing and FX turnover.
Note: FX turnover data for 2010 except for Japan as specified.
Source: HKMA, Westpac Economics, BIS. Yun (2005).

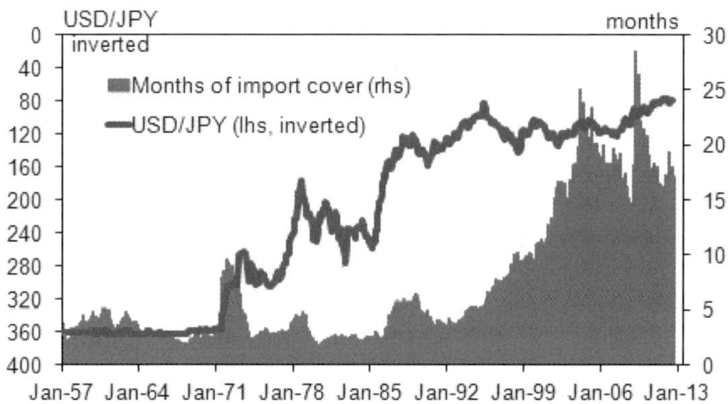

Figure 5. The exchange rate and FX reserve adequacy.
Source: IMF (2001).

steadily through to the mid-1990s to a little under one quarter of the total (Sato, 1999; Oi, 2003, Figure 1). The imprint of the substantial yen appreciation between 1985 and 1995 (Figure 5) can be read in the relative pathways for export and import denomination.

The literature on the underwhelming levels of yen trade invoicing and on the modest internationalization of the yen more generally has focused on the following arguments:

1. US dollar denominated commodities form a major proportion of Japan's import basket.
2. The nature of intra-firm trade between Japanese based firms and their offshore subsidiaries, and the presence of large trading companies in the resources space, both served to concentrate foreign exchange risk in the firms most equipped to handle it.
3. The immature state of foreign exchange markets in Asia, where Japanese firms are very prominent, and the "original sin" of its trading partners in the region (Eichengreen and Hausmann, 1999) which pushes them towards the US dollar.
4. The lack of non-resident holdings of yen and a low demand for non-resident borrowings in the yen.[9]
5. The wide use of "pricing to market" strategies among Japanese and Asian exporters.

These factors lead to a bias towards the use of a vehicle currency — the US dollar — for much of Japan's trade, rather than its own currency. The official committee on yen internationalization (Japanese Ministry of Finance, 1998) focused its recommendations on the availability of trade finance in Asia; deepening the corporate understanding of the risks inherent in foreign exchange and the advantage of home currency denomination; and using trade invoicing as a "door opener" to drive greater demand for yen financial transactions. These points all relate to what the committee noted was a "vicious cycle" of under-developed markets for yen leading to low transaction volumes and ongoing under-development. This indicates a sophisticated understanding of the dynamics of vehicle currencies outline above, which work to limit entry and sponsor incumbency.

Based on their reading of the situation, these are all sensible suggestions, but they lacked the required game changing jolt to turn the "vicious cycle" virtuous. Where might this jolt have emanated from?

---

[9]This point is made with reference to the non-financial sector in the 1990s and before. The famed "yen carry trade," whereby financial institutions funded themselves very cheaply in Tokyo and bought higher yielding assets elsewhere, which reached its heights during the Bank of Japan's original quantitative easing experiment in the early 2000s, is a special case.

There was one clear avenue of opportunity that was open to Japan to further the intermediate objective of establishing the yen as an international vehicle currency as a means of achieving the super-ordinate objective of establishing Tokyo as a first tier IFC. The official committee on yen internationalization states that "The currency used in invoices for trade transactions is determined by such factors as *relative market power*, the currencies in which *international commodities* are invoiced, and trade structures (*ibid.*, author's italics)."

Japan's strategists need not have looked far to find commodity markets where they had considerable market power, thereby taking advantage of one aspect of the currency invoicing outcome and breaking a legacy mindset that was holding back progress towards the IFC goal. The argument here is that Japan was too timid in working towards denominating its major commodity imports in yen, particularly where benchmark prices were negotiated rather than traded on an exchange. After all, just as it was the world's largest exporter of manufactures in 1985, it was the largest steel producer with almost one quarter of global output, and it was also the largest importer of fuel and mining products in the same year, narrowly surpassing the United States (Figure 6). While with hindsight we see that this was a temporary situation, we can be certain that many contemporary observers would have expected that ranking to persist having been caught up in the "Japan as number 1" euphoria of the times.

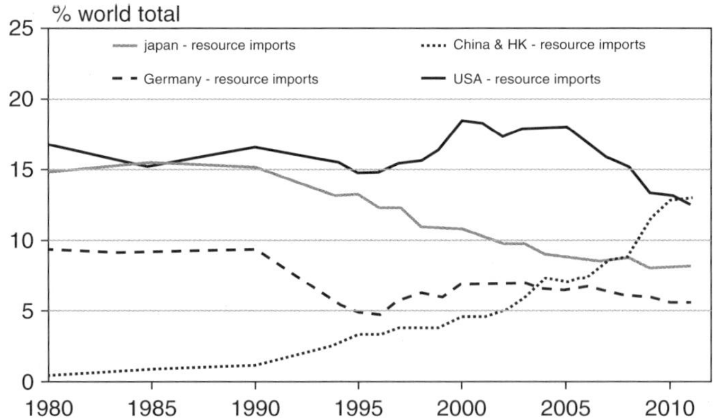

Figure 6. Resource import shares.

Note: Resource imports defined as "fuel and mining" products.

Source: WDI, WTO.

Japan was able to shape the trade in specific non-exchange traded commodities related to steel making to its liking in almost all ways but currency of denomination. Consider the international trade in iron ore and metallurgical (or coking) coal, the two major primary inputs for crude steel production. Until a few years ago, the price of these commodities was set at annual contract negotiations between the Japanese steel mills (the JSMs, often represented by the giant Nippon Steel as lead negotiator) and the major resources companies, principally the Australian headquartered global titans, BHP Billiton and Rio Tinto[10], and their forerunners. The contract period reflected the *Japanese fiscal year*, beginning on April 1st. *Japanese trading companies* had *substantial equity stakes* in joint ventures to develop the assets. The price negotiations were based on long term considerations, with statistical and anecdotal evidence arguing that neither side pushed for dramatic short run concessions based on cyclical shifts in negotiating power, even though the Japanese clearly had the benefit of inside information based upon their equity stakes in many major projects (Oczkowski, 1993).

The US Geological survey estimated that 82% of Australian iron ore exports went to Japan and the rest of Asia in 1985, with the remainder going to Western Europe (Kuck, 1985, p. 526). Even as late as 2002, Japanese imports of Australian iron ore exceeded those of China, who today dominates the trade.[11] If the various interested parties had been focused on internationalizing the yen as an overarching national goal (the Ministry of International Trade and Industry, the Ministry of Finance, the JSMs themselves, the major trading companies involved in the commodity trade, especially Mitsui and Mitsubishi, the major banks, the domestic consumers of steel and steel products, the various industry associations plus the influential peak business association *Keidranren*) then the JSMs would surely have been requested to negotiate hard for yen denomination of the iron ore and metallurgical coal contracts and would have

[10]The Brazilian company Vale, nee CVRD, was the largest producer of iron then as now, but Australia's proximity (lower freight costs) and stability (noting the unstable policy and economic environment in Latin America in the 1980s and 1990s) made Australia unambiguously the best contract partner.

[11]Customs data accessed via the CEIC database. The primary source for China is the General Administration of Customs and for Japan it is the Ministry of Finance.

been provided with whatever support was deemed necessary. An Australian dollar–Japanese yen foreign exchange swap line between the Bank of Japan and the Reserve Bank of Australia perhaps?

There would certainly have been some reluctance on behalf of the Australian sellers of the resource. An issue for Asian economies that have soft levels of foreign competition in their home markets is that there is little two-way trade conducted by foreign firms outside of the vertical production networks. Two-way transactions are vital as they create the incentive to invoice in the home currency of the trading partner as the firm has both revenues and costs in that unit. One-way transactions only — closed end importing or exporting by the foreign party — argues for either home invoicing by the foreign party or the use of a vehicle currency. For the major resource companies, it would have been costly to convert yen revenues to a currency in which they had obligations — wages, debt servicing, capital goods investment — to meet. Their yen cost bases would have been negligible — essentially running representative offices. However, if Japan simultaneously made great efforts to raise the level of yen invoicing of its exports, the conversion costs for the firm paid in yen would fall as the global market for the currency deepened. Another issue is that, when a currency is expected to appreciate in the longer run, as the yen certainly was in the 1980s, non-residents will be reluctant to accrue obligations in that currency, as they will either need to hedge, which is expensive, or run valuation risk, which is also potentially very costly.

Reform of international financial arrangements and the domestic financial system

At the time of US President Nixon's decision to cease US dollar convertibility to gold, thereby effectively ending the Bretton Woods fixed exchange rate system, the Japanese yen was fixed at ¥360 to the US dollar, exchange arrangements were still highly restrictive, a Glass–Steagall like separation between banking and securities business was in place, interest rates were regulated at repressive low rates and the economy ran small trade surpluses and small current account deficits. From the early 1970s forward, Japan progressively moved towards a more flexible exchange rate and a more open capital account.

Its domestic financial markets deepened appreciably as high household savings and high corporate profits generated virtuous circles of wealth creation. The economy began to produce consistent current account surpluses from the immediate aftermath of the first oil shock. The country's traditional post-war shortage of foreign exchange was reversed and foreign assets begun to build quite rapidly. Japan was a net international creditor in 1980 and it would become the world's largest international creditor in the decades to come. A great deal was achieved in a relatively short space of time. However, the sum of these achievements — added to the documented failure to establish the yen as a major vehicle currency — was not sufficient to establish Tokyo as a first tier IFC ahead of the nation's 1990s decline, which ultimately prevented further advance.

The yen appreciated against the US dollar (and in broad effective terms) in fits and starts in the 1970s. From the Bretton Woods fixed rate of ¥360 to the dollar that held through the 1950s and 1960s, it appreciated to ¥308 after the Smithsonian Agreement of December 1971; it was trading at ¥270 at the end of February 1973 after it was officially floated on the 14th of that month; it appreciated to ¥176 by October 1978. From that point the contractionary monetary policies of the Volcker-led US Federal Reserve sponsored US dollar strength deep in to the 1980s. The yen averaged ¥236 in the five and a half years of the 1980s leading up to the Plaza Accord of September 1985. Following this compact between the G5 nations to depreciate the US dollar, the yen appreciated rapidly, given the existence of a by now very large current account surplus.

The Japanese authorities attempted to manage the rate of currency appreciation throughout this period, which saw foreign exchange reserves rise from two months worth of import cover ahead of the Plaza Accord to five months worth of import cover in December 1987 (Figure 5). The G6 Louvre Accord of February 1987 (noting that Canada attended the Louvre but not the Plaza) temporarily stabilized the US dollar, but the yen kept rising after a slight pause, ending the year at ¥123. All told, by the end of 1987 USD/JPY had moved 66% in the yen's favor since the collapse of Bretton Woods.

While the yen was appreciating, the Japanese authorities were performing a sequenced and gradual opening of their capital account while moving more cautiously on financial deregulation (Aramaki, 2006, Table 1, pp. 186–191). The reform sequence pursued by the Japanese began with trade liberalization and the allowance of foreign direct investment inflows. The initial moves in these fields go back to the first days of independence from the administration imposed by the Allies.[12] That framework persisted through the 1960s, with some selective forms of portfolio capital inflow allowed from 1964, with general support for the progressive pursuit of capital account convertibility formalized in 1967 (Table 1).

Deregulation of cross border capital flow proceeded through the 1970s and was made both more complicated and more urgent by the demise of the fixed exchange rate system and the oil and financial crises of 1973–1974. However, reforms were not symmetric. They sought to increase capital inflows in the first instance, reflecting the

Table 1. Various reforms relevant for the IFC criteria.

	First post-war reform	Criterion fully met
Capital account convertibility	1967	1984
Unrestricted inward portfolio equity	1964	1973
Unrestricted inward portfolio debt	1964	1980
Unrestricted outward portfolio equity	1970	1980
Unrestricted outward portfolio debt	1970	1980
Floating currency	1971	1973
AAA status	1975 (gained status)	2001 (lost status)
Deregulated interest rates	1979	1993
Active central bank market making	1985	1996
Bond issuance by all forms of financial institutions	NA	1999
Banking/securities business separation	1992	1999
Foreign borrowing by local firms	1960	1964
Yen borrowing by non-residents	1970	1977
Outward direct investment	1969	1972

Sources: Aramaki (2006), McKay (1999), Standard and Poor's Financial Services LLC (2012).

[12]A fascinating insider account of some of the domestic economic reform conducted by the Allied administration can be found in Hadley (1970).

needs of the time, and were slower to liberalize outflows. There was even a period of temporary regression towards stronger regulation of capital outflow in times of stress (Aramaki, 2006). Reforms of the domestic financial system itself lagged behind those relating to exchange arrangements and exchange restrictions (Table 1). This strategy appears to describe a textbook path for a middle income economy looking to modernize while simultaneously maintaining domestic stability. *What it is not is the description of an economy with a super-ordinate goal to enter the top tier of IFCs within a decade or two.* This path of policy betrays the key point highlighted at the outset: Japan did not behave in the 1970s and first half of the 1980s as if it had a super-ordinate national goal of establishing Tokyo as a competitor for New York and London. And history shows that moving to do so later missed the window of opportunity.

Returning to Table 1 and considering the subsidiary IFC criteria outlined, it is easy to see that at the time when Japan's economic momentum and share of global aggregates was at its peak between 1985 and 1990, those related to the domestic financial system were not particularly competitive. Consider these criteria in turn against the Japanese experience:

> "A market making central bank-primary dealer complex in the key financing vehicles of the day — whether the discounting of bills of exchange, government securities on repo/reverse repo or commercial paper."

There was a flurry of activity on this front in the mid 1980s, with a yen denominated bankers acceptance market and money market certificates established and introduced respectively in 1985 and the introduction of commercial paper (CP) in 1987. However, a repo market was not established until 1996, well after the slowdown of the economy, declining asset prices and much publicized trading scandals[13] had began to sap international confidence in Japanese financial markets.

[13]The "loss compensation scandal" involved the revelation that 17 securities firms had been making their best clients whole on equity trading losses (a scandal that engulfed the heights of politics and the bureaucracy) was particularly damaging for the reputation of the financial markets. For further details see Char (1993).

> *"A broad variety of financial assets to cater for the appetites of a diverse domestic and international investor base. This tends to prioritize the development of non-bank, arm's length financing channels (direct equity and debt raisings principally). A broad variety of financial institutions to cater for diverse intermediation functions. These institutions will also have a global footprint. At the very least, an internationally competitive cluster of banking, insurance and funds managements firms must be present."*

Japan certainly had an active capital market through the 1980s, highlighted by the "*zaiteku*" (literally "financial technology") era (McKay, 1999), although it operated within an oligopoly structure. Japan inherited a strict separation between securities and banking business from the Allied occupation. This was both an "off the shelf" policy from the United States (the Glass–Steagall Act of 1933) and an attempt to limit the power of the *zaibatsu* banks in postwar Japan. The securities business grew to be dominated by a "big four" with a direct market share of Tokyo Stock Exchange turnover of around 40% and an indirect share close to 60% in the late 1980s (Char, 1993, p. 180). These firms enjoyed a very lucrative, protected underwriting business in the 1980s as the equity market boomed and large firms increasingly moved to raise funds directly.

On the banking side, the industry was also highly concentrated, but it was also strictly fragmented by activity, with distinctions between "long term credit banks," "city banks," "regional banks," "trust banks," "shinkin banks" and other deposit taking institutions. There was also a group of large but staid insurers and funds management firms. The strict separation between securities and banking business was abolished in 1992 and the banking compartments were progressively removed through the 1990s as well, leading up to the "big bang" financial system reforms of 1998 (of which more below).

Japanese banks did achieve a reasonable footprint in global finance by the end of the 1980s. Indeed, the market capitalization of Japan's major banks was world leading, courtesy of inflated balance sheet valuations from their cross shareholdings of equity and their exposure to the real estate bubble, and the equity bubble itself. Japan's share of the gross international financial exposures of the G4 (international assets plus international liabilities, Figure 7) grew sharply in the second half of the 1980s to be equal to the United

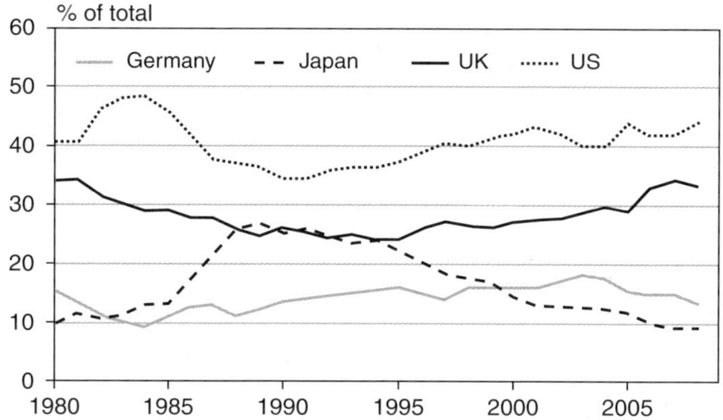

Figure 7. Shares of the G4 international financial position.

Note: Sum of each country's gross international assests and liabilities as a proportion of the G-4 total.

Source: IMF, Westpac.

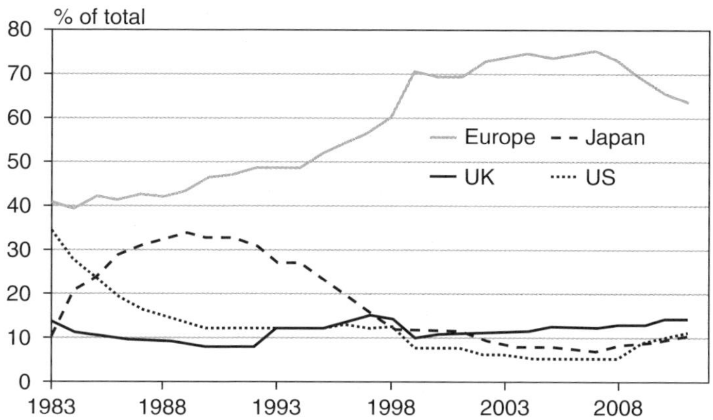

Figure 8. Shares of foreign bank claims: Total.

Source: BIS, Westpac.

Kingdom and well ahead of Germany. Japan's share of total cross border banking claims surpassed that of either the US or the UK in the 1980s, to be second only to the combined position of the Europeans, whose home economies would soon enter into a monetary union and provide the first genuine alternative to the US dollar as a global vehicle currency since the interwar period (Figure 8). Japan's

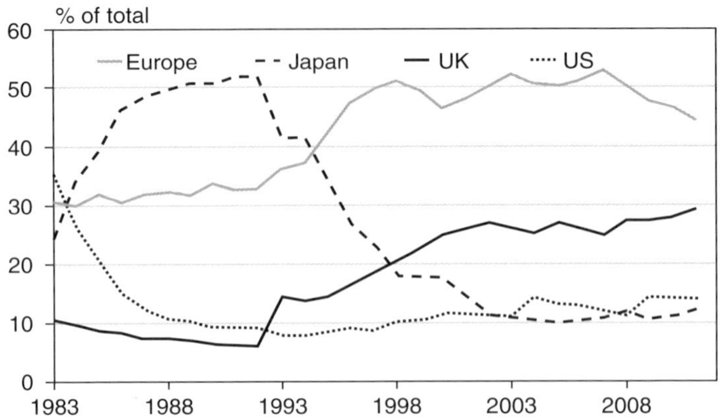

Figure 9. Shares of foreign banking claims on Asia.
Source: BIS, Westpac.

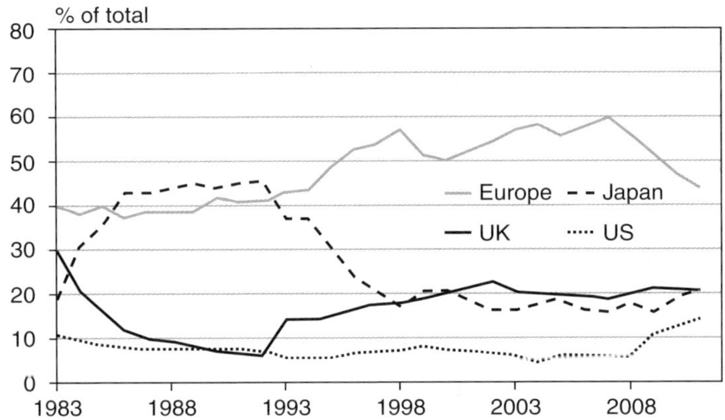

Figure 10. Shares of foreign banking claims: Offshore financial centers.
Source: BIS, Westpac.

international position was even more positive in two subsets of this data: claims on Asia and claims on offshore financial centers (hereafter OFCs, noting Singapore and Hong Kong are in both of these two categories, Figures 9 and 10). Note that the Asian crisis was not the peak for Japan's share of banking claims on Asia or on OFCs. The peak was early in the 1990s when Japan's domestic bubble burst and asset quality began to decline at home. So even as Japanese non-financial firms, particularly manufacturers, rapidly increased their direct investment in emerging Asian countries through the middle 1990s, Japanese banks were in retreat.

> "A regulatory framework that is seen as a credible check on excesses without stifling innovation. A legal framework that is transparent and predictable. Other support services such as accounting, IT, and specialist higher education offer economies of scale and scope to financial institutions that choose to base their activities in IFCs."

The "big bang" was an explicit effort to address Tokyo's shortcomings relative to London and New York. The reforms liberalized equity trading commissions and over-the-counter business; sought to accelerate competition across the institutional compartments previously kept separate; a new exchange for the listing of small, high growth companies was devised (MOTHERS) and a NASDAQ affiliated exchange was planned; and a new regulatory framework modeled on the United States' Securities and Exchange Commission was instituted. Later, the cross shareholdings of banks were forced to be divested, increasing the proportion of freely floating shares used for the purpose of calculating the composite market capitalization indices against which global fund managers benchmarked their performance.

> "A demonstrated ability to consistently and transparently allocate large amounts of capital to productive uses. A liquid market for anchor risk free assets in the home currency."

All these moves were positive but they were overshadowed by the dramatic rise in non-performing loans of the banking system as asset prices collapsed from their peak levels. The system entered a full blown solvency crisis ahead of the "big bang," amplified by the onset of the Asian Financial Crisis. The Japanese government's own large debt and the contingent liabilities emanating from the banking system served to undermine its status as a risk free issuer around this time. While the formal downgrade from AAA would not come until 2001 (Figure 11), foreign investors had seen enough well beforehand. These reputational losses were irreparable in terms of the first tier IFC criteria, noting that New York looked more formidable than ever at this time, while the introduction of the euro pushed the yen down

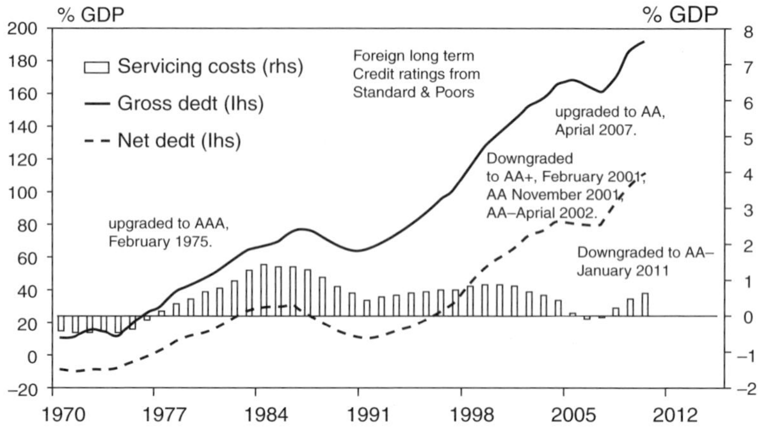

Figure 11. Japan's public debt and its credit rating.

Note: Author calculations.

Source: OECD (2013).

the pecking order from the moment of its formal arrival on January 1, 1999.

Conclusions on Tokyo's Ultimately Unsuccessful Bid for First Tier IFC Status

This chapter has argued that establishing Tokyo as a first tier IFC was never a super-ordinate goal of national economic policy until the middle 1990s, by which time the window of opportunity had truly closed. This late recognition prevented a strategic approach to maximizing the obvious potential inherent in its earlier bid. The reform decisions of policymakers in the 1970s and 1980s were too gradual, particularly in relation to financial system deregulation, and were thus ultimately ineffective in boosting the competitiveness and attractiveness of Tokyo to first tier levels before the weakness of the economy and the banking system prevailed over all else.

The inability to establish the yen as a competitive international vehicle currency, which was and is reflected in the low proportion of yen invoicing in Japan's own trade, is the mascot for Tokyo's *second tier* IFC status. Yet, perhaps it is unfair to criticize too much. Japanese policymakers could not have had perfect foresight of either a) what Japan would look like in 1985 from the perspective of 1973 or

b) what Japan would look like in 1998 from the perspective of 1985. Decisions were made at each time based upon visions of the future that were in the first instance both too cautious and too humble and in the second instance both too cautious and too proud.

With hindsight it can be shown that greater aggression towards the expansion of yen trade invoicing, if successful, might have instigated virtuous dynamics in the vehicle currency arena with the associated positive spillovers for Tokyo's IFC status. Even so, Japan's economy was never going to be larger than that of the United States, and thus, New York would have always retained the edge in scale over Tokyo. Furthermore, London had two centuries of experience as a first tier IFC. Tokyo sat at the center of a financially repressed, closed system in the 1950s and 1960s, and a system in transition in the 1970s and 1980s. That was not really a fair fight either. Tokyo would have moved closer to first tier IFC status in the late 1980s if Japan had prioritized the goal earlier and acted accordingly; but it would not have changed the ultimate result that Tokyo has settled down as a very important but not dominant centre for international financial activity.

Implications for Shanghai's Potential First Tier IFC Status

When Japan first had international financial openness thrust upon it by the demise of the Bretton Woods system, it had recently achieved the $8,000 GDP per head level (1990 international dollars). Conveniently, China achieved the same per capita living standard in 2011. Both economies experienced very strong rates of per capita economic growth leading up to the $8,000 GDP per head landmark. Japan quadrupled its GDP per head from $2,000 to $8,000 in 17 years, while China took one year less, beginning in 1995 (McKay and Song, 2013, Table 5.1). Figure 12 depicts some key relative fundamentals for the two economies at the $8,000 GDP per head level, with Japan serving as numeraire and South Korea included as a further point of comparison.

The figure shows that China's current structure and overall development characteristics differ in some fundamental ways from Japan's when it was an $8,000 per head economy. Japanese average education

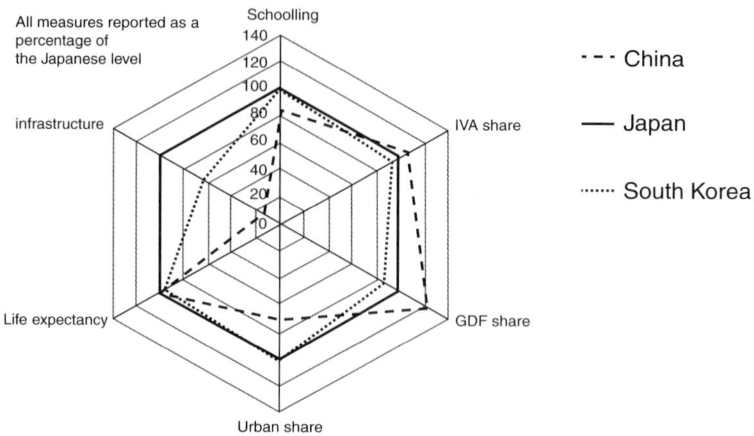

Figure 12. Selected economies at $8,000 GDP per head.

Note: All measures reported as percentage of the Japanese level. "Schooling" refers to average years of schooling per adult. "IVA share" and "GCF share" refers to the percentage of GDP accounted for by industrial production and gross investment respectively. "Life expectancy" is at birth. "Infrastructure" is open rail network length scaled by 2010 land area. "Urban share" is the percentage of the population classed as urban by the United Nations in their 2011 revision. All information on post second world war GDP and GDP per capita levels are from the Conference Board (2012), and are in 1990 Geary Khamis dollars.

Source: Adapted from Figure 5.2b in McKay and Song, 2013.

levels were greater than China's; Japanese urbanization was considerably greater and its infrastructure stock considerably deeper; while the share of overall activity in industrial production and investment in Japan was below the equivalent Chinese levels. The comparisons between China and South Korea are similar in absolute terms to the Sino–Japanese relativities, but the divergences are somewhat less pronounced. This implies that China's industrialization is less mature at the $8,000 per head level than it was at the same stage for its North Asian neighbors. Noting that China also exhibits a much higher export orientation today than Japan ever did, alongside a much great reliance on inward foreign direct investment in manufacturing; China has the luxury of a large current account surplus, while Japan still ran current account deficits at the $8,000 per head level; while China has a substantially higher rate of income inequality than did Japan. Ergo, there are a number of material points of difference between the two real economies at the starting points of their respective financial deregulation eras.

Put simply, Japan had a more balanced economy at the $8,000 per head level than China does today, which implies Japanese policymakers had fewer structural legacies to be taken into account in designing and adoption a holistic approach to financial reform. The situation in China is replete with structural legacies that must be acknowledged and incorporated into the design of policy.

The recent remarks of the new Premier, Li Keqiang, reported by official news agency Xinhua (2013b), are clearly in sympathy with this assessment. Speaking at a macroeconomic seminar on April 12, 2013, which brought together policymakers, scholars and industry representatives, Li stressed that the deepening of reform was vital to the sustainability of growth and that any counter cyclical efforts would be considered in the context of their longer term structural implications and their impact on the reform path. The exact reporting was as follows:

> "While effectively coping with short-term problems and *maintaining reasonable growth, more efforts should be made to improve the quality and benefits of development*, with a focus on promoting economic restructuring and upgrading, expanding employment and increasing people's incomes, ... the impetus for sustained development lies in deepening reform, *urging targeted policies to cure not only 'symptoms' but deeply-rooted problems* in the Chinese economy... If interim measures have to be carried out, *they should not set up barriers for promoting market-oriented reform and development in the future* (emphasis added)."

The State Council memorandum on income distribution reform, which cuts across all relevant aspects of macroeconomic decision making, released on February 5, 2013, was also very realistic. It stated that "deepening the income distribution reform is a systematic project that is arduous and complicated and concerns the reallocation of various interests. There is no way to accomplish it overnight." (*Xinhua News*, 2013a).

When Li urged "targeted policies to cure not only 'symptoms' but deeply-rooted problems" it is an acknowledgment that a redesign of the major parameters that describe the current capital allocation system ought to be on the agenda. Arguably, establishing a superordinate goal to raise Shanghai to first tier IFC status could play a galvanizing role in the reform process, assisting policymakers to move forward with focus and resolve.

Disentangling the complex web of the many tiers of the banking system, shadow finance, exchange arrangements and the exchange rate-monetary policy regime is no simple matter. It is not just that capital is too cheap for certain large firms. Household savers are poorly remunerated as a consequence of historically regulated deposit rates that often failed to compensate for inflation. A lack of financial market development and exchange arrangements that disallow most forms of private outward portfolio flows provides a limited menu of alternative investment options, leading to a crowded real estate investment market, which causes fundamental socio-economic problems of its own. Small, private firms often pay too much for their capital. Chinese firms are advantaged in foreign markets by the competitive exchange rate, raising export orientation, while importers are disadvantaged by it, lowering domestic absorption. If China addresses each of these shortcomings with a view towards achieving a more balanced and inclusive growth model, a happy consequence will be that Shanghai becomes a more viable candidate as a major IFC.

There has been much activity in the fields of domestic and international financial liberalization already (Huang, 2001; Ma, 2006; McKay, 2007; Hong Kong Monetary Authority, 2010). Greater flexibility in setting deposit and lending rates has been introduced, although they are not yet fully free. The domestic bond market has been encouraged as an alternative source of both private and public financing. Loan securitization and short selling have both been introduced. Exchange rate flexibility has been increased progressively after the peg to the US dollar was abandoned in 2005; foreign exchange reserve accumulation has leveled out; the supply of RMB now available outside the Mainland has increased rapidly as part of the trade settlement program, the centerpiece of the internationalization initiative; the Qualified Foreign

Institutional Investor (QFII) program, the Qualified Domestic Institutional Investor (QDII) program and a new Renminbi QFII program have been revamped or instituted; and outward flows of direct investment have continued to enjoy policy sponsorship. Furthermore, since the middle of 2012, the People's Bank of China (PBoC) has increasingly relied upon its open market operations to manage domestic liquidity and credit conditions, rather than the traditional administrative tools of required reserve ratios, window guidance and lending quotas. And in a further move towards sophistication, rather than issuing or purchasing bills, reverse repurchase agreements dominated open market operations in 2012, when liquidity was being increased, while repurchase agreements have been used in 2013 so far to keep liquidity from expanding too quickly.

All of this activity points in the right direction and improves China's standing on the IFC criteria outlined in the first section of the chapter. Yet moving more swiftly on interest rate liberalization, particularly with regards to deposit rates, would be a welcome move. An unintended consequence of the slow movement towards deregulation of interest rates has been the rapid growth of off balance sheet activity by the banks and a rise in the market share of non-banks in total credit supply. While such developments are desirable as part of an effort to deepen domestic financial markets, extraordinary growth in lightly regulated areas of the financial system unavoidably comes with heightened systemic risks. Japan's decision to move slowly on deregulation was exposed as a flawed approach from an IFC perspective (and any other perspective, to be fair, given the depth of the resultant problems) when accumulated financial risks burst to the surface in the early 1990s, and have served to hamstring the economy since.

Moving on to the monetary policy–foreign exchange nexus, in concert with the moves to increase the power of market forces in setting the domestic cost of capital, exchange rate flexibility has increased in material fashion since 2005, to the extent that the currency is an accepted element of the counter cyclical toolkit. While the daily volatility of the currency within the present band of plus–minus 1% remains low, there have been official statements that a further widening of the band is just a matter of time. To quote PBoC deputy governor Yi Gang directly, who spoke at an International Monetary Fund meeting in Washington DC on April 18, 2013:

> "Last year we increased the band for the exchange rate from 0.5% to one percent. I think in the near future we'll increase the floating band even further... In China, we all do this kind of reform in a gradual manner. The direction is clear." (*People's Daily Online*, 2013).

The desire to maintain a gradual approach to exchange rate flexibility emanates from China's structural legacies, the most obvious of which in this context is its high degree of export orientation, and the psychological difficulty of changing a winning formula. The success of China's gradual approach to financial reform through its transition era has been rightly celebrated. Yet when a new model is required, rather than a marginal evolution of business as usual, a bolder strategy becomes more appropriate. Given Japan's failure to establish the yen as a true international vehicle currency has been identified as a prime shortcoming in its first tier IFC bid, if China is serious about Shanghai's bid, then RMB internationalization should be advanced aggressively and move beyond trade settlement forthwith.

It was noted that Japan was temporarily the world's largest importer of fuel and mining products in the mid 1980s (Figure 6). The same figure shows that China (including Hong Kong) recently surpassed the United States to ascend to the same position. Given the United States' diminished expected appetite for imported fuels with the massive exploitation of its domestic unconventional gas and oil reserves (International Energy Agency, 2012: BP, 2013), and the expected upward trajectory in Chinese resource demand per capita as its development proceeds (McKay, Sheng and Song, 2010: UNDP, 2010), China's time as the number one importer of fuel and mining products will be anything but brief.

Like Japan in its high growth era, China's growth has taken a very metal intensive path, which in tandem with its great size, has put it in a very powerful market position in the international trade for iron ore (Sheng and Song, 2012). Indeed, China's abrupt rise to dominance in the market for steel making inputs served to fracture the Japan-centric institutional arrangements that had been developed over the previous decades. It does not take a great stretch of the imagination to surmise that a proportion of the international trade in commodities will be re-denominated in the RMB once its supply outside of the Mainland reaches a critical mass. Or less abruptly, once portfolio flows are substantially deregulated, China's onshore commodity exchanges (based in Shanghai) where prices will be quoted in RMB and trades settled in RMB, could become the locus of world trade in resources. Similar arguments might be made for the international trade in food staples and shipping contracts, echoing London's agglomeration benefits dating back centuries. Such developments would no doubt ignite the dynamics of "scale begetting scale" in the vehicle currency domain that Krugman has highlighted. Yet before we get too advanced in that direction, we must acknowledge the point made by the Japanese Ministry of Finance (1998): that a "vicious cycle" of under-developed markets for yen led to low transaction volumes and ongoing under-development that served to limit entry into the vehicle currency arena and to sponsor incumbency. This is a "chicken and the egg" problem that despite China's likely future scale advantages may still need a jolt to initiate the desired dynamics for the latecomer and their counterpoint, adverse dynamics for the incumbents.

To tackle the "vicious circle" of under-developed foreign exchange markets and turn the cycle "virtuous," China's exchange arrangements must be liberalized to allow offshore parties to acquire, accumulate, invest and hedge in the RMB in such amounts that transaction costs decline materially. In this regard, Ma and McCauley (2013) note that while China has become progressively more open financially over the last decade, it is significantly less open than India, a much smaller and less developed economy. A major difference between the two countries is that China's current account surplus allows it the luxury of choice in terms of the types of capital inflows it will allow, whereas, India's large external deficits (and the fact that the financing of the fiscal deficit has first call on the finite domestic savings pool) force it to be more open to both portfolio and lending flows. Recalling the discussion with regards to the Japanese sequence of international financial liberalization, as it spent the 1950s and 1960s with a current account deficit and a shortage of foreign exchange, exchange arrangements were oriented toward the attraction of foreign capital as well as the retention of domestic savings. China is presently seeking to retain private domestic savings and attract only high quality capital, while repelling most "hot money" style flows (McKay, 2007). It was only when Japan began to run consistent current account surpluses from the middle 1970s that it felt more secure in allowing private portfolio outflows (Table 1). In short, Japan's approach was an asymmetric one regarding inward and outward portfolio flows, with the former allowed first (during its external deficit era) and the latter almost a decade later, in its external surplus era.

China's current account surplus — diminished from the pre financial crisis peak above 10% of GDP but still significant at 2–3% of GDP in recent years — is thus a source of comfort for policymakers seeking to liberalize exchange arrangements. The counterpoint is of course the prospective vulnerability of the domestic banking system to a more competitive environment for depositor funds. As argued above, domestic interest rate liberalization is required to modernize and commercialize the Chinese financial system. Deposit leakages are a necessary evil in this process. The example of South Korea is instructive. After the Asian crisis, Korea successfully pushed through the middle income phase of its development to achieve high income status. One element of this process was that South Korea successfully transitioned from a repressed to a relatively open financial system over the last decade and a half, with banks replacing some of their deposits with wholesale financing, deepening domestic capital markets along the way, which in turn has accommodated a move towards an inflation targeting monetary policy regime. Furthermore, Korean Treasury bonds have become a highly traded asset by international investors with the liberalization of inward and outward portfolio flows, deepening capital markets further and increasing turnover in onshore foreign exchange markets and offshore trade in non-deliverable forward markets of the Korean won.

It is possible to infer a relationship between macroeconomic stability, GDP per capita and financial reform in developing economies. My abstract conception of this relationship is depicted in Figure 13. I have refrained from using actual values on the GDP per capita axis, as the precise point at which these hypothesized curves cross

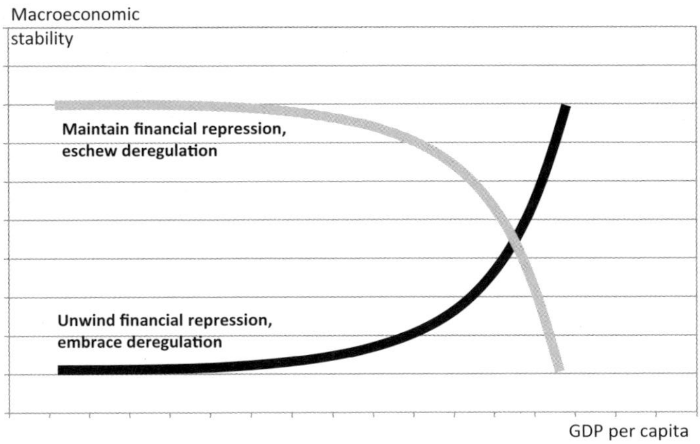

Figure 13. The relationship between macroeconomic stability, GDP per capita and financial reform in developing economies.

Note: Authors' own conception.

is unknowable, and may vary considerably based upon the strategy each individual economy has taken towards its financial system in the context of its industrialization. That said, recalling the initial discussion and peer review of China's industrialization path and mode, in this framework it seems entirely reasonable to pursue a gradual approach to financial reforms at a GDP per capita level of $2,000. However, at $8,000, the implicit cost-benefit analysis of that strategy, where macroeconomic stability is the ultimate objective, will be less clear cut. Cognizant as I am of the wisdom of the State Council, that "deepening reform is a systematic project that is arduous and complicated. There is no way to accomplish it overnight," (Xinhua News, 2013a) which are especially relevant sentiments regarding financial matters, I respectfully submit that the China of today, in search of a new model, cannot be far from the crossover point in Figure 13, if it is not already there. Korean policymakers perceived that they had persisted too long with the grey (conservative) schedule in Figure 13, and jumped onto the black (reformist) schedule, acknowledging the signal from the financial failures of the 1990s. The decision has been a good one. While Seoul never had a realistic aspiration to reach first tier IFC status, a similar leap from the grey to the black schedule at the opportune moment, alongside China's prospective dominance of real economy flows in coming decades, would be a powerful combination serving Shanghai's first tier IFC bid.

Deepening financial deregulation assists with the reduction of specific distortions that create rents and skew resource allocation (the low cost of capital for certain firms and industries), it would address asymmetric opportunities that lead to and inflame imbalances (improve entry conditions to boost competition, improve access to finance for private firms and households), and work to minimize macroeconomic risks, and enhance macroeconomic benefits, in a more general way (reducing systemic risk through increasing the proportion of capital allocated on commercial market principles). It brings risks of its own, which have collectively cowed many governments in emerging economies in recent decades (Calvo and Reinhart, 2000), with heightened exposure to foreign exchange and interest rate movements, foreign counterparties, new and complex instruments and greater market discipline for Chinese borrowers and lenders not used to such external oversight among the catalogue of "fears." Of course, successful internationalization of the RMB will reduce systemic foreign exchange risk, although as Cheung, Ma and McCauley (2010) illustrate, China's position as a large international dollar creditor means it is already extremely "long" foreign currency as a nation (primarily via the sovereign balance sheet at this point) and is consequently exposed to major valuation risks on its immense portfolio that cannot be realistically hedged either at the level of the exchange rate or at the underlying instrument level. It is worth recalling the enormous foreign exchange losses imposed on Japanese holdings of US dollar denominated assets in the decade following the Plaza Accord.

It was noted above that China's average schooling levels presently lag behind those seen in Japan and South Korea at the same income level. At the level of higher education, China has no universities in the top 200 social science departments, which is where global finance professionals are usually trained. Human capital is of course the backbone of an IFC once the policy infrastructure is put in place. So a shortfall here could possibly hold Shanghai, China back. However, Marginson (2012, p. 25), reports that Shanghai's schools were the best performed in the world across the three core disciplines of reading, science and mathematics in the 2009 OECD PISA tests. So while China as a whole is yet to reach the average levels of schooling seen in Japan and South Korea at $8,000 per head, Shanghai itself is something of a center of excellence in secondary education outcomes. This may translate into a strong next-generation white collar labor force. This dichotomy is noted in the most recent OECD survey of the Chinese economy (OECD, 2013, p. 91), which produces evidence that the quality of education delivery is highly variable by region and hukou status.

The national education figures raise a broader question about the adaptability of the current work force to a new model that is focused less on heavy industry and more on the consumption of services. Being home to a first tier IFC is of course one highly tangible expression of a complete transition to a services driven economy. Perhaps this image will resonate with policymakers as they ponder the optimal timing to enact the necessary steps required to pursue that goal. Or if that is too presumptive a statement, perhaps the establishment of a super-ordinate national goal to establish Shanghai as a first tier IFC by, say, 2030, can be seen to offer a focal point for reforms and to galvanize individual policymakers who may see the present program of rebalancing initiatives as somewhat nebulous and lacking a centre of gravity.

Conclusions

Tokyo never reached the first tier of IFCs. The basic failing in this quest was an inability to establish the yen as an international vehicle currency. Given the likely future scale of China's economic and financial footprint, it seems reasonable to venture that the RMB has an excellent chance to become a genuine international vehicle currency at some point, thus succeeding where Japan fell short. On the other hand, China is in the very early days of international and domestic financial reform, and Shanghai is presently extremely disadvantaged by a lack of indigenous expertise and experience in international finance, and some pronounced shortcomings across the vast majority of the soft infrastructure demanded of first tier IFCs. China, of course, has time on its side to build such expertise, as it will be the world's largest economy for at least the next two generations, a luxury never afforded to Japan. Even so, the imperative for a new growth model in China is more urgent than that, and the IFC goal may usefully serve as a galvanizing force in the overall reform process, assisting policymakers to move forward with focus and resolve.

References

Aramaki, K (2006). Sequencing of capital account liberalization — Japan's experiences and their implications to China. *Public Policy Review*, 2(1), 177–232.

Auboin, M (2012). Use of currencies in international trade: Any changes in the picture? World Trade Organization Economic Research and Statistics Division: Staff Working Paper ERSD. May.

Baker, M and C Michael (2005). London as an international banking centre, 1958–1980. In Youssef, C and E Bussiere (Eds.), *London and Paris as International Financial Centres in the Twentieth Century*, pp. 287–312. Oxford: Oxford University Press.

BP (2013). *Energy Outlook 2013: January 2013*. Available at http://www.bp.com/energyoutlook2030.

Calvo, GA and CM Reinhart (2000). Fear of floating. NBER Working Paper No. 7993. November.

Central Intelligence Agency (2012). *The World Factbook Online*. Available at https://www.cia.gov/library/publications/the-world-factbook/index.html.

Char, CJ (1993). Reforming Japan's securities markets: The loss compensation scandal. *International Tax & Business Law*, 10(2–3), 173. Available at http://scholarship.law.berkeley.edu/bjil/vol10/iss2/3.

Cheung, Y-W, G Ma and RN McCauley (2010). Renminbising China's foreign assets. CESIFO Working Paper No. 3009, Category 7. Monetary Policy and International Finance, April.

Cohen, BH (2005). Currency choice in international bond issuance. *BIS Quarterly Review*, June, 53–66.

Conference Board (2012). Total economy database^{TM}. January. Available from http://www.conference-board.org/data/economydatabase/.

Cui, L, C Shu and J Chang (2009). Exchange rate pass-through and currency invoicing in China's exports. HKMA China Economic Issues Paper No. 2/09, July.

Dobson, W and PR Masson (2009). Will the renmimbi become a world currency? *China Economic Review*, 20, 124–135.

Dooley, M, D Folkerts-Landau and P Garber (2003). An essay on the revised Bretton Woods system. NBER Working Paper No. 9971, September.

Eichengreen, B and Ricardo H (1999). Exchange rates and financial fragility. NBER Working Paper No. 7418, November.

Eichengreen, B (2011). *Exorbitant Privilege: The Rise and Fall of the Dollar and the Future of the International Monetary System*. Oxford: Oxford University Press.

Eichengreen, B (2012). When currencies collapse: Will we replay the 1930s or the 1970s? *Foreign Affairs*, Council on Foreign Relations. January/February.

Esteves, RP (2011). The *belle epoque* of international finance. French capital exports, 1880–1914. University of Oxford, Department of Economics. Discussion Paper Series No. 534. February.

Flandreau, M and F Gallice (2005). Paris, London and the international money market: Lessons from Paribas, 1885–1914. In Y Cassis and E Bussiere (Eds.), *London and Paris as International Financial Centres in the Twentieth Century*, pp. 287–312. Oxford: Oxford University Press.

Flandreau, M and C Jobst (2009). The empirics of international currencies: Network externalities, history and persistence. *The Economic Journal*, 119(537), 643–664.

Goldberg, LS and C Tille (2008). Vehicle currency use in international trade. *Journal of International Economics*, 76(2), 177–192.

Grassman, S (1973). A fundamental symmetry in international payments patterns. *Journal of International Economics*, 3(2), 105–116.

Hadley, EM (1970). *Antitrust in Japan*. Princeton: Princeton University Press.

Hong Kong Monetary Authority (2010). China's exchange rate reform: Past, present and future. Mainland Economic Monitor Special Note No. 06/2010. September.

Huang, Y (2001). *China's Last Steps Across the River: Enterprise and Banking Reforms*. Canberra: Asia Pacific Press.

International Energy Agency (2012). *World Energy Outlook* 2012. Available at http://www.worldenergyoutlook.org/pressmedia/recentpresentations/PresentationWEO2012launch.pdf.

International Monetary Fund (2001). Evolution of the SDR: Paper gold or paper tiger? Chapter 18 in *Silent Revolution: The IMF 1979–1989*, pp. 924–962. October 1. Available at http://www.imf.org/external/pubs/ft/history/2001/ch18.pdf.

Ito, T, S Koibuchi, K Sato and J Shimizu (2011). Currency invoicing decision: New evidence from a questionnaire survey of Japanese export firms. Center on Japanese Economy and Business Working Paper No. 293. Columbia University, Graduate School of Business.

Japanese Ministry of Finance (1998). *Internationalization of the Yen: Interim Report*, November 12. Council on Foreign Exchange and Other Transactions Sub-council on the Internationalization of the Yen. Available from http://www.mof.go.jp/english/international_policy/others/ks030707/index.htm.

Japanese Ministry of Finance (1999). *Internationalization of the Yen for the 21st Century*, April 20. Council on Foreign Exchange and Other Transactions. Available from http://www.mof.go.jp/english/about_mof/councils/customs_foreign_exchange/e1b064b.htm.

Japanese Ministry of Finance (2003). Enhancing Japan's status as an international financial center: Chairman's summarization of study group on the internationalization of Japan's financial and capital markets. July. Available at http://www.mof.go.jp/english/international_policy/others/ks030707/index.htm.

Kamps, A (2006). The euro as invoicing currency in international trade. ECB Working Paper Series No. 665, August.

Krugman, PR (1980). Vehicle currencies and the structure of international exchange. *Journal of Money, Credit and Banking*, 12(3), 513–526.

Kuck, PH (1985). Iron ore in United States Bureau of Mines. *Minerals Yearbook Metals and Minerals 1985*, 1, 517–540. Available at http://digicoll.library.wisc.edu/cgi-bin/EcoNatRes/EcoNatRes-idx?type=turn&entity=EcoNatRes.MinYB1985v1.p0536&id=EcoNatRes.MinYB1985v1&isize=M.

Lowe, P (2013). The journey of financial reform. Deputy Governor of the Reserve Bank of Australia, Address to the Australian Chamber of Commerce in Shanghai, April 24, 2013.

Ma G, (2006). Who foots China's bank restructuring bill? In R Garnaut and L Song (Eds.), *The Turning Point in China's Economic Development*, pp. 103–127. Canberra: Asia Pacific Press, Australian National University.

Ma, G and RN McCauley (2013). Is China or India more financially open. BIS Working Papers No. 410, April.

Marginson, S (2012). Emerging Asia and the future of the US–Australia alliance research and research universities in East Asia and Singapore. Presented at the Crawford School, Australian National University, August 30–31, 2012.

Maziad, S and JS Kang (2012). RMB Internationalization: Onshore/offshore links. IMF Working Paper WP/12/133, May.

McKay, H (1999). The logic of the developmental state: Alliance theory and the postwar Japanese political economy. Doctoral dissertation, University of Sydney.

McKay, H (2007). Reforming China's exchange arrangements: Monetary and financial sovereignty, sequencing and the foreign exchange market. In Garnaut, R and L Song (Eds.), *China: Linking Markets for Growth*. Canberra: Asia Pacific Press.

McKay, H (2012). The world economy in 2100: Five alternative visions of the future and the development of the alliance. Presented at the *Emerging Asia and the Future of the US-Australia Alliance: A stream of the US-Australia 21st Century Alliance Project Workshop*, Australian National University, Canberra, August 30–31, 2012. Available at www.ussc.sydney.edu.au.

McKay, Huw and L Song (2013). Chinese Industrialisation: Path dependence and the transition to a new model. In R Garnaut, C Fang and L Song (Eds.), *China: A New Model for Growth and Development*. Canberra: ANU E Press.

McKay, H, Y Sheng and L Song (2010). China's metal intensity in comparative perspective. In Garnaut, R, J Golley and L Song (Eds.), *China: The Next Twenty Years of Reform and Development*, pp. 73–98. Canberra: ANU E Press.

McKinnon, RI (1979). *Money in International Exchange: The Convertible Currency System*. Oxford: Oxford University Press.

McKinnon, R (1993). *The Order of Economic Liberalization*, 2nd Edition. Baltimore: Johns Hopkins University Press.

McKinsey Global Institute (2009). An exorbitant privilege? Implications of reserve currencies for competitiveness. MGI Discussion Paper, December.

Mitchie, R (2005). Financial phoenix: The city of London in the twentieth century. In Y Cassis and E Bussiere (Eds.), *London and Paris as International Financial Centres in the Twentieth Century*, pp. 15–41. Oxford: Oxford University Press.

Oczkowski, E (1993). An econometric analysis of price bargaining: The coking coal trade between Australia and Japan. Charles Sturt University Working Paper No. 9, October.

OECD (2013). *OECD Economic Surveys: China.* March, 2013.

Oi, H, A Otani and T Shirota (2003). The choice of invoice currency in international trade: Implications for the internationalization of the yen. Bank of Japan IMES Discussion Paper Series No. 2003-E-13.

Peng, W and C Shu (2010). *Currency Internationalization: Global Experiences and Implications for the Renminbi.* Hampshire: Palgrave-McMillan.

Prasad, E, T Rumbaugh and Q Wang (2005). Putting the cart before the horse? Capital account liberalization and exchange rate flexibility in China. IMF Policy Discussion Paper No. PDP/05/01. Washington, DC: International Monetary Fund.

Reszat, B (1993). Japan's financial markets: The lost decade. HWWA Discussion Paper No. 231, June. Available at http://www.hwwa.de.

Sato, K (1999). Trade invoice currency and pricing-to-market: Evidence for the limited use of the Japanese yen in the East Asian region. ICSEAD Working Paper Series Vol. 99–15, August.

Schenk, C (2005). Crisis and opportunity: The policy environment of international banking in the city of London, 1958–1980. In Y Cassis and E Bussiere (Eds.), *London and Paris as International Financial Centres in the Twentieth Century*, pp. 207–228. Oxford: Oxford University Press.

Siegfried, N, E Simeonova and C Vespro (2007). Choice of currency in bond issuance and the international role of currencies. ECB Working Paper Series No. 814, September.

Sheng Y and L Song (2012). China's iron ore demand and its determinants: A time series analysis. In Song, L and H Liu (Eds.), *The Chinese Steel Industry's Transformation: Structural Change, Performance and demand on resources.* Cheltenham: Edward Elgar.

Standard and Poor's Financial Services LLC (2012). Japan: Unsolicited ratings history. *S&P Capital IQ Global Credit Portal*, subscription service only.

Thimann, C (2010). Global role of currencies. In Peng, W and C Shu (Eds.), *Currency Internationalization: Global Experiences and Implications for the Renminbi.* Hampshire: Palgrave-McMillan.

Triffin, R (1978). The international role and fate of the dollar. *Foreign Affairs*, 57(2), 269–286.

United Nations Development Programme (UNDP) (2010). *China Human Development Report 2009/10. China and a Sustainable Future: Towards a Low Carbon Economy and Society.* Beijing: China Translation and Publishing Corporation.

United Nations Development Program (2013). *International Human Development Indicators.* Available at http://hdrstats.undp.org/en/indicators.

United Nations (2011). *World Urbanization Prospects, The 2011 Revision.* Available at http://esa.un.org/unup/

Union of International Railways (1991). *UIC Member Railway Statistics — Synopsis.* Available at https://www.uic.org/spip.php?article1350.

Union of International Railways (2001). *UIC Member Railway Statistics — Synopsis*. Available at https://www.uic.org/spip.php?article1350.

World Bank (2013). *World Development Indicators online*. Available at http://data.worldbank.org/topic.

Xinhua News (2013a). China to reform income distribution. Available at http://english.people.com.cn/90778/8122934.html.

Xinhua News (2013b). Premier stresses foresight in economic policymaking. Available at http://news.xinhuanet.com/english/china/2013-04/14/c_132308046.htm.

Xinhua News (2013c). Fact box: Highlights of China's income distribution reform plan.

Yun, S-H (2005). An essay on invoicing currency practices for Korean exports. *Bank of Korea Economic Papers*, 8(1), 75–101.

SECTION III

DESIGNING THE RIGHT FINANCIAL SYSTEM FOR CHINA

Chapter 7

The Great Accommodation: Chinese Central Banking in the New Millennium*

Junhui Qian and Wing Thye Woo

Introduction and Summary

The main objectives of People's Bank of China (PBC) are, in Governor Zhou Xiaochuan's words: (1) to maintain low inflation; (2) to keep appropriate economic growth; (3) to keep relatively low unemployment; and (4) to maintain external balance of payments. Among the four objectives, low inflation is the paramount one and receives the heaviest weight in policy deliberation (Zhou, 2012).[1]

However, PBC's low inflation agenda had to be carried out under the constraint of rapid expansion of the bank's asset sheet. From 2000 to 2012, PBC's foreign exchange reserve expanded almost 16 times, 21.3% annually in average. The external backdrop for the rapid accumulation of foreign exchange (forex) reserve, including the redistribution of world manufacturing activity, is obviously outside PBC's control. Even the domestic policies that lead to the over-accumulation of forex reserve, including exchange rate setting and policies for attracting FDI, are determined at a level of decision-making that is above PBC in the hierarchy of economic management.

*We are grateful to Professor Pan Yingli's encouragement and helpful discussions.

[1]It is highly credible that the Chinese government and PBC are hostile to inflation. First, the Party dominated the revolutionary war after a hyperinflation eroded the power base of the once mighty Nationalist regime. This historical association is a permanent warning to the Party leaders. Second, if that remote memory is not deterrent enough, the severe inflation in the late 1980s almost undermined the reform agenda led by Deng Xiaoping.

The PBC accommodated the extraordinary expansion of asset sheet with an unconventional expansion of liability sheet. We would call this action the great accommodation both for the scale of operations and for the happy result that no severe inflation occurred. From 2000 to 2012, the average annual inflation was a mere 2.3% and the maximum monthly inflation rate was 8.7% in February 2008, which was largely driven by a surge in food and energy prices. This was a notable achievement by PBC, given the rapid accumulation of forex reserve and the double-digit growth in real GDP during the same period.

During the great accommodation, required deposits together with central bank bills (since both are interest-bearing, we group deposits and bills together as debt financing) replaced currency issuance as the major financing instrument for the expansion of asset sheet. The central bank bill (CBB) was a major policy initiative for the sterilization of the position for forex purchase (PFP).[2] However, CBB proved to be inadequate for the flood of newly created liquidity through PFP. From 2006, PBC relied more and more on raising deposit reserve ratio of commercial banks, possibly for the lower interest cost and longer (infinite, indeed) lockup period on withheld liquidity.

The great accommodation was not without side-effects. The restrictive level of deposit reserve ratio for commercial banks was partly responsible for two recent developments: the financial disintermediation and the expansion of shadow banking system in China. Both developments would make PBC less powerful in its quantity-based liquidity management of the economy. It may well happen in the future that PBC's control of the formal banking system ceases to be relevant even when it remains successful.

The future of Chinese central banking relies on reforms on two fronts. First, China should allow a more flexible exchange rate

[2]The central bank bill is not an invention of PBC. Germany had something similar in early 1970s, when Bundesbank issued short-term treasury bills with an unconditional buy-back guarantee. In mid-1970s, the central bank of Philippines started to issue its own liabilities to conduct open market operations. Following Philippines, Indonesia introduced central bank bills in 1984, which subsequently became the major instrument for day-to-day monetary management. Taiwan also used central bank debt certificates in the 1980s to sterilize foreign reserve increases due to trade surpluses.

and abandon policies for encouraging exports and FDI. This would achieve some degree of balance of payments, so that the constraint of asset sheet expansion on PBC would be relaxed. Second, PBC should move from quantity-based to price-based central banking, targeting short-term interest rate rather than money supply. To make the transition successful, of course, many more reforms of the financial markets are needed.

In the rest of the chapter, we first lay out the challenges to PBC, especially since China joined WTO in 2001. In the section "The Changing Set of Policy Instruments," we describe the PBC's policy instruments, old and new. We then examine the changes in PBC's balance sheets during the great accommodation. In the subsequent section, we offer a set of recommendations for the future reform of Chinese central banking. The final section concludes.

Challenges to PBC

As a developing country in transition from command-based to market economy, China was prone to overheating e.g. Fan and Woo (1996). First, the rapid income growth created upward pressures on the price level. Second, the interest rate was kept artificially low to support state-owned enterprises. There were, indeed, several prolonged periods with negative real interest rate in the past three decades. Third, perhaps most importantly, the state sector and the local governments, generally operated under "soft budget constraints" and hence tended to over-borrow and over-invest. This soft-budget constraint situation created powerful pressures on the monetary authority to loosen credit. The relationship between inflation and rate of credit expansion is clearly visible in Figure 1. Indeed, despite the paramount weight on inflation, PBC had not been successful in reigning inflation during its early years as the central bank of China.

The passage of the Law of People's Bank of China in 1995 gave PBC the legal status of the central bank of China. Along with the transition of Chinese economy, PBC started to transform itself in the following years from conducting command-based banking macromanagement to market-based indirect central banking (Yi, 1999). In

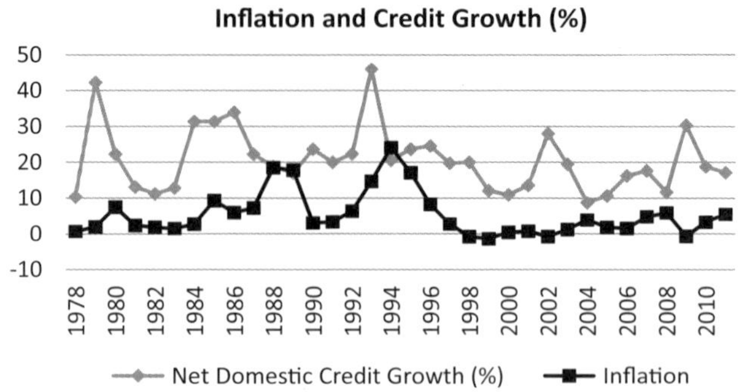

Figure 1. Inflation and credit growth, 1978–2011.

the new model, PBC targeted the money supply instead of total loans instead of controlling bank loans (Zhang *et al.*, 1997).

After China joined WTO in 2001, Chinese economic growth picked up and inflation pressures came back after the Asian financial crisis. The key challenge for PBC in the new millennium was to combat inflation pressure with the constraint that PBC had to purchase every dollar from the "twin surpluses" in the current account and the capital account of the balance of payments.

Exchange rate stability

Exchange rate stability itself, especially at an undervalued level, was not among the four objectives of PBC, but it was considered crucial for the objectives of keeping "appropriate economic growth" and "relatively low unemployment." In January 1994, to stimulate "external demand," PBC orchestrated a big depreciation of yuan from 5.8 to 8.7 yuan/dollar.[3] From May 1995 to June 2005, the yuan had been pegged to the dollar de facto at about 8.3 yuan/dollar (Figure 2), although it was allowed to fluctuate within the daily range of (−0.3%, 0.3%). On July 21, 2005, the yuan was officially unpegged from the dollar. But the cap on daily fluctuation remained. The yuan began

[3]Before the move, there were two exchange rates of yuan, one official rate of 5.8 yuan/dollar and the other unofficial adjustable (Tiao-Ji) rate. In Jan 1994 PBC unified the two rates and set the new official rate as 8.7 yuan/dollar.

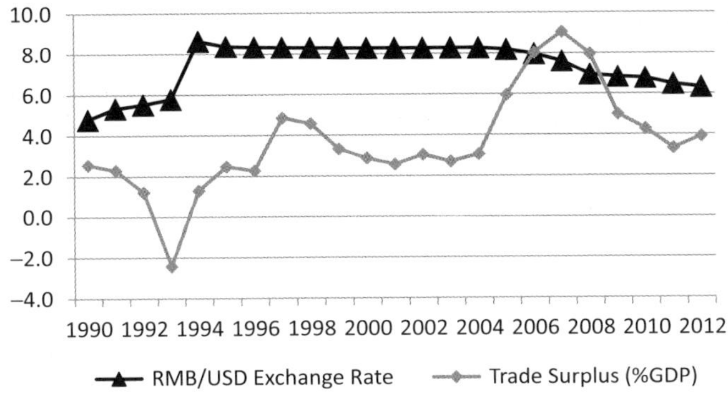

Figure 2. RMB/USD exchange rate and trade surplus of China (percentage of GDP), 1990–2012.

to appreciate slowly against the dollar, only interrupted briefly by the 2008 financial crisis.

It was, of course, PBC's job to intervene in the foreign exchange market to keep the yuan stably undervalued against the dollar. PBC had to purchase dollars from two main groups of sellers: exporters and foreign direct investors. In fact, it is mandatory that the foreign currency earned by exporters and brought in by FDI and foreign loans be converted into yuan. As this purchase of dollars by PBC necessarily resulted in yuan creation, PBC had to sterilize its effect on inflation.

"Twin Surpluses"

With the undervalued yuan, Chinese exporters made the best of the opportunities that are opened for them by China's joining WTO. For example, the trade surplus jumped from RMB 34 billion in 2001 to 44 billion in 2002, causing the current account surplus to increase from 2.6% to 3.0% of GDP. In 2007, the current account surplus reached 10.1% of GDP.

At the same time, FDI poured into China, partly attracted by preferential policies for foreign investment.[4] As a result, China had

[4]For example, FDI enjoyed a corporate tax rate of 15%, while the tax rate for domestic investment was 33%. In addition, FDI enjoyed various forms of tax deduction or exemption.

been running both current account and financial account surpluses from 1994 to 2011, with the exception of 1998 when the Asian financial crisis was in full swing. Yu (2010) has attributed this phenomenon of "twin surpluses" as mainly due to distortionary policies that encouraged export and FDI, in which the undervalued yuan and export subsidies played important roles.

Double-edged Sword

Forex reserve was considered essential for the modernization of China and economic growth. Without foreign currency, the argument was, modern machines could not be bought for the modernization of factories. Policies designed to promote export and those to attract foreign capital were both based on this simplistic view of economic growth. Local governments were all too happy to come up with such policies, since the bank dominated financial system under-supplied funding persistently but the dollar brought by export and FDI could be converted into yuan and local credit easily.

Of course, forex reserve was indeed essential for the facilitation of international trade and the stabilization of exchange rate. However, too much forex reserve and too much growth in forex reserve were curses to China rather than blessings.

First, the excess increase in forex reserve over the current account surplus in effect financed at least part of foreign investment by domestic saving[5] (See Figure 3). Sincc the interest rate received from forex reserve was necessarily lower than the return from FDI, this is a perverse kind of financial operation. It was thus ironical that the initial purpose of encouraging export and attracting FDI was to finance modernization of China. This perverse finance was pointed out by Chinese scholars as early as in mid 1990s, when "twin surpluses" first appeared e.g., Yu (1996). But all the talk of too much reserve accumulation was muted by the subsequent Asian financial crisis.

[5]To see this, consider the following accounting identity (omitting changes in gold and other foreign assets), nFDI + nOCI = ΔF-CAS, where CAS represents current account surplus, nFDI represents net FDI, nOCI represents net other capital inflow, and ΔF represents change in forex reserve. From 2001 to 2011, we have nFDI $>$ 0 and ΔF-CAS $>$ 0 in China.

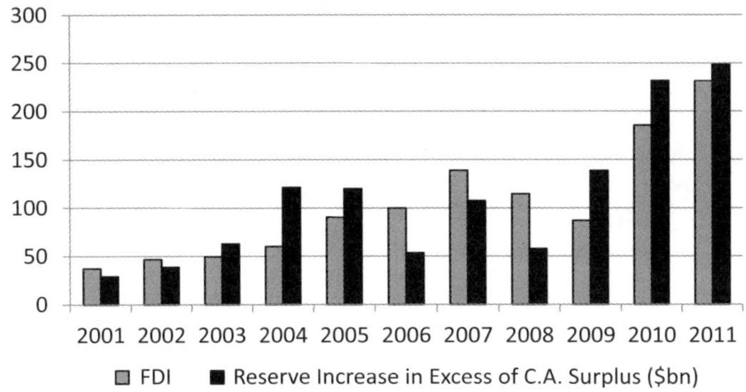

Figure 3. FDI and forex reserve increase in excess of current account surplus (in billion dollars).

Second, since the dollar was the dominant international reserve currency, the run-away accumulation of forex reserve ended up digging a "dollar trap" for China. A major depreciation of dollar would result in huge loss of wealth for China. And any attempt of switching to other types of reserves would only precipitate the feared crisis. It might even happen that China would have to keep the pace of dollar reserve accumulation just to keep dollar afloat, thus perpetuating wrong policies.

Third, the rapid increases in forex reserve and the associated RMB position for forex purchase were inflationary. Every dollar increases in forex reserve must be accompanied by an equivalent yuan creation by PBC, which is called "Position for Forex Purchase" (PFP) in the Table of "Sources & Uses of Credit Funds of Financial Institutions" published by PBC. Since 1994, money creation through increase in PFP had become major source of base money (high-powered money consisting of cash in circulation and reserve deposits in PBC) expansion.

As shown in Figure 4, PFP accounted for a mere 10.9% of money base, which was measured by "reserve money" in PBC's balance sheets, and 4.1% of M2 in 1993. These two ratios increased dramatically in the next 20 years. The first high was in 1997, when PFP accounted for 44.0% of money base (MB) and 14.8% of M2. From 1998 to 2000, these two ratios declined slightly, thanks to the pegged yuan/dollar exchange rate during the Asian financial crisis, when

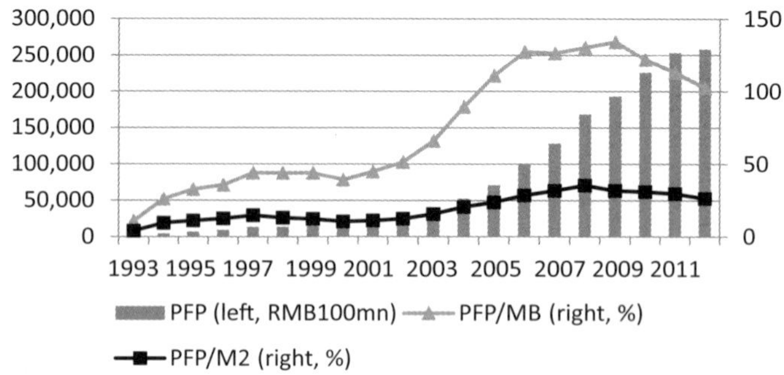

Figure 4. Position for forex purchase (PFP) and its share in money base (MB) and M2.

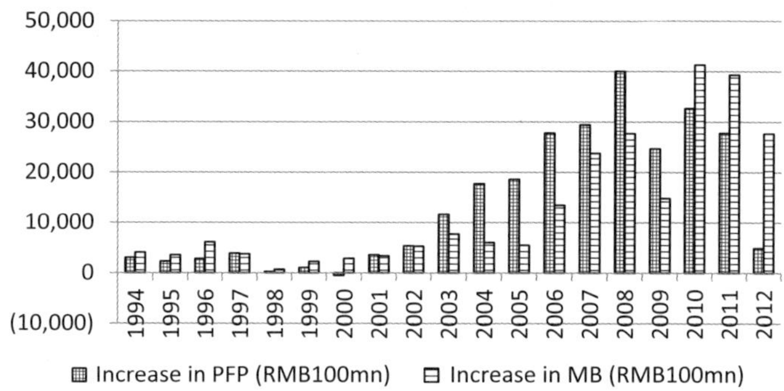

Figure 5. Increases in PFP and MB.

other Asian currencies depreciated substantially. From 2001, the year when China joined the WTO, PFP began to pile up in unprecedented scale. In 2008, PFP accounted for 130.3% of MB and 35.4% of M2. The ratio of PFP to M2 started to decline in 2009, but not because PFP stopped to pile up, but because the stimulus package at the end of 2008 unleashed massive credit expansion which led to dramatic increase in M2 (M2 increased 27.6% in 2009). Figure 5 compares the increases in PFP and MB. From 2001 to 2009, the increase in PFP consistently topped the increase in MB. In an extreme year of 2005, the increase in PFP was 339% of that in MB.

This was obviously a success story of PBC, maintaining a moderate growth in the high-powered base money during this period despite the rapid money creation through PFP. Before examining how PBC achieved this, we first describe PBC's policy instruments, old and new.

The Changing Set of Policy Instruments

Credit Plan and Credit Ceiling

In the pre-reform era, credit plan was the major monetary policy instrument. Along with cash plan and interest rates setting, credit plan was an integral part of centralized economic planning. After 1978, PBC began to experiment decentralized credit planning. However, decentralized credit planning proved to be vulnerable to pressures from credit-hungry state enterprises and local governments. As credit expansion and inflation got out of control in 1988, PBC reintroduced credit ceiling for banks. Credit ceiling thus became a major policy instrument of PBC, especially when the economy was in heated mode.

Credit ceiling was effective in controlling the inflation in late 1980s and again in early 1990s. However, it had all the limitations of command-based economic planning. The consensus was that credit ceiling was a necessary sin for the economy in transition and had to be phased out as institutional and market conditions improved. Indeed, PBC ceased to use credit ceiling in 1998.

Central Bank's Loan (CBL)

Central Bank's Loans (CBL) referred to PBC's loan to financial institutions, especially commercial banks. Before 1994, it was a major policy instrument for adjusting base money. When PBC wanted to tighten (expand) money supply, it reduced (increased) lending to banks. From 1994, CBL as a monetary policy instrument began to lose flexibility, as "twin surpluses" kicked in and rapid increases in PFP forced PBC to hold back CBL. After 1994, CBL was mainly used for injecting liquidity to financial institutions in distress or those already in debt-restructuring process.

Open Market Operations (OMO)

PBC experimented with trading treasury bonds in 1996, but only from 1998 did PBC begin to conduct open market operation (OMO) on large scale. In 1999 and 2000, when aggregate demand was weak, OMO became the major source of base money expansion (Wang, 2001). However, the ability of OMO was restricted by the amount of treasury bonds trading in the open market, which was very limited at the time. Furthermore, as the PBC's holding of bonds was even less, there was an asymmetry of OMO's effectiveness in expansionary and contractionary operations. If inflation became a worry, the ability of OMO to drain liquidity was very limited. This was, indeed, what happened after China joined WTO in 2001, when PFP began to pile up rapidly.

In addition to bond trading, PBC also conducted short-term repo to drain liquidity from market or reverse repo to inject liquidity. However, the same limitation, that is the limited supply of underlying assets, could be applied to repo and reverse repo operations.

Issuance of Central Bank Bill (CBB)

As PFP rapidly piled up, PBC must find ways to sterilize its effect and prevent rapid expansion of base money. One innovation was the issuance of Central Bank Bill (CBB). Unlike treasury bonds issued by the Ministry of Finance, CBB was issued by the monetary authority PBC and was not intended for financing government spending. The sole purpose of CBB was to sterilize the increases of PFP by draining liquidity from the interbank money market. CBB was of course interest-bearing. Since the interest payment was not backed by the fiscal authority, it is part of money creation by PBC.

CBB played a dominant role in containing inflationary pressure from the "twin surpluses." As Table 1 shows, CBB issuance increased from 193.75 billion yuan in 2002, representing 4.3% of BM, to 3.7 trillion yuan in 2008, which amounted to 47.0% of BM. At the beginning, CBB was mostly short-term bills. The average term was about six months in 2002. The short-term bills were soon found to be inadequate to "lock in" liquidity brought by the increases in PFP. In 2005, the average term was about 11 months, and it increased further to about 17 months in 2007. It was not uncommon in 2007 that PBC issued three-year bills.

Table 1. Summary of Central Bank Bill (CBB) issuances (2002–2011).

	Issuances	Total amount (RMB 100 mn)	Average term (year)	Average annual rate (%)
2002	19	1938	0.58	2.12
2003	63	7638	0.42	2.48
2004	105	15161	0.68	2.86
2005	124	27462	0.94	1.94
2006	97	36523	0.66	2.35
2007	141	40571	1.40	3.23
2008	122	42960	1.09	3.78
2009	71	38240	0.50	1.34
2010	114	42350	0.99	1.96
2011	100	14140	0.79	3.23

Source: Tonghuashun.

For reasons that we will analyze later in this chapter, PBC curtailed the issuance of CBB in 2011. The total amount of CBB issuances amounted only 6.3% of BM in 2011. In 2012, the issuance of CBB was stopped all together. Within less than a decade, CBB rose to dominance and fell back to negligibility.

Deposit Reserve (DR)

PBC introduced required deposit reserve (DR) in 1984, in an attempt to strengthen the control of bank loans. For the purpose, the minimum deposit reserve ratio was 40% for urban household deposits, 25% for rural household deposits, and 20% for enterprise deposits. Furthermore, since the deposit reserve could not be used in transactions and settlements at the time, banks were required to put additional settlement reserves (5–7%) in PBC. In 1985, PBC lowered DR ratio to 10% for all deposits. But the settlement reserve requirement remained until 1998.

The DR ratio was employed as a monetary policy instrument soon after it was introduced. The DR ratio was increased to 12% in 1987 and to 13% in 1988 to combat inflation. The move proved to be useful, thanks to the fact that money supply at the time was almost solely determined by bank loans.

In 1998, a major reform was introduced to DR policy. The DR account and the settlement reserve account merged into one. The

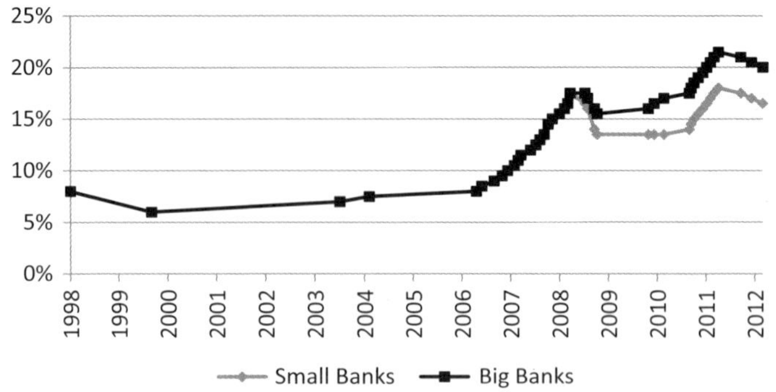

Figure 6. Minimum deposit reserve ratio (%).

required DR ratio was lowered to 8%, in an attempt to stimulate weak demand following the Asian financial crisis. But banks were allowed to deposit more in the new DR account ("Excess DR"), which is interest-bearing.

Since 2003, to sterilize the increase in PFP, PBC began to raise the required DR ratio, gradually at first, and aggressively from 2006 (Figure 6). The DR ratio was raised to 17.5% in mid-2008 from 8% in mid-2006, after 18 raises in about two years. The DR ratio was lowered to 15.5% at the end of 2008 when the whole world was deep in financial crisis. From 2010, when inflation pressure came back, thanks to the massive stimulus package enacted in 2008, PBC began yet another round of aggressive raises of DR ratio, from 15.5% in early 2010 to 21.5% in mid-2011 for big banks.[6] The ratio of deposit reserve to total liabilities increased slightly from 36.7% in 2003 to 37.5% in 2006, but increased dramatically since 2006 to 65.1% in 2012. There was little doubt that DR requirement had become the major monetary policy instrument in the past six years.

The Great Accommodation

In 1998, PBC stopped setting credit ceilings for the big state banks. Those for smaller banks were scrapped years earlier. This marked

[6]PBC began to set different deposit reserve ratio for smaller banks in September 25, 2008.

the PBC's transition from command-based to market-based central banking. In this new model of central banking, PBC manipulates its own balance sheet, instead of those of commercial banks, to indirectly influence the latter's operations. In this section, we examine PBC's balance sheet and study how PBC accommodated the surge in foreign exchange purchase without causing severe inflation.

Balance Sheet of PBC

Like commercial banks, a generic central bank's balance sheet is composed of liabilities and capital on the one hand and assets on the other. Table 2 gives a detailed description of the items in PBC's balance sheet, and Table 3 lists data for each item from 1999 to 2012.

The assets of PBC include foreign assets (FA), claims on government (CG), claims on private sector, and "other assets" (OA) that are largely out of sight of the public. FA include gold reserve and, importantly, forex reserve. Claims on private sector include those on other depository corporations (CODC), those on other financial corporations (COFC), and those on non-financial corporations (CNFC). The assets of PBC were once dominated by CODC, which

Table 2. Balance sheet of PBC: Items of assets and liabilities.

Assets	Liabilities
	Reserve money (RM, "Base money")
Foreign assets (FA)	Currency issue (CI)
Foreign exchange (Forex)	Deposits of other depository corporations (DODC)
Monetary gold (Gold)	
Other foreign assets (OFA)	Deposits of financial corporations excluded from reserve money (DFCXR)
Claims on government (CG)	Deposits of government (DG)
Claims on private sector	Bond issue (BI)
Claims on other depository corporations (CODC)	Foreign liabilities (FL)
Claims on other financial corporations (COFC)	Other liabilities (OL)
Claims on non-financial sector (CNFS)	
Other Assets (OA)	Own Capital (OC)

Table 3. Balance sheet of PBC (1999–2012).

	TA	FA	Forex	Gold	OFA	CG	CODC	COFC	CNFC	OA
1999	3535.0	1445.9	1406.1	1.2	38.5	158.3	1537.4	383.3	10.2	N/A
2000	3939.5	1518.9	1481.5	1.2	36.2	158.3	1351.9	860.0	11.0	N/A
2001	4254.1	1935.1	1885.0	25.6	24.5	282.1	1131.2	854.7	19.6	N/A
2002	5068.5	2282.0	2210.7	33.7	37.5	286.4	1228.8	724.0	20.7	526.6
2003	6152.2	3065.9	2984.2	33.7	96.3	290.1	1198.3	725.6	20.6	851.6
2004	7809.3	4639.8	4594.0	33.7	68.3	297.0	1042.4	886.5	13.6	930.0
2005	10367.6	6333.9	6214.0	33.7	86.2	289.2	816.8	1775.1	6.7	1146.0
2006	12857.5	8577.3	8436.1	33.7	107.5	285.6	651.7	2195.0	6.6	1141.3
2007	16914.0	12482.5	11516.9	33.7	931.9	1631.8	786.3	1297.2	6.4	709.8
2008	20709.6	16254.4	14962.4	33.7	1258.2	1619.6	843.3	1185.3	4.4	802.7
2009	22753.0	18533.3	17515.5	67.0	950.9	1566.2	716.2	1153.0	4.4	779.9
2010	25927.5	21542.0	20676.7	67.0	798.3	1542.1	948.6	1132.6	2.5	759.8
2011	28097.8	23789.8	23238.9	67.0	483.9	1540.0	1024.8	1064.4	2.5	676.3
2012	29453.7	24141.7	23667.0	67.0	407.7	1531.4	1670.1	1003.9	2.5	1104.2

	RM	CI	DODC	DFCXR	BI	FL	DG	OC	OL
1999	3362.0	1507.0	1420.1	N/A	11.9	N/A	178.6	36.7	N/A
2000	3649.1	1593.8	1539.2	N/A	0.0	N/A	310.0	35.7	N/A
2001	3985.2	1686.9	1685.3	N/A	0.0	N/A	285.1	35.5	N/A
2002	4513.8	1858.9	1913.3	N/A	148.8	N/A	308.5	22.0	75.4
2003	5284.1	2124.0	2255.5	N/A	303.2	N/A	495.5	22.0	95.7
2004	5885.6	2310.4	3563.3	N/A	1107.9	N/A	583.2	22.0	210.6
2005	6434.3	2585.4	3822.5	N/A	2029.6	64.2	752.7	22.0	1064.8
2006	7775.8	2913.9	4822.4	N/A	2974.1	92.6	1021.1	22.0	972.0
2007	10154.5	3297.2	6809.5	N/A	3446.9	94.7	1712.1	22.0	1483.7
2008	12922.2	3711.6	9189.5	59.1	4578.0	73.3	1696.4	22.0	1358.6
2009	14398.5	4155.6	10228.1	62.5	4206.4	76.2	2122.6	22.0	1864.9
2010	18531.1	4864.6	13648.1	65.7	4049.7	72.0	2427.7	22.0	759.2
2011	22464.2	5585.0	16879.2	90.8	2333.7	269.9	2273.4	22.0	643.8
2012	25234.5	6064.6	19169.9	134.9	1388.0	146.4	2075.3	22.0	452.6

TA: Total Assets, FA: Foreign Assets, Forex: Foreign Exchange, OFA: Other Foreign Assets, CG: Claims on Government, CODC: Claims on Other Depository Corporations, COFC: Claims on Other Financial Corporations, CNFC: Claims on Non-Financial Corporations, OA: Other Assets.

RM: Reserve Money, CI: Currency Issue, DODC: Deposits of Other Depository Corporations, DFCXRM: Deposits of Financial Corporations eXcluded from Reserve, BI: Bond Issue, FL: Foreign Liabilities, DG: Deposits of Government, OC: Own Capital, OL: Other Liabilities.

documented PBC's CBL operations. In 1999, CODC still accounted for 43.5% of all assets, while forex reserve accounted for 40.9%. In 2012, however, CODC's share dropped to 5.7% of total assets, while forex reserve rose to 82.0%. As discussed previously, the dramatic increase in the share of forex reserve was driven by the persistent "twin surpluses." As the "twin surpluses" were caused by industrial and trade policies that are largely outside PBC's domain, we may treat the change in the asset sheet of PBC as exogenous.

The liabilities of PBC include reserve money (RM, or base money), deposits of financial corporations excluded from reserve (DFIXR), bond issue (BI), foreign liabilities (FL), deposits of government (DG), own capital (OC), and "other liabilities" (OL) that are as opaque as OA. Unlike commercial banks, the central bank's liabilities are mainly in the form of base money and its own capital is often negligible. Typically, the dominant share of total liability is base money, of which the largest share is currency in circulation. In a normal year of 2006, for example, the share of currency in circulation in total liability was 88.4% for US Federal Reserve, 54.6% for European Central Bank, and 69.1% for Bank of Japan. For PBC, this share was 22.7% in 2006. For a more detailed cross-country study of central bank's balance sheet structure, see Wang (2010).

Debt Financing Replaces Currency Issuance

We may think of the liabilities of PBC, much like a commercial bank, as means of financing for asset acquisition. PBC's challenge was to manipulate its liability structure to achieve domestic price stability, at the same time finance the ballooning foreign asset acquisition, which was largely exogenous. The total liability or to borrow a term from corporate finance, total value of PBC, can be expressed as follows,

$$\mathrm{V} = \mathrm{C} + \mathrm{D} + \mathrm{E} \tag{1}$$

where C is currency in circulation, D is value of debt which includes CBB and deposits of government (DG) and financial corporations (DODC), and E is own capital (OC). Here we omit other items in the liability sheet such as DFIXR, which is negligible, and OL, which is opaque to the public.

A Simplified Diagram of PBC's liabilities

Liabilities of Central Bank

C	D	E
Currency	Deposit of Other Depository Corporations Deposit of Government Bond Issue	Equity

C is a zero-cost financing only available to a central bank. The monopoly use of C indeed defines a central bank. D is more expensive. The deposits of other depository corporations (DODC) bear interest, albeit low. Currently, the interest rate on required deposit reserve is 1.62% and that on excess reserve is 0.72%. Bond issue is even more expensive. Before each issuance of CBB, PBC would consult participants in the inter-bank market on the interest rate they would accept. A market-based interest rate is thus formed. We can see in Figure 7 that the interest rates on CBB and government bonds (one-year term) roughly move in tandem. Like many other central banks, E is small and exhibits little variation over time. Indeed, PBC's own capital has not changed from 2003 to 2012, while V almost quintupled during this period.

To characterize the dynamics of debt financing replacing currency issuance, we first define equilibrium for currency issuance.

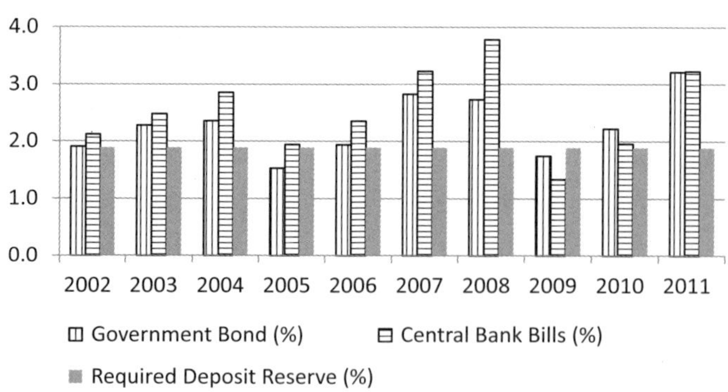

Figure 7. Average interest rate on government bonds (one-year term) and central bank bills.

Definition: *An equilibrium for currency issuance occurs when real demand for currency equals real balance of currency, that is C/P.*

Proposition 1. *Assume E is fixed and real demand for currency grows at rate c_t. If the total value of a monetary authority grows exogenously at a rate v_t, then the monetary authority achieves inflation π_t in the equilibrium of currency issuance if D expands at rate*

$$d_t = \frac{C_t}{D_t}\left(\frac{v_t}{\frac{C_t}{V_t}} - \pi_t - c_t\right).$$

The proof of the proposition is in the Appendix A. If we assume that real demand for currency is proportional to real GDP, then $c = g$, real GDP growth. Figure 8 illustrates the empirical validity of the proposition by charting the implied growth in D with data. Since $\frac{\partial d_t}{\partial v_t} = \frac{V_t}{D_t} > 1$, for each unit increase in v_t, d_t must increase more, given an inflation target and real GDP growth. In other words, PBC has to accommodate a quicker growth in total asset by an ever quicker growth in debt financing, either through raising required reserve ratio or issuing more central bank bills.

From Proposition 1 we may deduce:

Corollary 7.1. *The share of D in V expands if and only if*

$$v_t > \frac{C_t}{C_t + E_t}(\pi_t + c_t).$$

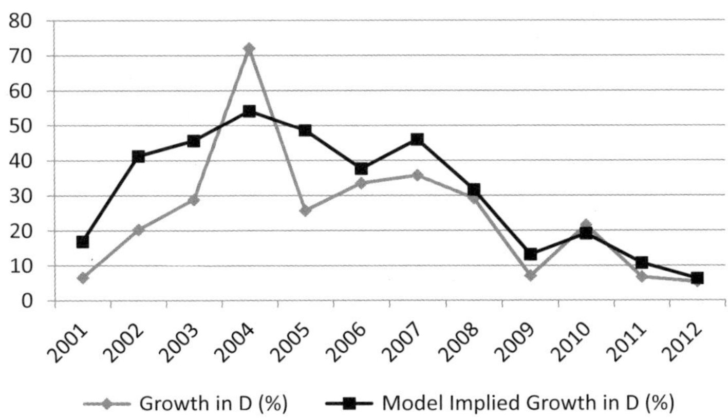

Figure 8. Growth in D financing and that implied in Proposition 1.

Since E is negligible relative to C, under the additional assumption $c = g$, it does not lose much accuracy to claim that the share of D expands if V expands faster than nominal GDP.

For PBC from 2001 to 2012, PBC's total value V expanded at an average compound rate of 17.6%, while average inflation was 2.5% and real GDP growth was 10.2%. Looking more closely, we find in Figure 9 that the growth rate of V were consistently higher than nominal GDP growth rate from 2002 to 2008. This occurred again in 2010.

Indeed, as shown in Figure 10, the share of D increased dramatically since 2003, when PBC formally began to issue CBB. In 2010,

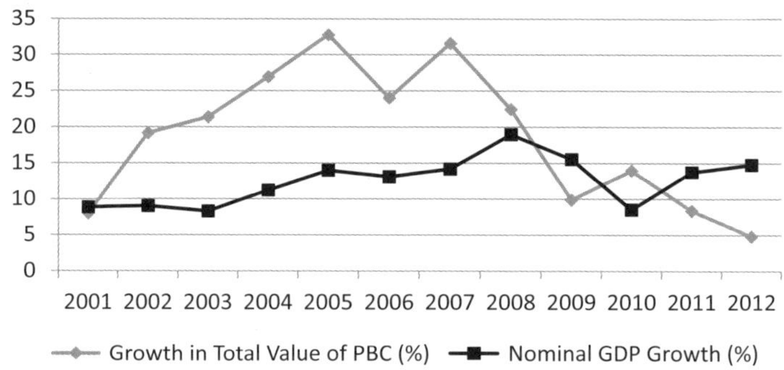

Figure 9. Growth in total value of PBC (V) compared with nominal GDP growth.

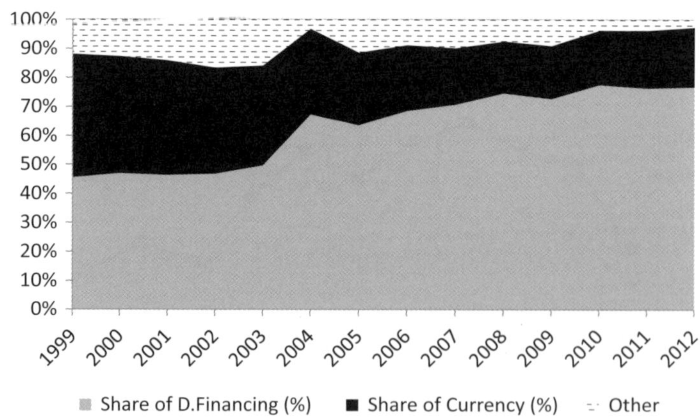

Figure 10. Liability structure of PBC (1999–2012).

the share of D reached an all-time-high of 77.6%. Correspondingly, the share of CBB declined from 42.6% in 1999 to a historic low of 17.9% in 2008, and rebounded only slightly to 20.6% in 2012.

The Rise and Fall of Central Bank Bills

The issuance of CBB was a major policy innovation during the great accommodation. Because of the limited supply of government bonds, the usual open market operation with treasury bonds was unable to drain the seemingly unlimited liquidity generated from forex reserve purchase. In September 2002, PBC converted its repo position into CBB, and, from April 2003, PBC began to issue CBB on a continual basis in the inter-bank market, with terms of three-month, six-month, one-year, and three-year.

As described in previous section, CBB issuance increased dramatically in the following several years, playing an increasingly important role in debt financing (D) of PBC from 2003 to 2006. Figure 11 shows that the share of CBB position in D increased from 9.9% in 2003 to 33.7% in 2006. From 2006 to 2012, however, the share of CBB declined all the way to 6.1%. In fact, PBC has stopped issuing new CBB since 2012. The inverted U-shape of CBB's share in D documented the rise and fall of CBB in the great accommodation.

The advantages of CBB over usual OMO with treasury bonds are obvious. With CBB, PBC's ability of draining liquidity is no

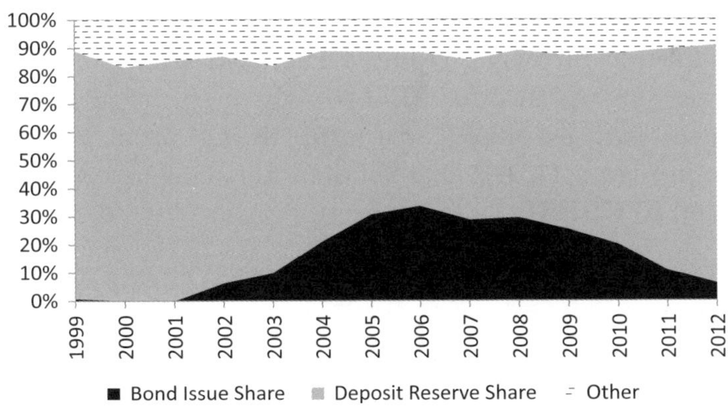

Figure 11. The rise and fall of bond issue.

longer bounded by the supply of operatable assets such as treasury bonds. However, PBC incurs a higher cost in issuing CBB, which bears a market interest rate, than, say, requiring DR. The cost difference between CBB and DR, indeed, may partly explain the fall of CBB.

From 2003 to 2011, the average interest rate on CBB was generally higher than the interest rate paid on required DR, which was a constant 1.89%. The only exception occurred in 2009, when demand for safe assets was unusually high after the financial crisis. In some years, interest rate on CBB was much higher than that on DR. In 2008, for example, the average interest rate on CBB was 3.78%, double of that on DR.

Unlike treasury bonds, the interest burden of CBB is not on the fiscal authority but on the PBC, and the interest payment is backed not by taxation but money creation. As PBC pays interest, the payment automatically adds to base money. From a long-term perspective, thus, there is little sterilization in the issuance of CBB. CBBs are similar to treasury bonds in that CBBs only transfer, but not lower, some of the current inflationary pressure to the future, just like treasury bonds only transfer, but not lower, current tax burden to the future. In the case of CBB, the delay of inflationary pressure was at most three years, a not-too-distant future indeed.

In contrast, the required DR bears a much lower interest rate, and equally important, the required DR may delay the current inflationary pressure to an indefinite distant future. As a result, there is *real* sterilization in raising required DR from a long-term perspective. It was thus natural for PBC to rediscover the merit of DR in 2006, when "twin surpluses" was in full swing. From 2006 to 2012, as shown in Figure 11, DR share of debt financing (D) reclaimed the lost ground to CBB.

Assessment

The surge in forex reserve purchase was a consequence of China's industrial and trade policies, which were largely outside PBC's control. PBC accommodated the great expansion of balance sheet *via* a structural twist to its liabilities such that growth in currency issuance was reined in and large pool of liquidity was locked in PBC's vault. From 2001 to 2012, China's inflation averaged 2.5% against the backdrop of an average 17.6% growth in PBC's total liability. The highest monthly inflation rate was 8.7% occurred in February 2008, which was driven by food and energy prices. This was a notable achievement of central banking in a tough place and tough era.

The great accommodation was not without cost. The frequent use of reserve requirement ratio as a monetary policy instrument meant reduced flexibility and profitability of commercial banks. Indeed, Abiad *et al.* (2008) classify a require DR ratio of equal or greater than 20% as "restrictive," a line China crossed in 2011. There were two kinds of developments in response to the rising reserve requirement ratio.

First, in a process called "financial dis-intermediation," many borrowers turned to other types of financing. In 2002, the share of bank loans in aggregate financing of the economy was 95.5%. The share dropped to 52% in 2012. In contrast, the share of corporate bonds increased from 1.8% in 2002 to 14.3% in 2012, and the share of trust loans increased from almost zero in 2002 to 8.15% in 2012. In recent years, indeed, trust became a significant player in financing and at the same time, an important destination for household savings.[7]

Second, banks moved more and more lending "off balance sheet." The usual instruments include entrusted loans, undiscounted banker's acceptance, and trust loans in cooperation with trusts. Financial innovation abounded, taking advantages of loopholes in regulations. For example, entrusted loans were originally one-to-one, meaning that one agent lends directly to another through a bank, which collected a processing fee without assuming any risk. In recent years, however, there appeared one-to-many, many-to-one, and even many-to-many entrusted loans. In these creative forms,

[7]Trust loan is a form of direct financing from trust investors to debtors. A trust company is, in legal terms, not responsible for bad loans. In practice, however, trusts guarantee payment of the principal at least, for fear of losing market or more seriously, losing their license. This implicit guarantee makes a trust a bank-like entity. It is not unreasonable that some characterize trust loans as shadow banking business.

banks could not escape responsibilities if loans became bad. These creative entrusted loans, indeed, had every characteristic of normal bank loans, except, they are "off balance sheet."

Some of these developments are favorable, such as the expanding role of corporate bonds. Indeed, there is still large room for the development of direct financing, either in the form of equity or bond. But some other developments are not so favorable. Many so-called financial innovations transform regulated activities into those under no or less regulation. In this process, traditional financial institutions such as banks, brokers, and trusts become part of the fast expanding shadow banking system. Without proper regulation and surveillance, the shadow banking system will make the entire financial system more vulnerable to internal and external shocks.

These developments could make PBC less powerful in influencing monetary and liquidity conditions of the Chinese economy. The reserve requirement ratio is a quantitative instrument only effective in the control of bank loans. As the role of bank loans becomes even smaller in the economy, reserve requirement would become less powerful in influencing aggregate financing of the economy.

Chinese Central Banking in the Future

The future of Chinese central banking will partly depend on the future of its asset sheet, which largely depends on China's trade and industrial policies. Therefore, part of the policy recommendations that we outline as follows will be outside PBC's usual domain. It is indeed not possible to reform Chinese central banking by reforming PBC's practices alone.

Balance of Payments

Policy makers should give higher priority to the external balance of payments (BoP) position. BoP equilibrium is listed as the No. 4 objective of monetary policy, but it was essentially ignored during the great accommodation. There are different interpretations of the meaning of the BoP equilibrium. One particularly strict definition of BoP equilibrium would require both current and capital accounts to be balanced individually.[8] A less strict definition of BoP equilibrium would require the sum of current and capital surpluses to be zero, which would amount to zero growth in forex reserve, an outcome that is consistent, one, with a current account surplus and capital account deficit, and, two, with a current account deficit and capital account surplus. Zero growth in forex reserve would, of course, always be guaranteed when PBC stops its intervention in the forex market, i.e., when the RMB floats freely against the other currencies.

While there is a growing consensus about the importance of BoP equilibrium, the issue of how much the exchange rate should be allowed to fluctuate remains contentious. There is a school of commentators who emphasize the role of "structural reasons" for the BoP imbalance. They would argue that the imbalance of trade is caused by the gap between saving and investment. Specifically, China saves too much over investment, e.g., Bernanke (2005). In the view of the structuralists, the value of the exchange rate is not important for the imbalance of trade, finding support from the fact that Chinese net export to the US kept expanding even after yuan began to appreciate since 2005.

The structuralists also see China's capital account surplus as the result of weakness in the Chinese financial sector. As the underdeveloped financial industry could not convert Chinese savings into domestic investment, the job has then been outsourced to the Wall Street. The Wall Street converts the cheap funding from PBC's forex reserve purchase into high-return FDI into China.

We are skeptical of the structuralist explanation that sees the amount of savings and investment as exogenous variables. We see the gap between saving and investment, and the amount of FDI into China as endogenous outcomes from two sets of distortionary state economic policies. In the first set of distortionary policies, the variables that should be considered exogenous are the value of the

[8]PBC's recent communications with the press seem to imply that PBC wishes to achieve this strict sense of BoP equilibrium. Vice Governor Yi Gang summarized PBC's recent policy directions as "expand internal demand, adjust structure, decrease surpluses, and achieve balances."

exchange rate; China's trade policy regime of export-promotion and import-substitution;[9] preferential policies toward FDI; and various subsidies to manufacturing sector in general (cheap energy, loose environmental protection, etc.). These policies start the chain reactions that finally lead to the persistent "twin surpluses." As in Yu (2010), we would argue that China should adopt a more flexible exchange rate, give equal treatment to all producers (exporters or not), give equal treatment to all industrial investors (foreign or domestic), and usher in reforms that promote market-based factor pricing with environmental considerations.

In the second set of distortionary policies, the primary policy variable that has raised savings to be above, and lower investments to be below, the free market level is the over-regulation of China's financial markets and the discrimination against the domestic private sector which together keep the financial markets underdeveloped as characterized by the limited terms of variety of financial products offered to the public, the disproportionately large amount of total credit allocated to state-controlled production units, and the near-total dominance in every type of legal financial activities by state-controlled financial institutions. Woo (2008) has argued that China's current account surplus exists because its dysfunctional financial system cannot intermediate the private savings into desired private investments. The private savings rate is high because China does not have the variety of financial institutions that would, one, reduce risks by pooling them and providing medical insurance, pension insurance, and unemployment insurance; and, two, transform savings into education loans, housing loans, and other types of investment loans that would enable the private investor to reap the high returns from China's fast-growing economy. The backward financial system in China has increased precaution-motivated savings and investment-motivated savings thereby raising the private savings rate in China 7.0 to 12.2 percentage points higher than in the US.[10]

[9]For example, tax rebates and preferential credit line for exporters.

[10]Woo's (2008) estimates are based on the empirical work of Liu and Woo (1994) who added a "financial sophistication variable" into the standard Modigliani-style private savings equation.

Opening of Capital Account and Diversification of Forex Reserve

China's forex reserve is much larger than needed for transactions and settlement in international trade and finance. It is also much larger than needed for "self-insurance" purposes. As the forex reserve is mostly in the form of long-term US treasury bills, it generally receives low interest, a return much lower than FDI in China, which is partly financed by Chinese saving. The over-accumulation of forex reserve thus leads to welfare loss for the Chinese public.

To reduce official holding of forex reserve and diversify the investment of forex reserve, we may rely on one simple reform: the opening of the capital account, especially outward security investments. In recent years, there have been some limited trials in opening security investment to private investors. For example, domestic financial institutions may apply for QDII (Qualified Domestic Institutional Investor), which allows qualified institutions to invest in equities and bonds abroad.[11] These trials can be enlarged gradually. In the end, everyone including retail investors should be allowed to invest abroad. Since the newly rich in China have strong incentives to diversify their assets internationally, the effects of opening capital account can be immediate and significant. First, the official holding of foreign currency will be transferred to private hands. Second, as the risk appetite of private investors naturally differs from that of the government, Chinese assets in the abroad will be diversified accordingly. Both developments would point to more efficient use of forex reserve.

Moving from Quantity-Based to Price-Based Central Banking

PBC should now move from quantity-based central banking to price-based central banking. The quantity-based central banking targets money supply, while price-based central banking targets market interest rate. Central banks in developed countries usually rely on

[11]Similarly, there is QFII (Qualified Foreign Institutional Investor).

price-based instruments such as US federal fund rate and ECB's refinance rate. In the case of US, the Fed announces a given federal fund rate which is subsequently backed by open market operations. In the case of euro area, ECB sets the refinance rate which subsequently becomes the benchmark rate for market participants. A central bank can directly and precisely control only the MB, a narrow form of money. However, the wider form of money is largely endogenous, and the supply of broad money is determined by market participants. The price-based instruments are favorable to modern central banking since they directly alter costs and incentives of market participants.

For PBC, it may not be a matter of choosing which is more favorable. The current trend may force PBC to move to price-based central banking. First, measurement of money and liquidity will become an issue as Chinese economy and financial market become more complex, making robust quantity-targeting difficult, if not impossible. Second, the most important policy instrument of PBC is now DR ratio, a quantitative tool most effective at controlling bank loans, but the role of bank loans is fast declining. Direct financing in the forms of equities and bonds will take more important share in aggregate social financing. And perhaps more importantly, shadow banking system is fast expanding, mainly driven by restrictions put on banks by PBC and other regulatory entities. The highly adaptable shadow banking system makes it impossible for PBC to target any quantitative measure by quantity restrictions on financial institutions. The quantity restrictions only drive more activities into shadow. Eventually, PBC has to target some interest rate.

PBC, indeed, has taken gradual steps to prepare for the new model of price-based central banking. First, interest rate adjustments have been used along with quantity-based measures in the past policy maneuvers. Market participants have learned to form expectations of movements in interest rates. Second, there has been important progress in the introduction of market interest rates. Interest rates in money and bond markets are already market-based. The same is true for interest rates on wealth-management-products (WMP), loans and deposits in foreign currency. Interest rate upper bound on bank deposit and lower bound on loans still remain, but the bounds have been relaxed recently,[12] giving commercial banks more freedom in setting interest rates. To introduce a market-based benchmark interest rate, PBC established SHIBOR (ShangHai Interbank Offer Rate) in early 2007. SHIBOR has already become an important benchmark rate for transactions in money and bond markets. Third, financial markets are now more developed. As an important development, PBC established the interbank funding market and the interbank bond market in as early as 1997. Over the subsequent years, these two markets grew rapidly. Trading volumes in the interbank funding market and the interbank bond market reached 33.4 trillion and 163.1 trillion yuan in 2011, respectively.

These are far from enough, however. To make the new model of price-based central banking work, PBC will need more developed financial infrastructure. First, PBC is in need of a target short rate. SHIBOR, as a rate formed in the interbank funding market, is not suitable for this role. Firstly, SHIBOR is not a risk-free rate per se. Secondly, the interbank funding market is a small one compared to the bond market, whether measured in trading volumes or number and type of participants. It is thus doubtable that PBC's policy can be effectively transmitted to the financial market through the funding market. A natural candidate for the target short rate would be repo rate on treasury bonds, which is generally regarded as risk-free. However, the bond markets are rather fragmented. There are three bond markets in China: interbank market, security exchange market, and over-the-counter market. Repo rates on a same asset can be very different in different markets. Institutional reforms should be introduced to allow arbitrage across different markets. In this way, we may achieve a unified bond market with diversified investors.

Second, treasury bond issuance needs to expand,[13] *not only in quantity and frequency, but also in more continuous term structure.* For the sake of tradability, book-entry treasury bonds should

[12]From June 2012, the interest rate upper bound on deposits is 10% higher than benchmark rate, which is still set by PBC, and the lower bound on loans is 30% lower than benchmark rate.

[13]This depends, of course, on whether there is need for deficit financing or not. The increase in treasure bond issuance may be accompanied by a tax cut.

dominate bond issuance.[14] At the same time, the Ministry of Finance should make bond issuance more regular and predictable, conditional on the fiscal conditions of the central government, so that the market may form better expectations.

Finally, the futures exchange market for treasury bonds should be restored. The futures market of treasury bonds is essential for hedging interest rate risk. China experimented with treasure bonds futures in early 1990s, but the experiment was unfortunately stopped following the notorious "327 treasure bond incident" in 1995. It is arguable that the failed experiment was indeed too early. But almost 20 years later, as interest rates become more volatile as liberalization forges ahead, the futures market for treasury bonds has become a necessity, for financial and nonfinancial institutions alike. The futures exchange for treasury bonds is also important for price (interest rate) finding. Indeed, for PBC, a well-functioning futures market for treasury bonds can be a powerful link in the transmission of interest rate policies to the entire financial system.

Conclusions

In this chapter, we document PBC's accommodation of forex reserve accumulation with an unconventional liability expansion, which avoided rapid expansion in BM and severe inflation. The unconventional expansion of liability was a process in which currency issuance was replaced by debt financing, which mainly includes issuance of CBB and frequent changes in the required deposits of commercial banks. These steps have been effective in the fight against inflation.

However, the use of these instruments has sowed the seeds for undermining their effectiveness. PBC's reliance on DR ratio, coupled with other regulations on banks, already set forth: (a) a dis-intermediation process, in which direct finance replaces bank loans; and (b) the expansion of shadow banking. In the end, PBC may end up in a position where its control of bank loans is no longer

[14]There are three types of treasury bonds in China: certified bond, book-entry bond, and bearer bond. Purchase of certified bond is equivalent to saving. Book-entry bond is most suitable for trading in modern exchanges.

effective in controlling the macro economy. For viable and better central banking in the future, policy makers should relax constraints on PBC by adopting a more flexible exchange rate, abandonment of export-promotion policies and preferential policies toward FDI, and the opening of the capital account. Opening the capital account, in particular, achieves reduction in, and diversification of the official forex reserve at the same time.

It should be stressed that besides the pricing reform of using a more market-determined exchange rate to restore independence to monetary policy and to reduce the trade imbalance, there should also be institutional reform that allows the private sector a greater presence in the different financial markets in order to improve financial intermediation that will translate more of the domestic savings into domestic investments and hence reduce the trade imbalance and the creation of liquidity. Equally important is that the strong growth of private Chinese financial firms will produce a more competitive and dynamic financial sector and a more efficient growth pattern for China.

Appendix

Proof of Proposition 1: Let R be real demand for currency and P be price level. Apply the equilibrium condition R = C/P, we write

$$D_t = V_t - R_t P_t - E_t.$$

Differentiate both sides of the equation with respect to t, we have

$$\begin{aligned} d_t &= \frac{dD_t}{D_t} \\ &= \frac{dV_t}{V_t}\frac{V_t}{D_t} - \frac{dR_t}{R_t}\frac{P_t R_t}{D_t} - \frac{dP_t}{P_t}\frac{P_t R_t}{D_t} - \frac{dE_t}{E_t}\frac{E_t}{D_t} \\ &= v_t \frac{V_t}{D_t} - c_t \frac{C_t}{D_t} - \pi_t \frac{C_t}{D_t}. \end{aligned}$$

Note that $c_t = \frac{dR_t}{R_t}$ is growth in real demand for currency, $\pi_t = \frac{dP_t}{P_t}$ is inflation rate, and that $\frac{dE_t}{E_t} = 0$ by assumption. Collecting terms yields the desired result. □

References

Abiad, A, E Detragiache and T Tressel (2008). A new database of financial reforms. IMF Working Paper WP/08/266, Washington, DC: International Monetary Fund.

Bernanke, BS (2005). The global saving glut and the US current account deficit. Homer Jones Lecture, Federal Reserve Bank of St. Louis, April 14. Available at www.federalreserve.gov/boarddocs/speeches/2005/20050414/default.htm.

Fan, G and WT Woo (1996). State enterprise reform as a source of macroeconomic instability: The case of China. *Asian Economic Journal*, 10(3), 207–224.

Liu, L-Y and WT Woo (1994). Saving behavior under imperfect financial markets and the current account consequences. *Economic Journal*, 104(424), 512–527.

Wang, G (2010). The analysis of central banking capability based on balance sheets of central banks. *Financial Review*, 1, 1–16.

Wang, Y (2001). On the reform of central banking practices of China. *Economic Research*, 11, 28–34.

Woo, WT (2008). Understanding the sources of friction in US–China trade relations: The exchange rate debate diverts attention away from optimum adjustment. *Asian Economic Papers*, 7(3), 65–99.

Xiaoyi (2013). On top-down reforms of foreign exchange reserve and foreign exchange management. *China Reform*, 5.

Yi, G (1999). Chinese monetary policy moving to indirect central banking. *Journal of Capital Market*, 10, 6–11.

Yu, Y (1996). The problem of the macro-management of capital inflow. *World Economics and Politics*, 10.

Yu, Y (2010). Witness imbalances — Twin surpluses, renminbi exchange rate, and the dollar trap. *International Economic Review*, 3, 7–44.

Zhang, XZ, CZ Wan, and WJ Jiang (1997). Experiences and existing problems of macro-financial management since 1993. *Financial Research*, 5, 1–8.

Zhou, X (2012). Main characteristics of China's monetary policy in the new millennium. Per Jacobsson Lecture, Tokyo.

Chapter 8

The Structural Friction in China's Banking System: Causes, Measurement and Solutions

Hongzhong Liu and Tai Qin

Introduction

The relationship between financial development and economic growth has been one of the most important issues in the economic literature during the recent two decades. A large literature has analyzed the direction of the causality between financial development and economic growth. Some researchers argue that economic growth is the reason for financial development: as the economy grows, demands for financial services increase, which leads to the development of the financial sector e.g., Jung (1986). Others, on the other hand, have argued the reverse. For example, Levine (2005) has identified five ways that financial systems can improve the resource allocation process and increase growth: facilitating risk amelioration, acquiring information about investments, monitoring managers and exerting corporate control, mobilizing savings, and facilitating transactions. Most of the recent theoretical and empirical literature supports the latter point of view.

This paper was sponsored by People's Bank of China Project "Study on Real Interest Rates and Related Issues."

The literature has employed many different kinds of proxies to measure the level of a country's financial development. von Furstenberg and Fratianni (1996) have pointed out that financial development can be gauged from two dimensions: quantity and price. In general, quantity-based indicators, specifically stock-flow ratios, are preferred in the literature; and price-based indicators, namely interest rates spread, are rarely used. For instance, when measuring the development of banking system, two categories of quantity-based indicators are commonly used in the literature, e.g., Levine *et al.* (2000), Chinn and Ito (2006), Eichengreen *et al.* (2011) and Hassan *et al.* (2011):

1. aggregate quantity indicators that reflect the size of the financial sector, e.g., liquid liabilities (like broad money) divided by GDP, and domestic credit/deposit divided by GDP; and
2. quantity indicators that focus on certain funding channels or capital flow destinations, such as domestic credit to the private sector as a percentage of GDP. This second type of quantity indicators focuses on the share of the resources allocated by financial intermediaries to the more efficient sectors in the economy, and thus reflects the structural features of the financial sector.

However, as von Furstenberg and Fratianni (1996) and Levine *et al.* (2000) pointed out, both of these two quantity-based indicators cannot show the efficiency of the financial sector in reducing information asymmetry and transaction costs, and hence cannot directly reflect the improvement of efficiency.

Price-based indicators, on the other hand, could identify the resource allocation efficiency of the financial sector directly. However, because of the practical difficulties in computing price-based indicators, they are rarely used in the literature. For example, the spread between the rate of return on productive investment and the rate of return on intermediated savings — constructed by von Furstenberg and Fratianni (1996) — is the only price-based indicator we know to have been used to identify the efficiency losses caused by the monopoly power of the financial sector and the incompleteness of financial markets in developing countries. However, this price indicator by von Furstenberg and Fratianni cannot be mechanically used to measure the degree of the efficiency in China's financial markets because, until very recently, the interest rates were tightly controlled in China[1]: the spread between deposit rate and loan rate is exogenous to a great extent and is not the result of resource allocation.

This chapter seeks to answer the following questions: How to assess China's financial development quantitatively? What reforms must be undertaken to deepen financial development in order to allocate resources more efficiently?

Interest rate control, state-owned banks and structural friction

We see one of the most critical problems in China's banking system to be the phenomenon that is described by:

1. the credit resources that the banking system allocates to the lower-risk enterprises (state-owned and state-controlled enterprises) representing a disproportionately large share of the banks' total credit assets; and
2. the productivity of the lower-risk sector being lower than the higher-risk sector (mainly the private-owned and individual enterprises).

This phenomenon of the resource allocation of the banking system being tilted toward the lower-risk and lower-efficiency sector has also been noted by Woo (2006), Brandt and Zhu (2010), and Song *et al.* (2011).

In our analysis, this dysfunctional phenomenon is caused by "structural friction" which is the inevitable product of two state policies: the policy of controlling interest rates and the policy of allowing the state-owned banks (SOBs) to have near total domination of the banking system. We make the case of our diagnosis by considering

[1]Though the loan rate can be floated around the benchmark in a relatively large range, the floating range of deposit rate is limited within 10% of the benchmark rate. So banks can still get a guaranteed loan-deposit spread income.

an economy that is made up of three sectors:

1. the lower-risk enterprise (LRE);
2. the higher-risk enterprise (HRE); and
3. the state-owned bank sector which provides financial intermediation services.

To operationalize our definitions of LRE and HRE, we base them on the ownership registration of enterprises[2]: LRE corresponds to state-owned and share-holding (including share-holding and limited liability enterprises, mostly state-controlled) enterprises and HRE corresponds to private, self-employed individual, collective-owned (most of which are in fact private-owned township and village enterprises) and other categories of enterprises. The assumption that the state-owned enterprises (SOEs) and state-controlled enterprises (SCEs) have lower default risk is based on the observation by Woo (1999) that these firms face soft-budget constraints which enable them to privatize their profits and socialize their losses to a great extent. When the SOEs and the SCEs are going into bankruptcy, the government tends to rescue them through several channels (like providing fiscal subsidies or recapitalizing them with fiscal funds). The other assumption that the productivity of LRE (represented by SOEs) is far below that of HRE is based on the empirical work of Woo *et al.* (1994)and Brandt and Zhu (2010).

We denote the interest rate charged on bank loans to LREs and HREs as $\mathrm{r_{LRE}}$ and $\mathrm{r_{HRE}}$, respectively. The risk of default of LREs and HREs are σ_{LRE} and σ_{HRE}, respectively. According to the assumptions, we obtain the relationships below:

$$\mathrm{r_{LRE}} < \mathrm{r_{HRE}}$$
$$\sigma_{\mathrm{LRE}} < \sigma_{\mathrm{HRE}}$$

The rational, Markowitzian bank would choose its loan portfolio by maximizing its utility which has the following function form:

$$\max_{w_{\mathrm{HRE}}} \mathrm{U} = \max_{w_{\mathrm{HRE}}} \left(\mathrm{r} - \frac{1}{2}\lambda\,\sigma^2\right) \tag{1}$$

[2] *China Statistical Yearbook* categorizes enterprises into 8 to 11 types including state-owned, collective-owned, self-employed individual, foreign funded enterprises, etc.

where r represents the average return rate of the loans portfolio, and σ^2 the average default risk:

$$\mathrm{r} = w_{\mathrm{LRE}}\,\mathrm{r}_{\mathrm{LRE}} + w_{\mathrm{HRE}}\,\mathrm{r}_{\mathrm{HRE}}, \tag{2}$$

$$\sigma^2 = w_{\mathrm{LRE}}^2\sigma_{\mathrm{LRE}}^2 + w_{\mathrm{HRE}}^2\sigma_{\mathrm{HRE}}^2 + 2w_{\mathrm{LRE}}w_{\mathrm{HRE}}\sigma_{\mathrm{LRE}}\sigma_{\mathrm{HRE}}, \tag{3}$$

where w_{LRE} and w_{HRE} are the shares of the credit allocated to LRE and HRE (relative to the total sum of the loan portfolio) respectively, which satisfy:

$$w_{\mathrm{LRE}} + w_{\mathrm{HRE}} = 1,$$

and λ is the risk aversion coefficient.

When the banking system is subject to interest rate control policy and is dominated by SOBs, the utility function Equation (1) has to be modified to take these two factors into account.

First, under the interest rate control policy, there is a ceiling of the interest rate that the commercial banks could provide to savers (since June 2012, the saving rate has been able to float within 1.1 times of the benchmark saving rate, and before that, floating upward is prohibited.). Although the floating range of the loan rate is much larger, there is a floor. (The People's Bank of China [PBoC] relaxed the floor to 80% and 70% of the benchmark loan rate in June and July 2012 respectively — and removed the floor completely in July 2013.) The loan rate can be floated upward to more than twice the benchmark rate. As a result, commercial banks can obtain a guaranteed saving-loan spread,[3] denoted $\bar{r}$. Because of this guaranteed spread (which is quite substantial), banks have less incentive to pursue high yield loan projects, especially when considering the higher risk and higher management costs related to such projects.

Second, in a banking system dominated by SOBs, the banks are not wholly focused on increasing their enterprise value, and the objectives of bank management are ambiguous. For instance, the top managers of state-owned commercial banks have chances to become officials of local government or regulatory authorities, and the odds depend on the stability rather than profitability of the bank. Another

[3]In July 2013, the loan rate floor control was abandoned, but loans were seldom priced on the floor rate, so the situation will be not much different in the near future.

example is the non-market-oriented appointment procedure of management, under which the manager may be dismissed just because of a single mistake, and the long-run economic performance is not the main consideration. Taking on higher risks is never an optimal choice for the management.

Because of the ambiguous multiple-objectives of the bank managers, they tend to show extreme risk-aversion, and are seldom attracted by the potential higher return of the higher-risk projects. In the utility function, the consequences are an additional risk aversion coefficient (relative to that in a market-oriented banking system), λ_A, and the insertion of the guaranteed saving-loan spread, $\bar{r}$, to give us the modified utility function:

$$\max_{w_{\mathrm{HRE}}} \mathrm{U} = \bar{r} + \max_{w_{\mathrm{HRE}}} \left[(r - \bar{r}) - \frac{1}{2}(\lambda + \lambda_A)\sigma^2 \right] \tag{1a}$$

Comparing Equation (1a) with Equation (1), we can find that: on one hand, the return of risk taking gets smaller, particularly, it is represented as $r - \bar{r}$ in Equation (1a), which is smaller than r in Equation (1); on the other hand, because of the much larger risk aversion coefficient ($\lambda + \lambda_A > \lambda$), the same risk will cause much bigger utility losses in Equation (1a). The result of the combination of smaller risk premium and larger risk disutility is the smaller total risk of the loans portfolio, in other words more loans are allocated to LRE.

In sum, because of the interest rate control policy and the ambiguity of the management objectives in SOBs which dominate the banking system, banks have less incentive to pursue higher return with extremely high degree of risk aversion. So based on the modified utility function, the rational banks choose to allocate more credit to LREs while reducing the resources to HREs, even though the latter could lead to potential higher return. Thus, in a banking system mainly consisting of SOBs and subject to interest control, the credit allocation is systematically distorted towards LREs, which is so called as structural friction. Faced with risk, the attitude of the bank sector is avoiding, rather than taking and managing it positively.

Figure 1 shows the economic logic of the analysis.

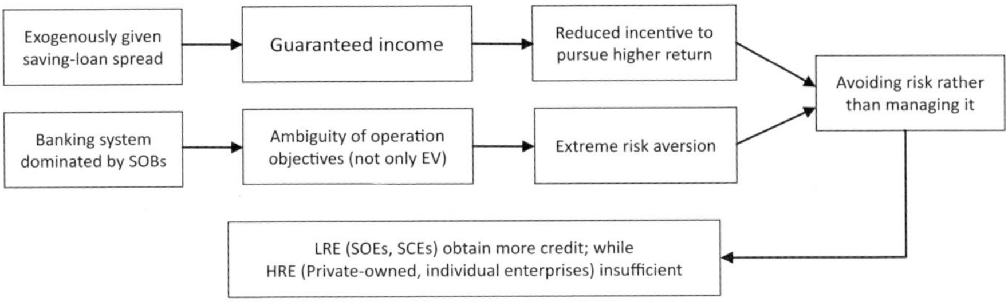

Figure 1. Causes of structural friction.

Measurement of Structural Friction

In this section, we construct a new indicator to measure the degree of structural friction in China's banking system. We proceed in three steps:

1. estimate the actual average interest rate (or actual loan rate) based on banking data; "actual" interest rate as contrasted with the official "benchmark" interest rate;
2. estimate the shadow interest rate (or shadow loan rate) based on actual financing demand; and
3. calculate the degree of structural friction as the difference between the shadow loan rate and the actual loan rate, i.e., the "Shadow-minus-Actual Spread (SAS)."

Construction of the indicator

Actual loan rate from the actual bank credit assets allocation

The rational commercial banks maximize the *modified* utility function presented in Section 2 and thus allocate credit assets between the two sectors. The result is the actual loan rate:

$$\mathrm{r} = w_{\mathrm{LRE}}\,\mathrm{r}_{\mathrm{LRE}} + w_{\mathrm{HRE}}\,\mathrm{r}_{\mathrm{HRE}} \tag{2}$$

Because the loan rate can be floated in a rather large range, it is not reliable to use the benchmark loan rate as a proxy of the actual rate. We make adjustments based on public information about the interest rate floating structure, in order to obtain a more precise proxy of the actual loan rate.

Shadow loan rate from the aggregate investment structure and real credit demand of enterprises

Enterprises' investment demands compose the majority of the demand for commercial bank loans. We denote the investment demand share of LRE and HRE as ν_{LRE} and υ_{HRE} (i.e., $\upsilon_{\mathrm{LRE}} + \upsilon_{\mathrm{HRE}} = 1$), then the shadow loan rate that reflects the average cost of funding the *entire* investment through bank loans is given by:

$$\mathrm{r}' = \nu_{\mathrm{LRE}}\,\mathrm{r}_{\mathrm{LRE}} + \nu_{\mathrm{HRE}}\,\mathrm{r}_{\mathrm{HRE}}, \tag{4}$$

where r′ is the "shadow loan rate."

Shadow-minus-Actual Spread (SAS)

If there is no structural friction, banks will price the risks of enterprises correctly, and allocate credit resources proportionately, which means that LRE and HRE would have roughly the same share in bank loans and in investment spending, i.e., ν_{LRE} and w_{LRE} will have the same values and SAS would equal zero. However, if the structural friction caused by interest rate control and the domination of SOBs exists, then banking system will tilt its allocation towards LRE, leading to $w_{\mathrm{LRE}} > \nu_{\mathrm{LRE}}$, and the actual rate will be smaller than shadow rate.

Specifically:

$$\text{Shadow-Actual Spread (SAS)} = r' - r, \tag{5}$$

which gives us:

$$r' - r = (\nu_{\mathrm{HRE}} - w_{\mathrm{HRE}})(\mathrm{r}_{\mathrm{HRE}} - \mathrm{r}_{\mathrm{LRE}}). \tag{6}$$

The more the banks tilt their credit allocation toward LRE, the larger is the SAS.

Estimation results

According to the availability of data, our sample is from January 2003 to December 2010.

Actual loan rate

Based on the (monthly average) one year benchmark loan rate, we estimate the actual average commercial bank loan rate by adjusting for the floating ranges and the corresponding share of commercial bank loans, which is reported by the central bank. The one-year benchmark loan rate comes from People's Bank of China, the floating ranges and corresponding shares come from *China Monetary Policy Report*, published by People's Bank of China. As the report did not include the floating ranges data until 2003, we set the start point of our sample as January 2003. The estimated actual loan rate compared to the benchmark rate is shown in Figure 2.

Shadow loan rate

According to Equation (4), in order to estimate the shadow rate r', we need to estimate the investment demand share of the two sectors ν_{LRE} and ν_{HRE}, as well as the loan return rate of each sector $\mathrm{r}_{\mathrm{LRE}}$ and $\mathrm{r}_{\mathrm{HRE}}$. As we have already estimated the actual loan rate r, according to Equation (2), we should obtain the proxies of the credit

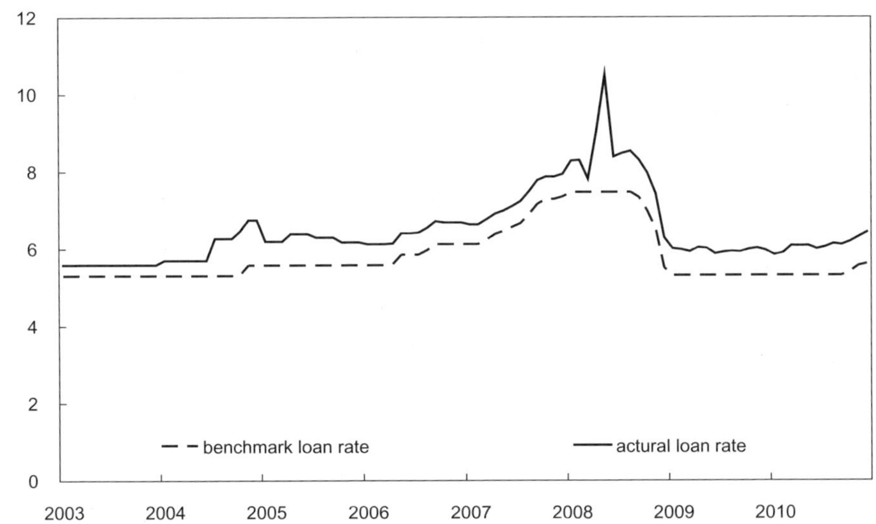

Figure 2. 1-year actual and benchmark loan rate (%).

assets share of the two sectors w_{LRE} and w_{HRE} before estimating $\mathrm{r}_{\mathrm{LRE}}$ and $\mathrm{r}_{\mathrm{HRE}}$.

The share in investment demand of the two sectors ν_{LRE} and ν_{HRE}

Fixed assets investment is the major part of investment in China. So we use the share of LRE and HRE in fixed assets investment as the proxies of their share in total investment.

The National Bureau of Statistics publishes enterprises' fixed assets investment by registration categories every year in *China Statistical Yearbook*. The share of LRE and HRE in fixed assets investment from 1995 to 2010 is reported in Figure 3.

Since 1995, LRE's share has been steady in general, and has experienced a slight increase; the minimum is 57% in 1996, and the maximum is 62% in 2010, the average is 60.78% in our sample. Correspondingly, the share of HRE decreases a bit.

The share in bank loan assets of the two sectors w_{LRE} and w_{HRE}

Based on the portions of fixed investment financed through domestic loans for each registration category, we can calculate the share in

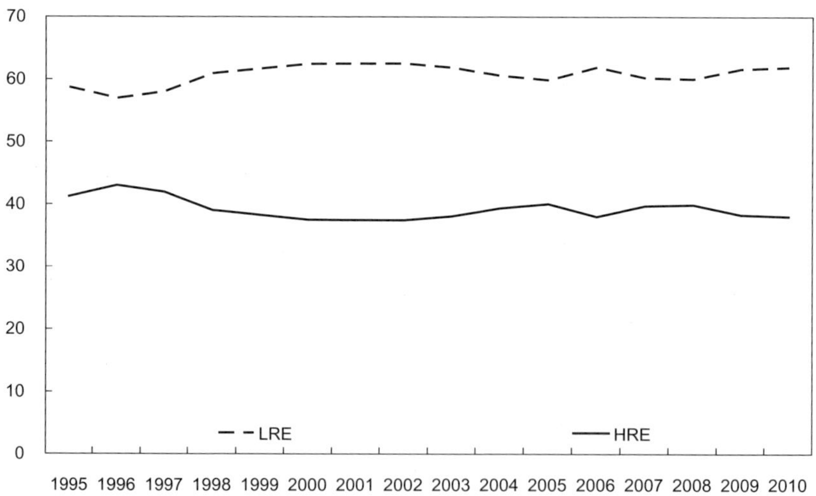

Figure 3. The share of each sector in investment demand (%).
Source: People's Bank of China, National Bureau of Statistics.

fixed investment loans of LRE and HRE. Considering the importance of fixed investment in the total bank loan assets, the share of LRE and HRE in bank loan assets can be approximated by the share just calculated.

Until the year 2004, enterprises' financing sources of fixed investment was published in *China Statistical Yearbook*, so we can make estimation directly.

The portion of fixed investment financed through domestic loans of the two sectors can partially reflect the existence of structural friction, which is reported in Figure 4. It is indicated that LRE composing of SOEs and share-holding enterprises shows relatively higher ability to raise fund from domestic credit market than HRE. From 1995 to 2003, the portion of LRE's fixed investment that comes from domestic loan market is within the range of 24%–26%, while domestic loan only accounts for 11.5%–16.5% of the fixed investment of HRE. This phenomenon verified the argument of Song *et al.* (2011) that non-state-owned enterprises are discriminated in financial markets and thus cannot acquire sufficient external financing, but can only rely more heavily on internal financing channels such as retained earnings and the personal savings of the entrepreneurs.

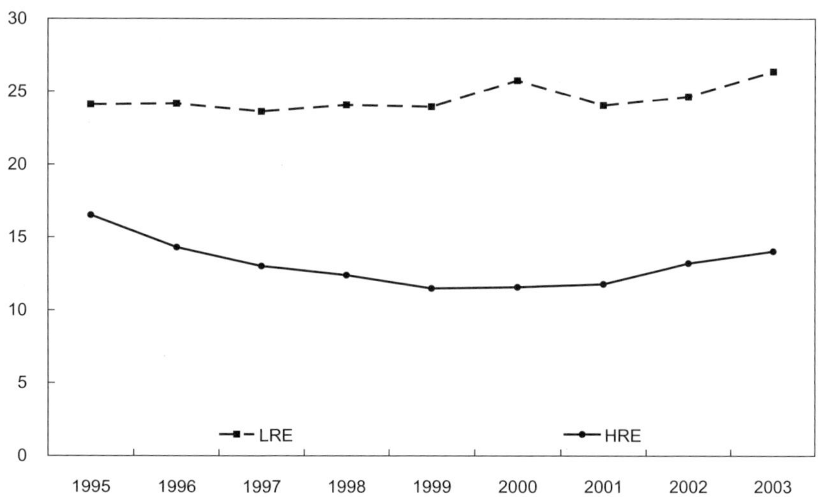

Figure 4. The portion of fixed investment financed by domestic loans of each sector (%).

However, beginning with the 2005 issue of the *China Statistical Yearbook*, the information that allowed the calculation of the data reported in Figure 4 was no longer released. So we used an extrapolation method for w_{LRE} and w_{HRE} which used the 2000–2003 period as the baseline.[4]

The estimated share of LRE and HRE in total bank loans is illustrated in Figure 5. It can be observed that before 2000, LRE's share in bank loans continued to rise, from 67.5% in 1995 to 78.8% in 2000, showing the increased tendency of credit allocation towards LRE; during 2000 and 2007, the share of LRE was maintained steady with a little decrease, to 75.3% in 2007; however, since 2008, the share of LRE has increased again to 77.7% in 2010 as a result of the "4 trillion" fiscal stimulation, which was allocated towards large state-owned projects operated by LREs.

Compare Figure 5 with Figure 4, we can find that LRE's relatively larger share in credit is related to its higher capacity to raise funds by loans. Figure 3 and Figure 5 together show that LRE's share in bank loans is 14.2% higher than its share in investment. Relative to investment structure, the loan structure is tilted systematically

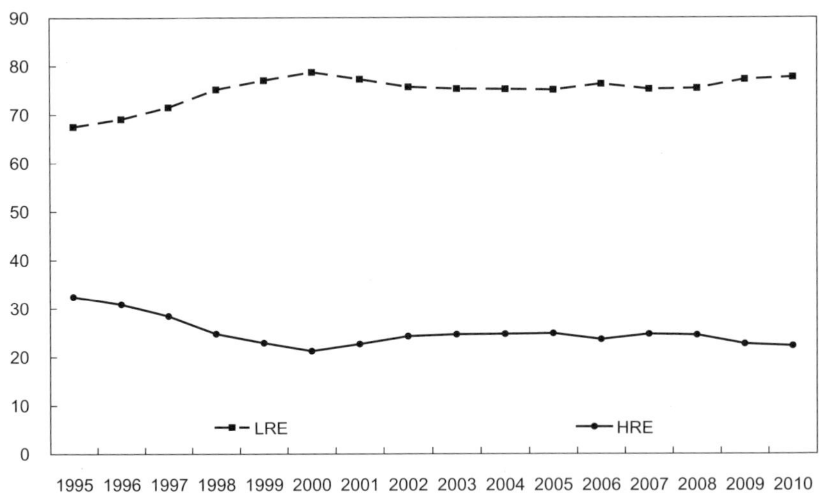

Figure 5. The share of each sector in banks' credit assets (%).

[4]The details of the extrapolation method are available on request.

and continually towards the lower-risk SOEs and share-holding enterprises, reflecting that the rational, risk-averse banks are minimizing their portfolio risk exposure under the interest rate control policy, and allocating too much to LRE, with the sacrifice of the external financing capacity of HREs. The difference between Figure 5 and Figure 3 indicates the existence of structural friction qualitatively.

Loan return of the two sectors r_{LRE} and r_{HRE}

We use the 1-year interbank yield to maturity of corporate bond (AA-) as the proxy of the loan return of LRE. The reasons include: first, the majority of the corporate bond issuers in the bond market are SOEs or SCEs, and most bonds are guaranteed, so the corporate bond market is a substitute for loan market (most of the loans are collateralized) for LREs to a great extent, and thus the corporate bond market yield could serve as a proxy of LRE's loan costs; secondly, the rating of bonds is correlated with the size of enterprises and the share controlled by state, the huge SOEs fully controlled by the central government will receive AAA rating, while smaller SOEs controlled by local governments will expect an AA rating, and the size and state-owned share of an average enterprise in banks' loan portfolio is similar to the AA rating ones; thirdly, the LRE share of the loan portfolio is far less liquid than the interbank corporate bonds, so we should also take liquidity premium into account. In sum, considering the features of the market participants, the credit rating issues and liquidity, we believe that the yield of corporate bonds with AA- rating is a good proxy of LRE's loan return.

As the corporate bond yield data before September 2008 are not available, we estimate the yield in earlier period by the risk spread method based on the treasury bond yield through the following formula[5]:

$$r_{\text{LRE}} = r_{\text{Treasury}} + \overline{RS_{AA-}}$$

[5]The key assumption of this method is the spread between the yields of AA-corporate bond and treasury bond is relatively steady, which could be observed from the available sample data.

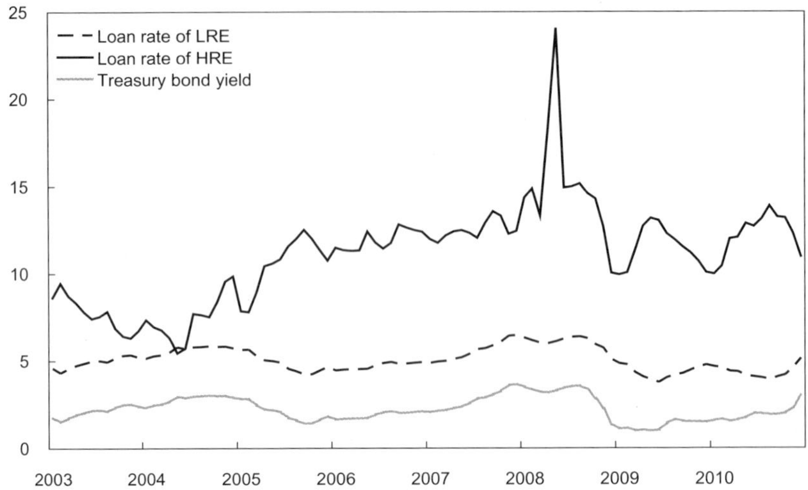

Figure 6. The loan rates of each sector (%).

where $\overline{RS_{AA-}}$ is the average risk spread between 1-year yields of interbank corporate bond (AA-) and treasury bond.[6] The estimated r_{LRE} is shown in Figure 6.

So far, we have already obtained the estimates of actual loan rate r, the share of each sector in bank credit assets w_{LRE} and w_{HRE}, and the loan return of LRE r_{LRE}. According to Equation (2), we can get to the estimated loan return of HRE r_{HRE}. The estimated result is also reported in Figure 6.

During the sample period, the loan return of HRE is systematically and significantly higher than that of LRE: the average of r_{HRE} is 11.1%, and the range is from 6.3% to 15.2% (except for those in April and May 2008, which are distorted by the potential statistic error of the loan rate floating share); r_{HRE} is 6.1% higher than r_{LRE} on average. This difference reflects the higher credit risk of the HREs, as well as the additional financing costs due to the banks' abnormally high risk aversion.

[6]The data needed for estimation comes from chinabond.com, which is sponsored by China Central Depository & Clearing Co., Ltd., and Wind.

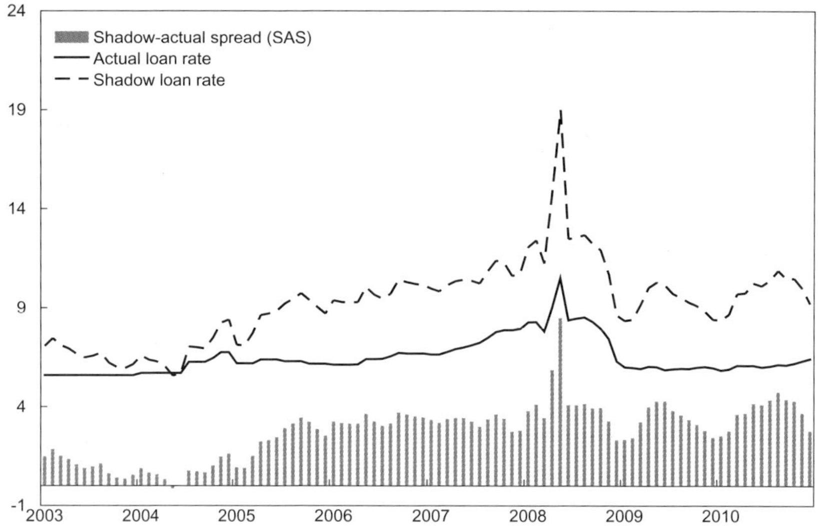

Figure 7. The actual and shadow loan rates and SAS (%).

Shadow loan rate

Given the estimated number of LRE and HRE's share in investment ν_{LRE} and ν_{HRE}, and their respective loan return r_{LRE} and r_{HRE}, we can compute the shadow loan rate r' based on Equation (4). Figure 7 presents the result.

Shadow-minus-Actual Spread (SAS)

Based on the calculation, the Shadow-minus-Actual Spread (SAS) is obtained from Equation (5), and it is also presented in Figure 7.

The trend in financial deepening

In the sample period, shadow loan rate varies from 5.7% to 12.7% (also except for April and May 2008, which are two outliers), the average of which is 9.26%. The actual loan rate, on the other hand, ranges from 5.6% to 8.5%, and averages to 6.5%. The SAS amounts to 2.76% during the sample period.

The intertemporal profile of SAS in Figure 7 gives a serious warning signal: the structural friction in the resource allocation of the banking system is getting worse in the sample period. Table 1 reports

Table 1. Shadow-minus-Actual Spread (SAS): Yearly average.

Year	2003	2004	2005	2006	2007	2008	2009	2010
SAS (%)	1.02	0.72	2.38	3.35	3.25	3.72	3.31	3.76

the annual averages of SAS. In 2003 and 2004, SAS is relatively small, around 1%. Since 2005, SAS has enlarged quickly. SAS reached 3.72% in 2008 and 3.76% in 2010.

This trend indicates that structural friction has not been mitigated with the rapid increase in the scale of bank assets. In contrast, this problem is getting more severe. Because the probability of the higher-efficiency, higher-risk sector to obtain the support from bank loans is getting smaller, the ability of banking system to promote the long-run economic growth of the economy is being reduced gradually.

Unjustified Complacency

It must be emphasized that the alarming trend in SAS reported in Table 1 has generally been overlooked in the usual discussions of China's financial system. This is because most of the usual discussions are based on quantity-based indicators but not price-based indicators of financial sector development.

In Figures 8 to 11, we show that the quantity indicators tend to give a rosier picture of the level of financial sophistication in China in the 2000s.

At the end of 2012, Figures 8 and 9 show that:

- China's outstanding domestic bank RMB loans and M2 were 7.3 times and 9.3 times respectively as those at the end of 1998;
- the ratio of RMB loans to GDP increased from 1.03 in 1998 to 1.21 in 2012; and
- the ratio of M2 to GDP rose even faster, from 1.24 to 1.88.[7]

[7]Compared with other countries, China's M2 as a percentage of GDP is larger. The higher level of this ratio may be related to the lower efficiency of capital when flowing in the real economy. However, the increase of this ratio should be considered as showing enhanced capability of the financial system to finance the real economy through transferring more deposit into loans or other channels.

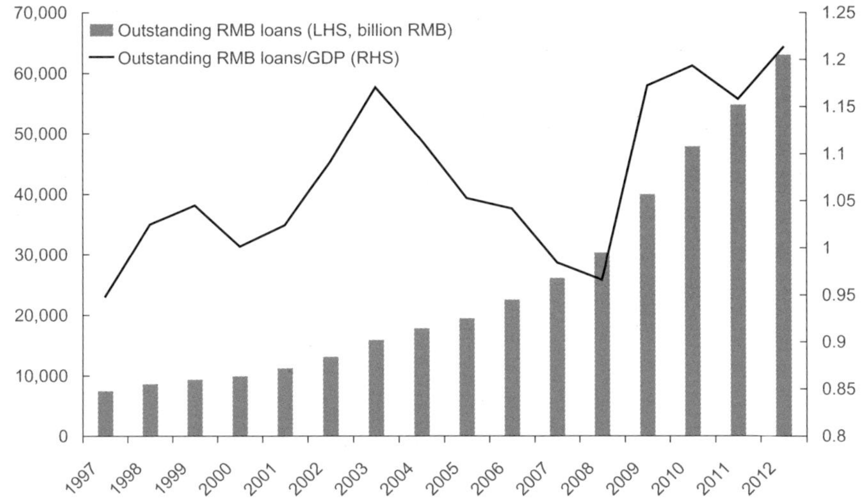

Figure 8. RMB loans.

Source: People's Bank of China, National Bureau of Statistics.

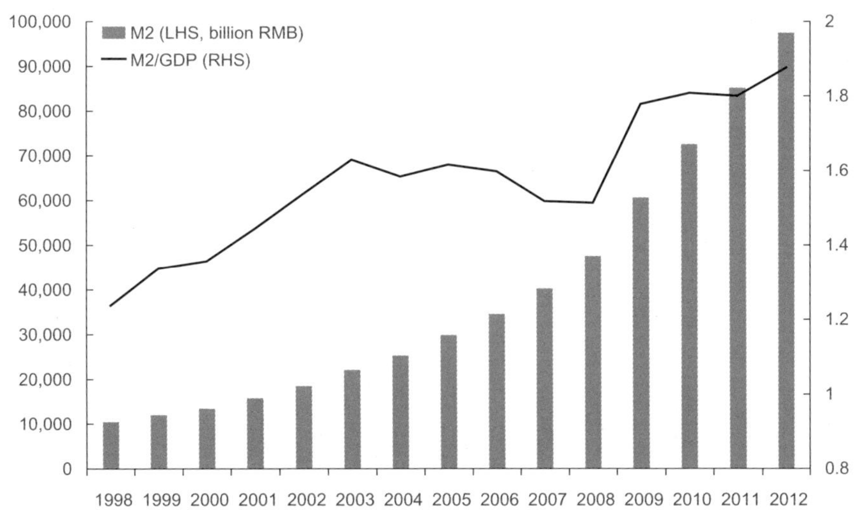

Figure 9. Broad money (M2).

Source: IMF, National Bureau of Statistics.

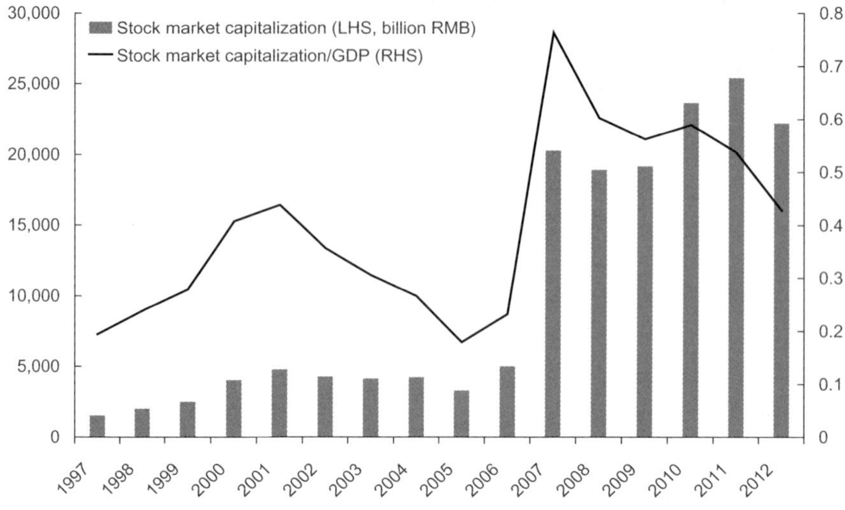

Figure 10. Stock market capitalization.

Source: Shanghai/Shenzhen Stock Exchange, National Bureau of Statistics.

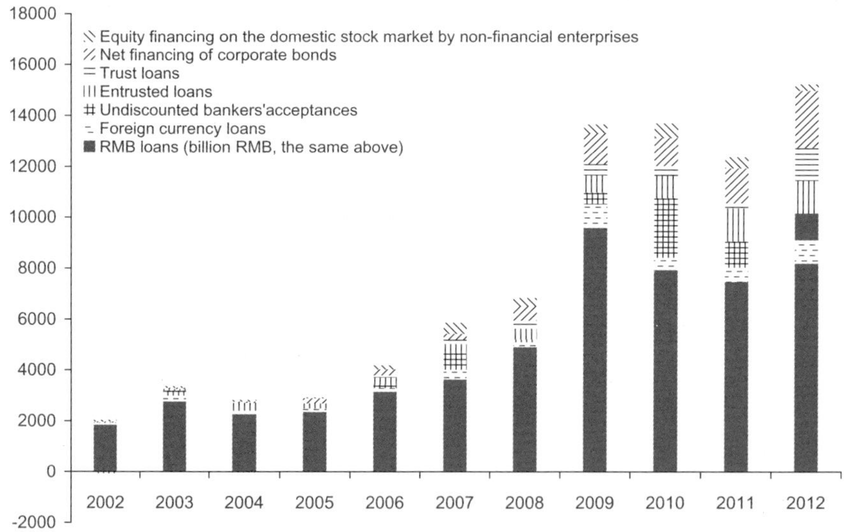

Figure 11. Aggregate financing of the economy.

Source: People's Bank of China.

For the stock markets, the total market capitalization of China's two stock markets in 2012 was 10 times more than that of 1998. Although the ratio of capitalization to GDP showed great volatility during the sub-period of 1997–2005 and 2006–2012, this ratio increased in general, the average of which shifted from 0.3 in the earlier sub-period to 0.53 in the latter sub-period (Figure 10). The aggregate financing of the economy (also called the total social financing) averaged 14 billion yuan in the 2009–2012 period, which is 3.5 times the amount in the 2002–2008 period. RMB loans accounted for 58% of the aggregate financing in 2012, compared to 92% in 1998, while during the same period, the share of corporate bonds increased from 1.8% to 14.3% (Figure 11).

In our opinion, the quantity-based indicators of financial sector development in China has generated an atmosphere of unjustified complacency about the harm that China's banking sector could inflict on future economy growth.

We urge urgent reforms to the banking sector in four areas:

1. the interest rate control policy should be abandoned by adjusting the ceiling on the deposit upwards gradually to reduce the policy-guaranteed deposit-loan spread so that the commercial banks have greater incentives to pursue potential higher returns;
2. the multiple operational objectives of the SOBs should be reduced to one primary objective, which is (risk-adjusted) profit-maximization, in order to eliminate the extreme risk aversion of SOBs;
3. the near-total domination of the banking system by state-controlled banks should be cut back by allowing domestic private banks, especially small and medium ones; and
4. the monitoring and regulating ability of the regulatory authorities must be improved in order to allow more market competition pressures.

In this process, the availability of credit for higher-risk, higher efficiency sector will be raised, the funding constraints relaxed, and the expansion of enterprises facilitated. As a result, the long-run perspective of the economic growth will be more optimistic, and the long-run profitability and competitiveness of the banking system per se will be improved.

References

Brandt, L and X Zhu (2010). Accounting for China's growth. IZA Discussion Paper Series, No. 4764, Institute for the Study of Labor, Bonn, Germany.

Chinn, MD and H Ito (2006). What matters for financial development? Capital controls, institutions, and interactions. *Journal of Development Economics*, 81, 163–192.

Eichengreen, B, R Gullapalli and U Panizza (2011). Capital account liberalization, financial development and industry growth: A synthetic view. *Journal of International Money and Finance*, 30, 1090–1106.

Hassan, MK, B Sanchez and J-S Yu (2011). Financial development and economic growth: New evidence from panel data. *Quarterly Review of Economics and Finance*, 51, 88–104.

Jung, WS (1986). Financial development and economic growth: International evidence. *Economic Development and Cultural Change*, 34, 333–346.

Levine, R (2005). Finance and growth: Theory and evidence. In Philippe, A and Steven, ND (Eds.), *Handbook of Economic Growth*, pp. xi–xv. Amsterdam: North-Holland.

Levine, R, N Loayza and T Beck (2000). Financial intermediation and growth: Causality and causes. *Journal of Monetary Economics*, 46, 31–77.

Song, Z, K Storesletten and F Zilibotti (2011). Growing like China. *American Economic Review*, 101, 196–233.

von Furstenberg, GM and M Fratianni (1996). Indicators of financial development. *The North American Journal of Economics and Finance*, 7, 19–29.

Woo, WT (1999). The real reasons for China's growth. *The China Journal*, 115–137.

Woo, WT (2006) The structural nature of internal and external imbalances in China. *Journal of Chinese Economic and Business Studies*, 4(1), 1–20.

Woo, WT, W Hai, Y Jin and G Fan (1994). How successful has Chinese enterprise reform been? Pitfalls in opposite biases and focus. *Journal of Comparative Economics*, 18(3), 410–437.

Chapter 9

Credit Rationing, Bank Bailouts, and the Deleterious Impact of Credit: Evidence from China*

Jean Louis Arcand

Introduction

Are Chinese households and firms excessively indebted? Figure 1 plots the relationship between outstanding loans, as a fraction of GDP, and GDP per capita at the county level, using data for the 2000–2005 period.[1] As should be obvious from the Figure, there is a very strong negative relationship between the stock of outstanding loans as a fraction of county GDP, and county GDP per capita. Moving from having a stock of outstanding loans equal to 20% of GDP to having a stock that represents 120% is associated with a fall in county GDP per capita of roughly 2,000 Yuan. Similarly, as illustrated in Figure 2, an equivalent change in the stock of outstanding loans is associated with a fall of 6% points in the annual growth rate of county GDP per capita.

In the light of the existing literature, which points to a strong positive causal link flowing from financial development to economic growth, Figures 1 and 2 may appear highly puzzling. Bagehot (1873) and Schumpeter (1911) were among the first to point out that finance plays a key role for economic development. Empirical work

*This chapter is based in part on joint work with Ugo Panizza and Enrico Berkes. I thank Tao Ran and Huang Yi for useful discussions. The usual disclaimer applies.

[1]I am deeply indebted to Professor Tao Ran of Renmin University of China for sharing his county-level dataset with me.

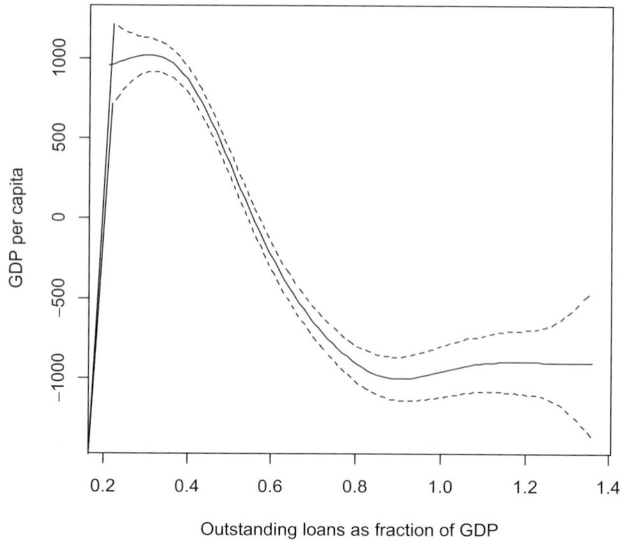

Figure 1. Semiparametric estimate of the relationship between outstanding loans, as a fraction of county GDP, and county GDP per capita.

Notes: Dashed lines are 95% confidence bands. Estimates control for year effects. Number of county-years: 8, 248; number of counties: 1, 658.

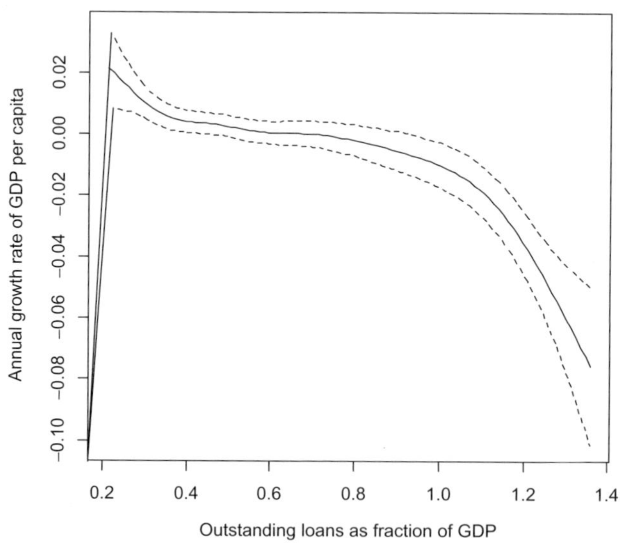

Figure 2. Semiparametric estimate of the relationship between outstanding loans, as a fraction of county GDP, and the annual growth rate of county GDP per capita.

Notes: Dashed lines are 95% confidence bands. Estimates control for year effects. Number of county-years: 8, 248; number of counties: 1,658.

by Goldsmith (1969) confirmed the presence of a correlation between finance and economic development but could not establish whether the link between these two variables was causal. Successive work by King and Levine (1993), Levine *et al.* (2000), Beck *et al.* (2000), and Rajan and Zingales (1998) provided convincing evidence that financial development has a causal effect on economic growth. There is now an enormous literature showing that finance does indeed play a positive role in promoting economic development and, while recent research has shown that not all types of credit are the same (with enterprise credit being the driver of growth, Beck *et al.*, 2008), most economists now believe in such a causal link (Levine, 2005).[2]

It is however possible that financial development may hinder economic growth, especially if the financial sector becomes "too large." In particular, there may be a threshold above which finance starts having negative returns. Proponents of this view include Martin Wolf who noted that there might be something wrong with a situation in which: "instead of being a servant, finance had become the economy's master" (Wolf, 2009), two former chief economists of the IMF (Rajan, 2005, and Johnson, 2009) who wrote influential articles on the potential dangers of large financial sectors, and a recent World Bank report (De La Torre *et al.*, 2011). Along similar lines, Tobin (1984) suggested that a large financial sector may lead to a suboptimal allocation of talents and to private returns that are much larger than social returns (for evidence in this direction see, Philippon and Reshef, 2008). In Arcand *et al.* (2012), we show that there is strong empirical backing for these claims using cross-country data, and that the marginal effect of financial development on economic growth becomes negative when credit to the private sector reaches 100% of GDP. In that paper, we show that our results are not only driven by volatility, banking crises or poor institutions.

It is easy to show, in a simple model without credit rationing and with exogenous probability of default, that the presence of a bank bailout will generate a level of credit that is greater than the social optimum. Here, I show that the same result applies when one allows

[2]There are, however, also papers that challenge this view (for a review see Panizza, 2012).

for credit rationing and endogenize the probability of default.[3] This model is particularly suited to the Chinese context in which bank bailouts are highly likely in the context of default, coupled with a relatively underdeveloped regulatory framework.

The Textbook Model

Consider an economy (in this case, a Chinese county) in which entrepreneurs who cannot post collateral produce by borrowing from competitive banks which, in turn, borrow outside of the county at an exogenous interest rate R and lend at a rate $r \geq R$. In such a setup, the capital stock K is equal to the size of the county's stock of loans. Entrepreneurs are successful with probability π and unsuccessful with probability $1-\pi$. The representative entrepreneur has the following production function:

$$Y = \begin{cases} AF(K) & \text{with probability } \pi \\ \delta K & \text{with probability } (1-\pi) \end{cases} \tag{1}$$

with $F' > 0$ and $F'' < 0$ and $\delta < (1+R)$ (i.e., failed projects have negative residual value).[4]

A social planner interested in maximizing the county's value added $V = \pi AF(K) + (1-\pi)\delta K - (1+R)K$ would choose the level of capital that satisfies the first order condition:

$$F'(K^{SP}) = \frac{(1+R)-(1-\pi)\delta}{\pi A}. \tag{2}$$

Now consider the decentralized equilibrium. When the project is successful, banks are paid back in full and get $(1+r)K$. When the project is not successful, they receive the residual value of the project and potentially a bailout: $(1+\gamma)\delta K$ ($\gamma \geq 0$ is the bailout; assume that $(1+\gamma)\delta K \leq (1+r)K$).[5] Competitive banks choose the interest

[3]A paper which presents a model that is similar in spirit to the one presented in what follows is De Gregorio and Guidotti (1995) who develop a simple model in which the presence of a government bailout and a poor regulatory framework lead to suboptimal screening and excessive lending.

[4]The results would not change if the production function were to include labor, with perfectly inelastic labor supply.

[5]In the next section, I also allow for imperfect creditor rights and discuss what happens when γ is negative.

rate that satisfies the zero-profit condition $(1+r)\pi+(1-\pi)(1+\gamma)\delta = (1+R)$, yielding:

$$r = \frac{(1+R)-(1-\pi)(1+\gamma)\delta-\pi}{\pi}. \tag{3}$$

Given limited liability, a firm's expected profits are given by $P = \pi[AF(K)-(1+r)K]$, with FOC $F' = \frac{(1+r)}{A}$. Using (3), one obtains:

$$F'(K^*) = \frac{(1+R)-(1-\pi)(1+\gamma)\delta}{A\pi} \tag{4}$$

Without distortions (i.e., with $\gamma = 0$), the decentralized equilibrium is equal to the social optimum (with $\gamma = 0$, $F'(K^*) = F'(K^{SP})$). In the presence of a bailout ($\gamma > 0$), one finds that the capital stock (and total credit) in the decentralized equilibrium is larger than the socially optimal level of capital.

The Credit Rationing Model

I now check whether the textbook result can be replicated in a model with credit rationing and endogenous default probability. In particular, I consider a simple economy where production takes place in two sectors, and where individuals supply labor inelastically and never save.

Given the zero saving assumption, firms finance investment by borrowing out-of-county at the exogenous interest rate R (as in the textbook model). The only role of the competitive financial sector is to screen projects and use its screening technology to intermediate out-of-county loans.[6]

I assume that the economy consists of two sectors. The first sector is composed of a large number of established competitive firms with a standard constant returns to scale technology: $y_c = F(K, L)$ (with $F_K > 0$, $F_L > 0$, $F_{KK} < 0$ and $F_{LL} < 0$). As output is non-stochastic, I assume that established firms can post collateral, guaranteeing that they will always repay their loans. Since loans to these firms carry

[6]I rule out any concerns related to the behavior of the exchange rate by assuming a common currency. I also assume, without loss of generality, no cost associated with screening projects.

no risk, the competitive banking sector will charge them an interest rate $r_c = R$ (with $F_K = r_c$, and $F_L = w$; where w is the wage rate). At this stage, the only reason for introducing this sector is to generate resources for the bailout.

Next, I build on Stiglitz and Weiss's (1981) credit rationing model and assume that the second sector is composed of monopolistic new entrants with the following stochastic production function:

$$y = \theta\sqrt{D}, \tag{5}$$

where D is the firm's stock of debt and θ is a random variable distributed according to the uniform density over $[0, N]$.[7] Given stochastic production, loans to firms in this sector are risky and the banks will charge an interest rate $r > R$. Total production is given by $Y = y_c + y$ and GNP is equal to $Y - (1 + R)(K + D)$, where $K + D$ is the size of the financial sector.

Social planner

The optimal level of debt is equal to the level of investment that maximizes domestic value added. Since the contribution to domestic value added of the traditional sector is fully determined by the exogenous labor supply and foreign interest rate, I only consider the innovative sector. The social planner's problem is:

$$\max_{\{D\}} \frac{1}{N}\int_0^N \theta\sqrt{D}d\theta - (1 + R)D. \tag{6}$$

The solution to this problem yields a level of debt and investment that maximizes social welfare, and which is equal to:

$$D^{**} = \frac{N^2}{16(1 + R)^2}. \tag{7}$$

The optimal level of debt is a negative function of the cost of funds R, and a positive function of productivity which, in turn, is determined by the upper bound of the distribution of θ.

---

[7] I choose a specific functional form because it is impossible to obtain a closed-form solution with a generic production function.

Decentralized equilibrium

Because of limited liability and the assumption that entrepreneurs have no equity capital, the profit of the representative entrepreneur is given by: $\pi = \max[\theta\sqrt{D} - (1+r)D, 0]$. Given the uniform distribution of θ, this yields an expected profit of:

$$E(\pi) = \frac{1}{N}\int_{\theta^*}^{N} [\theta\sqrt{D} - (1+r)D]d\theta, \tag{8}$$

where $\theta^* = (1+r)\sqrt{D}$ is the threshold level of the realization of the random variable above which the entrepreneur makes positive profits and is able to repay the loan. Performing the integration one obtains:

$$E(\pi) = \frac{\sqrt{D}}{2N}[(1+r)\sqrt{D} - N]^2. \tag{9}$$

In order to use Equation (9) to find the level of debt that maximizes profit, one needs to solve for the endogenous lending rate r. Given the assumption of a competitive banking system, this is the rate that equates a lender's expected profits, $E(L)$, to zero.

$E(L)$ is composed of three elements: (i) full debt repayment times the probability that the project will be successful; (ii) the recovery value times the probability that the investment will be unsuccessful; and (iii) the cost of funds. Formally:

$$\begin{aligned} E(L) = {} & \frac{1}{N}\int_{\theta^*}^{N} (1+r)Dd\theta \\ & + \frac{1}{N}\int_{0}^{\theta^*} [\theta\sqrt{D} + \gamma((1+r)D - \theta\sqrt{D})]d\theta - (1+R)D. \end{aligned} \tag{10}$$

The term in the first integral is the repayment if the investment is successful, while the term in the second integral measures what the lenders will recover in case of default; the third term in Equation (10) is the cost of lending. If $\gamma \neq 0$, the recovery value in case of default is different from the residual value of the defaulted project. As in the Economics 101 model, the parameter γ is crucial in this story because it introduces a wedge between the socially optimal level of debt and the market equilibrium. It will be shown that when $\gamma < 0$

the level of debt is too small with respect to the social optimum and when $\gamma > 0$ the level of debt is too big with respect to the social optimum.

One can think of γ as a combination of the strength creditors' rights (c) and government bailout (b) in case of default. To fix ideas, assume that $\gamma = (c + b - 1)$, with $0 \leq c \leq 1$ and $0 \leq b < 2$.[8] In this setting, $c = 1$ denotes a situation with perfect creditor rights (lenders can recover the whole residual value of the failed investment project) and $c < 1$ denotes a situation in which lenders can only recover a fraction of the failed investment project. Similarly, $b = 0$ denotes a situation in which the government never bails out lenders, and $b > 0$ denotes a situation in which the government offers a (possibly partial) bailout. I assume that the bailout is financed with a lump-sum tax on the first sector.

Consider, for instance, the case of a county with no creditor rights and no bailout. In this case, creditors will receive no payments in case of default: $(\theta\sqrt{D}+\gamma[(1+r)D-\theta\sqrt{D}]) = 0$ and $\gamma = -\frac{\theta\sqrt{D}}{(1+r)D-\theta\sqrt{D}} < 0$. With perfect creditor rights ($c = 1$) and no bailout ($b = 0$), instead, one gets $\gamma = 0$, and the bank will receive all the residual value of the failed investment project (i.e., $\theta\sqrt{D}$). Note that the presence of a positive bailout ($b > 0$) is a necessary but not sufficient condition for $\gamma > 0$. With a positive bailout ($b > 0$), creditors could receive either less than the recovery value (if $b < 1 - c$) or more than the recovery value (if $b > 1 - c$).

Performing the integration in Equation (10), one obtains:

$$E(L) = \frac{D[2N(r - R) + (1 + r)^2(\gamma - 1)\sqrt{D}]}{2N}. \tag{11}$$

Competitive lenders will choose the interest rate that sets expected profits equal to zero. Equation (11) is a quadratic in r and admits

---

[8] In order to avoid negative payments or payments which are greater than the original loan, it is also necessary to impose a joint constraint on c and b such that their sum guarantees that $-\frac{\theta\sqrt{D}}{(1+r)D-\theta\sqrt{D}} \leq \gamma < 1$ (we use a strict inequality, $\gamma < 1$, for technical reasons). Note that in case of default the denominator of the lower bound is always positive and $-\frac{\theta\sqrt{D}}{(1+r)D-\theta\sqrt{D}} > -1$.

two solutions:

$$r_1^* = \frac{N + \sqrt{\psi}}{\sqrt{D}(1-\gamma)} - 1; \quad r_2^* = \frac{N - \sqrt{\psi}}{\sqrt{D}(1-\gamma)} - 1, \tag{12}$$

where $\psi = N[N - 2\sqrt{D}(1+R)(1-\gamma)]$. For the time being assume that $\psi > 0$: I will later show that this condition holds in practice.[9] With $\psi > 0$ it is always true that $r_1^* > r_2^*$.

Since lenders are indifferent between interest rates (they always make zero profits), I pick the one that makes the borrower better off (any lender who charges a different interest rate would lose all customers). By substituting the expressions in (12) into (9) one obtains:

$$E(\pi_1) = \sqrt{D}\frac{[\sqrt{\psi} + N\gamma]^2}{2N(\gamma-1)^2}; \quad E(\pi_2) = \sqrt{D}\frac{[\sqrt{\psi} - N\gamma]^2}{2N(\gamma-1)^2}. \tag{13}$$

Since $\psi > 0$, $E(\pi_1) > E(\pi_2)$ if $\gamma > 0$ and $E(\pi_1) < E(\pi_2)$ if $\gamma < 0$ (if $\gamma = 0$, $E(\pi_1) = E(\pi_2)$). Whenever $\gamma > 0$, borrowers will prefer the higher interest rate and when $\gamma < 0$ borrowers will prefer the lower interest rate. The intuition for this is simple: inspection of Equation (9) reveals that $E(\pi)$ is quadratic (and $U-$shaped) in r. It is therefore, not surprising that a higher level of the interest rate is entirely compatible with higher borrower welfare.[10]

One can now maximize $E(\pi_1)$ and $E(\pi_2)$ with respect to D and solve for the optimal amount of debt. Consider first the case in which $\gamma > 0$ and expected profits are given by $E(\pi_1)$. In this case, the FOC is given by:

$$\frac{\partial E(\pi_1)}{\partial D} = \frac{[\sqrt{\psi} + N\gamma][N - 4\sqrt{D}(1+R)(1-\gamma) + \gamma\sqrt{\psi}]}{4\sqrt{D}\sqrt{\psi}(\gamma-1)^2} = 0. \tag{14}$$

Given the previous assumptions, when $\gamma > 0$, the first term in square brackets in the numerator and the denominator of (14) are both always positive. Therefore, one can find the optimal value of D by

[9]The assumption that $\gamma < 1$ is necessary to guarantee that the denominators in the interest rate equations are non-zero.

[10]In turn, the $U-$shape of $E(\pi)$ in Equation (9) stems from the linearity in θ of the integrand in Equation (8), combined with the limited liability assumption.

setting the second term in square brackets in the numerator equal to zero. This yields two solutions:

$$D_{11}^{*} = \frac{N^2[8 + \gamma^4 - \gamma(4 - \gamma^2)\sqrt{8 + \gamma^2}]}{128(1 + R)^2(\gamma - 1)^2};$$

$$D_{12}^{*} = \frac{N^2[8 + \gamma^4 + \gamma(4 - \gamma^2)\sqrt{8 + \gamma^2}]}{128(1 + R)^2(\gamma - 1)^2}. \tag{15}$$

Since $0 < \gamma < 1$, $\gamma(4 - \gamma^2) > 0$, and $D_{12}^{*} > D_{11}^{*}$.

At this point, one can substitute D_{11}^{*} and D_{12}^{*} into ψ and, after some tedious algebra, show that they satisfy the condition that $\psi > 0$. It is also easy to show that $\frac{\partial^2 E(\pi_1)}{\partial D^2} < 0$ and therefore, that the solution satisfies the second order condition for a maximum.[11] Appendix A shows that when $\gamma > 0$, expected profits are always higher with D_{12}^{*} and therefore, the borrower always prefers the solution with a higher level of credit.

Summing up, with $\gamma = 0$ the decentralized equilibrium is equal to the social optimum ($D_{11}^{*} = D_{12}^{*} = D^{**}$ where D^{**} was given in Equation (7)), but for positive values of γ, one finds that credit is always above the social optimum ($D_{12}^{*} > D^{**}$). The presence of a bailout leads to too much risk taking and to a level of debt which is larger than the social optimum (this does not necessarily mean that bailouts are never desirable, more on this below).

I now consider the case with $\gamma < 0$. In this case, $E(\pi_2) > E(\pi_1)$ and the borrowers will choose the lower interest rate r_2^{*}. Taking the first order condition, one obtains:

$$\frac{\partial E(\pi_2)}{\partial D} = \frac{[\sqrt{\psi} - N\gamma][N - 4\sqrt{D}(1 + R)(1 - \gamma) - \gamma\sqrt{\psi}]}{4\sqrt{D}\sqrt{\psi}(\gamma - 1)^2} = 0. \tag{16}$$

Since $\gamma < 0$, the first expression in square brackets in the numerator is always positive (and so is the denominator). One can thus

[11]Let $A = [\sqrt{\psi} + N\gamma]$; $B = [\psi/N + \gamma\sqrt{\psi}]$; and $C = (4\sqrt{D}\sqrt{\psi}(\gamma - 1)^2)$. Then $\frac{\partial^2 E(\pi_1)}{\partial D^2} = \frac{(A\frac{\partial B}{\partial D} + B\frac{\partial A}{\partial D})C - \frac{\partial C}{\partial D}AB}{C^2}$. Given that at D^*, B is equal to zero, the SOC simplifies to $\frac{\partial^2 E(\pi_1)}{\partial D^2} = \frac{A}{C}\frac{\partial B}{\partial D}$. Since $A > 0$, $C > 0$, and $\frac{\partial B}{\partial D} < 0$, one obtains $\frac{\partial^2 E(\pi_1)}{\partial D^2} < 0$.

find that value of D that maximizes profits by setting the second term in the numerator equal to zero. As this term is equal to the one considered earlier (in Equation (14)), one obtains the same solutions: $D^*_{21} = D^*_{11}$ and $D^*_{22} = D^*_{12}$. However, γ is now negative and $D^*_{21} > D^*_{22}$. The Appendix shows that with $\gamma < 0$, borrowers always prefer D^*_{21} (again, with $\gamma = 0$ one gets $D^*_{21} = D^*_{22} = D^{**}$).

One can now use the expressions in (15) to fully describe the size of debt under positive and negative values of γ.

$$D^* = \begin{cases} \dfrac{N^2[8+\gamma^4-\gamma(4-\gamma^2)\sqrt{8+\gamma^2}]}{128(1+R)^2(\gamma-1)^2} & \text{if } \gamma < 0 \\[2ex] \dfrac{N^2}{16(1+R)^2} & \text{if } \gamma = 0 \\[2ex] \dfrac{N^2[8+\gamma^4+\gamma(4-\gamma^2)\sqrt{8+\gamma^2}]}{128(1+R)^2(\gamma-1)^2} & \text{if } \gamma > 0 \end{cases} \tag{17}$$

It is easy to show that when $\gamma > 0$, there is always too much debt ($D^* > D^{**}$ because $\gamma^4 + \gamma(4-\gamma^2)\sqrt{8+\gamma^2} > 0$ and $(\gamma-1)^2 < 1$).

With $\gamma < 0$, the comparison between D^* and D^{**} is more complicated because γ increases both the numerator and the denominator of D^* (with $\gamma < 0$, $\gamma^4 - \gamma(4-\gamma^2)\sqrt{8+\gamma^2} > 0$ and $(\gamma-1)^2 > 1$). It can be shown, however, that when $-1 \leq \gamma < 0$, it is always true that $D^*/D^{**} < 1$ and when $0 < \gamma < 1$, it is always true that $D^*/D^{**} > 1$. Therefore, when $\gamma < 0$, the amount of debt is always too small with respect to the social optimum ($D^* < D^{**}$).

Equation (17) shows that bailouts are not necessarily a bad idea. The optimal bailout rule is $b = 1 - c$. Only with perfect creditors rights ($c = 1$) are bailouts never desirable. If $c < 1$ and the bailout is financed with lump sum taxes, society will be indifferent between setting $b = 1 - c$ and a reform that improves creditor rights. Improving creditors' rights will be the preferred option only if the bailout is financed with a distortionary tax. D^*/D^{**} is generally an increasing and convex function of γ. Thus, for any pair of γs with $|\gamma_i| = |\gamma_j|$ and $\gamma_i < 0$, $\gamma_j > 0$, the deviation from the social optimum is always larger when γ is positive. Therefore, in the presence of uncertainty on the value of c, policymakers should be conservative in offering bailouts because the costs of overshooting are larger than those of undershooting. This result would be strengthened if one were to assume that the bailout is financed with distortionary taxes.

However, it is straightforward to use the model to show that, under certain conditions, a distortionary tax on the second sector can restore the social optimum. In particular, if $\gamma > 0$ and $c = 1$, a Pigouvian tax equal to the cost of the potential bailout will make entrepreneurs internalize the cost of overborrowing and lead them to choose D^{**}. This is a result similar to that of Jeanne and Korinek's (2010) model of credit booms and busts.

Empirical Evidence

I now present empirical evidence which suggests that this mechanism may be at work in the Chinese economy, and which provides a formal test of the striking stylized facts presented in Figures 1 and 2.

Figures 3, 4 and 5 display the distributions of county-level GDP per capita, its corresponding annual growth rate, and the stock

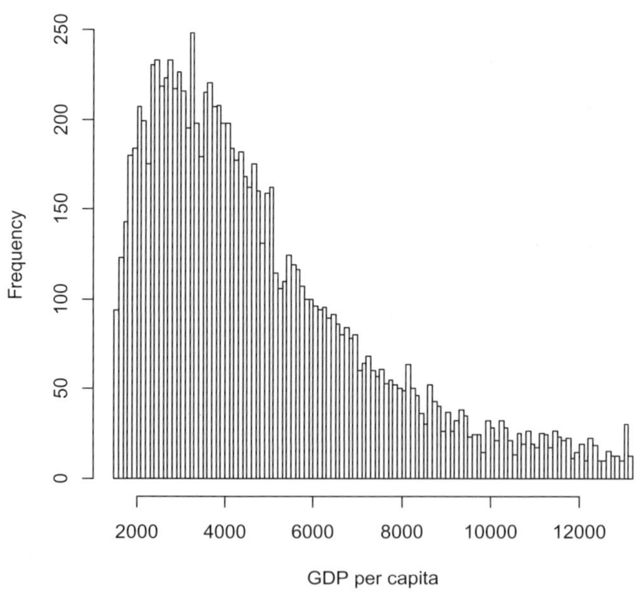

Figure 3. Histogram of GDP per capita at the county level, 2000–2005.

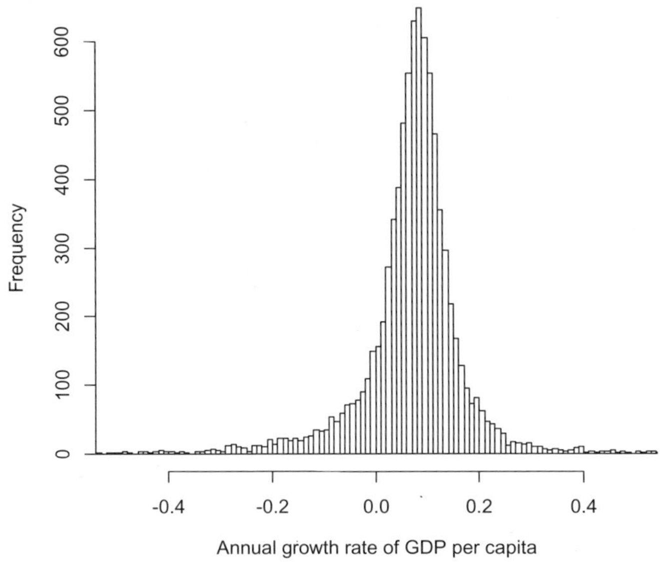

Figure 4. Histogram of the annual growth rate of GDP per capita at the county level, 2000–2005.

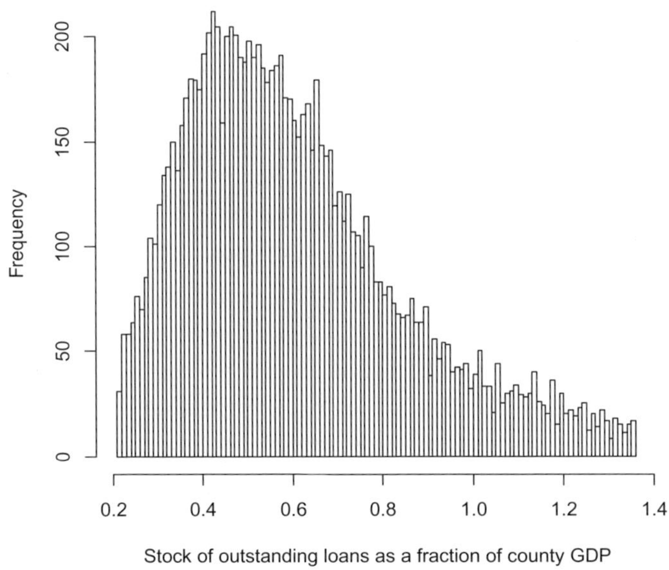

Figure 5. Histogram of the stock of outstanding loans, as a fraction of county GDP, 2000–2005.

of outstanding loans as a fraction of GDP, respectively. Over the 2000–2005 period, the mean level of county GDP per capita is equal to 4,836 Yuan, with a standard deviation of 2,549. This high degree of between-county heterogeneity is reflected in the annual growth rates, whose mean is equal to 0.070, with a standard deviation of 0.102. Note also that the level of outstanding loans as a fraction of county GDP is highly heterogeneous and ranges from 0.212 to 1.359, with a mean value of 0.605 and a standard deviation of 0.242.

The basic estimating equation is given by:

$$\ln Y_{it} = \ln Y_{it-1}\alpha + \ln D_{it}\beta + \mu_t + \lambda_i + \upsilon_{it}, \tag{18}$$

where Y_{it} is GDP per capita at time t in county i, and D_{it} is the outstanding stock of loans as a fraction of county GDP. The disturbance term is assumed to be given by $\mu_t + \lambda_i + \upsilon_{it}$, where μ_t are shocks common to all counties in a given year (that will be accounted for in all specifications presented below), λ_i represents county-specific time invariant unobservables and υ_{it} is a disturbance term that satisfies the usual assumptions. The equivalent representation in terms of the annual growth rate of GDP per capita is given by:

$$\ln Y_{it} - \ln Y_{it-1} = \ln Y_{it-1}(\alpha - 1) + \ln D_{it}\beta + \mu_t + \lambda_i + \upsilon_{it}.$$

Estimation is performed using the pooling, county-specific fixed effects, first-difference and difference-GMM estimators. Results are presented in Table 1. Data cover 1,658 counties over the 2000–2005 period.

Two results stand out. First, as shown by the large negative coefficient $(\alpha - 1)$ associated with $\ln Y_{it-1}$ in Table 1 (as long as one controls for county-specific, time invariant heterogeneity λ_i), there are extremeley strong convergence effects at work in the Chinese economy at the county level. The annual convergence rate η, using the standard formula $\alpha - 1 = -(1 - e^{-\eta})$ and the county-specific fixed effects results of column 2, is equal to 0.661. This is roughly one hundred times the rate reported using cross-country data in the seminal paper by Mankiw *et al.* (1992), ten times the rate reported by

Table 1. The impact of outstanding loans (as a fraction of county GDP) on the annual growth rate of county GDP per capita. Year dummies included in all specifications. Difference-GMM estimates use all available lags of GDP per capita and outstanding loans, starting at t-3, as instruments. Standard errors in parentheses.

Dependent variable	Annual growth rate of county-level GDP per capita			
Estimation method	Pooling	Fixed effects	First-diff	Diff-GMM
log initial GDP per capita	−0.013 (0.002)	−0.484 (0.009)	−0.937 (0.011)	−1.001 (0.144)
log outstanding loans	−0.025 (0.002)	−0.164 (0.006)	−0.232 (0.006)	−0.257 (0.064)
Sargan test of overid. restrict. [p−value]				20.43 [0.309]
m_1 test [p−value]				0.357 [0.360]
m_2 test [p−value]				2.706 [0.003]
$\overline{R}^2$	0.090	0.308	0.581	
Number of counties	1,658	1,658	1,658	1,658
Number of observations	8,248	8,248	8,248	5,194

Knight *et al.* (1993), and still five times the rate reported by Caselli *et al.* (1996).[12]

Second, the stylized facts displayed in the introduction in Figures 1 and 2 survive the move to formal empirical testing. Standard errors in all cases are extremely small and the parameter estimates are highly significant at the usual levels of confidence. The results presented in Table 1, based on the county-specific fixed effects results, imply that a 1% increase in the ratio of the stock of outstanding loans to county GDP leads to a 0.164% decrease in county GDP per capita or an equivalent decrease in its annual growth rate. The corresponding number based on the difference-GMM results is 0.257. These are very large numbers and imply that there may be a highly deleterious effect of debt on the economic performance of Chinese counties.

[12]Using the difference-GMM results yields what is essentially instantaneous convergence, since the coefficient $\alpha - 1$ is indistinguishable from 1.

Conclusions

In this chapter, I develop a simple model with endogenous default probability and credit rationing and show that the presence of a bailout leads to a level of loans which is "too large" with respect to the social optimum. Within the model, there are three factors that determine the size of the stock of loans: the productivity parameter N, the exogenous interest rate R, and the distortion γ. Therefore, counties with a large stock of loan are not necessarily in trouble, since it may simply be that their productivity is high. However, if the stock of loans is positively correlated with the county's political and lobbying power, γ could become endogenous, leading to a situation in which counties which have a naturally large stock of outstanding loans (because of high N) also end up having too big a stock of loans. This is the implicit message of Johnson (2009). The model developed in this chapter could thus serve as a building block for a political economy model aimed at endogenizing γ.

Inspired by the theoretical model, the preliminary empirical results presented here have identified what appears to be an empirical regularity that has hitherto gone unnoticed in the Chinese context: there is a large, negative, and statistically significant impact of outstanding loans on the economic performance of counties. Further research will investigate the precise mechanisms through which this result obtains, and will potentially focus on the functioning of the rural banking sector, as well as regulatory issues.

References

Arellano, M and S Bond (1991). Some tests of specification for panel data: Monte Carlo evidence and an application to employment equations. *The Review of Economic Studies*, 58(2), 277–297.

Arcand, JL, E Berkes and U Panizza (2012). Too much finance. IMF Working Paper WP/12/161, June.

Bagehot, W (1873). *Lombard Street: A Description of the Money Market.* History of Economic Thought Books, McMaster University Archive for the History of Economic Thought, Ontario, Canada.

Beck, T, R Levine and N Loayza (2000). Finance and the sources of growth. *Journal of Financial Economics*, 58(1–2), 261–300.

Beck, T, B Buyukkarabacak, F Rioja and N Valev (2009). Who gets the credit and does it matter? Household vs. firm lending across countries. Policy Research Working Paper No. 4661, The World Bank.

Caselli, F, G Esquivel and F Lefort (1996). Reopening the convergence debate: A new look at cross-country growth empirics. *Journal of Economic Growth*, 1(3), 363–389.

De la Torre, A, A Ize and S Schmukler (2011). *Financial Development in Latin America and the Caribbean: The Road Ahead.* Washington DC: World Bank.

De Gregorio, J and P Guidotti (1995). Financial development and economic growth. *World Development*, 23(3), 433–448.

Goldsmith, RW (1969). *Financial Structure and Development.* New Haven, MA: Yale University Press.

Jeanne, O and A Korinek (2010). Excessive volatility in capital flows: A Pigouvian taxation approach. *American Economic Review*, 100(2), 403–407.

Johnson, S (2009). The quiet coup. *The Atlantic*, May.

King, RG and R Levine (1993). Finance and growth: Schumpeter might be right. *Quarterly Journal of Economics*, 108(3), 717–737.

Knight, M, N Loayza and D Villanueva (1993). Testing the neoclassical growth model. *IMF Staff Papers*, 40(3), 512–541.

Levine, R (2005). Finance and growth: Theory and evidence. In Aghion, P and S Durlauf (eds.), *Handbook of Economic Growth*, Vol. 1, pp. 865–934. Amsterdam: Elsevier.

Levine, R, N Loayza and T Beck (2000). Financial intermediation and growth: Causality and causes. *Journal of Monetary Economics*, 46(1), 31–77.

Mankiw, GN, D Romer and D Weil (1992). A contribution to the empirics of growth. *Quarterly Journal of Economics*, 107(2), 407–437.

Panizza, U (2012). Finance and economic development. *International Development Policy.* (Forthcoming).

Philippon, T and A Reshef (2008). Wages and human capital in the US financial industry: 1909–2006. Mimeo, New York University.

Rajan, RG and L Zingales (1998). Financial dependence and growth. *American Economic Review*, 88(3), 559–586.

Rajan, RG (2005). Has financial development made the world riskier? In *Proc. Symp. Federal Reserve Bank of Kansas City.* Jackson Hole, WY: Federal Reserve Bank of Kansas City.

Schumpeter, JA (1911). *A Theory of Economic Development.* Cambridge, MA: Harvard University Press.

Stiglitz, J and A Weiss (1981). Credit rationing in markets with imperfect information. *The American Economic Review*, 71(3), 393–410.

Tobin, J (1984). On the efficiency of the financial system. *Lloyds Bank Review*, 153, 1–15.

Wolf, M (2009). Why dealing with the huge debt overhang is so hard. *Financial Times*, January 27.

Appendix A. Proof That When $\gamma > 0$, the Firm Will Choose D^*_{12} (and When $\gamma < 0$, the Firm Will Choose D^*_{21})

By substitututing D^*_{11} and D^*_{12} into $E(\pi_1)$, we get:

$$E(\pi_1(D^*_{11})) = \frac{N^2\phi_1(4\gamma - 2\sqrt{2}\phi_1)^2}{256\sqrt{2}(1+R)(\gamma-1)^2}$$

$$E(\pi_1(D^*_{12})) = \frac{N^2\phi_2(4\gamma - 2\sqrt{2}\phi_2)^2}{256\sqrt{2}(1+R)(\gamma-1)^2}$$

$$\phi_1 = \sqrt{8 + \gamma^4 - \gamma(4-\gamma^2)\sqrt{8+\gamma^2}}$$

and

$$\phi_2 = \sqrt{8 + \gamma^4 + \gamma(4-\gamma^2)\sqrt{8+\gamma^2}}.$$

Considering the positive roots, we have $sign(\phi_2 - \phi_1) = sign(\gamma)$. Let us now write:

$$\frac{E(\pi_1(D^*_{11}))}{E(\pi_1(D^*_{12}))} = \frac{\phi_1(4\gamma - 2\sqrt{2}\phi_1)^2}{\phi_2(4\gamma - 2\sqrt{2}\phi_2)^2} = \varphi(\gamma)$$

Given that $E(\pi_2(D^*_{21})) = E(\pi_1(D^*_{12}))$ and $E(\pi_1(D^*_{11})) = E(\pi_2(D^*_{22}))$, it is always true that when $\gamma < 0$, $\frac{E(\pi_2(D^*_{21}))}{E(\pi_2(D^*_{22}))} > 1$ and that the borrower will always prefer D^*_{21} over D^*_{22}.

Chapter 10

The Options for Reforming the Renminbi Exchange Rate Regime

Xinru Wu, Yingli Pan, Zhichao Zhang, Jing Nie and Si Zhou

Historical Evolution of RMB Exchange Rate System

In December 1948, the People's Bank of China (PBC) was established in what is today Shijiangzhuang, Hebei province, and began to issue the RMB (Renminbi). Since then, the RMB exchange rate system has passed through a variety of stages. The process is characterized at different times by the adoption of a single currency peg (dollar or pound), or by pegging to a basket of currencies. In addition, there were also periods of multiple exchange rates. Table 1 summarises the evolution of the exchange rate regime.

Figure 1 shows visually the historical tracks of the RMB exchange rate regimes and the RMB against the US dollar exchange rate.

The "Pro-Cyclicality" of the RMB Exchange Rate Fluctuations over the Past Two Decades

Klau and Fung (1996) have pointed out that the effective exchange rate index can serve various purposes, such as a measurement of

This chapter is a partial output of the research project on "The evolution and reconfiguration of the international monetary system." We acknowledge gratefully the financial sponsorship from Mr. Shi Zhengfu, Chairman of Comway Capital Group and Director of the Research Center of New Political Economy of Fudan University. We have benefited from constructive comments from Yu Yongding, Chen Ping, He Dong and other scholars. Wang Wei of Shanghai University of Finance and Economics, Liu Jianfeng and Deng Yanfei helped with some data collection.

Table 1. Chronology of the RMB exchange rate system.

Period	Basic characteristics of exchange rate system and exchange rate adjustment
October 1949 to March 1955	RMB exchange rate was under a managed float arrangement.
March 1995 to December 1971	After the monetary reform on March 10, 1955, the RMB pegged to the US dollar ($1 was worth between ¥2.46 and ¥2.6) to adapt to the Bretton Woods System.
December 1971 to August 1974	After the USA closed the "gold window" on August 15, 1971, the RMB shifted to peg to the HKD and GB pound. The RMB appreciated in value against the dollar.
August 1974 to December 1985	The RMB was pegged to a basket of 15 currencies. On July 8, 1980, $1 was worth for ¥1.45.
January 1981 to January 1985	From 1981, China had multiple exchange rates. An internal exchange rate was set for settlements of foreign trade; and the official exchange rate had frequent and small-scale fluctuations against the US$ to make RMB depreciate. By January 1985, $1 could exchange for ¥2.8.
January 1985 to December 1993	In early 1985, the internal settlement price of foreign trade was replaced by foreign exchange swap prices. 80% of the trade account transactions were conducted through the swap centres all over the country. The official exchange rate was characterized by infrequent yet wide-range currency movements with depreciation being the main trend. The value of US $1 went from ¥2.8 in January 1985 to ¥5.7 in December 1990. On April 9, 1991, the Chinese government announced the implementation of a floating exchange rate system and began to adopt the fine-tuning adjustments of the floating with high-frequency, narrow-range and mainly depreciation. In October 1986, the International Monetary Fund (IMF) classified China as following a managed floating system for the first time.
January 1994 to July 20, 2005	China unified the exchange rates in January 1994 at $1 for ¥8.7, and established the unified inter-bank foreign exchange trading centre. China began to implement the "single, managed floating exchange rate regime based on market supply and demand." However, from May 1995, especially after the Asian financial crisis in mid-1997, the RMB exchange rate was pegged at around $1 for ¥8.27. In December 1996, China achieved basic current account convertibility of the RMB, but kept foreign exchange

(*Continued*)

Table 1. (*Continued*)

Period	Basic characteristics of exchange rate system and exchange rate adjustment
	controls with policies of compulsory settlement and conditional sale. In 1999, the IMF classified the Chinese system as a pegged exchange rate system according to the de facto performance.
July 21, 2005 to July 2008	China announced the implementation of "a managed floating exchange rate regime based on market supply and demand with reference to a basket of foreign currencies." In these three years, the RMB appreciated accumulatively by 21% against the US dollar. On August 14, 2007, China began to implement the voluntary exchange settlement system.
July 2008 to June 18, 2010	In order to deal with the global financial crisis, the Chinese government again pegged the RMB to the US dollar ($1 exchanging for about ¥6.83).
June 21, 2010 till now	On June 19, 2010, the PBC re-launched the managed floating exchange rate regime that was originally announced on July 21, 2005. China allowed the RMB/dollar exchange rate to move around the central parity 0.5% each way daily. On April 16, 2012, the upper limit of the daily range of the RMB against the US dollar rose to 1%. On May 2, 2012, the central parity of the RMB was $1 exchanging for about ¥6.27.

Sources: Author's compilation based on Zhang Zhichao (2005), Zhang Daozheng (2005), Lin and Schramm (2003), and on information from PBC.

international competitiveness, or the operation goal of stabilization policy. This raises the question, has the RMB exchange rate been mostly a measure of price competitiveness, or a policy instrument to promote economic stability? Our conclusion is that, although the RMB exchange rate regime has undergone various changes over the past 20 years, it has been mainly a passive price index rather than an active policy tool. We base our conclusion on three sets of evidence that unanimously show the "pro-cyclical" nature of the RMB exchange rate changes. If the RMB were being used as a policy tool, the exchange rate fluctuation should be "leaning against the wind."

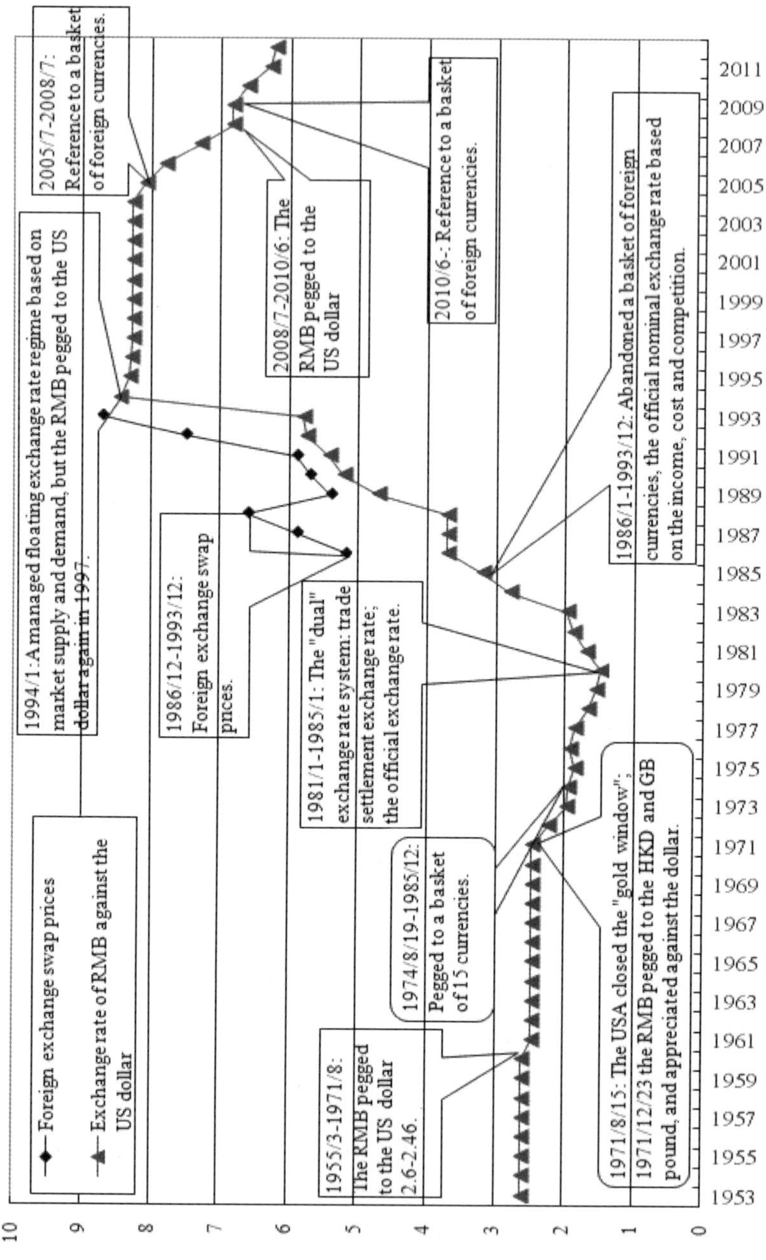

Figure 1. History of RMB exchange rate system and the exchange rate of RMB against the US dollar (1953–2012).

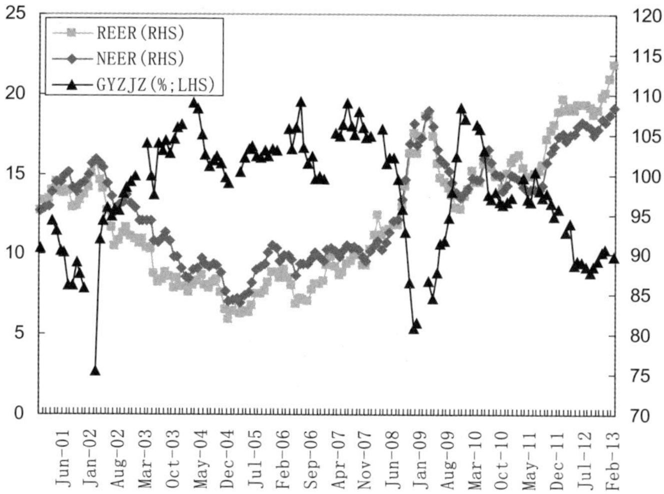

Figure 2. Monthly changes of RMB effective exchange rate and added value of industrial production (December 2000 to February 2013).

First, the "pro-cyclicality" of the RMB exchange rate is revealed when we look at its level with the monthly changes in the value added of industrial production, see Figure 2, over the 147 months from February 2000 to February 2013. It can be seen that when the industrial value-addition was experiencing rapid growth of 15% month on month, the RMB nominal and real effective exchange rates remained at a relatively low level (as for example from March 2003 to June 2008), hence further stimulating the industrial growth. However, when the growth rate of industrial added value (GYZJZ) slowed down, the nominal effective exchange rate (NEER) and real effective exchange rate (REER) were rather high (as from December 2000 to December 2001, from December 2011 to February 2013, and during the global financial crisis), thus exacerbating the decline of industrial production.

Second, we can come to a similar conclusion through investigating the relationship between the level of RMB effective exchange rate and the movements of the purchasing managers' index (PMI) of the Chinese manufacturing industry, see Figure 3. The manufacturing industry PMI, released through the website of the China Federation of Logistics and Purchasing Association, reflects the overall economic

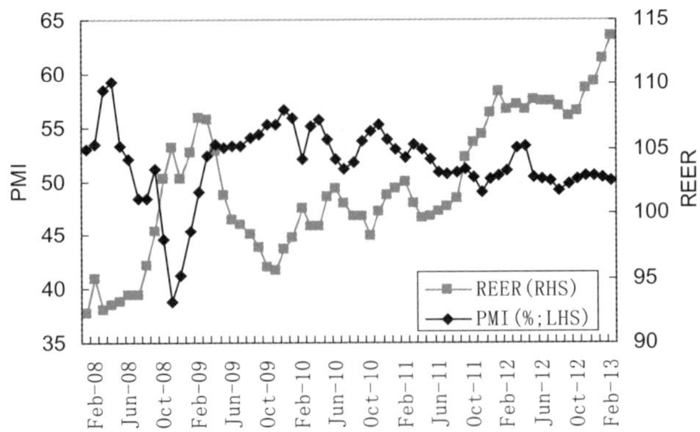

Figure 3. RMB real effective exchange rate (REER) and PMI index of manufacturing industry (January 2008 to March 2013).

situation in terms of eight aspects: production, new orders, commodity prices, inventory, employees, order delivery, new export orders and imports. In the 63 months from January 2008 to March 2013, when the PMI was above the break-even line of 50 (i.e., the economy was in a boom phase), the REER was rather low (for example, January 2008 to June 2008, March 2009 to May 2011), thereby exacerbating the overheating of the economy. Conversely, when the PMI was around or even lower than 50 (i.e., the economy was sluggish in terms of growth), the REER remained at a high level, thus accentuating the slowdown.

Third, Figure 4 demonstrates the levels of the NEER and the producer price index (PPI) from January 2006 to February 2013. It can be seen that when the PPI was significantly higher than 100, that is, during phases of rapid rises in product price, the NEER was low (i.e., the RMB was weak against other currencies). When inflation was high, export prices were low and contributed to inflation. Conversely, when the PPI was significantly lower than 100 (i.e., when the economy was going through deflation), the NEER remained high, which could only exacerbate the deflation.

These three facts demonstrate that the RMB exchange rate has not played a role in stabilizing domestic prices. Therefore, we need to confront the important issue of how to conduct effective reform of the RMB exchange rate mechanism, so that it becomes a policy tool for stabilizing price and economic growth.

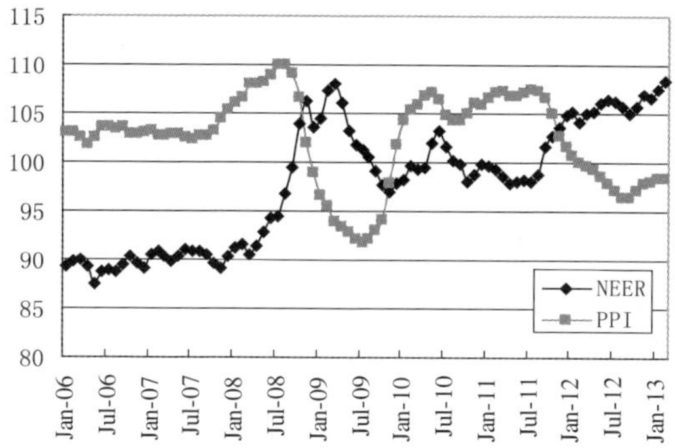

Figure 4. RMB nominal effective exchange rate (NEER) and PPI (January 2006 to February 2013).

Economic Theory and the Singapore Experience

We have formulated recommendations for the management of the RMB over two time horizons: the medium-run and the long-run. Our recommendations draw on the theoretical literature on the management of the exchange rate and on the experience of Singapore in exchange rate management.

On the theoretical side, Williamson (1985) and Williamson and Miller (1987) have advocated exchange rate target zones, with ±10% around the fundamental equilibrium exchange rate. The works of Krugman (1991), Anthony and MacDonald (1998), Bertola and Svensson (1993), and Duarte *et al.* (2013) have shown that the exchange rate band becomes a practical way to stabilize the exchange rate around the central parity as well as around the edge of the band.

On the practical side, Wilson and Ren (2009) and Wlliamson (1998), among others, have concluded that for over 30 years, Singapore has scored a successful record of effective management of the exchange rate, in a framework described either as "dynamic target zone management" or "Basket, Band, and Crawl" (BBC). Basket refers to the fact that the Monetary Authority of Singapore (MAS) manages the NEER of the Singapore dollar (NEER or trade-weighted nominal exchange rate index [TWI]), which is the average weighted level of the Singapore dollar (SGD), against an unpublished trade-weighted basket of currencies of the major trading partners. Band refers to the range within which the NEER is allowed to float in order to ensure appropriate flexibility and also to accommodate short term fluctuations in the exchange rate. Crawl indicates that the exchange rate target is crawling; that is, the central exchange rate parity is adjusted regularly based on economic fundamentals in order to avoid excessive deviation from the fundamentals of the Singapore dollar (See for example Khor *et al.*, 2007 and Peebles and Wilson, 2005).

RMB Exchange Rate Management in the Medium-Run: A Dynamic Target Zone Approach

The PBC has described the current RMB regime as "a managed floating exchange rate based on market supply and demand with reference to a basket of foreign currencies." Our recommendation is that the current regime should take the specific form of a dynamic target zone in the medium run, adopting a modified form of the Singapore approach to exchange rate management.

The Singaporean experience and its applicability to China

Although Singapore has set a good example of undertaking the "BBC" system, two important concerns must be factored into China's implementation of its own form of BBC. First, unlike the small economic size of Singapore, China is the world's second largest economy, and so the same use of a non-transparent system (e.g., the weights of the basket are not published) by China could generate negative attention by the rest of the world on China's motivations (e.g., beggar-thy-neighbor behavior or legitimate domestic stabilization).

Second, unlike Singapore, China is not a fully fledged free-market economy; albeit that the Chinese economy already has attained a considerable degree of openness. The historical evidence shows that under the relatively rigid exchange rate arrangements, the monetary policy in China, including quantity of money and the interest rate level, is under many constraints. Therefore, even if China does not adopt the exchange rate as a major policy tool to the extent that Singapore has done, China should at least adopt exchange rate policy as a complementary policy, by appropriately increasing the exchange rate flexibility in order to compensate for the temporary incompetence of interest rate policy and monetary policy.

Design of the dynamic target zone for RMB exchange rate

Determination of the central parity exchange rate

The central parity of the RMB exchange rate target zone is represented in the form of NEER with reference to REER. According to the Balassa–Samuelson effect and the difference between the domestic and foreign production productivity, the central parity should maintain an appreciation in the range of 1.5% to 2% each year. The reason is that the annual growth of China's labour productivity (usually manifested by per capita income) is about 8%, which is about 2.5% higher than in Europe, America, Japan and other developed economies, and 3.5% higher than the overall level worldwide. This leads to the conclusion that the REER of RMB should maintain an annual appreciation of about 1.5% to 2%. This figure is similar to the opinion expressed by Mussa (2008), who believes that the differences in labour productivity between China and its main trading partners is 3% each year, and proposes that the long-run equilibrium path of the RMB exchange rate is to maintain the growth of the REER at about 2% each year. It is worth noting that Singapore depreciated its currency during domestic economic depression and external crisis, while during the economic boom it usually permitted an annual appreciation in the range of 2% to 3%, in order to protect domestic prices and exports from the impact of imported inflation.

Options of "policy bandwidth" in the exchange rate target zone

Learning from Singapore's experience, this chapter argues that the optimal system of RMB exchange rate management is not to choose a point target of fixed value, but rather to choose a moving range known as the "policy bandwidth," which would allow the RMB exchange rate to float within the crawling band. Figure 5 demonstrates the historical trend of nominal and REER of RMB and the dynamic target zone of effective exchange rate management since the exchange reform in 1994. The upper and lower

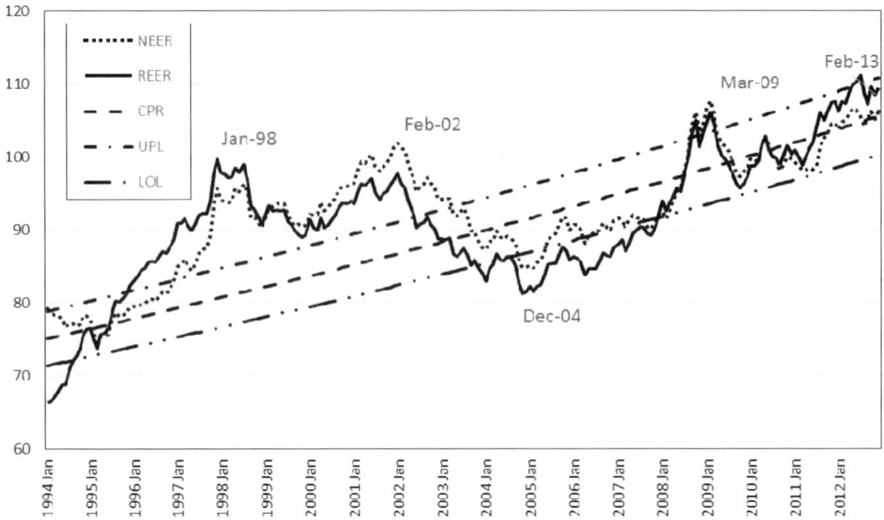

Figure 5. Dynamic target zone for management of RMB effective exchange rate.

limit lines in the figure represent the "policy bandwidth" of the RMB effective exchange rate. We can see that the central parity exchange rate (CPR) grew at the speed of 1.8% per year (or 0.15% per month), while the upper and lower limits (UPL, LOL) were about +/−5% of the central exchange rate respectively, representing the "policy bandwidth" that allowed the effective exchange rate changes.

There are some reasons for setting the width of policy range at +/−5% of the CPR as a temporary measure. Huang *et al.* (2005) estimate that a 10% depreciation of the RMB REER would promote China's real GDP growth by 1% to 2% based on the data for 1987–2003. According to this view, if we want to control the potential speed of economic growth within a range of around +/−1%, then the RMB REER should allow a changing range of around 10%. Furthermore, Cline (2008) and Cline and Williamson (2010) estimate that the elasticity of changes of RMB REER to the ratio of China's current account balance to GDP to be 0.3 to 0.45. Hence, we may in normal situations control the ratio of the balance of China's current account to GDP to be around +/−3% and allow the REER to fluctuate in a range of 10% to 6.6%, that is, 3%/0.3 to 3%/0.45, respectively.

Therefore, from the perspective of internal and external balances and taking full consideration of the impacts of RMB effective exchange rate fluctuations on economic growth, price stability and the balance of payments, it is both prudent and appropriate to set the width of the "policy band" of RMB effective exchange rate to be around the central parity at +/−5%. From the empirical data over the past two decades, we know that if the effective exchange rate exceeds the target zone as shown in Figure 5, it will cause either economic overheating with inflation (June 2004–June 2008), or economic decline with deflation (January 1998–March 2003). This also indicates that the "policy bandwidth" of +/−5% in operation recently is appropriate in general. However, with the strengthening of Chinese economic capacity and the loosening of capital controls, the width of "policy band" can be gradually extended to +/−10% in the future.

Operation approaches of the target zone management

Although the effective exchange rate refers to the ratio of one currency to a basket of currencies, its management does not require us to intervene the price movements of all the currencies on the foreign exchange market, but only with those of the major currencies in the basket. Under the existing market structure, the PBC needs only to set the central parity of the RMB against the US dollar through China's Foreign Exchange Trade Centre, and to meet the excess demand in the market or absorb the excess supply as necessary, which can be achieved through keeping the effective exchange rate within the target zone or policy range. Specifically, when NEER exceeds the upper limit of the target zone as in Figure 5, the rate of exchange of RMB against the US dollar should depreciate; in the opposite case, the RMB should appreciate against the US dollar.

China's Exchange Rate Regime: Long-Term Options for the Future

The selection of a particular form of RMB exchange rate regime is an endogenous process, determined by both national interests and possible global responses.

China's manufacturing sector makes up half of its national economy, enabling China to become a "world factory" in the global network of production and distribution. This structural characteristic makes it necessary that the RMB exchange rate arrangements should contribute to the stability of the enterprise production costs and create a stable policy environment for China's foreign trade, dominated by raw materials and manufactured goods. This is an important prerequisite to ensure the national competitiveness and sustained growth, as well as a key to safeguard China's national interests.

In terms of global repercussions, the "New Triffin Dilemma" has indicated that the current over-reliance on the dollar international monetary system lacks long-term sustainability. As an emerging economic power, China should promote the internationalization of RMB and participate in the re-construction of the international monetary system. Therefore, China's exchange rate system should comply with the reforming trend of the international monetary system and contribute to the internationalization of RMB.

In short, we should choose an RMB exchange rate regime that plays a role in promoting RMB internationalization and the reform of international monetary system. The chosen RMB exchange rate regime can also contribute to the steady growth of the real economy and foreign trade in China's manufacturing goods.

Specifically, the long-run exchange rate regime should meet the following two requirements. First, the RMB should be independent of other currencies and abandon the over-close connection with the US dollar. Over the past two decades, the issuance of RMB has mainly depended on the central bank's acquisition of the US dollar and other foreign currencies; in fact, in the recent decades, the issuance of RMB has largely been backed by $3.3 trillion of foreign reserves that China has accumulated. The US dollar thus becomes the basis of the RMB value, and the RMB is essentially a substitution coupon of the US dollar. If this situation does not change, there will be no genuine RMB internationalization, and discussion about reforming the current international monetary system, which is over-reliant on the dollar, will be no more than empty talk.

Second, with regard both to RMB internationalization and to the stabilization of the national economy, the purchasing power, or currency value of RMB, should remain basically stable. The stability of RMB purchasing power in terms of raw materials and manufactured products is conducive to steady production costs and competitiveness of Chinese enterprises, and contributes to the long-term survival and sustainable development of the manufacturing industry. Furthermore, stability of the currency value is crucial to RMB internationalization and to playing the roles of international currency. Otherwise, the redistribution of wealth caused by inflation or deflation would undermine worldwide confidence in the RMB.

To achieve this, we propose the following three elements for the basic structure of the RMB exchange regime:

1. Make explicit the value basis of RMB and set the RMB price according to a commodity basket composed of a series of important means of production and materials so as to maintain the basic stability of the purchasing power of RMB against the commodity basket.
2. Strengthen the independence of the Chinese central bank and transform the monetary policy framework to one of "generalized inflation targeting," which can stabilize the RMB's purchasing power in terms of the above commodity basket, so as to guarantee and strengthen the market confidence.
3. Achieve the free floating of exchange rate in general to adapt to the needs of RMB internationalization and capital account liberalization, and perform a buffer function as a "firewall" to mitigate impacts of possible external shocks brought about by the floating exchange rate.

For construction of the proposed commodity basket, in principle it should take into consideration at least the following essentials:

1. These commodities are critically important for China's production and livelihood;
2. They are suitable for a long period of storage; and
3. For the component commodities, China's production and storage capacity of them should achieve a certain share in the world total.

We construct the commodity basket according to the CRB Index (Commodity Research Bureau Index), adding and deleting some commodities and changing the weights as appropriate to the specific case of China. The CRB Index, a commodity price index established in 1956 by the "Commodity Research Bureau" set up by the American Jiler Brothers in 1933, is the leading index to reflect commodity futures prices, and the benchmark to measure changes in worldwide commodity futures prices. The CRB index is updated every 15 seconds, a frequency that cannot be matched by the other price indexes such as the PPI and CPI, which are released at the monthly frequency. Moreover, the CRB index leads the CPI and PPI in terms of the changing trend, which makes it a pre-warning index reflecting inflation. CRB index futures price data comes from the Chicago Board of Trade (CBOT), the New York Mercantile Exchange and Commodity Exchange (COMEX), the New York Mercantile Exchange (NYMEX), and the London Metal Exchange (LME). The original CRB index commodity basket included 28 commodities (26 commodity futures and two spot commodities). Since then, it has undergone more than 10 revisions. In 1973, the CRB index became a purely futures price index, after the spot commodities were excluded. In 2005, the modified CRB index included three categories and 19 commodities futures contracts, with weights distributed as follows: 39% energy (23% crude oil, 5% heating oil, 5% unleaded gasoline, 6% natural gas), 41% agricultural products (6% soybean, 1% wheat, 6% corn, 5% cocoa, 5% coffee, 5% cotton, 5% sugar, 1% orange juice, 6% live cattle, and 1% bacon hogs), and 20% metal (6% gold, 6% copper, 6% aluminium, 1% silver, 1% nickel). Among these commodities, orange juice, live cattle and bacon hogs are not appropriate for constructing the commodity basket of proposed for the value base of China's RMB.

It should be pointed out that to maintain the basic stability of the RMB against the purchasing power of a basket of commodities does not mean to keep fixed the value of RMB: we can allow the RMB to change its value against the basket by a certain rate per year (e.g., 2%), based on fluctuations of the production cost of the component commodities, purchasing and storage costs, etc. We can also allow the price of the commodity basket to decline in a certain range. To some extent, depreciation of the price of the commodity basket can help alleviate pressure on the RMB exchange rate brought about by international commodity price movements.

Conclusions and Recommendations

This chapter has examined the changes of RMB exchange rate regime over the past 60 years, with particular reference to the "pro-cyclical" pattern of RMB exchange rate fluctuations since 1994. When China encountered economic downturn and deflation, the RMB exchange rate was overvalued; conversely, during periods of over-rapid economic growth and rising inflation, the RMB exchange rate was undervalued. This indicates that China does not use the exchange rate policy as a tool to stabilize domestic prices, and this should be redressed.

We then identified the medium-term and long-term choices of RMB exchange rate regime. In the medium-term, we recommend that China draw on Singapore's experience and implement an exchange rate management with the characteristics of "BBC." Specifically, we suggest setting up a dynamic target zone for management of the effective exchange rate where the central parity rate (based on the Balassa–Samuelson hypothesis about relative labor productivity growth) maintains an annual 2% appreciation in terms of the REER. Meanwhile, taking into account the exchange rate elasticity of the current account and the objective of basic balance in the current account, the width of the target zone should be set to allow $+/-5\%$ fluctuation for the movements of the RMB exchange rate around the central parity exchange rate.

In the long-term, we recommend that China implement a monetary regime that combines a floating exchange rate system and generalized inflation targeting. The value of the RMB should be established in terms of a basket of commodities, to strengthen the independence of the Chinese central bank and to strengthen international confidence in the Chinese RMB as an international currency. China should also allow a RMB exchange rate that can freely float in normal situations, to achieve internal and external balances, and to protect against the impacts of external price shocks and economic disturbances on the domestic economy.

References

Anthony, M and R MacDonald (1998). On the mean-reverting properties of target zone exchange rates: Some evidence from the ERM. *European Economic Review*, 42, 1493–1523.

Bertola, G and L Svensson (1993). Stochastic devaluation risk and the empirical fit of target-zone models. *Review of Economic Studies*, 60, 689–712.

Cline, WR (2008). Estimating consistent fundamental equilibrium exchange rates. Working Paper Series, No. 08–6, Peterson Institute for International Economics.

Cline, WR and J Williamson (2010). Estimates of fundamental equilibrium exchange rates. Policy Briefs, No. 12–14, Peterson Institute for International Economics.

Duarte, Andrade and Duarte (2013). Exchange rate target zones: A survey of the literature. *Journal of Economic Surveys*, 27(2), 247–268.

Huang, WY, RL He and SX Chen (2005). An empirical study on the relationship between economic growth and RMB real exchange rate. *Journal of Dalian Maritime University* 4, 50–54.

Khor, HE, J Lee, E Robinson and S Supaat (2007). Managed floating exchange rate system: The Singapore experience. *Singapore Economic Review*, 52, 7–25.

Klau, M and SS Fung (2006). The new BIS effective exchange rate indices. *BIS Quarterly Review*, March, 51–65.

Krugman, P (1991). Target zones and exchange rate dynamics. *The Quarterly Journal of Economics*, 151, 669–682.

Lin, G and RM SCHRAMM (2003). China's foreign exchange policies since 1979: A review of developments and an assessment. *China Economic Review*, 14, 246–280.

Mussa, M (2008). IMF surveillance over China's exchange rate policy. In Goldstein, M and NR Lardy (Eds.), *Debating China's Exchange Rate Policy*, pp. 279–335. Washington, DC: Peterson Institute for International Economics.

Monetary Authority of Singapore (2001). Singapore's Exchange Rate Policy. Singapore: Monetary Authority of Singapore.

Peebles, G and P Wilson (2005). Don't frighten the horses: The political economy of Singapore's foreign exchange rate regime since 1981. Singapore Centre for Applied and Policy Analysis Working Paper No. 2005/06.

Svensson, L (1992). An interpretation of recent research on exchange rate target zones. *Journal of Economic Perspectives*, 6, 119–144.

Williamson, J (1985). *The Exchange Rate System.* Washington, DC: Institute for International Economics.

Williamson, J (1998). The case for a common basket peg. In Collignon, S, J Pisani-Ferry and YC Park (Eds.), *Exchange Rate Policies in Emerging Asian Countries.* London: Routledge.

Williamson, J (2001). The case for a basket, band and crawl (BBC) regime for East Asia. In Gruen, D and J Simon (Eds.), *Future Directions for Monetary Policies in East Asia.* Sydney: Reserve Bank of Australia.

Williamson, J and M Miller (1987). *Target and Indicators: A Blueprint for the International Coordination of Economic Policy.* Washington, DC: Institute for International Economics.

Wilson, P and NS Ren (2009). Managing exchange rate volatility: A comparative counterfactual analysis of Singapore, 1994–2003. *The Singapore Economic Review*, 54, 543–568.

Zhang, DZ (2005). Determination of RMB exchange rate: A purchasing power parity perspective. *Forum on World Economics and Politics*, 2, 52–58. (In Chinese).

Zhang, ZC (2005). Regime shifts in RMB exchange rate policy: A historical perspective. In Zhang, LQ (Ed.), *Reform of Exchange Rate System: International Experience and China's Choice*, pp. 113–130. Beijing: China Finance Publication House.

Chapter 11

The Internationalization of the renminbi is in Accordance with China's National Interests and Global Responsibilities*

Yingli Pan, Yingfeng Xu and Jun Wu

Introduction

The internationalization of the renminbi (RMB) is a controversial issue among Chinese economists and policy makers. The issue of controversy is whether the Chinese government should actively push RMB internationalization. In fact, the term used in official parlance is to push forward "the cross-border use of the RMB," not "RMB internationalization." Partly, this term is motivated by some strategic considerations. Also important is the reality that Chinese economists and policy makers have not sorted out how to relate RMB internationalization to reforming the international monetary system and liberalizing and opening China's financial sector. Therefore, they have not formulated a comprehensive strategy to push forward RMB internationalization.

Broadly speaking, there are three distinct views on the question of whether the Chinese government should actively promote

*This chapter is a partial output of the research project on "The evolution and reconfiguration of the international monetary system." We acknowledge gratefully the financial sponsorship from Mr. Shi Zhengfu, Chairman of Comway Capital Group and Director of the Research Center of New Political Economy in Fudan University. We have benefited from constructive comments from Yu Yongding, Chen Ping and He Dong and other scholars. Wang Wei of Shanghai University of Finance and Economics and Liu Jianfeng and Deng Yanfei of the Institute of Contemporary Finance, Shanghai Jiaotong University helped with some data collection.

RMB internationalization. The first view approves the proactive role of the Chinese government. There are proponents of such a view both within and outside China. International investors and many prominent foreign economists would like to see a faster pace of RMB internationalization, because the liberalization of the capital account as an integral part of RMB internationalization would make RMB available as another major international reserve currency and make RMB-denominated assets available as an additional asset class for the portfolios of global investors. As a result, the heavy pressure on the US dollar in international financial markets can be relieved.[1] Those proponents in China believe that RMB internationalization would help raise China's status in global political and economic power, and would yield the international seiniorage revenue for China and reduce foreign exchange risks in cross-border receipts and payments for the private sector, and furthermore would speed up and facilitate the liberalization of China's domestic financial sector.

The second view opposes the proactive role of the Chinese government in pushing RMB internationalization. A prominent representative of the negative view is Lin (2012), former senior vice president and chief economist of the World Bank. He does not believe that the Chinese government should promote actively to make the RMB into an international reserve currency prematurely. He is concerned that the opening of the capital account amounts to a self-dismantling of the financial Great Wall shielding the domestic financial sector from global financial shocks, potentially triggering a financial crisis in China. Yu (2011) also shares the concern that the proactive involvement of the Chinese government in RMB internationalization is a kind of destructive enthusiasm, i.e., "trying to help the shoots grow by pulling them upward."

[1]Bergstein of Peterson Institute of International Economics opined in 2009 that RMB internationalization would relieve the pressure on the US dollar. An official of Japan's finance ministry supported RMB internationalization in an interview in Washington DC in March 2013. Eichengreen (2011) believed that RMB internationalization would benefit both the Chinese economy and the global economy. Many scholars hold the view that RMB internationalization is in line with the emergence of a multi-polar global economy.

The third view takes a middle position, advocating that a gradual but steadfast approach to internationalize the RMB. The proponents of the middle view recognize the risks and challenges inherent in the process of internationalizing the RMB. Therefore, it is important to handle properly the interaction between RMB internationalization on the one hand and the restructuring of the Chinese economy and the reform and opening of the domestic financial sector on the other and sequence various financial reforms accordingly. Subachi and Driffill (2010) points out that it is a tricky challenge to proceed with RMB internationalization under restricted capital flows. In this context, the offshore financial center of Hong Kong plays a critical role. Prasad and Ye (2012) thinks that the most challenging task in RMB internationalization is to find the right sequence of various financial reforms. GAO Haihong (2011) proposes that RMB internationalization should start from a regional basis, make full use of the off-shore financial center of Hong Kong in the context of China's restricted capital account, and let the RMB play a major role of an anchor currency in coordinating exchange rate policies among East and South East Asian countries. Murase (2011) points out that at present, the backdrop for RMB internationalization is the segmentation of the onshore and offshore markets and therefore, it is necessary to separate the use of RMB in real business from that in financial investment in the process of RMB internationalization.

The use of the RMB in the cross-border settlement of trade payments occurs mainly on the side of China's imports, as a result, meeting the demand for RMB assets from international investors and speculators who anticipate the RMB to appreciate. The accumulation of RMB money in offshore financial centers such as Hong Kong tends to accentuate the pressure for China to increase foreign exchange reserves involuntarily and accumulate the capital loss risk from dollar depreciation. In this context, the roadmap for internationalizing the RMB remains hazy and there lacks a coherent theoretical analysis of the consequences of various options for RMB internationalization. Yu (2011) points out that the essence of RMB internationalization is the liberalization of cross-border capital flows. Therefore, China should pause with the current program of RMB internationalization and thoroughly evaluate the experience in the past few years. There is an extensive literature discussing the costs, benefits and pre-conditions of RMB internationalization. But there has been inadequate attention given to the relationship between RMB internationalization on the one hand, and the reform of the current dollar-centered international monetary system on the other. There are few studies that have touched in a systematic way the issue of what should be the immediate targets at the present stage and the final goal of RMB internationalization, the issue of how to situate RMB internationalization against the backdrop of reforming the international financial architecture, and the issue of how to proceed practically in the face of unstable and volatile global financial markets.

This chapter attempts to present a systematic analysis of RMB internationalization in the context of reforming the global financial architecture. The second section spells out the global significance of RMB internationalization. The third section analyzes how RMB internationalization should interact and be coordinated with restructuring the Chinese economy on the one hand and reforming and liberalizing the domestic financial sector on the other. The fourth section delineates the strategic objectives of RMB internationalization. The fifth section presents two major findings for the pre-conditions and potential of RMB internationalization. The sixth section explores the strategy of pushing forward RMB internationalization and outlines the key areas with which China should be focused at the present stage. The final section gives concluding remarks.

The Global Significance of RMB Internationalization

It contributes to form a more stable international monetary system based on multiple reserve currencies

Over the past three decades, a multi-polar world economy has emerged, resulting from the forces of globalization. Table 1 lists the average growth rate of G-20 economies over three sub-periods of 1980–1990, 1991–2000, and 2001–2011. The growth of the US, Japan and Europe, or the G-7 economies, all fell behind emerging markets. In contrast, at the front of the growth league are China, India, Indonesia, Argentina, Turkey and Brazil.

Table 1. Real GDP growth of G-20 economies (%).

Country	1980–1990	1991–2000	2001–2011
China	9.2	10.5	10.4
India	5.7	5.6	7.4
Indonesia	6.6	4.4	5.3
Argentina	−0.9	4.7	5.0
Russia	—	−3.6	4.9
Turkey	4.6	3.7	4.4
South Korea	7.8	6.2	4.1
Saudi Arabia	0.2	2.8	3.6
Brazil	2.3	2.6	3.6
South Africa	2.0	1.8	3.5
Australia	3.4	3.4	2.9
Mexico	2.5	3.5	2.0
Canada	2.8	2.9	1.9
United States	2.9	3.4	1.6
United Kingdom	2.3	2.9	1.6
Euro zone	2.3	2.2	1.4
France	2.3	2.0	1.2
Germany	2.3	1.9	1.1
Japan	4.5	1.1	0.6
Italy	2.5	1.6	0.4

Source: World Bank — WDI Online.

Table 2 shows the global share of G-20 members' GDP measured at purchasing power parity (PPP). Collectively, the global share of the US, Japan and Europe declined from 60.26% in 1980 to 44.37% in 2011, a drop of 15.89 percentage points. In contrast, the global share of China, India, South Korea, Turkey and Indonesia rose from 6.7% in 1980 to 24.33% in 2011, an increase of 17.63 percentage points. The average annual growth of China's GDP over the past 30 years was as high as 10%, and the global share of China's GDP at PPP expanded from 2% in 1980 to 13.98% in 2011.

This trend in the shifting of the global economic center of gravity from North American and Europe to Asia will continue and may even accelerate. Johansson *et al.* (2012) provides the latest projection for the long-term economic growth of the global economy over the next 50 years on the basis of assuming reasonable progress made in

Table 2. G-20 economies' share in the global economy (%).

Country	1980	1990	2000	2011
Euro-zone	29.54	27.16	24.94	20.37
United States	22.59	22.54	23.32	18.60
China	2.00	3.54	7.04	13.98
India	2.40	2.99	3.79	5.58
Japan	8.13	9.30	7.76	5.40
Germany	6.31	5.78	4.99	3.97
Russia	—	4.66	2.36	3.73
Brazil	3.42	3.04	2.88	2.84
France	4.28	3.93	3.61	2.84
United Kingdom	3.84	3.66	3.62	2.82
Italy	4.25	3.92	3.46	2.44
Mexico	2.17	2.02	2.12	2.17
South Korea	0.74	1.34	1.90	1.85
Canada	2.21	2.12	2.06	1.72
Turkey	0.78	0.94	1.39	1.53
Indonesia	0.78	1.05	1.17	1.39
Australia	1.10	1.15	1.19	1.10
Argentina	1.10	0.69	0.79	0.89
Saudi Arabia	1.30	0.88	0.85	0.85
South Africa	0.94	0.79	0.70	0.69

Data source: WDI.
Note: GDP is measured in current international dollar (PPP).

structural reform and fiscal consolidation. Their projection[2] is that the global economy would grow at an average annual rate of 3%. Non-OECD economies would grow at an annual of 7% over the next 10 years, 5% over 2020s, and gradually slow down to 2.5% by 2050. The average annual growth of OECD economies would be in the range of 1.75%–2.25%. As a result, relative economic power would shift fundamentally. In terms of the 2005 international dollar at PPP, the two economies of China and India would exceed the total of the G-7 economies, expanding seven times over the next 50 years, surpassing the total of all OECD economies. The global share of the Chinese economy would be 17% in 2011, 28% in 2030 and 2060. The global share of the Indian economy would be 7% in 2011, 11% in 2030 and 18% in 2060. In comparison, the global share of the US

[2]Johansson *et al.* (2012).

economy would fall from 23% in 2011 to 18% in 2030 and 16% in 2060. The total global share of the US, Japan and Europe would fall from 47% in 2011 to 34% in 2030 and 28% in 2060. Similar projections are also made by Lyons (2010) and Ignazio *et al.* (2011). It may appear that these projections take a sanguine outlook for China and other emerging markets. But such projected trend growth of emerging markets is fairly reasonable, so long as it is not severely disrupted by major social and economic crises.

A multi-polar global economy needs a multiple reserve currencies system

There exists a structural mismatch between the demand for and supply of reserve assets. In our opinion, the Triffin dilemma has an important limitation. The Triffin dilemma is predicated on the presumption that the demand for reserve assets grows proportionately with global trade, while the supply of dollar reserve assets relies on the injection of dollars from US current-account deficit. As US external deficit appears to be unsustainable, international confidence in the US dollar as a store of value would dissipate. Hence, the Triffin dilemma arises. There is an important limitation regarding the applicability of the Triffin dilemma to the present global economy. The original Triffin hypothesis does not make a distinction between the reserve assets demand based on trade transactions and the reserve assets demand arising from global financial investment.

As a matter of fact, the global liquidity demand required for international trade does not need to expand proportionately with global trade. Theoretically, imports can be paid with exports. So long as trade is balanced, there is no need for the liquidity used in trade settlements to expand proportionately with the value of global trade. Practically speaking, there are many ways to economize the global liquidity need for trade settlements. Global liquidity may expand through orderly raising special drawing right (SDR) quotas. It is possible to set up global or regional clearing systems. All these measures may reduce global liquidity need for trade settlements. In the literature on reforming the international monetary system, most proposals are preoccupied with the transactions-based global liquidity demand. There has not been adequate study of the demand for and supply of international reverse assets in the realm of international financial investment. Perhaps, this inclination in the existing literature for focusing narrowly on the global reserve assets demand for trade settlements reflects the lingering influence of the original Triffin doctrine.

The demand for and supply of dollar assets arise from global payments imbalances. If such payments imbalances are mainly driven by the cross-country differences in short or medium-term economic cycles, there is no need for alarm or worry. The various financing facilities provided by the international monetary fund (IMF) should be capable of funding temporary payments imbalances, offsetting external shocks and improving social welfare. However, global imbalances pose an entirely different challenge if the resulting demand for international reserve assets reflects a cautious self-defense response to the unstable and volatile global financial environment. In that case, the core issue in reforming the global financial architecture is to create a stable global financial environment. However, the intricate knot difficult to untangle in global rebalancing is that global imbalances reflect long-term structural imbalances in the global distribution of the productive capacity of tradable goods and services. In our opinion, financial assets are essentially the media through which purchasing power is transferred from those people who are post-adolesents and have savings to themselves when retired. In today's globalized economy, the increasing demand for international reserve assets from emerging market and developing economies reflects their need for safe and liquid financial assets which would enable these economies to enjoy higher levels of consumption of tradable goods and services of equal value in the future. The real challenge lies in the fact that against the background of economic globalization, there exist substantial imbalances in the global distribution of the productive capacity of tradable goods and services resulting from highly mobile capital technology and immobile labor and land.

The contradiction between a multi-polar global economy and the unipolar international monetary system is deepening. The economies with expanding productive capacity of tradable goods and services are selling their surplus output to those economies with stagnating and shrinking productive capacity of tradables in the current and future periods. This implies systematic risk of default for a large part of international reserve assets. Farhi *et al.* (2011) propose a modern version of the Triffin dilemma. On the one hand, there is an increasing demand for global reserve assets from emerging market and developing economies, but on the other hand, the supply of liquid and safe reserve assets in the form of US government bills and bonds comes from US fiscal deficit and rising debt. At some point in the future, ever-rising US government debt would erode global confidence in the safety of dollar reserve assets.[3] Once that critical moment comes, a collapse of the current global monetary and financial system cannot be ruled out. This is the fundamental source of global financial instability. And that is the core challenge confronting the global community.[4]

The most realistic direction for reforming the international monetary system is to move towards a multiple reserve currencies system. This is also a common proposal sanctioned by many international think tanks. A multiple reserve currencies system has many advantages over the current dollar-dominated system. It is more compatible with the emerging multi-polar global economy. It allows countries to diversify their portfolio of foreign exchange reserves assets. It meets the demand of emerging market and developing economies for more reserve assets. It will exert more global discipline on the monetary policy of major reserve currency economies. The main disadvantage lies in the inherent exchange rate instability resulting from the competition among major reserve currencies and mercurial international capital flows. Because economic cycles are not synchronized across major economic blocs, current and expected future yield differentials would induce large portfolio reallocations among major reserve currency assets by international investors as well as the foreign exchange reserve portfolios of central banks. When international capital flows become too large and result in excessive

[3]Pan (2011).

[4]Our view is corroborated by that President Obama approved the Manufacturing Revival Act in 2010 and many other advanced also attempt to enhance the tradability of their service activities.

movements in major exchange rates beyond the levels consistent with fundamental determinants, chaos in global financial markets may ensue, threatening the stability of the international financial system.

While there is a widely shared agreement on the realistic direction of moving towards a multiple reserve currencies international monetary system,[5] current major reserve currency economies, especially the US, do not have much enthusiasm in such a proposal. Therefore, as pointed out by many scholars and international think tanks, the initiative to push forward a multiple reserve-currency system has to come from emerging market economies, especially China. In addition to government-led initiatives, the natural selection by market forces is another important driver. However, there are also many scholars and think tanks (the UN proposal) who are more concerned with the inherent instability of a multiple reserve-currency system and do not put it at the top of the option list for reforming the international monetary system.[6]

What need to be done in order to make the multiple reserve-currency system a feasible replacement for the current system? There are two major pre-conditions. One is that the RMB is successfully internationalized and becomes a stable and attractive alternative international reserve currency. The other is that a stabilizing mechanism can be set up and institutionalized for the multiple reserve-currency system.

We believe that the Chinese government should take the initiative to promote the reform option of moving towards a multiple reserve-currency system with a built-in stabilizing mechanism. The challenge is how to institutionalize a built-in stabilizing mechanism. In our view, the built-in stabilizing mechanism has three major attributes. First, there exist multiple reserve currencies compatible with the emerging multi-polar global economy. The reserve currencies consist of the currencies of major economic blocs. The currencies of other economies or economic blocs experiencing strong economic

[5] Angeloni *et al.* (2011) and Prasad and Ye (2012).
[6] UN (2009).

growth may also be encouraged to join the reserve currency pool. It is important that the international monetary system is enhanced by the inclusion in the reserve assets pool of the currencies of most dynamic big economies. Second, each major reserve currency provides a stable anchor for the relevant regional economic bloc so that major reserve currencies are more complementary than competitive to each other. Third, major reserve currency economies cooperate actively and closely to attain exchange rate stability and stabilize international capital flows. With effective global coordination and cooperation in monetary and exchange rate policies, it is possible to attain a smooth transition into a multiple reserve-currency system and avoid the destructive competition among major reserve currencies and the resulting global systemic financial risk.

If the realistic direction for reforming the international monetary system is to move toward a multiple reserve-currency system with a built-in stabilizing mechanism, then the two critical drivers are the internationalization of the RMB and the global monetary coordination to stabilize exchange rates and capital flows. In this context, RMB internationalization will provide a new stabilizing force in the formation of a stable three-pillar reserve currencies system. On the other hand, effective global coordination in monetary, exchange rate and financial policies will create a favorable global financial environment for RMB internationalization.

Toward re-balancing of the global economy

There has been extensive debate on the causes of global imbalances and their role in causing the 2008 global financial crisis. Broadly speaking, there are three views on global imbalances involving Asian economies.

One view[7] as expounded by Chairman Bernanke of the US Federal Reserve Board is the global saving glut narrative. According

[7]The proponents of this view include Mussa (2004), Roubini and Setser (2004), Blanchard *et al.* (2005), Bernanke (2005), IMF (2006, 2007), Obstfeld and Rogoff (2007), and Yoshitomi (2007).

to this view, global imbalances are mainly caused by excessive saving in China and other Asian economies and their currency manipulation. According to the logic of this view, more appreciation of Asian currencies, especially the RMB, would have ameliorated global imbalances substantially. This is also the official position of the US government. That is why the US government constantly exerted pressures on China to allow the RMB to appreciate against the US dollar.

The second view attributes global imbalances to the asymmetry in the outlook for economic growth and that in financial development.[8] On the one hand, the US economy and Europe grew slowly because of the aging of their population and a slowing down in innovation output. On the other hand, emerging Asian economies enjoyed strong growth, partly as a result of the dividend of their relatively young population, and their strong growth also pulled up the economies of commodity exporters such as Saudi Arabia and Russia. However, many of these fast growing economies do not have a highly developed financial sector that can provide safe and liquid financial instruments to hold their savings. As a result, they turned to invest in US government debt securities. In turn, their strong demand for safe dollar securities pushed down the interest rate in the US and other advanced economies, providing a breeding soil for financial bubbles.[9] The preference for safe dollar assets is explained by the depth and liquidity of US financial markets, which accounted for 50% of global totals (In other economies, a large portion of business equities are held by government or large families and are not available for foreign investors) and better legal protection available for international investors.[10]

The third view[11] believes that the 2008 global financial crisis has much deeper roots. Fundamentally, it is caused by the inherent flaw of the current international monetary system which depends critically on the US dollar, while the US economic power has been on the

[8]See Caballero *et al.* (2008a), Mendoza *et al.* (2009), Cooper (2007).
[9]See Caballero *et al.* (2008b).
[10]See Cooper (2007).
[11]Pan Yingli (2010).

wane. The apparent demand for safe US dollar assets from emerging market and developing economies is only a superficial symptom of the underlying flaw of the current international monetary system. As discussed, the accumulation of dollar reserve assets in emerging market and developing economies is sourced from their current-account surpluses, which reflect, in turn, the imbalances in the global distribution of productive capacity of tradable goods.

How should global imbalances be corrected? This requires joint adjustments in the US, Europe and Asia, though in different directions according to their own circumstances.[12] The US and Europe need to expand their productive capacity and curtail their credit-fueled excessive consumption so that deficit economies can gradually move into external balance dynamically over time.[13] Asia needs to stimulate their domestic demand, both household consumption and business investment, and at the same time, develop further their domestic financial institutions and markets so that they can meet the rising demand for liquid and safe saving instruments. There is much room for expanding consumer credit, education loans, and infrastructure financing which will make their economic growth more sustainable and capable of resolving the inter-generational transfer of wealth and purchasing power in their own economies or within the Asian region. For the Asian region, it is important to have an alternative global reserve currency which is both liquid and safe and supported by the strong legal protection of private properties. Which Asian currency can play such a role? The US dollar is already overburdened. Like the British pound, the Japanese is only a marginal reserve currency. The current debt crisis in the euro zone renders it an infeasible option to develop an Asian regional currency following the euro model. Therefore, the RMB has the potential to play the irreplaceable role of a core regional reserve currency. Therefore, it is strategically important to develop the offshore financial center

[12]We do not touch the adjustment of major commodity exporters, for their adjustment tends to be automatic and passively responding to commodity prices.

[13]Examples include Obama's Manufacturing Revival Act and other advanced countries efforts to raise the tradability of many service activities.

of Hong Kong and the onshore financial center in Shanghai, especially the government bond market which is available to international investors. The emergence of the RMB as a reserve currency will play an important constructive role in global re-balancing. The development of the financial centers in Hong Kong and Shanghai with the RMB being the vehicle currency will help to relieve the demand pressure on the US dollar for global liquidity, especially from emerging market and developing economies. In this way, an emerging international monetary system based on three major reserve currencies will be more stable and superior to the current dollar-dominated system.

The dollar experience as the leading reserve currency shows that issuing a global reserve currency is a double-edged sword. Thanks to the "exorbitant privilege" of a global reserve currency, the level of real exchange rate would be higher than otherwise, resulting from the global demand for financial assets denominated in that reserve currency. Therefore, the reserve currency economy is likely to experience the Dutch disease. A while ago when The Netherlands discovered North Sea oil and natural gas, its currency appreciated substantially. As the currency appreciation erodes the international competitiveness of Dutch manufactured exports, resources shifted from the tradable sector to the non-tradable service sector, shrinking its manufacturing productive capacity. As a result, employment declined and social instability ensued. This scenario is an outcome that China should attempt to avoid. As the most populous country, it is necessary that China should strive to keep a balance between tradable and non-tradable sectors so as to render economic growth sustainable and should not allow its manufacturing sector to shrink too much as a result of currency appreciation. As a matter of strategy, the wise approach to internationalize the RMB is to promote its use mainly in Asia instead of posing a challenge to the dominant role of the US dollar in global trade and finance. The international monetary system that relies mainly on one single reserve currency is inherently unstable and that reserve currency country tends to suffer extensively from the Dutch disease-styled structural imbalances. In contrast, a multi-reserve currency system would be more stable and resilient, because the pressure is dispersed among all the three major reserve currencies, instead of concentrating on one single currency.

The Logical Coherence between RMB Internationalization, Restructuring of the Chinese Economy and the Liberalization of China's Domestic Financial Sector

While spectacular progress has been made since China started to reform and open its economy 30 years ago, it is widely acknowledged that the past export-led and financially-repressed growth model is no longer sustainable. This growth model has its own logic, largely conditioned by the legacy of centrally planned industrialization before 1978 and also shaped by the gradual approach of reform and opening. However, the past growth model can no longer continue. Given the stagnation of advanced economies, continued strong export demand can no longer be counted. China's environment has been severely degraded. Therefore, for the next 10 or 30 years, it is paramount that China alters its growth model by implementing deep and comprehensive institutional reforms. Concurrent with RMB internationalization, it is paramount that China's growth model must shift from the export-led model to domestic demand-driven model and the Chinese financial sector must be reformed and upgraded into a more efficient, diversified and open sector. The economic and financial transformation of China is the internal counterpart of RMB internationalization, while the latter is the external manifestation of an emerging rebalanced economy and liberalized and internationally competitive financial sector.

Two important policies implemented before 1978 have far-reaching impact even today. One is the population policy. In the 1950s, large families were encouraged with no effective promotion of contraception and family planning. Later on, towards the end of 1970s, alarmed by the tightening of resource constraints and the fast growth of population, China introduced a compulsory one-child family planning policy. As a result, there are two significant periods in which population dividends are released: 1975–1985 and 2000–2012. In the first period, there was pressing employment pressure because the industrialization emphasizing heavy industry did not create adequate jobs in cities, so millions of young school graduates were sent

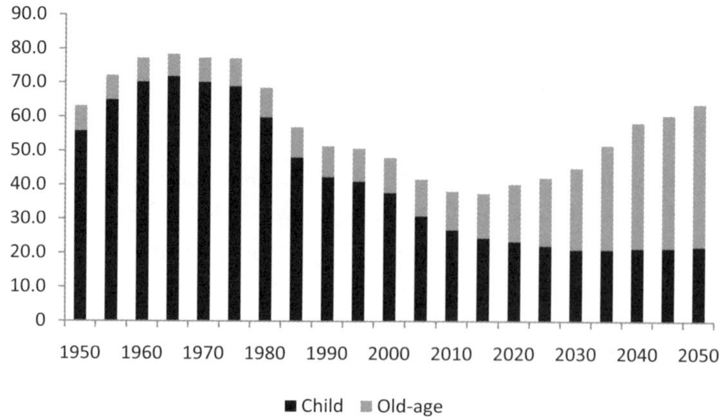

Figure 1. China's dependency ratio of population: 1950–2050.
Source: United Nations, World population prospects: The 2010 revision.

to work with farmers as a way to relieve the employment pressure. In the second period, the working age population expanded rapidly and peaked. Facilitated by FDI that brought in foreign capital, technology and market access, especially after China acceded to the World Trade Organization (WTO), and supported by high domestic saving rate, employment of abundant cheap labor generated strong economic growth at about 10% a year.

The other relevant pre-1978 policy is that following the experience of Soviet Union's industrialization, China extracted substantial rural surplus from peasants by keeping government procurement prices of agricultural produce low and the prices of industrial goods high, the so-called "price scissors" policy.[14] In the early days of China's industrialization, the country was poor and national saving was inadequate. So such extraction of rural surplus was the only way to fund the development of heavy industry and feed an expanding urban population. Given the political context of the cold war in that period, such a heavy-industry first development strategy has its own historical rationale. However, an important legacy from that period is a dual rural-urban political and economic structure in the

[14] Price scissors refer to the practice to suppress the procurement prices for agricultural produce and raise the prices of farming inputs so that agricultural surplus is extracted and becomes industrial profits, which form the main revenue source of the state and are used to fund capital accumulation.

Chinese society with a large rural-urban income gap.[15] Because low rural income restrained rural consumption, it became necessary to reply on investment and export demand to create jobs and propel economic growth. The presence of abundant rural surplus labor provided a favorable environment for the subsequent export-led growth model. That accounts for China's apparent advantage of cheap labor in global trade. China's accession to the WTO provided the opportunity to bring out this huge growth potential through making manufactured exports.

Another two policy initiatives implemented during the reform and opening period also have significant impact on the Chinese economic performance. One is the particular fiscal system introduced in 1994 that let the central government and local governments share tax revenue, especially value added tax (VAT). The revenue-sharing scheme provides a strong incentive for local governments to expand their GDP. The other policy initiative is financial repression with which the government keeps the cost of capital low through interest rate controls and its direct influence over state banks. Low capital cost has made it feasible to undertake industrial investment on a large scale.

In 1994, the current fiscal system characterized by centralized political power and decentralized economic power was introduced to replace individually negotiated profit retentions with a unified corporate income tax and a flat rate VAT tax. It specifies a way to share fiscal revenue between the central government and various levels of local governments. Local governments had a strong incentive to expand local GDP from which they can share part of tax revenue. There are major ways to expand local GDP. One way is to attract industrial investment projects, from both domestic companies and foreign investors, especially top 500 multinational corporations. The other way is to expand urban boundary and develop real properties commercially. Because rural land can be acquired at a fixed cost set administratively and real estate properties can be sold at ever rising prices, urban development and housing construction are very profitable to both local governments that get large land sale revenue

[15]In 1978, China's urbanization rate was only 17.92%, so rural population accounted for 82% of the national total (Liu, 2013).

and developers. Hence, local governments have a strong incentive to expand their local GDP and government officials are mainly promoted according to their GDP performance metrics. As a result, there has been an irresistible tendency towards industrial investment and urban construction. The plus side of such an incentive system is strong economic growth, while the down side also results in duplicative production lines, excess capacity, local protectionism, excessive competition among Chinese companies and unduly dependence of Chinese industrial production on external markets.

Financial repression is mainly motivated to keep capital cost low and channels funds mainly to enterprises on government's priority list, often large state-controlled enterprises. Priority borrowers mainly consist of large manufacturers, real estate developers and infrastructure projects. There is no denying that financial repression has played a critical role for China's successful industrialization and strong economic growth. However, low capital cost has also led to many undesirable structural imbalances such as over-dependence on bank funding, excess productive capacity in manufacturing, a bubbling housing market, and other structural distortions. Though it is impossible to pin down accurately, credit risk has been accumulated to levels worthy of serious concern, increasingly significantly contingent government liabilities.

At present, China is at a critical juncture. Under the mounting pressures from depleting resources and degrading environment, shrinking external demand, a shrinking value of its foreign exchange reserves and wide-spread social tensions, the past growth model supported by the four pillars of cheap labor, cheap capital, cheap environmental costs and global markets is no longer sustainable. It is now imperative and urgent that China must undergo another transformation of its economy.

The main requirement of this transformation is to shift the gravity from export demand to domestic demand, to turn extensive growth into intensive growth sourced from rising productivity. At the center of this transformation is the allocation of capital. And that is where the role of finance comes in. The transformation of the financial sector lies at the core of economic transformation.

The main requirements of developing a more efficient modern financial sector is to change the role of government from keep capital cost low for business borrowers to more effective protection of creditors and small investors, to fight against financial frauds, to loosen and eventually lift numerous obstructive regulations, and to promote the expansion of non-bank intermediation through financial markets. Fundamentally, the task is to accumulate safe and high yielding financial instruments through which the inter-generational transfer of purchasing power can be realized so as to meet the challenge of an aging society.

There is logical consistency between the economic and financial transformation of the Chinese economy on one hand and RMB internationalization on the other. RMB internationalization is to extend the use of RMB outside China in invoicing and valuation, transaction settlements, and value storing. The rise of emerging reserve currencies also entails increasing competitiveness in providing financial instruments which are safe, liquid, high-yielding and convenient to use. Safety requires political stability and strong legal protection of private properties. At the aggregate level, the real yield on financial assets depends on economic growth potential and efficiency in resource allocation, which is critically impacted by the effectiveness of the financial sector. Finally, liquidity and ease of use depend largely on the depth and size and openness of the domestic financial sector. Globally, liquidity and ease of use overseas also depend on the global reach and service quality of China's banks and other financial institutions. Therefore, the transformation of China's domestic financial sector is a necessary pre-condition of a successful RMB internationalization. Conversely, RMB internationalization also points the direction for transforming the Chinese financial sector.

The Strategic Objectives of RMB Internationalization: Immediate Targets and Final Goal

The national interest and basic objective of RMB internationalization

Most emerging market and developing economies are handicapped by the "original sin" in that their international trade and investment are generally invoiced and denominated not in their own domestic currency. Therefore, they bear the exchange risk and often suffer substantial losses from exchange rate fluctuations. The Asian currency and financial crisis in 1997 is a revealing illustration of the substantial risk resulting from the original sin. The background for this Asian currency and financial crisis is sudden large withdrawal of foreign capital from Thailand, when the US dollar started to appreciate after 1995. Before the crisis, Thailand's baht was closely pegged to the US dollar. With a large current-account deficit, outflow of foreign capital quickly caused a depletion of foreign exchange reserves. When Thailand ran out of international liquidity in 1997, it had no choice but to abandon the dollar peg, triggering the currency crisis and a calamitous depreciation of the Thai baht. Because Thailand's banks were exposed to substantial foreign debt denominated the US dollar with most of their assets in the local currency, the currency collapse brought down many domestic banks. This financial crisis spread to many other Asian economies is a telling case of developing economies weighed down by foreign debt in foreign currencies. Reversing the appreciation trend in late 1990s, the US dollar entered a phase of depreciation in 2002–2007.[16] With the RMB pegging to the US dollar initially, China benefited from a gain in trade competitiveness and experienced strong export-led growth. However, the resulting large accumulation of US dollar reserves exposed China to huge capital loss risks. Attempting to avoid the pitfall of running out of international liquidity, many Asian economies chose to insure themselves by accumulating dollar reserves. But they could not avoid the capital loss from dollar depreciation. It is impossible for small weak economies to make their currencies into reserve currencies. They earnestly need coordinated global efforts to manage and stabilize the value of major reserve currencies. In comparison, China is now the second largest global economic power and has the potential to avoid the original sin risk *via* RMB internationalization.

Therefore, we believe that the core national interest in internationalize the use of the RMB lies in shielding from the original sin

[16]According to a report (2011) of the research institute of *China Business News*, the US dollar depreciated 75.6% in terms of the basket of 16 commodities.

risk. If their international trade and finance can be denominated in the RMB, Chinese global companies, financial institutions and governments can avoid exchange rate risk and gain a currency advantage. It is not correct to regard a potential seigniorage benefit as the core national interest of turning the RMB into a global reserve currency. There is no free lunch in enjoying the status of a global reserve currency. Corresponding to the seigniorage gain is the global responsibility of providing a public good. If a country only wants to gain from seigniorage without shouldering the implied global responsibility, then the loss of confidence and ensuing currency collapse will not be far away.

Therefore, even though economists often use the share in global foreign exchange reserves as the proxy indicator to reflect the international status of a reserve currency, it is not really correct to equate RMB becoming a reserve currency with China's national interest. The hallmark of a successful RMB internationalization is that RMB is widely used as its invoicing function in international trade and finance. Only in this way, China can avoid foreign exchange risk, and that is the long-run fundamental interest of China. Pushing the RMB into a reserve currency by opening domestic financial markets and liberalizing the capital account would enable international investors and foreign central banks can hold RMB assets, diversifying away the dollar risk and sharing the fruits of China's fast economic growth. In comparison, that objective should be regarded as offering an incentive to induce wider use of the RMB in international trade and finance. This can also be regarded as a way to relief the pressure on US financial markets and a global responsibility for China to safeguard the stability of the international monetary system. Though the invoicing function and value-storing function cannot be strictly separated and are interdependent on each other, as far as China is concerned, the invoicing function should really be the primary goal, while the value-storing function is secondary, serving as the means of realizing the primary function. In the process of internationalizing the RMB, it is important to handle the interaction between these functions properly. It is necessary to avoid liberalizing the capital account prematurely and as a result, to be forced to abandon RMB internationalization halfway.

The final goal of RMB internationalization

The issuer of a global currency plays, in a way, the role of a regional or global bank that provides liquidity with short-term liabilities and long-term assets.[17]

The US currently plays such a role as a global bank. On the one hand, it attracts low-cost funds (similar to bank deposits) from the rest of the world by providing safe and liquid government debt that carries very low yield to international investors, on the other hand, it undertakes, through its multinational corporations and global banks, direct investment and acquire risky financial assets in the rest of the world (similar to long-term bank loans and obtain high returns).

As a global bank, the issuer of a global currency provides short-term liquidity to the global economy and allocates financial funds globally in seeking profits and balancing the global economy. Therefore, the country playing the role of a global bank must possess three advantages:

(1) it has a solid credit standing in the rest of the world based on a strong economy, sustainable fiscal management, and strong legal protection of private properties;
(2) it provides liquidity to international investors in the form of a deep and liquid market for its government debt and quasi-government debt; and
(3) its multinational corporations and global financial institutions have the capacity to allocate resources globally in an effective way because of their strength in technological innovations and in managing funds and risks on a global scale.

Measured against that ideal of a global bank, the US has three weaknesses in playing its role as a global bank. First, the US economy is structurally deficient. Because its domestic economy is concentrated in defense industry, food production, financial activity and other activities supporting US's global hegemony, it has been under-produce tradable goods, resulting in trade deficits continuously in

[17]He Dong of Hong Kong Monetary Authority proposed the concept of issuer of an international currency plays the role of a bank. See He (2012a).

the past three decades. As a global bank, it may soon become insolvent (US external liabilities to non-residents exceeding US overseas assets). Unless this trend is checked and reversed, the US may be exposed to the risk of "a bank run."

Under the influence of the Triffin dilemma, some people have a mistaken notion that the injection of global liquidity is from the trade deficits of the reserve currency country. But according to the internationalization experience of the British pound and the US dollar, the main driver of their currency's internationalization is capital-account surplus, not current-account deficit.

> *The injection of a global currency does not necessitate that the reserve currency issuer runs a current-account deficit. On the contrary, the net foreign assets (cumulative current-account balance) of the issuer must be kept above a stable positive level in order to maintain the value of the reserve currency. In effect, the injection of the reserve currency is a process of maturity transformation through the issuer's capital-account and external balance sheet. It plays the role of a bank. Just as a commercial bank should avoid a bank run, the issuer must a certain degree of capital adequacy (in the form of net foreign assets).* (He, 2012b)

To highlight the "exorbitant privilege" of the US as the "global bank," Figure 1 shows how much the US has gained from issuing the dominant global reserve currency. Over the period of 1996–2010, US cumulative current-account deficit is $6,981.2 billion. However, its net foreign assets decreased only by $2,306.8 billion. Therefore, the US gained $4,674.4 billion from the financial effect. This financial effect captures the total impact on external financial assets and liabilities of financial operations and valuation changes. In the case of the US, a major source of the financial effect is the valuation effect of changes in the value of the US dollar. Most US external debt is denominated in the dollar, while its direct investment is denominated in other currencies. As a result, dollar depreciation would reduce the real value of US external debt and raise the value of US external real assets. The financial effect also captures capital gains and losses from the trading activities of portfolio investment. How does the US realize such enormous gain? A critical factor is dollar depreciation. Out of the total financial effect of $4,674.4 billion, $3,795.2 (81.2%) occurred in the 2002–2007 period when the dollar depreciated against

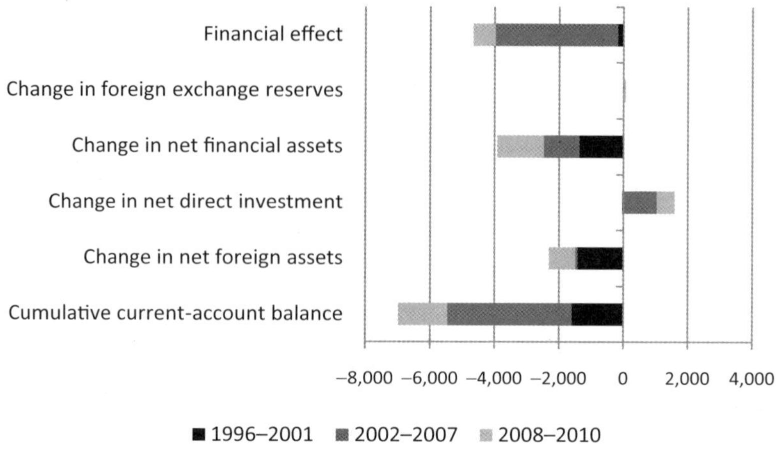

Figure 2. US's change in net foreign assets in 1996–2010 ($ billion).

Source: Lane and Milesi-Ferretti (2006) updated dataset of external wealth of nations.

other major currencies, including the RMB. Another $700 billion was gained in the three years of 2008–2010. Over the period of 1996–2010, US's external net direct foreign investment stock actually increased by $1,565.1 billion. However, US external net financial liabilities increased only by $3,918.5 billion. That is why US net foreign assets decreased only by $2,306.8 billion.

Second, the ability of the US government to tax the capital gains of it multinational corporations and global financial institutions is under challenge. The logic of serving as a "global bank" on a sustainable basis dictates that the national government of the issuer should be able to share the high returns of its multinational corporations and global financial institutions so as to cover the operational costs of protecting its overseas economic interests and maintaining a global military presence. If the US cannot effectively tax the gains made by US multinational corporations and global financial institutions, then it would be impossible to sustain the confidence and capital adequacy of such a global bank.

Third, the ability of US as the "global bank" to serve the real global economy is being questioned. The legitimacy of earning a return for a bank lies in the intermediary role it plays in moving financial funds and real resources from less efficient uses to more efficient uses, thus creating additional wealth from the real economy. It is necessary that the global community should prevent financiers from making excess returns from manipulating markets or maintaining monopoly market power through raising the leverage of themselves and the whole economy without improving or even distorting global resource allocation. Financial institutions profit from the bubbles they engender by raising the leverage of themselves and the whole economy and then shift the costs of the popped bubble onto the fiscal burden of many governments. This is the important background for this global financial crisis.

Therefore, the final goal of RMB internationalization should be to enhance global confidence in the Chinese government, to improve the liquidity to global investors of Chinese government debt securities, and to strengthen the capacity of Chinese multinational corporations and global financial institutions in global financial intermediation and resource allocation. At the same time, it is important to avoid the Dutch disease as displayed in the US experience of serving as a "global bank" in the structure of the Chinese economy, the divergence between capital interests and national interests, and the divergence between the vested interests of financial institutions and the interests of the global economy. In this way, RMB internationalization can promote efficient allocation of global resources, whereas a balanced global economy would enable China to play the role of a regional or global bank increasingly, maximizing national interest compatible with the interests of the global economy.

To illustrate where China should be heading and how far it must go in internationalizing the RMB, Figure 2 presents a comparison of global power in 2010 in four dimensions. China is compared to the other four major reserve currency powers: US, UK, Japan, and the euro-zone as represented by the sum (Euro-4) of the four largest member countries (Germany, France, Italy and Spain). The first dimension is economic size as measured by GDP in the US dollar. In 2010, the pecking order is as follows. The US is the largest at $14,419 billion. Collectively, the GDP of Euro-4 is in the second place at $10,297 billion, China is in the third place at $5,931 billion,

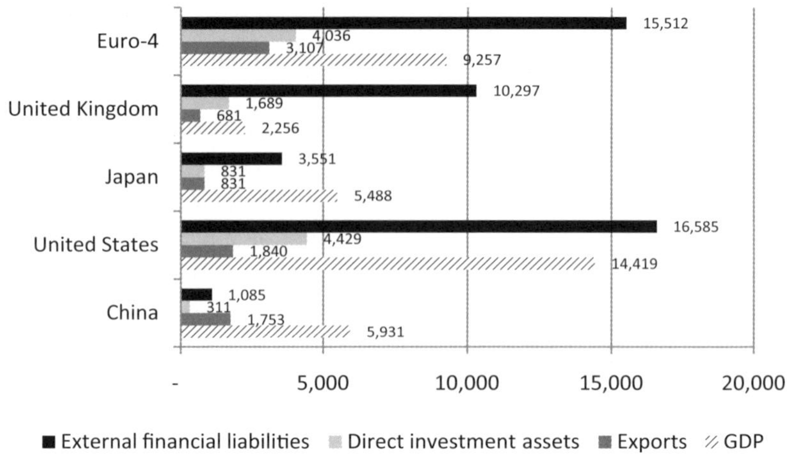

Figure 3. Comparison of global economic power, 2010 ($ billion).

Source: Lane and Milesi-Ferretti (2006) updated dataset of external wealth of nations and World Bank's WDI dataset.

Japan is close behind at $5,488 billion, while the UK is the smallest at $2,256 billion.

The second dimension is exports in the US dollar, a more relevant measure of the influence in global markets. Euro-4 is now the largest at $3,107 billion, though a big part of their exports is internal trade among themselves. The US is in the second place at $1,840 billion, though it is the largest on the national basis. China is next to the US at $1,753 billion. Actually, China has surpassed the US in merchandise exports, but the US has a large volume of service exports. So in total, the US still edges out China.

These two dimensions reflect global power in the real business space. By these yardsticks, China has already stood closely next to the US and the euro-zone in the supply to the rest of the world of goods and services in general, exports in particular. However, for reserve currency power, the next two dimensions are, perhaps, more important.

The third dimension is the stock of external foreign direct investment. On the side of the real economy, this indicator reflects a country's control over the global-supply chain, or alternatively, can be regarded as the supply to the rest of the world of technology and managerial knowhow. On the side of the financial space, this indicator captures real earning assets for a "global bank" in intermediating cross-border financial funds. By this measure, the US is in the first place at $4,429 billion. Euro-4 is in the second place at $4,036 billion. Being a much smaller economy by the size of GDP, Britain is in the third place at $1,689 billion. In comparison, Japan and China are far behind. Japan's external direct investment assets are at $831 billion, while China is at the bottom at $311 billion, even though this is a very large increase from $116 billion in 2007.

The fourth dimension is external financial liabilities, which are total external liabilities minus direct investment liabilities or the sum of external portfolio investment liabilities and other (bank) debt. From a bank perspective, this is analogous to the source of funds (deposits). It measures how much financial funds a country controls or intermediates in global financial markets. For a reserve currency issuer, this reflects its global financial power in supplying financial assets (saving instruments) to the rest of the world. In this regard, the US tops the pecking order list at $16,585 billion, while Euro-4 is the close second at $15,512 billion. In 2007, the order was reversed. Euro-4 was the largest at $16,240 billion, while the US was at 15,362 billion. More impressive is the financial power wielded by Britain. With its GDP only at $2,256 billion, it intermediates funds as large as $10,297, in the third place closely. The corresponding number for Japan is $3,551 billion, while that for China is $1,085 billion. It is clear that there is a long journey for China in bringing up its global financial power in line with its global economic power.

It is a lofty goal to internationalize the RMB and there is a long journey to cover. However, so long as we have clear objective, we can design an optimal roadmap and approach the final goal step by step.

The Precondition and Potential for RMB Internationalization

How large is the potential for the RMB to become an international currency? Here we briefly report the simulation result of a recent study of ours.[18] Our panel regression study covers eight

[18] Wu, Pan and Zhu (forthcoming).

reserve currencies (US dollar, euro, pound sterling, Deutsch mark, Japanese yen, French franc, Swiss franc and Dutch guilder). The dependent variable is the share of a currency in global total foreign exchange reserves. The sample period is from 1965 to 2010. The independent variables include GDP global share, export global share, import global share, stock market capitalization, bond market depth, turnover in the foreign exchange market, capital-account openness (Chinn-Ito index), real interest rate, inflation differential, exchange rate volatility, and currency appreciation. Table 3 lists some recent value of the variables used in our study.

We have found that the global share of a reserve currency is positively related to economic size, capital account openness and currency appreciation, but negatively related to exchange rate volatility. We estimated three models. Model 1 is a baseline full model incorporating all the independent variables, Model 2 adds network

Table 3. Recent data of reserve currency global share and explanatory variables.

	US Dollar	Euro	Pound	Yen	Swiss Franc	RMB	Year
Share global FX reserves (ratio)	61.50	26.20	4.00	3.80	0.10	NA	2010
Size of economy and trade							
GDP global share (ratio)	0.28	0.17	0.04	0.12	0.01	0.09	2010
Exports ($ trillion)	1.37	2.85	0.48	0.63	0.20	NA	2009
Imports ($ trillion)	1.67	2.80	0.53	0.48	0.10	1.06	2009
Financial markets							
Stock market capitalization ($ trillion)	13.40	7.83	2.33	3.30	1.00	NA	2009
Government bond market ($ trillion)	35.85	NA	4.39	36.83	0.46	NA	2009
FX turnover (total = 200%)	84.85	39.07	12.88	18.97	6.36	NA	2010
Capital-account openness	2.48	NA	1.00	1.00	NA	0.16	2010
Currency stability							
Real interest rate (%)	2.00	NA	−2.00	4.00	3.00	0.00	2010
Inflational differential (%)	−0.47	0.23	2.10	−1.47	−0.57	0.84	2010
Exchange rate volatility	0.11	0.14	0.17	0.20	0.17	0.12	2009
Currency appreciation (%)	0.16	−0.08	0.31	−0.19	−0.10	−0.21	2009

Source: COFER, WDI, BIS, IFS.

externality, and Model 3 retains only economic size and network externality. Once network externality is included, most other variables turn out to be insignificant, except economic size. Hence the specification of Model 3. The main finding is that the global share of a reserve currency depends on issuer's economic size and network externality as well as expected appreciation.

We performed a simulation to project the potential for the RMB for the period of 2011–2025. We assumed three possible scenarios: optimistic, middle and pessimistic outcomes and made projection of the time path of independent variables. Table 4 reports the simulation result.

The simulation suggests that the optimistic scenario of Model 1 gives the most sanguine projection: RMB global reserves share may approach 26.4% by 2025, close to that of the euro (27.6%). The incorporation of network externality significantly pushes down RMB's potential to the range of 9.7–12.7%, which still exceeds the peak level of the Japanese yen (8.4%) in 1991. Model 3 yields the most conservative projection in the range of 2.97–4.45%. We believe that incorporation of network externality is essential. We tend to regard that the middle scenario of Model 2 is most likely. In 2025, RMB's global share may rise to 11%, surpassing that of the Japanese yen and becoming the third largest reserve currency.

The Strategy to Push forward RMB Internationalization and the Important Steps at the Current Stage

The experience of currency internationalization indicates that the size of a country and the network effect are of great importance to the internationalization of a currency. To a certain extent, the latter depends on the role played by that country in global trade and investment in the real economy. We believe that on the basis that China is the second largest economy, the largest trader and recent rapid pace of outward foreign direct investment, the conditions for internationalizing the RMB are basically ripe.

To a large extent, the success of RMB internationalization depends on the stability in China macroeconomic environment and

Table 4. Simulation for the RMB global share in foreign exchange reserves, 2011–2025.

	Model 1			Model 2			Model 3		
	Scenario 1	Scenario 2	Scenario 3	Scenario 1	Scenario 2	Scenario 3	Scenario 1	Scenario 2	Scenario 3
2011	0.0718	0.0701	0.0692	0.0063	0.0062	0.0061	0.0002	0.0002	0.0002
2012	0.0836	0.0800	0.0782	0.0129	0.0125	0.0124	0.0003	0.0004	0.0004
2013	0.0960	0.0902	0.0874	0.0197	0.0191	0.0188	0.0007	0.0007	0.0007
2014	0.1089	0.1009	0.0970	0.0270	0.0259	0.0253	0.0012	0.0012	0.0011
2015	0.1225	0.1119	0.1068	0.0346	0.0329	0.0321	0.0020	0.0019	0.0019
2016	0.1344	0.1212	0.1128	0.0424	0.0401	0.0387	0.0031	0.0029	0.0029
2017	0.1467	0.1308	0.1189	0.0505	0.0473	0.0453	0.0046	0.0044	0.0042
2018	0.1596	0.1406	0.1251	0.0589	0.0547	0.0519	0.0067	0.0062	0.0060
2019	0.1729	0.1507	0.1312	0.0676	0.0622	0.0584	0.0093	0.0086	0.0081
2020	0.1867	0.1611	0.1375	0.0766	0.0699	0.0649	0.0127	0.0115	0.0107
2021	0.2010	0.1718	0.1439	0.0859	0.0778	0.0713	0.0171	0.0151	0.0137
2022	0.2159	0.1827	0.1504	0.0956	0.0859	0.0778	0.0222	0.0193	0.0171
2023	0.2313	0.1941	0.1570	0.1056	0.0942	0.0842	0.0284	0.0242	0.0209
2024	0.2474	0.2056	0.1636	0.1161	0.1026	0.0906	0.0359	0.0298	0.0251
2025	0.2641	0.2176	0.1704	0.1269	0.1113	0.0971	0.0448	0.0362	0.0297

the financial system and the sustainability of China's economic growth. Keeping certain levels of surplus in the current account would help to keep the RMB dollar exchange rate stable or a downward trend, which would attract inflow of foreign capital and realize maturity transformation of borrowing short and lending long in the capital account. Full convertibility of RMB in the capital account should be a natural final end of RMB internationalization, not its pre-condition.[19]

Therefore, China should promote economic and financial transformation and sustainable development with institutional reforms. Under the environment of incomplete capital account opening, China should promote the use of the RMB in the pricing, settlement and transactions of overseas real economic activity with the help of the offshore RMB financial center in Hong Kong and exporting of China's capital in order to expand network externality. When condition is ripe, it is possible to rapidly increase the supply of RMB to the rest of the world and break the network advantage of the incumbent reserve currency. The link worthy of special attention is to rapidly expand the scale effect of overseas use of the RMB.

We propose the following strategy of RMB internationalization: to foster steadfastly overseas demand for the RMB in the early phase and rapidly release large supply of the RMB in the later phase. The focal point in the early phase of foster international demand for the RMB steadfastly under incomplete liberalization of the capital account is to enlarge China's commercial presence overseas, accelerate domestic economic and financial transformation, and push forward, starting from Asia, global management of exchange rates and short-term cross-border capital flows, creating the appropriate condition for substantially expanding the supply of the RMB to the rest of the world in the later phase.

---

[19]Adaire Turner, former Chairman of British Financial Services Authority, pointed out in an interview by China Business News that the liberalization of the capital account is the rational ending point (of RMB internationalization). China ample reasons for a gradual approach.

Foster extensive China's commercial presence overseas

The core of successfully pushing forward RMB internationalization and forming the network externality is to expand the invoicing function of the RMB in international trade and finance. It is necessary that Chinese companies and financial institutions active participate more actively in global trade, investment, production and financial activities and acquire the leading position gradually. This is the micro basis of a successful RMB internationalization. In the absence of rapid overseas expansion of Chinese companies and financial institutions, it is very likely to form asset price bubbles if international investors who want to profit from anticipated RMB appreciation are allowed to hold liquid marketable RMB assets (securities and real estate properties). Once foreign capital exits en masse, bubbles may burst and a financial crisis may occur in China, aborting the process of RMB internationalization.

Now is the strategic opportunity for China to expand the overseas commercial presence of Chinese companies and financial institutions. With three trillion plus dollars of foreign exchange reserves and direct supply of RMB outside China, there is ample supply of funds for Chinese companies and financial institutions and the global financial crisis has created many opportunities for them. China needs to streamline related policies to remove policy barriers to overseas investment by private businesses. This would contribute to the adjustment of China's economic structure and industry upgrading and the strategic allocation of China's external assets.

Accelerate the pace of economic transformation

In two senses, the restructuring of the Chinese economy can be taken as the pre-condition of RMB internationalization. First, international experience and our regression study reported, prove that a powerful and globally competitive capacity to export manufactured goods is the material foundation for a currency's internationalization. At present, China's global shares in manufactured exports are driven mainly by low production costs. This model is becoming increasingly unsustainable. Now there are strong pressures for wages, the prices of raw materials, land usage costs, and capital cost to rise.

With increasing opening of low-income countries, revival of US manufacturing and new technology in extracting traditional energy, the cost advantage of China's manufactured exports is fast disappearing. Therefore, it is important to eliminate administrative monopolies, to deepen the reform of large state-controlled enterprises, to consolidate many competitive industries to remove disorderly and vicious competition among Chinese companies, to form large and strong Chinese industrial leaders and promote them to become global leading companies. These steps require fundamental institutional reforms and upgrading industries on the basis of technology.

Second, only when economic transformation is completed, there will be a sustainable engine for strong economic growth. China's manufacturing capacity is the largest in the world. A large part of China's exports depend on the unsustainable excessive consumption in the US and Europe. As the economic power of the US and Europe declines and their fiscal space shrinks, China's continued strong export demand is no longer attainable. Therefore, it is crucial to develop China's domestic markets as to provide demand to drive economic growth. On the other hand, China's traditional economic growth model of high input and low output is bumping up against the constraint of environment. Only the technological progress and improvement in economic efficiency brought about by institutional reforms can provide the growth engine on the supply side. Such a successful economic restructuring can sustain the confidence of international investors in Chinese economic growth and laying a firm foundation for expanding overseas demand for the RMB.

Actively push forward the market-oriented reform of the administratively controlled financial system

The financial system characterized by administrative monopolies is an important component of China's industrialization strategy. Such a system is designed to enable the financial sector and favored companies to acquire funds at lost costs at the expense of the interests of depositors and small and medium-sized investors. At present, excess capacity has already appeared in China's manufacturing sector, housing sector and many infrastructure supply sponsored by local governments such as the high-speed railway. On the other hand, a large middle class is needed to develop domestic consumer market and many service activities. Furthermore, the administratively controlled financial system has become the bottleneck preventing the intermediation between household saving and investment in new high growth industries. The role of government must change from supporting enterprises with subsidized credit to protection of creditors and investors. The pro-market reform of the financial system has the effect of hiding wealth among people. The sources of funding investment must be widened to enable new high-growth industries and the service sector that represent the future direction be funded on a sustained basis so that Chinese households may share the fruits of economic growth.

The main areas for financial reform are:

(1) Relax the threshold for private capital to enter banking and restructure the banking sector to ensure a balanced development between large banks and small banks under the protection of a sound deposit insurance system so that high quality banking services are accessible to households and small and medium-sized enterprises.
(2) Reform the initial public offering (IPO) rules, price setting mechanism and underwriting practice and beef up financial supervision and legal deterrence for financial crimes and frauds and the three "public-ness" and efficiency of the stock market.
(3) Complete interest rate liberalization and gradually reduce and eventually eliminate interest rate subsidies and push commercial banks to upgrade their operational model and raise their international competitiveness.
(4) Deepen the market for local government and corporate bonds and explore the opening of that bond market to international investors through qualified foreign institutional investors (QFIIs) in order to provide a mechanism for the RMB outside China to flow in.
(5) Reform the exchange rate regime to de-peg the RMB off the US dollar, to reduce the weights of the dollar and the euro in RMB's anchoring basket and increase the weights of other large Asian economies and commodities exporters. Keep the trade-weighted RMB exchange rate within a narrow band and let a stable RMB

exchange rate play a positive role in China's foreign trade and investment.

(6) Re-assess the items and sequence of capital-account opening, clean up China's policies towards foreign investment and improve the effectiveness of managing short-term capital flows. Maintain the flexibility to impose a transactions tax on short-term capital flows either independently or jointly with other Asian economies, even after the capital account is completely opened.

Delineate the strategic role of Hong Kong and Shanghai and develop the offshore and onshore RMB bond market

China possesses a unique advantage in having two financial centers of different nature and at different levels of development in Hong Kong and Shanghai. These two financial systems should actively complement, assist and interact with each other in the process of internationalizing the RMB. As a result of the fragility of the global financial environment and the Chinese financial system and the special arrangement of "one country, two systems," the open financial markets in Hong Kong are not yet fully integrated with the mainland markets before the complete opening of the capital account.

In the strategic roadmap of the Chinese government in promoting RMB internationalization, the strategic role of Hong Kong is to serve as an offshore financial center. Its medium-term goal is to extend its reach in Southeast Asia and Central Asia, facilitate the development of an international financial market in Asia for RMB denominated assets and enhance RMB's standing as a key currency in Asia. The strategic role of Shanghai is an onshore financial center and its medium-term objective is to solidify the soundness of the infrastructure foundation for financial markets and to improve its function as mainland's financial center, increasing its operational efficacy and its global operational capability.

According to the strategy of RMB internationalization, the immediate breakthrough essential for building the RMB financial center in Hong Kong and Shanghai is to nurture and develop the international market for RMB bonds. Hong Kong has a special role to play in developing the RMB bond market because it has the advantage of strong protection of private property rights, an effective market discipline mechanism imposed by mature investors and a range of related professional services. The task for developing Hong Kong's RMB bond market should be focused on China's local government bonds that need closer monitoring and more market disciplines (at the same time reform the fiscal system of Chinese local governments to make it more transparent) and RMB bonds issued by international borrowers. Taking into consideration of the inter-bank rate and the yield curve in Hong Kong, the Chinese central government may place a sizeable volume of central government's short-term bills and long-term bonds in Hong Kong.

However, the main body of government bonds and quasi-government bonds should be located in Shanghai so that the central bank can conduct effective open market operations and maintain the independence of China's monetary policy. Rapidly developing RMB government bond market is an urgent task of strategic significance. Therefore, two steps should be taken now. First, the People's Bank of China should change quickly its current operational mode of injecting base money through sterilizing its purchases of foreign exchanges and make open market operations more compliant with international standards subject to the condition that China's international payments should be kept in relative balance. Second, while China's capital account is still not completely open, it is possible to let foreign central banks to enter the onshore RMB government bond market so that some RMB outside China can flow into the mainland. At the same time, it is necessary to increase the scale and scope of QFIIs in order to raise the incentive to spread the overseas use of the RMB.

Proceed from Asia in reforming the international monetary system and creating a stable global financial environment

Many Asian economies were the victims of the current international monetary system in the past and will face common challenges from global financial speculation and volatile exchange rates resulting from global liquidity flooding. Therefore, most Asian economies share common interests and positions in international monetary cooperation and coping with the instability of the current international monetary system. The Chinese government should play a leading role. We propose that major Asian economies can explore to move towards more effective intra-regional cooperation of monetary and exchange rate policies so as to stabilize bilateral exchange rates and levy a common Tobin tax on financial transactions within Asia. The revenue from the Tobin tax can be placed in an Asia financial stability fund and a regional development fund.

The next 10 years can be regarded as the first phase of building up energy and steadfastly creating international demand for RMB. Afterwards, RMB internationalization may enter a new phase of releasing substantial RMB supply quickly to the global economy after Chinese corporations and global financial institutions have built up their overseas network, the economic and financial transformation is successfully completed, the RMB becomes the invoice currency in many bilateral agreements, the global financial environment is relatively calm or alternatively extremely turbulent. Only then may the Chinese government proclaim full RMB convertibility in the capital account, increasing RMB supply through trade imports, overseas direct investment and issuance of RMB bonds to international investors and rapidly expand the scale economy of RMB internationalization and RMB's global reach.

Conclusion

The present chapter explores the global significance of RMB internationalization, strategic goal and the roadmap for implementation. We believe that, against the background of the gravity center of the global economy moving towards Asia and a multi-polar global economy being formed, the main reform direction should be to create a multiple reserve currencies system that has an internal stabilizing mechanism. RMB internationalization is an integral component of this reform package. The integration centered on the RMB of Asian financial markets will promote the rebalancing of the global economy, forming a three-pillared stable configuration.

The primary objective of RMB internationalization is the invoicing function of the RMB in international trade and finance in order to remove the exchange rate risk for Chinese companies and financial institutions, while the ultimate goal lies in enabling China to become a "regional bank" or a "global bank" that will contribute to rebalance the global economy and increase global welfare in a way China's national interest merging with global interests.

Our regression study of eight reserve currency experience shows that network externality and economic size play a decisive role in determining the global status of a reserve currency and a stable exchange rate and an open capital account helps the currency internationalization process. The simulation for the next 15 years indicates that the RMB has the potential to surpass the peak level of the Japanese yen and approaching the euro status. International experience suggests that RMB internationalization should proceed in two phases. In the early phase, the key task is to transform the Chinese economy and the financial system and foster international demand for the RMB, whereas in the later phase when the condition becomes ripe, the task is to open the capital account and substantially release RMB supply to global use. This two-phased approach would help to enlarge network externality and keep risk under control.

There are several caveats in this chapter. China's economic and political system is substantially different from that of other major reserve currency economies. The present chapter did not attempt to assess the impact on RMB internationalization of a major shift in China's system. Next, the global monetary and economic environment and geopolitics are subject to substantial uncertainty and risks. We did not incorporate a robustness analysis covering such uncertainties and risks.

References

Bernanke, BS (2005). The global saving glut and the US current account deficit. The Federal Reserve Board. *The Sandridge Lecture*. Richmond, VA: Virginia Association of Economists.

Bi, SS (2003). *Frontier Problems Report on China's Rural Farmers*. People's Daily Publishing House.

Caballero, RJ, E Farhi and PO Gourinchas (2008a). Financial crash, commodity prices and global imbalances. NBER Working Paper No. 14521.

Caballero, RJ, E Farhiand and PO Gourinchas (2008b). An equilibrium model of "global imbalances" and low interest rates. *American Economic Review*, 98(1), 358–393.

Camdessus, M, A Lamfalussy, T Padoa-Schioppa, S Aleksashenko, H Al Sayari, JT Boorman, A Crockett, G de la Dehesa, A Fraga, T Gyohten, X Hu, A Icard, H Koehler, G Ortiz, M Ramos, YV Reddy, EM Truman and PA Volcker (2011). Reform of the international monetary system: A cooperative approach for the twenty first century. *Global Journal of Emerging Market Economics*, 3(2), 185–193.

Cooper, RN (2007). Living with global imbalances. *Brookings Papers on Economic Activity*, 38(2), 91–110.

Eichengreen, B (2009). Out of the box thoughts about the international financial architecture. IMF Working Paper No. 09/116.

Eichengreen, B (2011). *Exorbitant Privilege: The Rise and Fall of the Dollar and the Future of the International Monetary System*. New York, NY: Oxford University Press.

Farhi, E, PO Gourinchas and H Rey (2011). Reforming the international monetary system. Centre for Economic Policy Research (CEPR), London.

He, D (2012a). Triffin dilemma and currency internationalization. October 10.

He, D (2012b). RMB internationalization: A primer, Hong Kong Institute for Monetary Research (HKIMR), Hong Kong, July.

Liu, HS (2013). China's potential economic growth rate the next 20 years from the viewpoint of population factor. *Haitong Securities Research*, 1.

Ignazio, A, A Bénassy-Quéré, B Carton, Z Darvas, C Destais, J Pisani-Ferry, A Sapir and S Vallée (2011). *Global Currencies for Tomorrow: A European Perspective*. CEPII Research Reports No. 2011-01.

IMF (2011). Global financial stability report: Grappling with crisis legacies. World Economic and Financial Surveys, September.

Johansson, A, Y Guillemette, F Murtin, D Turner, G Nicoletti, C de la Maisonneuve, G Bousquet and F Spinelli (2012). Looking to 2060: Long-term economic prospects for the world. OECD Economic Policy Papers No. 3.

Lane, PR and GM Milesi-Ferretti (2006). The external wealth of nations mark II: Revised and extended estimates of foreign assets and liabilities, 1970–2004. IMF Working Paper No. WP/06/69.

Lin, Y (2012). China's next 20 years. *China Business Daily News*, Special Series on Strategic Observation, January 1.

Lyons, G (2010). The super-cycle report — Special report. Standard Chartered Global Research Department, London.

Mendoza, EG, V Quadrini and J-V Rios-Rull (2007). Financial integration, financial deepness, and global imbalances. NBER, Working Paper No. 12909.

Obstfeld, M and K Rogoff (2007). The unsustainable US current account position revisited. In Clarida, RH (Ed.), *G7 Current Account Imbalances: Sustainability and Adjustment*, pp. 339–366. Chicago, IL: University of Chicago Press.

Pan, Y (2010). *International Financial Centre: International Experiences and China's Future*. Shanghai, China: Truth & Wisdom Press & Shanghai People's Publishing House.

Pan, Y (2011). The dual risk of China's export-oriented strategy and the wealth illusion. *Exploration and Free Views*, 3.

Prasad, ES and L Ye (2012). The renminbi's role in the global monetary system. IZA DP No. 6335.

Subacchi, P (2012). To change or not to change: The transition period of the international monetary system. In *International Conference on Reform of International Monetary System and RMB Internationalization*, organized by China Society of World Economics & Shanghai Jiaotong University, September 27.

Subacchi, P and J Driffill (Eds.) (2010). Beyond the dollar: Rethinking the international monetary system. A Chatham House Report. The Royal Institute of International Affairs, London.

United Nations (UN) (2009). Report of the Commission of Experts of the President of the United Nations General Assembly on Reforms of the International Monetary and Financial System. New York, NY: United Nations.

Wu, J, Y Pan and Q Zhu. The conditions and potential of RMB as an international reserve currency. *China Finance Review International*, forthcoming.

Xie, P (1996). *The Choice of China's Financial System.* Shanghai, China: Far East Publishers.

Yu, Y (2011). To administratively promote RMB internationalization is to spoil things by excessive enthusiasm. *China Business Daily News*, July 4.

Zhang, J (1998). *The Structure and Evolution of China's Financial System.* Taiyuan, China: Shanxi Economy Press.

Chapter 12

Reforming China's Rural Financial Market

Xi Zhu

Financial services are of great importance to the investment and consumption of rural households. In recent years, operational income is still the main source of rural households despite the sharp increase of their income from working as migrant workers. For those who are engaged in agricultural production, such as planting grain crops or breeding livestock, there exists a time lag between input and output periods. For those who are engaged in non-agricultural production, the required investment size always exceeds their liquid assets. In these cases, active credit markets are favorable to rural households for production financing or consumption smoothing.

Furthermore, there are great uncertainties in rural households' production and income: agricultural production is vulnerable to weather, disaster, etc. And the demand and price of agricultural products and petty commodities are volatile. Thus, in rural areas where insurance market is undeveloped, credit market could also play a role as insurance. As a matter of fact, a poorer rural household has more urgent demand for credit. To realize the potentially profitable investment opportunity, or avoid the adverse impact of excessive reduction in consumption, he has stronger desire to relieve liquidity constraint through credit market. To summarize, it is clear that providing timely and effective financial service benefits the rural households' income, welfare and sustainable development.

From the macro perspective, the accessibility of credit also helps to relieve the degree of income inequality. Banerjee and Newman (1993) and Galor and Zeria (1993) found that in a incomplete financial market, financial institutions will only offer loans to those rich people who are able to provide collateral. These rich people can then use loans to start new business, make an investment, etc., thereby obtain a higher income and accumulate more wealth; on the contrary, due to the lack of effective mortgage/collateral, poor people are still kept away from financial institutions even though they have good investment projects. So they have no choice but to earn wages by providing labor for the rich, or to maintain simple production. Such means of living makes the wealth accumulation of poor people very slow. Although they work hard, it is still difficult for them to change the existing production pattern without financial support. In contrast, the advantage of rich people is continuously being enhanced — they get more and more support from financial institutions while accumulating their wealth, thus their income grows faster. The absence of credit markets results in the Matthew effect (the rich people become richer while the poor get poorer). Thus, establishing an efficient rural financial market could not only satisfy the financing demand of rural households and increase their income and welfare, but reduce the gap between the rich and the poor, thereby promoting the harmonious development of national economy.

This chapter looks at rural financial reform from the view of farmer credit, which has not gotten sufficient attention by now. The core of establishing modern rural financial system is to satisfy the investment demand of rural households and facilitate their effective investment, thereby increasing farmer income and developing modern agriculture. Why the existing rural financial institutions fail to effectively serve low or middle income rural households? In our opinion, one of the most important reasons is that the products and services do not match the households' investment demand. The win–win situation and mutual benefit between rural household and financial institution cannot be achieved unless the household investment project's return rate, risk, constraint and other features are well understood, and novel financial systems, including new financial institution, financial product and financial service are created according to these features.

The remaining part of this chapter is arranged as follows. The first section summarizes main problems in current rural financial market. The second section briefly reviews the process of rural financial reform. The third section explores the challenges which rural financial reform confronts from the perspective of rural household's credit. In the fourth section, several key issues in improving financial service to rural households are discussed. The last section summarizes the whole chapter.

Main Problems in Rural Financial Market

After 30 years of effort, China has preliminarily established a rural financial system including commercial, policy-based and cooperative formal financial institutions. At present, the suppliers of rural household's credit could be classified into two types — formal and informal. Formal suppliers include rural credit cooperatives, commercial banks, postal savings bank, microcredit companies which emerge in recent years, etc. Rural credit cooperatives are the main force among them. Informal suppliers include private lenders, such as relatives and friends, mutual-aid organizations (i.e., rotating savings and credit association), usurers, etc.

We first investigate the main characteristics of rural credit by analyzing the survey data of 1,000 rural households at the National Fixed-point Survey (NFS) during 2003–2009. The sampling proceeded in three stages. At the first stage, 10 representative provinces were selected from all provinces according to the development of the regional economy, which included Liaoning, Jilin, Jiangsu, Fujian, Shandong, Henan, Hubei, Sichuan, Gansu and Xinjiang. At the second stage, 18 villages were randomly chosen from each selected province. The villages whose endowments of land or populations were too large or small were excluded from the selection process. At the last stage, approximately six rural households were randomly drawn from each village, resulting in a total of 1,000 selected households. The wealthiest and poorest 5% of rural households were excluded from the selection process. This database included detailed information on these households from 2003 to 2009, including income, expenditures, credit activities, production and operational activities, and basic information on the environment (village and province). However, this data set was limited by the lack of weight information in the surveys; thus, the data may not be representative of the entire rural population in China. While we believe that the results of this chapter provide useful information about rural credit markets in China, one should exercise caution in generalizing any of the results.

Basic characteristics of rural credit

Table 1 shows the provincial distribution of sample households by loan categories from 2003 to 2009. It shows that 194 households borrowed money annually, amounting to 19.4% of the sample households, and 68 households annually received credit from formal sources, accounting for 35% of the total borrowing households. Though most rural households borrowed from informal sources, inter-provincial differences were also apparent. Liaoning showed the smallest share of borrowing households at 4.0%, while Jilin and Hubei showed the highest, at 35.6% and 40.7%, respectively. Jilin's high borrowing rate may stem from a greater access to formal sources than other provinces. Hubei's high borrowing rate may be attributed to its low rural household income, which encourages a shared-risk strategy of "relationship-credit."

Table 2 shows the annual distribution of households by loan categories from 2003 to 2009. It shows that the percentage of borrowing households in the total sample decreased from 24% in 2003 to 16.2% in 2009. The percentage of households borrowing from formal sources dropped sharply, from 11.9% in 2003 to only 3.2% in 2009. These rates show that credit rationing from formal sources was the main source of increased credit rationing.

Table 3 reports the distribution of loans by sources (from 2003 to 2009). It shows that 18.5% of total loan volume came from formal sources. As the households borrowing from formal sources represented 35% of all borrowing households, the average loan amount from formal sources was lower than that of informal sources. Table 3 also shows that loans from Rural Credit Cooperative Unions accounted for 77.2% of the total formal loan volume from 2003 to 2009, while loans from commercial banks and other

Table 1. Provincial distribution of households by loan categories.

Province	Households	Borrowing households (1)	Non-borrowing households (2)	Households that borrow only from formal sources (3)	Households that borrow only from informal sources (4)	Households that borrow from both formal and informal sources (5)	$\frac{(1) \times 100\%}{(1) + (2)}$
Liaoning	100	4.0	96.0	0.6	3.1	0.3	4.0
Jilin	100	35.6	64.4	15.1	14.4	6.0	35.6
Jiangsu	100	15.1	84.9	0.0	14.7	0.4	15.1
Fujian	100	16.7	83.3	2.4	11.9	2.4	16.7
Shandong	120	13.3	106.7	1.3	10.7	1.3	11.2
Henan	120	27.3	92.7	2.1	20.0	5.1	23.5
Hubei	60	24.4	35.6	1.3	21.4	1.7	40.7
Sichuan	100	20.7	79.3	2.9	13.1	4.7	20.7
Gansu	100	14.6	85.4	1.6	11.0	2.0	14.7
Xinjiang	100	22.3	77.7	3.1	5.9	13.3	22.3
All	1000	194.0	806.0	30.4	126.2	37.2	19.4

Note: Formal sources include commercial banks, which mainly include Agricultural Bank of China (ABC), Rural Credit Cooperative Unions and official institutions that offer loans supporting rural poor. Informal resources refer to the private credit activities (informal sources), mainly including loans occurred between households, and between private credit institutions or companies.

Table 2. Annual distributions of households by loan categories.

Year	Households	Borrowing households (1)	Non-borrowing households (2)	Households that borrow only from formal sources (3)	Households that borrow only from informal sources (4)	Households that borrow from both formal and informal sources (5)	Percentage of borrowing households
2003	1000	240	760	54	121	65	24.00
2004	1000	212	788	35	122	55	21.20
2005	1000	198	802	46	118	34	19.80
2006	1000	203	797	38	134	31	20.30
2007	1000	192	808	6	148	38	19.20
2008	1000	151	849	17	111	23	15.10
2009	1000	162	838	17	130	15	16.20
All	7000	1358	5642	213	884	261	19.40

Note: Formal sources include commercial banks, which mainly include Agricultural Bank of China (ABC), Rural Credit Cooperative Unions and official Institutions that offer loans supporting rural poor. Informal resources refer to the private credit activities (informal source), mainly including loans occurred between households, and between private credit institutions or companies.

Table 3. Distribution of loans by sources.

	Formal sources			Informal sources	
	Amount (yuan)	Share (%)		Amount (yuan)	Share (%)
Total amount	2,860,956	100	Total amount	12,630,393	100
Banks	452,471	15.8	Between households	10,815,637	85.6
RCCUs	2,209,739	77.2	Private credit institutions	393,883	3.1
Others	198,746	7.0	Other institutions	1,420,873	11.3
Formal loans/ total loans		18.5	Informal loans/ total loans		81.5

Note: Banks refer to loans from national-owned commercial banks, especially ABC; RCCUs refer to loans from Rural Credit Cooperative Unions; Private credit institutions refer to loans from rural cooperative foundation, rotating saving and credit associations, and private banks, which are not granted by government; Other economic institutions mainly include capital goods provider, private firms (for example, town and village owned enterprises), state-owned or town and village owned departments.

formal institutions only accounted for 15.8% and 7.0%, respectively. The table shows that the Rural Credit Cooperative Unions were the most important formal sources, along with the nationally owned commercial banks. After the Agricultural Bank of China (ABC) left the rural areas in 1997, the Rural Credit Cooperative Unions assumed a more important role for rural Chinese households. The loans granted between rural households amounted to 85.6% of total informal loan volume, while the informal loans from private credit institutions and other economic institutions only amounted to 3.1% and 11.3%, respectively. The latter two add up to less than 15%, which is much lower than those of other developing countries. For example, this combined figure is 43.8% in Pakistan, 39.7% in Bengal, and 41.9% in India. The data show that loans between households were the most important channel of informal loans, which indicates that the personal relationship between borrowers and lenders was crucial in Chinese rural credit markets (Shi and Chen, 2002). The data also reveal that most Chinese rural households resorted to a single borrowing source, partly because of the ineffective strictly regulated rural credit market in China.

Main problems of rural financial market

By summarizing the above facts, one could find that the key problem in China's rural financial market is the serious lack of credit supply, which results in the difficulty for rural households to get credit. Past reform did not fundamentally change the market. Financial service is always a weak sector of socialized service system in rural areas, and has become a bottleneck restricting rural economic development.

We can examine the performance of rural financial market by evaluating the performance of formal financial institutions. Yaron (1992) suggested using a double standard — service coverage and self-sustainability — for measuring rural financial institutions. Coverage is an indicator to measure the scale and depth of the service provided by rural financial institutions for target clients (rural households and rural enterprises), while self-sustainability measures the long-term business sustainability of rural financial institution, including ownership, governance, management, finance, etc. Zeller and Meyer (2002) improved it by proposing a triple standard — coverage, self-sustainability, and impact. Impact emphasizes the effects of the service provided by a financial institution on the borrower's income, welfare, and social status.

Most rural households are still subject to severe credit constraint. It is very hard for them to obtain loans from formal financial institutions like rural credit cooperatives. According to the study of Li and Zhu (2007) on 3,000 rural households at the NFS, the proportion of rural households who have credit demand but cannot be satisfied is close to 70%. The scarce loan tends to be allocated to rich rural households. 30% of the rural households with the highest income obtain about a half (48.3%) of the total borrowings, whereas the poorest rural households could hardly get the loan. The hundred-county survey carried out by the Development Research Center of the State Council (DRCSC) also confirmed the result. It showed that 70% of the 3,026 return migrants put financing as the dominant obstacle for starting a business in their hometown (Cui, 2008).

Sustainability is a difficult task for formal rural financial institutions. Because of the excessive intervention of government in the past, the quality of rural financial institutions' assets has deteriorated, and some of these institutions have great difficulties to keep operating. Take the case of rural credit cooperatives for example. Within three years after the Asian financial crisis, the ratio of total non-performing assets almost reached 50%. To support rural credit cooperatives and urge them to reform, the government provided them with a large amount of loans and bills from the central bank at a relatively low interest rate since 2003.

The mechanism reform of rural credit cooperatives relieves the financial deficit to a certain degree, but it is still very difficult for low and middle income rural households to get credit. Some investigations show that many rural credit cooperatives act more like commercial banks by neglecting the poor and favoring the rich. The basic mode of rural finance is the government-led subsidized credit system. The government prescribes the target and scale of loan, and sets the interest rate. Formal rural financial institutions are used as the loan-issuing window, and not operated as demand-driven institutions. The government pays most attention to the quantity of loans but less attention to the quality. This rural credit system just lacks allocative efficiency (Zhu and Li, 2006).

Review of the Process of Rural Financial Reform

There have been four stages to rural financial reform.

Stage 1 (1978–1993)

The government restored and established new financial institutions, and constructed a financial market with diversified and competing institutions. The major measures included:

(i) Restoring ABC;
(ii) Restoring the status of cooperative financial institution for rural credit cooperatives (under the supervision of ABC); and
(iii) Relaxing the regulation of private credit, and establishment of private cooperative institutions, etc.

During this period, the rural credit issued by formal institutions grew rapidly. The private cooperative institutions also developed quickly, which reduced the number of private usurers by substitution effect.

Stage 2 (1994–1996)

The government began to commercialize the big four state-owned banks, and to implement rural financial reform to establish a rural financial system to service agriculture and rural economy. The main measures included:

(i) Establishing Agricultural Development Bank of China in 1994, which manages special-purpose loans like funds for purchasing agricultural products, loan for rural poverty alleviation and loan for agricultural integrated development. It was an effort to separate policy-based financial business out of all businesses of ABC and rural credit cooperatives;
(ii) Accelerating the process of commercializing of ABC; and
(iii) Accelerating the process of commercializing rural credit cooperatives. It was planned to finish the establishment of county-integrated cooperatives in 1994 and set up lots of rural credit cooperative banks in 1995. But the implementation fell far behind the plan.

During this period, rural economy was driven by the soaring investment demand. Since there was wide gap between capital supply and demand in a short term, the interest rate increased to a high level. Rural cooperative foundations (RCFs) were established, and, under the intervention of local government, they invested heavily into the township and village enterprises. While their size expanded rapidly in the process, greater and greater risks accumulated. In consequence, their operation performance fell dramatically, and, at the end of 1996, the central government was forced to clean up the RCFs.

Stage 3 (1997–2003)

The State Council unveiled the *Decision on the Rural Financial System Reform* (1996) to separate out the rural credit cooperatives from the ABC, and gave them the right to develop independently again. Two important measures were taken to control financial risks: (i) the big four state-owned banks withdrew from grass roots of rural areas, which worsened the shortage of rural finance; (ii) informal financial activities were suppressed and even prohibited. In January 1999, the State Council ban all RCFs.

Stage 4 (2003–present)

The government launched a new round of financial reform to reform of rural credit cooperatives and introduce more financial institutions into rural areas:

(i) Rural credit cooperatives were managed by provincial governments;
(ii) Allow diversified pattern of property right arrangement and organizational form, so that different rural credit cooperatives may select different property patterns and organizational forms.
(iii) Widen the range of interest rates for rural credit cooperatives.
(iv) Provide capital support to rural credit cooperatives through special bills issued by the central bank. Payment of these bills was linked to the reform performance of rural cooperatives, which formed a strong incentive for institutional reform.

The pilot reform of rural credit cooperatives was quite effective. Their capital adequacy ratio increased significantly, which enhanced their capability to bear risk.

Various new rural financial institutions have emerged, e.g., village banks, micro-credit companies and rural mutual-aid funding associations. By the end of September 2012, 858 new rural financial institutions had been established, among which 799 were village banks. The microcredit companies — which grant loans but could not accept deposits — developed even faster. By the end of March 2013, there were 6,555 micro-credit companies with the loan balance amounting to 635.7 billion Yuan.

Rethinking the Challenges of Rural Financial Reform

We think that the challenges that rural financial market faces are much more severe than other markets, and we discuss the four main challenges below.

Improper governmental intervention

In the past, the government did not understand the credit demand of rural households. For example, it thought the return to rural households' investment was very low, thus the high interest rate charged by private source was the exploitation to rural households. So it controlled the interest rate of loans charged by rural financial institutions and specified the minimal scale requirement for rural credit. For the convenience of regulation, private capital was prohibited to enter rural financial market. However, those were misunderstandings of rural households. The agricultural production is no longer the old self-sufficient pattern. They have turned to the new commercialized pattern which satisfies social demands. And the non-agricultural production has created very considerable returns. These are proved by many recent empirical studies of rural households' investment behaviors. Even in the western areas of China, the income from non-agricultural investment of rural households also increases rapidly. From the survey of some poor regions of China, we find that the return on investment of rural households who were not credit constrained is 17.34%, while return of those constrained is 49.57% (Zhu *et al.*, 2010). In fact, owing to the short production period and relatively high return rate of project, some rural households are able to bear the high interest rate.

The improper government intervention led to a "three-failure" result in the rural financial market. (1) The subsidized interest rate which is lower than the interest rate of market often crowded out poor rural households. Since most of the loans was captured by those who were richer and more powerful. Such an allocation would intensify income inequality in rural areas.

(2) Rural financial institutions' development was limited. Most state-owned or quasi-state-owned institutions were regarded as a window through which loans were issued, and no attention was paid to the quality of loans. Meanwhile, they were poorly managed, where most managers and employees did not possess professional skills of a commercial bank. So these formal institutions had poor operating efficiency, getting into trouble in operation. On the other hand, private institutions could hardly compete with formal institutions since their unsubsidized interest rate were much higher. Besides, they were restricted to enter rural financial market by laws and regulations.

(3) The government had to pay for the great losses of formal rural financial institutions. Formal financial institutions assumed the task

of issuing low-interest-rate policy loans. It was virtually impossible for the government to find out whether the losses were incurred by interest rate restriction or operating efficiency. As a result, formal financial institutions lacked the incentive to improve operation, which made the likelihood of loss increased. In the end, all the losses were paid by the government.

Information asymmetry

Rural financial market is more vulnerable to the problems of adverse selection and moral hazard, while satisfying plenty of scattered investment demands of rural households. The credit rationing phenomenon arising from information asymmetry (Stiglitz and Weiss, 1981) also applies to rural households' financing in China. Since it is difficult for banks to observe a household's type, too high interest rate would either attract lots of high-risk customers (adverse selection), or induce customers to make too high-risk investment (moral hazard). So banks usually keep the interest rate lower than the equilibrium level. Even though rural households are willing to pay an interest rate higher than that in the market, they are still rationed. Consequently, lots of demands in the market keep unsatisfied, and the investment opportunities are wasted.

The routine tool adopted by formal financial institutions to solve such information asymmetry is wealth or cadre rating. It is a collateral mechanism. The institutions require borrowers to have the ability to provide collaterals in advance so that they do not need to bear the risk of adverse selection or moral hazard. However, most of rural households lack effective collaterals. Rural households possess the land use right rather than the ownership of land. The mortgage of land use right is very hard to handle. Futhermore, there are few special guarantee institutions providing guarantee for rural households. And the evaluation cost for handling mortgage is too high.

High transaction cost

Rural households mainly engaged in small-scale agricultural or non-agricultural investments. Their income is much lower than that of urban households. The population density in rural areas is relatively lower. Thus, rural financial market faces more barriers than general financial markets.

(1) The transaction cost of financial intermediaries is increased because of population decentralization and small loan scale in rural areas. (2) Rural financial market is seriously segmented due to weak infrastructure and socialized service in rural areas. The segmented market increases the cost of potential loan providers to acquire information and limits the scope of diversifying risk. (3) The investment risk of rural households is high. Most agricultural investment and production have a seasonal pattern, which are vulnerable to natural disasters. The price of agricultural products in China often fluctuates dramatically with the change of supply and demand. Non-agricultural investment also faces with various unknown risks arising out of the constraints of resource, market, information, etc. All these factors would increase the risk and cost of rural financial institutions under an incomplete insurance market.

Both information asymmetry and transaction cost increase the business cost of traditional formal financial institutions in rural areas. On the one hand, they are lack of information of rural households' qualification, capability, etc. And they cannot offset such risk through collateral mechanism. On the other hand, they have to pay excessively high transaction cost caused by dispersed rural households, small-scale demand and high risk. This is why credit rationing always happens. However, it leaves a large number of rural households who have effective investment opportunities excluded from financial service. Under credit rationing, the return on investment of many credit constrained rural households is much higher than those who are not constrained. Financial institutions are inclined to provide credit for rich households. A lot of investment opportunities are wasted and the income inequality of society is intensified.

Key Issues in Providing Credit to Rural Households

We think the new round of rural financial reform makes great progress in the following two aspects: (1) Improving the financial performance of existing rural financial institutions. (2) Introducing new rural financial institutions. But rural households still have great difficulty in getting loans. Major financial institutions, such as rural credit cooperatives, do not have the incentive to serve rural households after the commercialization reform. Tackling this problem remains as a great challenge to further reform.

The difficulty for rural household to get loans has kept for a long time. People used to think that profitable investment opportunities are scarce in rural areas, and the return to these investments is low. Thus when providing loan for rural households, it is impossible to satisfy both rural households' effective demand and institutions' business sustainable requirement. This is in fact a misunderstanding on the investments of rural households. By investigating rural households' investments, we find that it could achieve high return. What counts is that we need to have a better understanding of their demand, clarify the barriers to their financing, thereby design suitable mechanism and product to satisfy such a demand. In summary, future reform needs to pay more attention to the following issues.

Focusing on satisfying the developmental demand

The financing demand of rural households can be roughly classified into two types in terms of investment — survival demand and developmental demand. The survival demand comes from the purpose of satisfying survival expenditure. Return to such projects is low or even zero, which could not cover the interest cost. The developmental demand comes from the purpose of earning a higher income. Return to such projects could be much higher than the market interest rate.

In fact, it has been proved by a large amount of researches and practices that there is much effective developmental demand in rural areas. Since the 1980s, the microfinance revolution develops and grows very fast. Represented by Grameen Bank in Bangladesh, it has spread to many developing countries, and even poor regions in developed countries. It has a far-reaching influence on rural financial pattern. It was recorded in the 2007 annual report of Microcredit Summit Campaign that microfinance clients' number increased by 29% each year from 1997 to 2006. In 2006, 3,316 microfinance institutions served 133 million poor clients who were rejected by traditional banks. The microfinance maintained an impressively high repayment rate when serving the poor. Take Grameen Bank for example, its repayment rate kept at 95–98%.

The development of microfinance provides us important implications. It shows that rural households also possess entrepreneurship. As long as rural financial institutions focus on meeting their developmental demand, it is feasible to satisfy the effective demand of rural households when maintaining the business sustainability. It is true that in China's dual society, rural households fall into the vulnerable group, which needs fiscal, financial and other supports. But financial support should not focus on the past commanded credit pattern without regard for program efficiency. Such credit does not have a definite target. It does not differentiate between demands. It seemed that it charged a low interest rate and alleviate poverty. But it was likely to be obtained by a minority of mighty groups. It covered a small scope, which was unfair and unsustainable. For developmental credit, the issuance hinges on the quality of projects of rural households. It creates positive incentives for rural households to increase their income. It also ensures reasonable return for financial institutions.

Allowing appropriately high interest rate

High interest rate was viewed as the exploitation of rural households in the past. So the government regulated financial institutions by restricting the interest rate. But things were not necessarily so. The formation of high interest rate in rural financial market has two reasons. One comes from the characteristics of rural households' demand. Rural household's credit usually has a small scale, high degree of dispersion and high risk, vulnerable to the changes in weather, market, etc. It becomes worse that problems of information asymmetry (adverse selection and moral hazard) in rural financial market cannot be resolved by conventional tools such as collateral and guarantee from rural households. Therefore, compared with those enterprise clients, the loans to rural households require higher transaction and information costs. The other reason for high interest rate comes from market monopoly. In rural areas, the credit suppliers tend to have monopoly advantage. This monopoly may take shape by the scarcity of financial institutions, or the information advantage that the suppliers equip (for example, usurers tend to be locals).

It is clear that high interest rate is reasonable to a certain degree due to the demand features of rural households. But part of the high interest rate probably arises from the rent caused by monopoly. For the former, we should acknowledge it and allow the institutions to gain normal returns. For the latter, we need to eliminate it by breaking the supply pattern of rural financial market, introducing lots of new financial institutions. In this process, the allowance of appropriately high interest rate is a necessary prerequisite. Only competitive returns could attract more financial institutions to serve rural areas.

The current interest rate of rural unsecured micro-loan in China ranges between 15% and 20%. Take Ali-loan (oriented to small and micro business) created by Alibaba as reference. Its interest rate is about 18%. Practice demonstrates that the developmental demand of rural households could afford such an interest rate.

Introducing diversified specialized financial institutions

It is not enough to allow high interest rate. Private financial institutions (i.e., rotating savings, usurers, and so on) have existed in rural areas for many years. The interest rate level they charges is very high, but it does not attract more capital to serve rural areas. The problem lies in adverse selection and moral hazard in credit market. Under information asymmetry, simply increasing interest rate will only attract more high-risk clients and encourage rural households to take unfavorable hidden actions after obtaining loans. Hence, in order to solve these problems, innovations of mechanism and product based on the demand features of rural households must be created.

It is an established fact that rural households are short of effective collateral and guarantee in the rural areas. This could hardly be changed within a short period. So tradition tools to solve information asymmetry by means of collateral and guarantee does not work. Under such constraints, the only way is to introduce diversified specialized financial institutions and realize innovations of mechanism and product.

After a new round of reform, rural credit cooperatives have been substantially improved in financial sustainability. But in the current reform, credit cooperatives tend to be integrated into provincial rural credit cooperatives or restructured into commercial banks. It makes them pay more attention to business profit. They have stronger incentive to serve small-medium enterprises or rich rural households than to serve ordinary ones.

The rapid development of new rural financial institutions injects fresh vitality into rural finance. But these institutions, such as microcredit company, village bank, etc., also have stronger incentive to serve small-medium enterprises and rich rural households, same as credit cooperatives. Although the introduction of these new institutions has been a significant progress in rural finance compared with the past, effective service for ordinary rural households is still insufficient. Maybe for ordinary rural households, these institutions are still too large.

The hope of future rural finance lies in a large number of diversified specialized financial institutions. Different institutions have different advantages in information and transaction cost. They could be commercial, cooperative, policy-based, or public welfare-based. They could have different type of property structure, organization scale and operating pattern to satisfy the diversified demand of rural households. Institutions like microcredit organization, which provide financial products and services meeting the demand of rural households, are most useful in rural areas. These institutions understand the rural household's demand well, and have worked out many mechanisms and products suitable for them. Taking CFPA Microfinance, a microcredit institution under China Foundation for Poverty Alleviation, for example, it advocates the international principle of double base-line management over microfinance and pays equal attention to both financial performance and social performance. In 2012, it issued 137,000 micro loans, among which 69.1% with loan amount less than 10,000 yuan, and the average loan amount was 9,859 yuan. It had accumulatively issued 540,000 micro loans, with a total amount being over 4.1 billion yuan. It benefited nearly 1.5 million poor people. As shown by its annual report, the loan balance in 2012 was 0.85 billion yuan, and the ratio of risk loans longer than 30 days was 0.23%. Its business is developing steadily, and its loan quality is good.

Incentive policy support and moderate classified regulation

In a country with dual structure, agriculture, village and farmer are always at the disadvantaged position. It is a formidable task to provide financial support to them, especially to rural households. In consideration of the strategic objectives of social equality, food security, etc., suitable policy support should be provided for them. But we are opposed to the past commanded credit pattern, which will only lead to lose–lose situation for households and institutions. On the one hand, limited financial resource cannot be available for ordinary rural households. On the other hand, financial institutions suffer significant losses, and it is impossible to differentiate policy-related loss from operating loss.

A suitable pattern is incentive policy support. The government could grant appropriate subsidies to institutions engaged in rural finance. For instance, give tax exemption to financial institutions serving ordinary rural households, offer discounted interest rate for loan business to rural households, etc. The core purpose is to increase the incentives of institutions to serve rural areas by adjusting price leverage such as tax and subsidies, rather than directly commanding institutions to issue loans as what we did in the past. These policies would incur the efficiency loss to a certain extent. But rural households could get more financial resources at the cost of such loss.

Furthermore, moderate classified regulation should be implemented over rural financial institutions. The China Banking Regulatory Commission now implements classified regulation in rural areas, but the intervention is too excessive. For example, new financial institutions like village bank must take existing banking financial institutions as main founders. Micro-credit companies can only grant loan, but cannot absorb deposits. These policies can control risk well, but it restricts the access and development of new rural financial institutions. In the future when the condition becomes mature, these restrictions may be relaxed to attract more capital.

Only then there could be better development of rural financial institutions.

Conclusion

To summarize, the objective of reform is a diversified modern rural financial system that satisfies the effective investment demand of farmers in rural areas, and realizes the business sustainability of financial institutions. There are four sets of actions to achieve this dual goal.

First, financial services should mainly aim at satisfying the investment demand of rural households, rather than at expanding coverage. Only in this way can it be possible to realize the sustainable development of financial institutions. There is plenty of developmental demand of rural households. Most rural households could benefit from it.

Second, rural finance should allow a high interest rate due to the high information and transaction cost for credit business in rural areas, high interest rate is necessary for rural financial institutions to realize adequate profits. Judging from return on investment, rural households could afford such an interest rate. What they really concern is the availability of loans.

Third, problems such as adverse selection and moral hazard in loan transaction must be resolved by introducing more diversified and more specialized financial institutions, which could stimulate mechanism innovation and product innovation. The traditional loan pattern does not work well because of the lack of suitable collateral. We should especially allow private capital to enter rural financial market because private lenders (and small-medium financial institutions) have stronger capacity to adapt and more potential to develop in rural areas.

Fourth, the government should reduce improper intervention into the operations of rural financial institutions, and give them positive policy support and moderate its regulation.

It is worth mentioning that it is impossible to resolve the problems faced by agriculture, village and farmer (*san nong wenti*) by simply relying on rural finance. For example, the poorest rural households lack suitable investment opportunities, and so financial market reform cannot help the poorest households much. We need to implement a comprehensive program of aid (e.g., in health and education) and reform (e.g., land ownership and household registration system) in order to bring prosperity to rural China.

References

Banerjee, A and A Newman (1993). Occupational choice and the process of development. *Journal of Political Economy*, 101(2), 274–98.

Cui, C (2008). Return migrants' entrepreneurship in the 21st century. *Jingjiyanjiucankao*, 31, 40–43.

Galor, O and J Zeria (1993). Income distribution and macroeconomics. *Review of Economic and Studies*, 60, 35–52.

Li, R and X Zhu (2007). An empirical analysis of rural households financial constraints and its welfare loss. *Jingjiyanjiu*, 2, 146–155.

Li, R, Q Li, S Huang and X Zhu (2013). The credit rationing of Chinese rural households and its welfare loss: An investigation based on panel data. *China Economic Review*, 26, 17–27.

Shi, Q and K Chen (2012). An empirical analysis of farmer's credit behavior in less development areas. *Nongyejingjiwenti*, 2002, 10, 29–35.

Stiglitz, JE and A Weiss (1981). Credit rationing in markets with imperfect information. *American Economic Review*, 71, 393–411.

Yaron, J (1992). Successful rural finance institutions. T. W. B. D. papers.

Zeller, M and RL Meyer (2002). *The Triangle of Microfinance: Financial Sustainability, Outreach, and Impact.* Baltimore, MD: Johns Hopkins University Press.

Zhu, X and Z Li (2006). Efficiency analysis of rural credit since reform. *Guanlishijie*, 7, 68–76.

Index